CAMBRIDGE SERIES ON
HUMAN–COMPUTER INTERACTION 3

A Theory of
Computer Semiotics

Cambridge Series on Human–Computer Interaction

Managing Editor, Professor J. Long,
Ergonomics Unit, University College, London.

Editorial Board
Dr. P. Barnard, Medical Research Council,
Applied Psychology Unit, Cambridge, UK
Professor H. Thimbleby, Department of Computer Science,
University of Stirling, UK
Professor T. Winograd, Department of Computer Science
Stanford University, USA
Professor W. Buxton, Rank Xerox Ltd, Cambridge EuroPARC, UK
Dr. T. Landauer, Bellcore, Morristown, New Jersey, USA
Professor J. Lansdown, CASCAAD, Middlesex Polytechnic, UK
Professor T. W. Malone, MIT, Cambridge, Massachusetts, USA
Dr. J. Grudin, MCC, Austin, Texas, USA

A Theory of
Computer Semiotics

Semiotic approaches to construction and assessment of computer systems
Updated Edition

Peter Bøgh Andersen
University of Åarhus

CAMBRIDGE
UNIVERSITY PRESS

CAMBRIDGE UNIVERSITY PRESS
Cambridge, New York, Melbourne, Madrid, Cape Town,
Singapore, São Paulo, Delhi, Tokyo, Mexico City

Cambridge University Press
The Edinburgh Building, Cambridge CB2 8RU, UK

Published in the United States of America by
Cambridge University Press, New York

www.cambridge.org
Information on this title: www.cambridge.org/9780521393362

© Cambridge University Press 1997

First published 1997

A catalogue record for this publication is available from the British Library

ISBN 978-0-521-39336-2 Hardback
ISBN 978-0-521-44868-0 Paperback

CONTENTS

Preface to second edition

1. What is computer semiotics?

Semiotics is the science of signs and their life in society. A sign is anything that stands for something else for someone.

Semiotics treats all kinds of signs: verbal language, pictures, literature, motion pictures, theater, body language. Computer semiotics is a semiotic discipline that studies the nature and use of computer-based signs.

The motivation for the discipline comes from the nature of computer systems: although in many respects computer systems can be conceived as tools in analogy with typewriters, pencils, brushes and filing cabinets, they differ from these tools by not primarily existing or being used as physical objects, but as signs. The pencil of the drawing program is no real pencil that can be used to chew on, it is merely stands for a pencil, represented by a collection of pixels on the screen. Computer systems resemble other media by primarily acting as carriers of meaning.

Even if computer systems basically are symbolic tools, this symbolic nature has only attracted serious attention in recent years.

The reason for this is threefold: from being a tool only for specialists, computers have now been integrated into many occupations, and therefore the demands for interpretability have risen. The mode of operation and the meaning of the data must be easy to grasp for the secretary or the manager whose time should not be spent deciphering cryptic codes but writing agendas or making decisions. A good interface has become a necessary prerequisite for a good system.

The second reason is that computers are beginning to be used as media with functions similar to the textbook (educational systems, on-line manuals), the letter (e-mail), the newspaper (presentation systems), the telephone (conferencing systems), and the film (games), where the importance of the sign concept and semiotics is well established. In addition, hardware developments like high-resolution color screens, sound, and real-time video, begin to require skills of system developers that compare to the handicraft of professional artists or film-makers.

The third reason is that complex production processes are more and more being controlled by means of computers. The physical components and processes are no longer accessible to the operator, and this increases the demands to the interface, since the operators often have to rely solely on the computer-based signs when making decisions.

1.1. Computer systems from a semiotic point of view

Like any other theoretical framework, semiotics has its strong and weak sides. It can discuss some aspects of computer technology in a systematic and precise fashion, but must leave other aspects untouched. The general distribution of tractable and non-tractable aspects follows from the basic concepts of semiotics, namely the *sign* — something that stands for something else — and *semiosis*, the process whereby signs are created and used. Only those parts of reality that live the double life of a sign can be treated scientifically by semiotics.

The predicate "sign" does not denote an inherent feature of an object, but rather a specific way of treating it. In fact, almost anything can be used as a sign by someone. Clouds can be taken as a sign of rain, smoke as a sign of fire, footprints as a sign of a human, clothes as a sign of life-style. However, it is a fact that some objects are particularly popular as signs and obtain value solely from this function. This is true of letters, vocal sounds and pictures whose primary reason for being is to function as signs. It is not true of clouds and footprints that occur independently of whether someone uses them as signs or not. Still other objects are not primarily used as signs, but regularly participate in secondary semiotic processes. This is true of many artefacts; although the primary purpose of cars is transportation, the meaning of the design is important to the buyer since it signifies social status and life-style. However, even the most dashing design cannot sell a car that cannot run.

Computer systems resemble letters more than clouds and cars because their primary function is to enter into semiosis. A payroll system stands for employees and wages, a flight reservation system for planes, seats, and flights, a geographic information system for buildings and streets, an economic model for incomes, expenditures and taxes, and an action game for soldiers, guns and combat. If such systems cannot participate in semiosis and their data cannot be interpreted as employees, wages, planes, seats, houses, streets, etc., they are normally considered faulty.

Note that we do not as yet require the systems to stand for *true* properties of their domain. This requirement is only sensible for some kinds of systems but not for others. For example, the employee can rightfully expect that the payroll system correctly accumulates the amount of money he has received up till now, and the geographical information systems should not place a house on a location where the real town has a road. But in other cases, truth is not relevant: you cannot get your money back because the your action game does not assert true facts about reality.

In still other cases, a system may contain data that *creates* the state of affairs they stand for and for this reason cannot be true of false. This is e.g. true of the booking data of flight reservation systems: booking a seat on a flight does not reflect a pre-existing state of affairs, but creates a social obligation involving passenger and company: the company promises to let the passenger occupy the seat and transport him to the agreed destination, whereas the passenger promises payment in return. However, the system will also contain data that is intended to be taken as true statements about the present or the future: for example the number of seats of a plane or its destination.

Thus, the main motivation for creating a discipline of computer semiotics is that the primary function of computer systems is to work as sign-vehicles. The reason why I am not proposing a discipline of aeroplane-semiotics is that the main purpose of aeroplanes is transportation and not semiosis. For this reason semiotics can be expected to reveal basic and important properties of computer systems but not of aeroplanes.

Our discussion has also exemplified how semiotics can be useful for designing and understanding computer systems, namely by offering more precise concepts for understanding semiosis. If it is true that computer systems are primarily used as sign-vehicles, then non-semiotic approaches will have to deal with the same phenomena as semiotics do. We will expect to find semiotic concepts in other approaches, although used in a more naive and less systematic way, and this is indeed true.

One example is object-oriented design and programming. The method distinguishes between a computer model and a domain of the model, the computer model being similar to aspects of its domain. The classes of the model are said to correspond to collections of objects in the domain, the instances of the classes to objects of the domain, methods of the classes to actions and events in the domain, and variables of the classes to properties of the domain objects.

In the notion of "model" there is a clear invitation to see a computer system as a collection of true statements about the domain, but a systematic semiotic analysis of real computer based signs reveal a more complex picture. Let us start by classifying the computer model as a signifier and the domain as the signified, assuming that the model is taken by designer or user to stand for some aspects of its domain. But since we know there are many kinds of relationships between signifier and signified, we will not stop here but insist on a careful analysis of the relationship between signifier and signified. In some cases we will classify data as statements about the domain and relate them to the class of *representative* signs; but in other cases we will see them as forces that change the domain (*directive* or *commissive* signs) or discover that they stand for fictive phenomena. In short, we replace the simple idea of "modelling" by a more detailed description of signifier-signified relations.

A closer look at semiosis will have the same effect. The computer *model* is assumed to stand for the domain, but to whom? The model itself, in the shape of source code and diagrams, is normally only perceived by systems developers, and thus can only be said to stand for the domain to this group of people. Users have no contact with the global model in their daily work, but only interact with small pieces of model *executions*. The semiosis taking place here is very different from the one system developers experience, and there is absolutely no reason to expect that the meanings created during systems development automatically migrate to the use situation.

Putting systems development under the semiotic microscope reveals new interesting sign-types. We quickly discover that it is only a half-truth that the source code stands for the domain. Many lines of source code turn out to stand for the computer hardware or software. As an illustration to this, suppose we have an object such as *employee*:

```
class Employee {
    string Name, Address;
    int WageType, TaxDeduction ;
    int AccumulatedIncome;
    virtual void Payment(int Amount){....}
}
```

The variables and methods of this object can easily be taken to stand for domain features: an employee has a name, lives at an address, pays so much tax, has earned a certain sum and can receive a payment. But the object must also contain a method for displaying itself on a screen, say *Display(),* and this method will contain code specifying where to place the variables on the screen, say *Print(Name, 10, 20)* that prints the name on line 10 starting in position 20. Now, "10, 20" does not stand for the domain, but for a location on the hardware.

Besides references to hardware, the code contains many references to other pieces of code, i.e. references to itself. Consider a definition of *Display():*

```
virtual void Display(){
  Print(Name, 10, 20);
  Print(Address, 11, 20);
  Print(AccumulatedIncome, 12, 20);
  }
```

The definition says that performing "Display" is the same as performing the "Print"-method three times, where "Print" refers to the definition of "Print" somewhere else in the code. Thus, calling the "Print" method implies a reference to its declaration. In general, most uses of concepts in programs involves a reference to another location in the program where the concept is defined; and the definition normally uses new concepts for which the same is true. The unravelling of such references to references is routinely performed by any compiler (where the process is called "linking") .

Instead of having one sign-type standing for the domain, we find ourselves with at least three sign types distinguished by their reference: domain, hardware or software, and real programs reveal even more layers than three.

We can also begin wondering which forces maintain the relation between signifier and signified. What guarantees, for example, that instance #0099 of class *employee* in fact represents me? It probably turns out that the relation between #0099 and myself is guaranteed by a *conventional* rule: I just happen to have the name *Name* and live at the street named *Address,* but I and my street could easily have had other names. Signs that are based on conventional relations between signifier and signified are called *symbols* (this class includes the natural languages), but botanizing a bit more reveals another type of signs that is not based on a convention but rather on a cause-effect relation. We only have to visit the local power plant to discover signs that are not entered into the computer by a human following a set of conventions, but are produced mechanically by a gauge measuring pressure and temperature in boilers. This sign type is called *indexes* and includes the clouds, smoke and footprints mentioned before.

Thus, semiotics furnishes a more precise vocabulary and enables us to discover differences we might otherwise not have noticed. In addition, it helps us comparing computer systems to other kinds of sign-systems.

1.2. The environment from a semiotic point of view

It follows from the preceding arguments that semiosis requires some agent, psychic, social, biological, or mechanical, to whom the signifier stands for the signified. In addition, it is an empirical fact that different agents interpret the same signifier differently. To the computer scientist, a *queue* is a storage structure differing from another storage device called a *stack* in the manner in which elements are entered and released; the former uses the first-in/ first-out principle, whereas the latter is based on a first-in/ last-out convention. To a supermarket customer, however, a queue is a hindrance to getting the goods out of the shop, and certainly does not contrast to a stack. In general, semiosis depends upon the context of situation and its needs for distinctions. In the same organisation, the word "customer" can mean "entity which orders goods from the company", "places to which goods are delivered", "entity responsible for payments for delivered goods", and "entity towards which marketing actions are directed" (Goldkuhl 1984). The actual set of active meaning distinctions depends upon the action repertoire of the organisational unit. EDI and its attempts to create standards for common business transactions is a striking example of the order of magnitude of contextual variation.

In order to fulfil their purpose, computer systems must be understandable, but building an understandable system is just as difficult as writing an understandable book, because of the context-dependence of semiosis. For decision support systems the demands to understandability are even stronger because they must work as a guide for action.

Understanding in a context of action involves selection among a situation-specific set of alternatives. If the set is viewed as the complexity of the situation — large set, large complexity — then understanding can be defined as a reduction of complexity. The complexity depends upon the situation: in a bus we face a simple binary decision — staying or getting off — whereas other situations, such as conversations, present us with many options of continuation.

If information is to help us reduce complexity, we must be able to relate it to the options of the situation; otherwise it would have no bearing on our decision. Therefore, understanding a new sign involves relating it to the existing sign-system of the context.

A simple example suffices to illustrate the point: the monthly printout of my bank account most often identifies payments by means of a short name of sender or receiver of payments: travel agencies, shops, pubs, employers, etc. Although the names are not unique — shops with the same names exist in other towns — they are normally sufficient since they enable me to identify the unit within the restricted set of activities that constitute my daily life. I very seldom shop in other co-operative stores than our local one. The bank could of course identify the transaction uniquely by entering a transaction number, but this number cannot be related to my daily sign-system, which contains items such as "Co-operative Store Lystrup", "Pharmacy Lystrup", "Klemens Bookshop", but certainly not numbers such as "A12324XY".

Understanding can fail for two main reasons:

1.   The sign conforms to the principles of my semiotic system but happens not to find any hooks to relate to. For example, I read "Bookshop

Lystrup" and fail to make sense of it because Lystrup does not have any bookshop.

2.   The sign does not conform to the principles of my semiotic system, but uses one that is based on different classification principles. An example is using precise transaction numbers instead of sloppy short names.

Number 2 error is by far the worse because it is most difficult to correct. The reason is that classification principles can be deeply buried in the software and may require a major reprogramming effort to change.

It is not always easy to find the operative principles of classification of a given domain. A set of actions can be grouped according to the place or time, according to the object they concern, according to the instrument they use, or according to abstract process features of the actions themselves. Should we group *eating* together with *TV-watching* because both occur in the living room, or should *eating* belong to *cooking* because their object is food? Or maybe *eating* is more like *sleeping* since both reproduce our body?

It is definitely not a good idea for the systems designer to invent his own classification scheme without trying to understand some of the principles of the domain praxis.

The point of all this is that we need a framework for comparing the semiotic structure of a computer system to that of the context of situation. Compared to psychology or sociology, semiotics has an advantage that it can describe both entities, system as well as context, by means of the same set of concepts.

2. New developments

After this description of desiderata for a computer semiotics, I shall comment on some of the work that has been done after the first edition of this book (plus some work I did not know about when writing it) and indicate how some of it relates to the book. The following is list of books and papers that treats computer systems from a semiotic point of view; however, it is *not* complete but represents what I have come across myself.

ANDERSEN, P. BØGH & B. HOLMQVIST (1990a). Interactive Fiction. Artificial intelligence as a mode of sign production. *AI and Society 4*, 291-314.

ANDERSEN, P. BØGH & B. HOLMQVIST (1990b). Narrative computer systems. The dialectics of emotion and formalism. Paper presented at the conference *Computers and Writing III*, Edinburgh. 1990. Swedish translation in *Computerkultur — computer-medier — Computer-semiotik [Computer culture — computer media — computer semiotics]*, ed J. F. Jensen, 101-130. Nordic Summer University 1990.

ANDERSEN, P. BØGH & P. ØHRSTRØM. Hyperzeit. *Zeitschrift für Semiotik* 16(1-2), pp. 51-68.

ANDERSEN, P. BØGH (1986). Semiotics and informatics: computers as media. In *Information technology and information use. Towards a unified view of information and information technology,* ed P. Ingwersen, L. Kajberg and A. Mark Peitersen, 64-97. London: Taylor Graham.

ANDERSEN, P. BØGH (1990). Towards an aesthetics of hypertext systems. A semiotic approach. In *Hypertext: concepts, systems, and applications,* ed A. Rizk, N. Streitz and J. André, 224-238. Cambridge: Cambridge University Press.

ANDERSEN, P. BØGH (1991). A semiotic approach to construction and assessment of computer systems. In *Information systems research: contemporary approaches & emergent traditions,* H.-E. Nissen, H. K. Klein, R. Hirschheim (eds.), 465-515. Amsterdam: North Holland.

ANDERSEN, P. BØGH (1992a). Computer semiotics. *Scandinavian Journal of Information Systems.* Vol. 4: 1992. pp. 3-30.

ANDERSEN, P. BØGH (1992b). Vector spaces as the basic component of interactive systems. Towards a computer semiotics. *Hypermedia* 4(1), 53-76.

ANDERSEN, P. BØGH (1993). A semiotic approach to programming. In: Andersen, Holmqvist & Jensen (1993), pp. 16-68.

ANDERSEN, P. BØGH (1994a). Katastrophen und computer. *Zeitschrift für Semiotik* 16(1-2), pp. 29-50.

ANDERSEN, P. BØGH (1994b). The semiotics of autopoiesis. A catastrophe-theoretic approach. *Cybernetics & Human Knowing 2(4),* 1994.

ANDERSEN, P. BØGH (1995). The force dynamics of interactive systems. Towards a computer semiotics. *Semiotica* 103-1/2,5-45.

ANDERSEN, P. BØGH (forthcoming a). Dynamic logic. To appear in *Kodikas/ Code.*

ANDERSEN, P. BØGH (forthcoming b). Semiotics and Artificial Intelligence Research. In: *Handbuch der Semiotik.* R. Posner, K. Robering, T. A. Seboek (eds). Berlin/ New York: W. de Gruyter.

ANDERSEN, P. BØGH, B. HOLMQVIST & J. F. JENSEN (ed.) (1993) *Computers as media.* Cambridge: Cambridge University Press.

ANDERSEN, P. BØGH, P. HASLE & P. AA. BRANDT (forthcoming). Machine semiosis. In: *Handbuch der Semiotik.* R. Posner, K. Robering, T. A. Seboek (eds). Berlin/ New York: W. de Gruyter.

AURAMAKI, E., E. LEHTINEN & K. LYYTINEN (1988). A Speech-act-based office modelling approach. ACM Transactions on office information systems (6/2), 126-152.

BOLAND, J. R. (1991). Information system use as a hermeneutic process. In *Information systems research: contemporary approaches & emergent traditions,* ed H.-E. Nissen, H. K. Klein, R. Hirschheim, 439-458. Amsterdam: North Holland. Amsterdam.

BRANDT, P. Aa. (1993) Meaning and the machine. Towards a semiotics of interaction. In: Andersen, Holmqvist & Jensen, 1993, 128-141.

DECLÉS, J-P. (1989). Intermediate representations in the cognitive sciences. *Semiotica* 77(1/3): 121-135.

FIGGE, U. L. (1991). Computersemiotik. *Zeitschrift für Semiotik 13(3/4)*, 321-330.

FINNEMANN, N. O. (1993). *Tanke, Sprog og Maskine. [Thought., Language, and Machine]*. Copenhagen: Akademisk forlag.

GOLDKUHL, G. Understanding computer-based information systems through communicative action analysis. HUMOR 1984-12-06.

GORN, S. (1968). The identification of the computer and information sciences: their fundamental semiotic concepts and relationships. *Foundations of Language 4:* 339-372.

HASLE, P. (1993). Logic grammar and the triadic sign relation. In: Andersen, Holmqvist & Jensen, 1993, 104-128.

HOLMQVIST, B. & P. BØGH ANDERSEN (1991). Language, perspective, and design. In *Design at Work,* J. Greenbaum & M. Kyng (eds.), 91-121. Hillsdale: Earlbaum.

JORNA, R. J. (1990). Wissensrepräsentation in künstlichen Intelligenzen. Zeichentheorie and Kognitionsforschung. *Zeitschrift für Semiotik 12/1-2,* 9-23.

JORNA, R. J., B. van HEUSDEN & R. POSNER (eds.) (1993). *Signs, Search and Communication.* Berlin/New York: W. de Gruyter.

JØRGENSEN, K. G. (1993). The shortest way between two points is a good idea: Signs, Peirce, and the thorematic machines. In: Andersen, Holmqvist & Jensen, 1993, 92 - 104.

LAUREL, B. *Computers as Theater.* Reading, Mass.: Addison-Wesley 1991.

MATHIASSEN, L. & P. BØGH ANDERSEN (1984). Semiotics and informatics: the impact of edp-based systems upon the professional language of nurses. In van der Veer (ed.), *Readings on Cognitive Ergonomics - Mind and Computers.* 226-247. Berlin: Springer-Verlag. Also in *Journal of Pragmatics* 10(1986): 1-26.

NADIN, M. (1988). Interface design: A semiotic paradigm. *Semiotica 69:* 269-302.

NAKE, F. (ed.). (1993). *Die erträgliche Lichtigkeit der Zeichen. Ästetik, Semiotik, Informatik.* Baden-Baden: Agis-Verlag.

NAKE, F. (ed.). (1994). Zeichen und Gebrauchwert. Beiträge zur Maschinisierung von kopfarbeit. Bericht 6/94. Universität Bremen, Fachbericht Mathematik und Informatik.

OUELLET, P. (1989). Semiotics, cognition, and artificial intelligence. Special issue of *Semiotica. Semiotica 77.*

PIOTROWSKI, D. (1990). *Structures Applicatives et Language Naturel. Recherches sur les fondements du modele: "Grammaire Applicative et Cognitive".* Ph.D. thesis, Ecole des Hautes Etudes en Sciences Sociales, Paris.

PIOTROWSKI, D. (1993) Structuralism, computation and cognition. The contribution of glossematics. In: Andersen, Holmqvist & Jensen, 1993, 68 - 91.

RASMUSSEN, J. (1986). *Information processing and human-machine interaction.* New York: North-Holland.

SOUZA, C. SIECKENIUS DE (1993). The semiotic engineering of user interface languages. *Int. J. Man-Machine Studies 39,* pp. 753-773.

STAMPER, R. (1973). *Information in Business and Administrative Systems.* London: Batsford.

STAMPER, R. (1991). The Semiotic Framework for Information Systems Research. In Nissen, Klein & Hirschhaim (eds.), *Information Systems Research:*

Contemporary Approaches & Emergent Traditions, 515-528. Amsterdam: North Holland.

STAMPER, R. (1992). Signs organizations, norms and information systems. *Proc. Third Australian Conference on Information Systems.* 21-55. Wollongong, Australia.

STAMPER, R., L. KECHENG & K. HUANG (forthcoming). EDI systems design from semiotic perspective (University of Twente, Enschede, The Netherlands).

ZEMANEK, H. (1966). Semiotics and programming languages. *CACM 9/3,* 139-143.

2.1. Saussure versus Peirce

The first thing to note is the diversity of the semiotic framework. The most important distinction is between the two main traditions normally associated with the two fathers of semiotics: the European tradition founded by F. de Saussure and developed by L. Hjelmslev and A. J. Greimas, and the American tradition based on the works of C. S. Peirce and C. W. Morris. The present book is written within the European tradition, but both traditions are clearly productive in computer semiotics.

The two traditions differ in many respects. The European tradition evolved from the science of linguistics, whereas the American tradition was originally a part of a much more comprehensive philosophical system. Although the European tradition lacks the philosophical foundation of the American tradition, it is more operational and precise in its methodology. I have always found it very difficult to use Peircean semiotics for concrete purposes, and as a help for analysing and designing computer systems I definitely prefer the European version.

Their sign-concepts are different too. The European tradition works with a binary sign consisting of *signifier* and *signified*, whereas the Americans need three parts: the *representamen* (roughly corresponding to the signifier), the *object* (related to the *referential* aspect of the signified) and the *interpretant* (the *sense* aspect of the signified). The representamen stands for the object in the specific manner indicated by the interpretant.

The interpretant is a difficult concept to understand, although, paradoxically, it is one of Peirce's most fertile inventions. As said above, the interpretant indicates the specific way in which representamen and object are related, but the interpretant is also a reaction of an interpreter to the sign: for example, if the representamen is Mona Lisa whose object is La Gioconda, then possible interpretants range from comments of museum guests to books on the history of art. In both cases the interpretant specifies the relation between representamen and object. But, as the example shows, interpretants are themselves signs and therefore generate their own interpretants (comments on comments, books referring to books), which recursively generate their interpretants, etc. in infinity. Semiosis is unlimited, the process is infinite.

The reason why the European school does not have an interpretant is that it is a theory about the social aspects of signs. Since it focuses on the super-individual sides, it abstracts individual subjects away.

The problem for the Europeans is that it is very difficult to ignore interpretants when dealing with computers, because computer systems are interactive, which makes the physical response of the user a part of the semiosis. Whereas the user is only *psychically* active with older media, he is both psychically and *physically* active when using computers. Although the visual shape of a pencil in a drawing program is an important part of semiosis, the fact that the user can move it and use it to draw is an even more powerful reason for him to accept that the pixel-pattern represents a pencil.

For the same reason, the interpretant is indispensable when we deal with communication in organisations. For example, orders require an explicit response from the person ordered, and we can even *define* orders as a sign-action dependency where the action depends on the sign. The sentence "Close the door" is an order whether or not it is followed by the closing of the door. But the closing of the door is not an interpretant of an order if not preceded by the sentence. In other words, orders concern actions that would not have been done, had not the sentence been uttered.

Peircean semiotics was used in one of the earliest attempts to apply semiotics in design of computer systems, namely Nadin (1988) who classifies the interface as representamen, functionality ("type of computer system") as object, and context and values as interpretant. But although the interface, with the user as the interpreter, does seem the most obvious field to use semiotic methods, it is certainly not the only one. There are many interpreters at work in the design and use of computer systems. In fact, systems development mainly consists in writing and reading, so semiotics may not only shed light over the interface, but may also inform technical concepts such as program verification, program specification, compilation, etc., as we shall presently see.

The notion of interpretant in fact seems to be generally useful for analysing software systems. Hasle (1993) suggests that translation relations in Montague grammar can be classified as interpretants. The object of the representamen "man" is its sense *man'* (its intension). But the intension *man'* enters a new sign-relation as representamen whose object is a real individual (its reference or extension). The interpretant of this new sign is a possible world, since only a choice of a possible world can relate the sense of "man" to its reference. Thus, the object of a word is its sense — a method for finding referents, given a possible world; and the object of a sense is a real referent of the chosen possible world.

This idea is further elaborated in Andersen, Hasle & Brandt (forthcoming) where operational semantics and compilation are analysed along these lines. See Fig. 1.

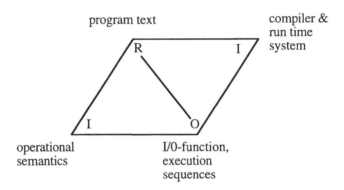

Fig. 1. Compiler and program.

The program text is a representamen (R) whose object (O) is execution sequences, i.e. sequences of machine operations. There are two different kinds of interpretants (I), namely an *intentional* and a *causal interpretant*. The intentional interpretant is identical to an operational semantics that specifies how the program text should translate into execution sequences. The compiler and run time system is a causal mechanical interpretant (Gorn 1968) that physically converts the program text into execution sequences. The idea is now that the causal interpretant must specify the same object as the intentional interpretant.

This type of analysis can give new insights in the semiotic variety of large software systems mentioned in Section 1.1. If we analyse program texts and their use we quickly discover a rich set of different sign types, a specimen of which is shown in Fig. 2.

The *program text* is typically ambiguous in that it has two different objects and two different interpretants. As we saw in Fig. 1, the program execution is one object of the program text, since a program text must specify a set of executions with the aid of an operational semantics and a corresponding compiler. But it must also count as a general description of the domain, based on system description conventions, for example the convention mentioned above that object instances signify entities in the domain, object methods events, and object variables properties of entities.

The two different interpretants can be described empirically by studying conventions for constructing identifiers and comments, since these two sign-types are not determined by the causal interpretant, but can be varied freely.

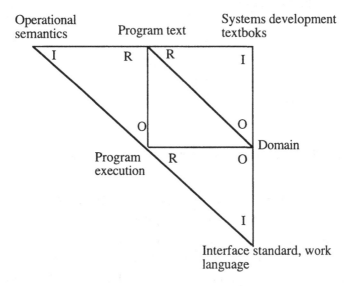

Fig. 2. Programs, executions, and users.

As suggested in Section 1.1, the *domain* itself is also ambiguous; on the one hand it is the object of the program text, on the other hand it is the object of program executions, with an interpretant based on the interface standard and the work language in the organisation. The former version of the domain is constructed by the system developers based on a reading of the whole text. The latter version is built by the users, typically based on experience with a small fraction of system executions and with their work language as an important interpretant. One wonders whether it is really the same domain we are talking about. Does the system developers' domain coincide with the users' domain, or are we really dealing with two different objects?

Although the Peircean sign-concept is clearly useful for understanding the global structure of software systems, the European tradition for dealing with concrete texts shows its strength when we get down to actual programming and concrete design. Examples of this are Andersen (1990, 1993) and Piotrowski (1990, 1993). Both authors use the three basic glossematic functions *constellation*, *determination*, and *interdependence* as a basis for understanding programming. Andersen applies them to object-oriented programming, whereas Piotrowski discusses applicative languages.

Specifying and implementing the relations between the main components of a system, say components that signify actions, tools, and material, can serve as an example. The relation between the three components can be described as a *determination* (an entity A is said to determine entity B if A can occur only if B occurs), and a possible principle is that actions determine tools which determine material.

material

tool

action

Fig. 3. Determination between actions, tools, and materials.

Since the glossematic functions are ontological, describing the conditions for some entity to exist, our analysis is ontological. Actions cannot exist if the tools do not exist (e.g. sawing is impossible without tools for sawing), and tools cannot exist if there is no material they can transform (saws cannot exist if the world does not contain material that can be sawed). The converse is not true: we can have material without having tools for manipulating it, and we can have tools without using them. The determination depicted is categorial, pertaining to types, but the dependence also implies restrictions on the instances: the concrete material constrains the possible tools, and the individual tool delimits the possible actions that can be performed.

This analysis can be manifested in various ways, e.g. as a guide for implementation or for interface design.

There are many ways of implementing the abstract ontological relations. For example, the *material* class may contain the definition of the *tool* class which again contains the definition of the *action* methods. This is one way of ensuring that tools do not make sense outside the context of material, and that actions are meaningless outside the tool context.

```
class material {
  class tool {
   virtual void action;
  }
}
```

The specific constraints can be implemented by specialising the classes:

```
class paper: material {
  class pencil: tool {
   virtual void action { // definition of drawing }
```

```
}
class brush: tool {
 virtual void action { // definition of painting }
 }
}
```

Only in the subclass *paper* are *pencil* and *brush* defined, and only in *pencil* is *drawing* defined.

When the ontology analysis is applied to programming, we deal with the existence of system objects in RAM, whereas if we use the same concepts in interface design, existence means: visible, available to the user.

My conclusion is that both the European and the American semiotic tradition are useful in computer semiotics.

2.2. *Organisational setting*

I have emphasised that semiosis depends upon the organisational setting, and that there is a need to relate systems design to organisational setting in a systematic fashion. The work of Ronald Stamper, Stamper (1973, 1991, 1993) and Stamper, Kecheng & Huang (forthcoming), seems relevant in this connection. Although Stamper's approach is highly original, his main orientation is towards Peircean semiotics.

I select two main ideas from his work, namely his theory of levels of information systems and his ontology charts that aim at describing the domain of the information system.

Major level	Minor level	Definition
Signified	Social world	Beliefs, expectations, commitments, contracts, law, culture.
	Pragmatics	Intentions, communications, conversations, negotiations.
	Semantics	Meanings, propositions, validity, truth, signification, denotations,...
Signifier	Syntactics	Formal structure, language, logic, data, records, deduction, software, files,...
	Empirics	Pattern, variety, noise, entropy, channel capacity, redundancy, efficiency, codes
	Physical world	Signals, traces, physical distinctions, hardware, component density, speed, economics.

Information systems and their context are described in 2 main levels, corresponding to the signifier-signified dichotomy. Each level is divided into 3 minor levels, yielding a total of 6 levels.

The higher levels presuppose the lower ones. Consider for example introduction of EDI, electronic data interchange, that enables automatic ordering, buying, and payment. Before anything else we need to install hardware and connect it by means of nets through which physical signals can travel (physical world). After we have succeeded in making signals travel from one computer to another, we must ensure reliable transmission, for example removing the negative effects of noise by means of redundancy (empirics). Having ensured reliable transmission of identifiable signals, we must fix a protocol of communication between the two computers, that is: we must design the formal syntax of communication (syntactics).

Having done this, we must agree on the meaning of the messages: e.g. what does is mean to sell or buy something? What is a customer? What is a payment? These semantic questions are solved by universal standards such as EDIFACT. Now that we can correctly send an order from one machine to another and know what it means, the next task is to align the working procedures of the buyer and seller to the new electronic market (pragmatics). And finally, we are curious to learn what changes in our organisations will follow. For example, will the closer co-operation cause employees to feel that they are really working in one, not two, organisations (social world)?

On the seventh day we rest.

The terms *syntactics*, *semantics*, and *pragmatics* are borrowed from Peirce, but the other three have been added by Stamper himself. However, it seems that the extra levels can be defined theoretically by looking at the Saussurean/Hjelmslevian sign-concept.

	Form	**Substance**
Content (signified)	Semantics	Pragmatics and Social world
Expression (signifier)	Syntactics	Empirics and Physical world.

As said above, the European sign-concept is articulated into signifier and signified — expression and content — but this distinction is combined with a form-substance distinction, giving us a total of 4 categories.

The *form* aspect of a sign consist of those features that commute. A feature commutes if exchange of the feature with another causes a change on the other plane of the sign. The form aspect can also be said to describe the essence of a semiotic system — the relations and units that define the identity of a system. Phonemes are an example of a form category, since exchange of one phoneme with another must cause a change of meaning.

The *substance* aspect deals with variations and statistical patterns — habits, norms, conventions — that do not commute and do not serve to define system identity. At the expression level, statistical, auditory and physical descriptions of phonemes belong to substance descriptions, whereas style and received syntactic usage are examples of content substance.

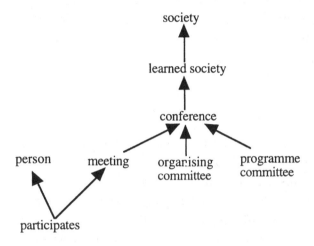

Fig. 4. Ontology chart.

Another original invention is Stamper's system description tool, the *ontology graphs*. The basic concept is the affordance-concept borrowed from Gibson. Invariants of a phenomenon are said to *afford* or make possible for an agent some repertoire of actions. For example, being in a car prevents you from walking but makes driving possible. Stamper's ontology graphs are made up of affordances that create other affordances. For example, the existence of a learned society makes conferences possible, which again affords organising committees, programme committees, and meetings which again together with the existence of persons enable the action "participate" (a person participates in a meeting) to occur. If we write affordance as an arrow, we can diagram this as shown in Fig. 4.

Ontology charts are used as database schemas to automatically generate a database in which data about the domain can be stored and used for further inferences.

Stamper's radical constructivism shows up as the requirement that each diagram must have a responsible agent at the root: a person, an organisation, or simply society. The purpose is to emphasize that the whole diagram is a construction for which some agent must take responsibility. For example, the institution of learned societies ontologically depends upon the existence of a society: learned societies are social constructions, not natural phenomena.

As the reader may already have noticed, Stamper's ontology diagrams are very similar to my use of the glossematic functions. In fact, his basic relation of affordance corresponds to the equally basic glossematic *determination*. Fig. 3 can easily be interpreted as a ontology graph where material affords tools which again afford actions.

Task analysis could proceed according to similar principles. Each time a certain task has been accomplished, a new set of affordances are opened. For example, opening the hood of my car enables me to check oil, to change filter, or to replenish water.

2.3. Dynamics

Computer systems are similar to film in that time and change are important features. A program execution is in fact a sequence of states $\Sigma = <S_1...S_n>$ where S_1 contains the input-values of the variables and S_n the output-values. Each state change S_i, S_{i+1} is uniquely specified by the program text.

A program text specifies a (possibly infinite) set of state change sequences $\{\Sigma_1...\Sigma_i...\}$ whose members share a set of common features but differ in other respects. Their common features are described by the program text, and the deviations are due to different inputs.

Example: the code below is a method of a movie-object playing a movie-file until it is finished. The object contains a *state* variable and keeps performing the method *Idle()* until the state is different from the constant *MSMovieRunning*.

```
Movie::PlayUntilEnd()
{
  while (state == MSMovieRunning) Idle();
}
```

The method specifies an infinite number of executions: performing Idle() one time, performing it two times, performing it three times, etc., the number of times being determined by the length of the input movie-file. How do the two main semiotics traditions treat such dynamic phenomena?

In *Peircean semiotics* the dynamic aspect of computer systems is naturally seen as a *logical* process, because logic, in a broad sense, is an integrated element of Peirce's theory. Peirce distinguishes between three kinds of logical processes, *deduction, induction,* and *abduction*.

In deduction we produce a result from a rule and a case of the rule (*All the beans from this bag are white* (Rule), *These beans are from this bag* (Case) gives us *These beans are white* (Result)).

In induction we use the case and the result to produce the rule (*These beans are from this bag* (Case), *These beans are white* (Result) gives us *All the beans from this bag are white*(Rule)).

Finally, in abduction we have a rule and a fact in need of explanation. The explanation is given by assuming that the fact is a case of the rule (from *All the beans from this bag are white* (Rule) and *These beans are white* (Result, needing explanation) we infer that *These beans are from this bag* (Case)). Abduction is a qualified guess, a kind of backward reasoning.

As noted in Jørgensen(1993), semiosis itself is a logical process. In the case of symbols, for example, the association of representamen and object is based on a convention, i.e. a rule. So if we know the convention, e.g. that an aeroplane can be signified "plane" in English (Rule), and if we are presented with the word "plane" (fact in need of explanation), we use abduction to figure out that speaker probably had an aeroplane in mind. The point is that the guess could be wrong, and that he really meant "surface". One may add, that we sometimes not only guess at the object, but also at the rule, i.e. the interpretant. This is the case in poetry.

Databases and expert systems, which are traditionally interpreted as collections of facts from which new facts can be inferred, are, so to speak, already prepared for a Peircean treatment. Examples can be found in Jorna et al (1993) that deals with expert systems, and in Stamper's theory that focuses on information systems (e.g. data bases) in organisations.

The basic rule in Stamper's framework is modal norms of the form

```
If <condition> then
  <some agent> is permitted/forbidden/obliged to do <action>
```

Norms are assumed to define organisations as well as the formal information systems they use. An organisational norm could be

```
If <loan is less than some amount> then
  <a bank clerk> is permitted to do <authorise the loan>
```

whereas a computational norm could be

```
If <the movie has not stopped> then
  <the movie object> is obliged to do <keep running the movie>
```

Thus, at least for some types of applications, Peircean semiotics contains concepts that can be specialised to handle computational processes too. However, it is not clear that all computer applications are fruitfully seen as inferential systems. Although Prolog, the standard logic programming language, is suited for some purposes, procedural languages (e.g. Pascal or C) and functional languages (e.g. LISP) perform better and are easier to use in other areas.

Whereas the Peircean tradition has a built-in dynamics, the *European tradition* has always had problems with accounting for processes. The reason is that it is mainly interested in general and stable structures and tends to overlook the idiosyncrasies of concrete language usage.

However, this does not mean that European structuralism has no concepts for processes in the sense of elements that follow each other in time. In fact, the concept of *syntagms* (elements that occur simultaneously, as opposed to paradigms which are elements that exclude each other) is intended to describe text processes. Traces of program executions can be viewed as a text that can be analysed as any other text. A syntagmatic analysis of this text will reveal the invariant features of the text and therefore count as a process specification.

As an example, consider again the behaviour of the movie-object above whose code says that whenever the state equals *MSMovieRunning* the *Idle()* method must be performed. Since it does not prevent *Idle()* from being performed if the state does not equal to *MSMovieRunning* and since other objects may indeed call *Idle()* even if the state is different from *MSMovieRunning*, it follows that the condition and action of the while-loop forms a *determination*, the state determining the action. We know such dependencies from language where we can have nouns (the *head*) without adjectives (the *modifier*), but not adjectives without nouns. Such constructions are called *hypotagms*, and in the case of the movie controller the action plays the role of the head with the state as its modifier.

In general, a while-loop can be described as a hypotagm whose modifer is the condition of the loop and whose head is a paratagm consisting of one or more instances of the action of the loop.

Modifier	Head		
Condition	Action	....	Action
state == MSMovieRunning	Idle()	. . . .	Idle()

The real problem is that structuralism is only interested in the stable properties of a given set of processes. It offers good methods for investigating the set in a systematic fashion and gives principles for extracting the regularities, but since it lacks concepts for agents, it cannot ask and answer questions about the genesis and development of the processes. It can produce good snapshots of states of the process, but finds it difficult to relate one snapshot to another.

This weakness is well known and has motivated recent attempts to combine the European semiotic tradition with catastrophe theory:

PETITOT, J. & R. THOM (1983). *Sémiotique et théorie des catastrophes. Actes Sémiotiques 5(47/48)*. Paris: Institut National de la Langue Francaise.

PETITOT, J. (1985). *Morphogenese du sens I*. Paris: Presses Universitaires de France

PETITOT, J. (1989). On the linguistic import of catastrophe theory. *Semiotica 74(3/4):* 179-209.

THOM, R. (1990). *Semio Physics. A sketch*. Redwood City, CA: Addison-Wesley Publ. Comp.

WILDGEN, W. (1982). *Catastrophe Theoretic Semantics*. Amsterdam: John Benjamins Publ. Comp.

WILDGEN, W. (1985). *Archentypen-semantik*. Tübingen: Gunter Narr Verlag.

In the last paragraphs I shall sketch a possible way of establishing dynamics right in middle of the heart of Saussure and Hjelmslev. At the same time I shall integrate semiotics explicitly with sociological theory because of the need demonstrated above to relate semiotic and organisational analyses. The theory I am using is the sociology of Niklas Luhmann:

LUHMANN, N. (1984). *Soziale Systeme*. Frankfurt am Main: Suhrkamp.

LUHMANN, N. (1986). Social system's autopoiesis. In: F. Geyer & J. van der Zouwen (eds.), *Sociocybernetic Paradoxes*. London: SAGE Publications, 172-192.

LUHMANN, N. (1988). *Erkenntnis als Konstruktion*. Bern: Benteli Verlag.

LUHMANN, N. (1990). *Essays on Self-Reference*. New York: Columbia University Press.

Some of the suggestions below are described more fully in Andersen 1994b and forthcoming a.

I want the theory to account for the following phenomena:

- *Form/substance:* as discovered by Hjelmslev, semiosis involves a simultaneous introduction of distinctions in two continua, the content and the expression substance. In this way the two substances are supplied with critical points, the transgression of which makes a qualitative difference — causes a catastrophe to happen. The two sides of the sign are conceived as phase-spaces analogous to the phase-space of water whose pertinent dimensions are temperature and pressure. If water is heated above a certain level, it crosses a critical limit and turns into gas — a quantitative change becomes qualitative. However, instead of having one isolated phase-space, we have two spaces, the expression and the content plane, that are coupled in such a way that one passes a critical limit whenever the other does it.

- *Context-dependence of semiosis:* there is no doubt that semiosis is highly context-dependent. Words and sentences do not have fixed meanings, but interact with the context of situation in a complex way. Now, since semiosis consists in the interaction of two coupled phase-spaces it follows that at least one of them must exist in many types. Since change of context normally changes contents but leaves the expression level intact, the content plane is assumed to contain many systems, each one representing a specific context of situation.
- *The self-sufficient nature of semiotic systems:* although the model must account for contextual variation, it must retain Hjelmslev's insight that semiotic systems contain an immanent logic that preserves their identity and structural stability. Although semiotic systems can be perturbed, there are limits that cannot be transgressed if the system is not to disintegrate.
- *Communication is indirect:* communication cannot be described as a message that travels from one head to another through a suitable channel, because the same sign can elicit different responses with different people at different times. Communication is more like a perturbation that disturbs the stability of the receiver; the receiver tries to compensate for the disturbance but the actual compensation is heavily dependent upon the present state of the receiver.

I follow Luhmann in postulating three main systems: the *social* system containing signifiers corresponds to Hjelmslev's expression plane, the *psychic* system contains signifieds and corresponds to the content plane; the *biological* system, representing our bodies, is ignored by Hjelmslev. Each system is a phase-space whose dimensions reflect the relevant dimensions of the sign: the dimensions of the social system includes phonemic and syntactic features, those of the psychic system semantic features. Each system is supplied with a force-field that defines the equilibria of the individual system if any exist.

Catastrophe theory uses polynomials to describe the force field and lets the inhabitants of the field move according to the gradients of the field. The system is in equilibrium if the gradient is zero. The polynomials are parametrized, and it is possible to change the equilibrium conditions by changing the parameters.

Below is shown an example from the expression plane. The curve (an x^4 polynomial) visualises the potential, and the black dot represents the signifier "she". In Fig. 5 the signifier is at rest in the leftmost minimum. Then the potential is perturbed and changes shape so that two minima appear (Fig. 6). Still the pronoun is at rest in the leftmost minimum, but in Fig. 7 something new happens; as we keep perturbing the potential, the left minimum suddenly disappears, "she" becomes unstable and rolls down into the right minimum. We see how a continuous change (the deformation of the potential) causes a sudden qualitative change (the movement of the signifier from the left to the right minimum).

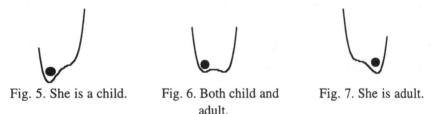

Fig. 5. She is a child. Fig. 6. Both child and adult. Fig. 7. She is adult.

Now, suppose that nouns such as "child" and "adult" are located on the x-axis and that the parameter change represents the passing of time: my daughter gets older. Suppose furthermore that the location of "she" relative to the nouns on the x-axis represents the subject-predicate syntagm. Then the sudden jump of the dot represents the distinction between the senses of "she is a child" and "she is an adult" — suddenly I realise that my daughter has grown up, I have to change my attitude to her, and in particular have to describe her differently.

In the example, the perturbation of our small semiotic universe came from its environment, but there will also be internally generated forces representing syntactic rules. For example, we may want to have adjectives determine a noun, ensuring that no sentence is in equilibrium if it contains an adjective without a noun. This can be done by assigning a noun-attracting potential to all adjectives. If a noun is around, it will be caught by the adjective and form a noun phrase.

A system cannot directly influence the inhabitants of other systems. Thus signifiers cannot directly influence signifieds, which rules out the conveyor-tube model of communication. A system can only *perturb* another system by influencing its "energy landscape". The resulting drift towards a new equilibrium is the perturbed system's own doing and depends upon the structure of the global field before perturbation. The field parameters that can be changed by the environment are called the system's *boundary*.

In a Peircean framework, the boundary parameters correspond to the *interpretant*, the perturbation is the *object* (in our example the age of my daughter) and the compensation is the *representamen*, since it results in the formation of a new syntagm, "she is adult".

In a Hjelmslevian framework, the boundary parameters and the potentials constitute the *form* whereas the perturbation itself is the *substance*. The reason for this is that the behaviour of the potentials articulates the space of possible perturbations by defining the boundaries at which catastrophes happen.

If there are n dimensions in the system, each inhabitant is represented by n coordinates $x_1...x_n$. Denote this as a vector $\mathbf{X}$. The energy-landscape is composed by a set of potentials of the form $P(\mathbf{X}, a_1...a_m)$ where $a_1...a_m$ represent the boundary. The gradient is the derivative of P, $P'(\mathbf{X}, a_1...a_m)$. The new state of the system at time t, $\mathbf{X_t}$, is calculated as the old state $\mathbf{X_{t-1}}$ minus the gradient, so the system trajectory is defined by the iteration

$$\mathbf{X_t} = \mathbf{X_{t-1}} - P'(\mathbf{X_{t-1}}, a_1...a_m)$$

Apart from the fact that the theory fulfils the desiderata listed above, it has additional advantages.

For example, although the system is susceptible to external influences, it retains its own immanent forces, and the combined effect of external and internal forces is well-defined: it is simply the vector sum of all gradients. Also, the old dichotomy between the system and its use has disappeared, since the system has now been re-shaped in a dynamic form that precisely defines its use.

Finally, the theory predicts a set of phenomena that seem very plausible. One such phenomenon is a mutual amplification of processes of content and expression plane. A small change in the content system perturbs the expression system, causing signifiers to begin to move slowly. This movement perturbs the content system and possibly amplifies the original movement, which again amplifies the signifier movement, etc., etc. The result is that the structural coupling between the systems schematises and amplifies the original movement of the signified. This explains why language use is not only a matter of externalising thoughts but also a way of clarifying or distorting thoughts. Therapy works because speaking our mind changes it.

I am not sure whether the mathematics of catastrophe theory actually turns out to be the best formalism for this type of theory. We need to investigate the properties of other types of dynamic systems, for example those studied by chaos theory, and to do empirical studies of the dynamics of communication in order to make a motivated choice.

Returning to computer semiotics, we now take this general conception of signs and semiosis and use it in the specific case of computer systems. In this view, a computer system is a social system, consisting of signifiers, that enters a structural coupling with minds and bodies (psychic and biological systems) during use. As before, the system objects are points in a multi-dimensional phase-space. A subset of these dimensions can be manifested in the interface-substance of the system: for example, an object may have a location on the screen, it may have a color, a transparency, a font type and font size, an icon, etc., etc. Object-oriented systems lend themselves easily to this interpretation. In fact, the objects of interface editors such as Hypercard and Supercard are defined as a bundle of more than 100 properties.

Programming such systems means to define the force-field and the boundary through which the user can disturb the field. The idea is elaborated in Andersen 1992b, 1994a, 1995, and has been used in practice to construct a multimedia system about the Viking age that is currently running in a Danish museum.

PART I. THEORY

I.1

The Structuralist Heritage

I start with a reassessment of selected linguistic traditions. Since they were developed to meet needs other than those I want them to serve, a careful re-examination is not out of place.

I.1.1. Empirical characteristics of two work languages[1]

The first issue I shall take up is simply whether they are able to handle the language variety in which most computer systems must function, namely the languages of people at work, and in order to do so we need to know what a "work language" is.

The car repair shop

The typical Danish car repair shop is a small scale enterprise, consisting of the owner and a couple of skilled workers, possibly an apprentice and a book-keeper, as well.

Most of the work can be performed by one worker alone, so cooperation is seldom a physical necessity. Planning and execution of the work proce-dure is integrated. The mechanic performs both tasks. Personal relationships between employer and employee survive, such as the master-journeyman relationship. Normally, a small stock of tools is used: hammers, screwdrivers, nippers, etc.

In the early eighties, I investigated communication in a small repair shop, and the following pages are based on this project[2]. The research was done in collaboration with one of the mechanics employed in the garage. A tape-recorder placed on a bench recorded the conversation that took place during work. (Everybody in the garage knew about the recording.) The mechanic also produced written descriptions of whole working days.

The analysis of the data took 1 1/2 years. The mechanic was employed as an assistant teacher in an advanced course at the university. The reason why this analysis of 15 pages took so long was that the speech recorded was so

---

[1] This section is based on Holmqvist & Bøgh Andersen 1987.
[2] See Bøgh Andersen 1977a.

context dependent that most of the important events were not expressed but had to be supplemented by the mechanic: I had to learn the secrets of car repair in order to understand why sentences were uttered, and what they meant.

The work situation - a mixture of verbal and non-verbal actions

This experience is very nicely illustrated by the first example I give, a conversation serving to coordinate work: work coordination. Try to read the following:

1   A: Bent[1]
     B: Yes
     A: Couldn't you come over here for a minute () couldn't you just - you shouldn't put in the lamp or the bolt until I
5   () the nut to the hole, see /.../
     B: Yes, it should be a bit further towards you
     A: Towards me
     B: Yes
     B: A little bit more
10   B: Higher up (towards you) -
     straight up - there, right there...(it has to be there) -
     there right there (...)
     B: I've got hold of it
     A: You've got hold of it
15   B: Yes, let go
     A: Are you sure?
     B: Yes
     A: Because I wouldn't like to let go if
     B: Oh yes
20   A: It's all right, then you are finished with this one now, but can you see the next one too?
     B: Yes, -a little further out and up, a little - higher up
     towards you
     A: Try and hold it
25   B: Yes
     A: It's OK
     B: Can I start to screw?
     A: Yes - I think it's there
     B: Hold it
30   A: It's not me that has to hold it, it's you

---

[1] A man's name.

B: I see

A: That's it, was that all?

B: Yes

Example 1. Work coordination.

The text does not convey much meaning just by reading it, and the stock in trade of linguistics also fails to yield interesting results. The reason is that something is missing - the text does not feel complete.

What is missing is the non-verbal work that is coordinated by means of language. When this is supplemented, the text becomes completely understandable: A wants to mount the rear light of a car by means of a bolt and nut. The nut must be positioned over the hole from inside the car. Then the bolt is put through the hole from outside, and if it catches the nut, the rear light can be screwed on. It is not possible for one man to do this, so A gets hold of B, places himself in the car, and tries to move the nut over the hole; he cannot see the hole, but from the outside B can see when the nut is covering the hole, and he directs A's movements, and finally inserts the bolt.

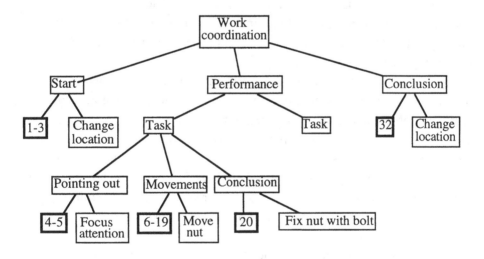

Fig. I.1.1. Analysis of car repair

Note first that the repair plan is not communicated - A presupposes that B can reconstruct his plan by merely looking at the state of the car. It is in fact generally true that a mechanic can reconstruct the work that is going on by simply looking at the car.

Note also that many utterances are not sentences: during the actual work, the utterances consist of adverbials of direction and place, and it would be difficult to extrapolate them into complete sentences, since they would never occur in this situation. The goal of the work is to place the nut over the hole, and A repeatedly performs actions of the type "move nut *in some* direction", while B furnishes the missing adverbial. Half of the "proposition" is realized as presupposed action, and half of it is verbalized.

The same principle of mixing verbal and non-verbal acts is found in the overall structure of the text[1] (Fig. I.1.1).

The large constituents of the conversation seem to be controlled by text linguistic rules: lines 1-3 (*A: Bent. B: Yes. A: Couldn't you come over here for a minute*) establish the coordination, and line 32 (*A: That's it, was that all, B: Yes*) ends it by verbal means, and the two subtasks each consisting in fixing a bolt and nut are marked symbolically at their boundaries (*It's all right, then you are finished with this one now, but can you see the next one too?*). However, the sequence of utterances within each "movement part" (*Higher up (towards you) - straight up - there, right there...(it has to be there) - there right there (...)*) is not governed by any text-linguistic rules, but depends entirely upon the way A moves the bolt. Thus, the work coordination consists of both verbal and non-verbal acts, the verbal acts sometimes having the independent function of marking the rough outline of the conversation, such as establishing and ending temporary social bonds and making transitions from one task to another, sometimes being completely dominated by non-verbal acts.

There is a clear influence of non-verbal acts upon the morphology of the utterances. For example, the progress of the job influences the modality system, since there is a tendency to use polite phrases when establishing a type of cooperation: A asks B *couldn't you come over here,* rather than using imperatives like *come here!* However, when the cooperation is established, naked orders begin to abound, the directions from B to A not any longer being qualified by politeness markings. The reason is that within the cooperation, B acquires authority because of his physical position: he can see something that A cannot see.

Syntax furnishes another example. The syntax in this example is very simple, consisting of short utterances, many of them based on the same schema. In the Danish text, there were mainly three kinds of adverbials of direction:

- a description of the new movement in relation to the preceding one (*a little - higher*)
- a description of the new movement in relation to the common system of orientation (*further out*)

---

[1] The diagram displays a part-whole analysis of the work process. Thus, the work coordination conversation is analyzed into three major parts: start, performance, and conclusion. The verbal parts are set off by boldface boxes.

- a description of the new movement in relation to the person doing the movement *(towards you)*

This syntactic structure is due to the fact that utterances and movements occur closely after each other, an utterance referring back to the preceding movement and controlling the subsequent one. The typical constituent in the conversation contains both utterance and movement:

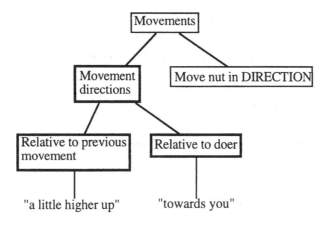

Fig. I.1.2. Utterances and actions.

Problem solving

In the work coordination example, strong expectations about what will probably happen are built into the context, and therefore the mechanics need only short and "incomplete" indications of what to do, but in other situations where the expectations are weaker, more elaborate means of expression are used. In the following problem solving situation the boss contemplates what to do in an ambiguous situation; he seems to be thinking aloud and giving orders at the same time

While you're going to get two short pieces anyway, then you can try and find out if they can be stripped, if they can't then you can try and get two new drums.

Example 2. Problem solving.

and later

Because if they can strip them, then they must mount oversized linings themselves, you know, but if they can't strip them, then we'll see, then we will have to get one pair of linings, and then hope that they have the bits over there.

Example 3. Problem solving.

Here we have subordinate sentences, whole sentences and logical conjunction. Even if many types of work situations generate schematized speech, there are situations that require more elaborate usage, as also observed by Falzon 1983 and 1984 in his study of flight controllers.

The problem to be solved is the following: the driver has waited too long and the linings are worn away, and there are three solutions: to mount ordinary linings, to turn the drums and mount oversized linings, or to buy new drums and mount ordinary linings.

The garage does not have the necessary gear to settle the question, and this ambiguous situation gives rise to various types of communication that aim at creating consensus about the situation. Among those are the following comments that illustrate the imaginative usage of rhetorical devices that is also a part of work language:

E: Oh hell, they are damned bad, the other side is just as worn

A: Yes, I can see that

E: Damn it, it has worn the lining clean off one of the shoes. There are only the rivets left.

B: It must have new drums, there is nothing else to do

B: Well, in the rear things are better

/.../

B: There is no doubt about it, the drums must be stripped, in any case, we need two new front drums

A: Oh

B: This is the worst I have ever seen

A: You can use them as sandpaper

A: He has driven long enough with these

B: I have never seen anything like this before

A: They are much worse on the other side

E: There are only the rivets left

B: Have you ever seen anything like this before

A: No, not that I know of

A: It looks very bad

B: Yes it does, doesn't it

A: It'll probably be too thin if it is stripped

B: It certainly will

Example 4. Work comments.

Note the repetitions, the exaggerations, the rhythmic patterns, and the metaphorical expressions. Utterances about the bad condition of the brakes are repeated in variations throughout the text, and *There are only the rivets left* is an exaggeration, since some of the lining remains. Finally, the sandpaper metaphor is used to drive home the point.

The purpose of this conversation is not as "pragmatic" as the work coordination (fix the lights in the easiest way) or the problem solving example (get hold of the necessary bits). Its function is rather to create a consensus, the speakers persuading themselves and their colleagues to agree on a certain interpretation of an ambiguous situation.

Mutual teaching in a shared context of work

Since a car is a sufficiently complicated piece of machinery to require some degree of specialization in the garage, mutual instruction is not uncommon, but the teaching process has its own special features. Here is one example:

K: How the devil should this [an ampmeter] be plugged in?

B: You just take off a battery cable

K: I just take off a battery cable

B: And then put...oh it doesn't matter, and then plug it in there, between...

K: Oh between the eh two cables

B: No, not above, definitely not above, but, you know, between the battery and the cable, between the battery and the cable

K: Oh, that way

K: And then you rev up, you see

K: Yes

B: Then it suddenly swings up

K: Then it swings up to amp

B: It must go up (K: ten?) to about eighteen-twenty

(K: eighteen-twenty)

B: Yes

Example 5. Instruction.

B, the "teacher", does not simply answer the question. He reconstructs K's working process, and describes the procedure in a fairly detailed way. K asks about a part of the repair job (plugging the meter in), and B responds by describing the whole job. Reconstruction of plans as a part of answering questions is common, but has its special features in the garage: since K and B have received a similar education and B is able to see how far K has proceeded, reconstruction of the intentions of the questioner can be very reliable. Also, it is important to B that the message gets through, since there is only one ampmeter in the garage, and if K damages it, it will concern B personally. Note also that B's speech is narrative and specified with respect to time, place, and person *(and then, you, there)*. It does not give causal explanations *(if-then)* and does not contain general statements. The reason is that this teaching is embedded in a concrete working process.

Note also how K participates actively in the instruction process: he interrupts several times and tries to complete the sentences of the "teacher" - possibly in order to show that he is not totally ignorant about the subject. Receiving and giving advice in a work context is problematic, since employees are supposed to be competent in their work, cf. Wynn 1979.

The Postal Giro

From the small Danish repair shop, we will now enter its diametrical opposite, namely the large Postal Giro in Stockholm, and take a brief look at the work language there. In contrast to the repair shop, the Postal Giro is a large enterprise with approximately 5,000 employees. It is owned by the state, but administratively and economically independent. The work is bureaucratic, fragmentized, routinized, and to some degree computerized.

In this section the Postal Giro is described as it looked in the early eighties. In 1986, work was reorganized and computer technology introduced, and the result of this change is described in Part III.

The data comes from a research project[1] conducted in one of five almost identical units called *accounting departments.* A department employs approximately 350 persons, all working together in a large office landscape. These people are divided into six *sections*, each of which performs one particular task. E.g. one section takes the customers' paying-in forms and prepares them for optical reading and computer processing; after the real accounting in the computer is done, the receipt forms are paired with the statements of account, put in envelopes, and mailed back to the customers.

This may sound simple enough, but in reality the work consists of a large number of subroutines, and an intricate system for the division of labor and the circulation of personnel between different tasks of the section exists: each afternoon, the section leader writes a new work schedule, allocating each person to a task. When workers arrive the next morning, they read the schedule, and confirm by their signature that they have seen it.

In addition to the above six sections, five other sections take care of certain problems common to the whole department.

Although there are routine workers and semi-skilled workers, no objective social differences exist between them. Routine workers should be able to do all types of work within the department if necessary, and routine workers go to the special sections and help out according to a fixed schedule.

The organizational hierarchy is rather simple. A male director presides over the whole department, his office being elsewhere in the building. In the de-

---

[1] Holmqvist 1986, Holmqvist & Källgren 1986, and Holmqvist & Bøgh Andersen 1987.

partment, two female supervisors are responsible for the whole department, and each section has two female section heads and one instructor. With these exceptions, the rest of the 45 employees in a section have the same tasks.

Since the women start working in the department with only little training, differences of experience and skills of course exist, but they are not formalized in titles and wages.

In the repair shop, each role is occupied by one or two persons, and each mechanic plans and executes his own work. The Postal Giro is very different in that a large number of workers are collectively organized in one role, with very few acting in other roles. Planning and execution of work are kept apart, planning being done in special departments, and execution taking place on the shop floor.

Communication in a rule-governed work place

A main difference between the repair shop and the Postal Giro is that the latter is highly rule-governed: the normal routine is known by everybody, and ordering is done by means of written schedules. The tacit standing order is that all material coming in in the morning has to be taken care of and sent back to the customers the same day. Verbal ordering is rare; it is always a request for working overtime, and comes from the department director through the loudspeaker:

> May I ask for the attention of all accounting departments. Due to the large amount of material we have today, especially as concerns the opening of cheque envelopes after coding is finished, I have to ask personnel with a short day to stay on for another forty-five minutes.   *Example 6. Ordering.*

The expression *a short day* refers to the working time schedule. Every second day you work between 8 and 12 AM; these days are called *short days*. The other days you stay on from 8 AM until all material is processed, and these days are *long days*.

On first hearing, this utterance resembles an order allocating a group of employees *(personnel with a short day)* to a task *(opening cheque envelopes)*. It is not. The employees know what to do and in what order: first coding, then opening the envelopes; it is the same routine every day. They also know which workers should prolong their duty, and that a large amount of material can be the only reason for them to do so. So the only new information is *45 minutes overtime.*

On the surface, the allocation of jobs is done by the director. In reality, the employees themselves do it from their knowledge of the organization, the schedules, and the tasks. If all ordering had to be made explicit, the Postal

Giro would break down immediately. In an organization of this size, management cannot possibly have sufficient knowledge to control the work explicitly.

To a large extent, work has to be organized by the collective of workers. Therefore, knowledge of the organization is an important qualification in Postal Giro employees, and a potential basis of power. In the repair shop, with its few employees and loose rules, organizational knowledge of this kind is not important.

Distribution of work is also highly routinized. The section head each day writes a schedule for the personnel in her section, the workers read it in the morning, and follow it during the day. However, there are exceptions.

Some section or special unit can be unpredictably short of people, so that workers have to be taken out of their schedule and transferred. In the following example, the supervisor S enters a section to see if she can transfer someone to another unit:

S: They are short of people at cheque control. Can anyone go over there?
A: I was there last week
B: I have to be at the dentist at eleven o'clock
S: But in the afternoon they have a part timer coming
B: Well, I'll go then

Example 7. Work distribution.

Why does this interaction look the way it does? Is it due to lack of authority on the part of the supervisor? Are A and B lazy and unwilling? No, but a lot of shared organizational knowledge is presupposed. These people act in a universe of discourse with at least the following common knowledge: the task of cheque control is carried out in a specific part of the big office landscape; it is a task that skilled workers master, but it is not a part of their daily routine. It is mainly a task for specialists and routine workers should take part in it according to an elaborate, special schedule. When a change in this schedule is called for, there are certain general rules to be referred to: for instance, if someone has had her regular turn, she should not have to do it again too soon. In this example, the supervisor has both the obligation and the power to move persons between different tasks, but she cannot do it haphazardly. She has to do it within the framework of the given rules. However, she cannot keep the schedules for 350 employees in mind, and so she turns to someone she believes to be available and asks for information, i.e. for the preconditions of redistributing work. Like the mechanics, the employees at the Postal Giro also solve problems, but problem solving has its own features due to the intricate network of rules:

A: Are you going to keep that one?

B: I don't know, there was a number I changed that I had to look up in the book. Am I supposed to change it on the list?

A: Piss on it

Example 8. Problem solving.

If the context is not known, this way of solving the problem may appear rather drastic. However, the expression *piss on it* is not an expression of irresponsibility. On the contrary, A is making a qualified decision, taking into account the amount of work to be done, and judges the problem to be less important. She knows it will be handled by someone else some other day or in another department.

In this particular office a lot of knowledge is conveyed in this way, by giving small hints about what to do in more or less unique situations. Problem solving and instruction are difficult to separate, as there exist a range of situations, from those that are symbolically marked as instruction to those that are explicitly marked as problem solving, such as the following:

A: I have to ask about this one. What do I do with this one [shows a form]. Own deposit of 300,000.

S: What strange things are turning up today: we have never had anything like this before. I'll have to go and ask [walks away with the form, returns after a little while without it]. No. It was meant for CR, you got it by mistake.

Example 9. Instruction.

CR is short for the English phrase "credit revision", and denotes a special unit in the department, and S is the section head.

The expression *to ask* is a conventional way of marking the situation as a problem solving situation: "Here is a situation I cannot solve without qualified help from the supervisor and the section head". The uniqueness of the situation is repeatedly confirmed by the section head, and she herself uses the catchword *to ask*.

Interference of contexts

In the preceding, I have treated work language as a unique language variety, in order to emphasize its characteristic features. But the work place is of course not a closed world, and contains traces of conversations that do not belong to work proper. An example of this is situations where utterances are not meant in a literal way. In the following example, a worker has left the reception desk in order to fetch materials from a department downstairs. Not all material is delivered to the department. Sometimes the workers have to get it themselves:

A: What do you mean, leaving the reception when no one else is there?
B: Well, I have to since nobody else is going down to fetch it.

Example 10. Control check.

In the initial analysis, this example was classified as *control check* (verifying that the task is carried out correctly or in the manner ordered). The first suspicion arises when one realizes that the two participants are peers: will peers really check each other's work? Are they entitled to reprimand each other? Again, it seems more likely that they are playing a game. They are using a pattern of interaction that belongs to another context. In the present example, the expressions used remind us of the power relationship between parent and child in a family situation, but the family context is used metaphorically. In the real family situation, parents actually mean what they say when reprimanding their children, and they have the power to demand actions and give reprimands. The workers at the Postal Giro Office do not have that power basis. A reprimand from a co-worker does not oblige one to anything but to defend oneself by answering with another reproach. The same pattern can be found in arguments between brothers and sisters, fighting for equality. However, in the Postal Giro the matter at issue, the tasks, is equally distributed from the beginning by means of the written schedule, so there is really nothing to fight about. It is a game played with tongue-in-cheek aiming at reproduction of a relation of solidarity.

In the repair shop, similar interferences between contexts were recorded. The mechanics often talked while working, and the conversations resemble those patterns we use in our leisure time. However, norms from the two contexts, the working context and the leisure context, may conflict. On the one hand, the mechanic is paid by the master and should work while he is paid. Therefore he should continue working when chatting with his boss. On the other hand, it is impolite not to concentrate one's attention on one's interlocutor, and hence one should stop working while talking.

Summary

The data from the two projects can be summarized as follows:
Communicative and non-communicative acts are highly interdependent

- Non-communicative and communicative acts are often mixed together in the same unit. There are no nice pure texts to work with, but rather a fusion of speech and action.

- The communicative acts cannot be planned in advance since they are elicited by non-communicative acts. The "discourse structure" is often not linguistic, but related to the work task.
- Communicative and non-communicative acts replace each other. Instead of saying something the workers do it.
- Interpretation of communicative acts is often impossible without knowledge about the non-communicative ones.
- The morphology of utterances depends upon the task in which they are embedded.

The work organization deeply influences what is said and how it is said

- The employees' knowledge of the organization and its schedules is important in large scale enterprises. Common knowledge about the organization is necessary to interpret the utterances, and outsiders without the necessary organizational knowledge (e.g. researchers) run the risk of interpreting the utterances incorrectly.
- Common knowledge about tasks and methods makes communication superfluous.

Reproduction of skills, knowledge and norms is an important function of the work language

- Mutual teaching among the employees takes place during normal work, and many work processes also have a teaching aspect: "look at me; this is the way things should be done".
- Some situations are symbolically marked as teaching or problem solving situations, but many conversations have both functions. Decisions are taken as paradigmatic for future situations.
- Communication types serving to reproduce consensus about past and present events are intertwined with types that are more directly related to actual work.

Work language patterns interfere with patterns originating from non-work contexts

- Conversation patterns from other contexts are used metaphorically in the working context; this metaphorical character is evidenced by the fact that the utterances are not to be taken at face value. People do not mean what they say.
- Norms from different contexts may conflict.

Technological and organizational change at the Giro[1]

The preceding descriptions of the Postal Giro cover the period up to 1986, but all this is now history, since the department is undergoing large organizational and technological changes that aim at changing the strict division of labor responsible for the norm underlying the problem solving conversation in example 8: *somebody else will take care of the problem.*

As early as the seventies, management projects discussed and planned the introduction of computer technology in the organization, and around 1980 the union entered the negotiations with its demands. There turned out to be two major kinds of disagreements that are relevant to the topic of this book:

Decentralization: both parties wanted some kind of decentralization and to change the assembly line work organization. According to Grip and Sundström 1984: 100, management wished only to integrate the accounting and investigation departments with the addition of parts from Registration and Revision, while keeping the other special units intact. However, the union was for more radical changes: they wanted to create "mini-giros", each consisting of five sections of groups of about 20 persons, integrating accounting, revision, registration and investigation, and having resources for planning and development of organization, market, economy, etc. One interpretation is that the union wanted to change the organization to a service organization, while management stuck to a more production-oriented interpretation.

Electronic scanning of paper forms: management wanted to get rid of all paper by optical scanning of the paying-in forms. All subsequent work involving the cards would by done by means of electronic card images on a video screen. The union demanded that the basis of data recording should still be the paper forms, so that a direct feeling of the amount of work remained intact.

The actual system (called the PGP-system) installed in autumn 1986 was a compromise between these views. On the organizational side, management views seem to have prevailed, while the union succeeded in preventing electronic scanning of paper forms.

On the hardware side, the old coding machines have been replaced by O(ptical)C(haracter)R(ecognition)-machines that read the preprinted information of the paying-in forms and store an electronic representation on a shared disk. From the disk, the card records go to six work stations, where the remaining data is input. The records are returned to the disk, and trans-

---

[1] Grip & Sundstrøm 1984.

mitted to a large IBM computer via a local network. The equipment also includes tape units and printers.

I was able to follow parts of this process together with Berit Holmqvist, one of the researchers from the first project, in a project called "Professional language in change". In the late spring and autumn 1986, data[1] was collected in the same section of the same department, and the two projects, providing snapshots of the language before and after computerization, give a unique opportunity to study the effects of computerization upon the language and work. The process is fully described in Part III, but I shall draw upon it for examples throughout the book.

I.1.2. Other work languages

The characteristics of the work languages of the repair shop and the Postal Giro Office are probably typical of two large groups of work types: handicraft work and routine clerical work. Together with assembly line work[2], these work types can be classified as *product-focused* work. In product-focused work, communication is only a means for producing some commodity, the workers getting paid for manufacturing this commodity, not for talking or writing.

However, there is another large class of work types, *communication-focused* work, where the relation between communicative and non-communicative acts is reversed: the main purpose is communication, and non-communicative acts are only means for communicating. Obvious examples of this class are journalists, teachers, and publicity experts, but a closer scrutiny of work practices reveals that many other occupations belong here: for example managers spend most of their time talking.

The distinction between communication- and product-focused jobs is not ontological but historical, since it is caused by a particular division of labor

---

[1] In the follow-up project, we gathered the following data:
Work language recordings. The data is obtained with a small recorder hidden in a suitcase and include six transcripts, ranging from five to ten pages each.
*Loudspeaking.*We asked one of the workers to tell us what she did while working. We got two recordings of this type. In one of them we took screen-dumps (about 50) in order to relate her descriptions to the screen-images.
Interviews. A computer scientist interviewed one of the project managers and one of the "advisers". The interviews were taped and transcribed.
Paper documents. We collected as much paper material as possible. Besides the requirement specification, the most important written material is the manuals that were placed at the workstations. We added some of the manuals for older systems for comparison.
Screen dumps. Besides the 50 screen dumps from the loudspeaking session, I went systematically through the system and took dumps. However, the documention is not complete, since there are images that I could not get into without damaging the ongoing work process.
[2] A description of the work language at the Volvo factories can be found in Andersson 1983. Tway 1976 describes communication habits in a china factory.

that can be changed, and the organizational change at the Postal Giro is a good example of this. Before the organizational change, the accounting departments at the Postal Giro had no contact with customers, this contact being assigned to special departments, and one of the objectives of the change was to reduce the rigidity in this division of labor so that the accounting departments also provide some customer service.

The work languages of communication- and product-focused jobs may be expected to differ. For example, in communication-focused jobs, text linguistic rules may be expected to play a more independent role, since they specify the communicative skills paid for. Teachers are expected to master the intricate language game of classroom interaction, and managers that of negotiation.

The present book only covers product-focused work, and when I speak of work language it should be taken as an abbreviation of "work language of product-focused work". Data on communication-focused work can be found in Falzon 1983 and 1984 (flight controllers), Kaasbøl 1986 (nursing[1]), and Wynn 1979 (customer service).

I.1.3. Adapting the structuralist framework

After having outlined the characteristics of work languages, the central language variety of this book, I shall adapt the theoretical framework described in the introduction to this type of language.

However, adapting the structural linguistic tradition to the study of work languages is not without complications. As mentioned in the introduction, structural linguistics is based upon the concept of *immanence*. Language should be analyzed as a structure *sui generis,* and psychological, sociological or historical factors are irrelevant for linguistic analysis as such. This methodological presupposition does not tally with the main conclusion that can be extracted from Section I.1.1, namely that *in work language the center of gravity lies outside the language itself.* In the two work languages exemplified there, utterances acts interact with work tasks, they have concrete purposes related to the tasks, and since speech is part of wage labor, it is subject to demands of efficiency.

These features are not so pronounced in all language varieties. In the coffee break, for example, speech is an end in itself, it may have no purpose except passing the time in a pleasant way, and efficiency is not important. If jokes are told, they may have an elaborate linguistic structure, since language

---

[1] Kaasbøl's work is a part of a larger Norwegan project called the Florence-project. It was conducted by the Institute of Informatics, Oslo University, and investigated computer applications in hospitals.

is the main means for communicating the point and making the audience laugh, whereas in work language, large parts of the meaning need not be expressed, since they can be inferred from the shared knowledge of the speakers.

I believe that language varieties like literary and mass communicative texts are much easier to analyze immanently, and probably these texts have been the conscious or unconscious points of reference for structural linguistics.

However this may be, I find theoretical problems arising now; although there is a lot to be said in favor of the principle of immanence, it needs a critical examination to be useful in the present context, and in the following I will describe the difficulties in more detail and indicate the solutions adopted in this book.

The next sections describe how the book deviates from classical structuralism, and is mostly written for linguistic readers. All points will be taken up later, and the following summary is sufficient for those who want to skip directly to Section I.2.

Summary

The basic problem is to connect symbolic acts to their context. Loosely said, a *symbolic act* is an act that people take to mean something different from itself, because they know a code they can use to interpret it. The most important variety is the *verbal acts* we perform every day when we talk or write, but other acts also count as symbolic: for example, a hand waving is a symbolic act, since we can assign the meaning "hello" to it. But not all acts are symbolic; hammering most often does not signify anything else than hammering; we move our hand in order to fix the nail, not because we want to tell a person something.

Not all symbolic acts are intended as such by the actor. Although facial expressions are covered by a standard common code, we sometimes loose control and may perform a symbolic act like frowning or smiling without intending it.

When the symbolic act is intended as such by the actor, I shall sometimes use the term *communicative act*.

In a place of work, these non-symbolic acts are closely intertwined with the symbolic ones, but linguistics provides very few methods for understanding and describing these relationships. Although in practice the symbolic and non-symbolic parts of our work belong closely together, theory places them on isolated islands.

The standard solution I adopt is simply to extend linguistic terminology from describing relations between symbolic acts, to cover relations between symbolic and non-symbolic acts ("saying and doing"), or between two non-symbolic acts.

Another departure from standard linguistics consists in choosing the *register* and not the *national language* as the basic subject. A register is the language used in a particular type of situation like solving problems, coordinating work, buying and selling, making love, etc., while the national language is the language(s) characteristic of a particular country. The practical reason for this is that we design computer systems for particular work situations, like writing, filing, or drawing, so it is the language people use here, and not their total language, we are interested in, unlike grammars and lexicons that often treat a whole national language.

Thus, when I use the term "language" I do not normally mean the conventional national languages, but much smaller languages associated to situation types.

I shall not exclusively use the *concept* "language" about spoken or written language, but take it to cover any set symbolic acts and their underlying patterns. The characteristic of a language, in this broad sense, is that it consists of two sides, an expression and a content side, like a coin consists of its front and back. Each side must consist of parts such that exchanging one part for another on one side causes a change on the other side.

Consider for example the word *signified*. On the content side, we can isolate three minimal units *signi* (sign) - *fi* (suffix used to build a verb out of a noun) - *ed* (the past tense). On the expression side, we can isolate four syllables sig-ni-fi-ed which again consist of 9 letters. If on the expression side we replace the initial *s* with a *d* we get *dignified* which obviously causes a change on the content side.

Many everyday phenomena besides spoken and written language have this property: I have already mentioned gestures and facial expressions, but clothes, pictures, hairstyles, and computer systems in so far they are interpreted by users, belong here. All these phenomena are therefore languages in the broad sense. It is the broad sense of language that makes it feasible at all to transfer linguistic and semiotic concepts to computers.

However, in order to preserve terminological clarity, I shall mostly use the *term* "language" about the spoken and written variety, and the *term* "semiotic system" about all the other phenomena. Thus, a language (in the narrow sense) is a special kind of semiotic system.

The last point to be mentioned is that we need to develop concepts for understanding why and how language changes. The reason is that designing computer systems implies changing the language of the users to larger or lesser extent, since they must learn new terminology and often also learn to look at and describe their work differently than they used to. Successful systems development presupposes that the users are able to adopt and use the new concepts in their daily life.

There are many hypotheses about the nature of language change; in this book, I assume that language change is connected to the register and caused by changes in its associated situation type. For example, introduction of new tools and materials in the car repair shop changes the lexicon of the mechanics.

I.1.3.1. Integrating descriptions of symbolic and non-symbolic acts

The theory must be capable of describing both symbolic and non-symbolic acts and their interrelations. In the two work places I described, the two types of acts were mixed, the latter type filling the largest span of time and providing motivation for the former.

In neither case was immanent analysis of the language practically possible, so written descriptions of the work were provided. In the Postal Giro case, a flow description of the written material was made; in the repair shop project, some car repairs were singled out for description via a means/ends analysis borrowed from AI. In both projects, the utterances were classified according to their function in the tasks and the work organization.

The two cases differed in the way necessary knowledge about the work was provided. In the repair shop case, professional knowledge about car repairs was embodied in the mechanic employed in the project. He was also the major source of work-specific knowledge when I analyzed the tape recordings. In the Postal Giro case, quite the opposite strategy was employed. The researchers wrote a rigid description of the working process, viewed both as a flow of material and as a working day as experienced by the typical worker, before any linguistic research was begun.

The first strategy served excellently to make explicit exactly what knowledge about the working context is required to understand what is said. The second strategy allowed the researchers to analyze the speech single-handedly, since, to a certain degree, they had become a part of the working context.

But these methods are clearly subject to Saussure's and Hjelmslev's criticism of the "philological" method that borrows methods from other disciplines, has no theoretical foundation of its own, and is only able to describe the historical, social or psychological context of language, but never language itself. Both authors advocate a strict division of language from its context:

My definition of language presupposes the exclusion of everything that is outside its organism or system - in a word, of everything known as "external linguistics".

Saussure 1966: 20

To establish a true linguistics, which cannot be a mere ancillary or derivative science, something else must be done. Linguistics must attempt to grasp language, not as a conglomerate of non-linguistic (e.g. physical, physiological, psychological, logical, sociological) phenomena, but as a self-sufficient totality, a structure *sui generis*.

Hjelmslev 1963a: 5-6

On the one hand, their arguments seem still valid: language should be described by concepts fitted for this object of study, and not by concepts developed for studying other objects. On the other hand, the preceding sections all have proven the impossibility of studying work language apart from its non-symbolic context.

The solution of the dilemma is to separate two issues which Saussure and Hjelmslev lump together:

(1)   language should be studied by methods and concepts that reflect the characteristic features of language, and not by methods and concepts reflecting characteristic features of other objects of study.

(2)   language should be isolated from non-language and studied separately.

In this book I accept the first proposition, but reject the second one. Methodologically, it means that I use linguistic concepts to describe those parts of the context which influence language[1].

The following simple example illustrates the method. I want to distinguish giving an order from other communicative functions, and decide that the characteristic feature of ordering is that it can elicit an action that would not have occurred without the order. Consider for example the part of example 6 that expresses the order *45 minutes overtime,*

I have to ask personnel with a short day to stay on for another forty-five minutes.

In this particular case, the utterance and the action, *staying on for 45 minutes,* both occur, but the utterance would still count as an utterance if the workers had gone home. In that case the utterance would simply be a disobeyed order. Then what are the combinations between utterance and action that characterize the order? The following combinations all retain the "order" relationship between utterance and action:

+utterance + action (the order is obeyed by performing the action)

---

[1] Hjelmslev in fact saw this kind of "widening of scope" as a logical consequence of his approach, cf. Hjelmslev 1963: 127.

+utterance - action (the order is disobeyed, the action is not performed)
-utterance - action (the action is not performed be.'ause not ordered)

but we cannot have

-utterance + action (the action is performed without any order)

since one of the defining characteristics of orders and requests is that the hearer would not perform the action in the absence of the request[1].

If the latter combination occurs, the relation between utterance and action is not ordering but something else. Thus, I define orders by their function to non-symbolic phenomena, rejecting principle 2 above. But since I accept principle 1, that language should be described by methods that reflect its characteristic features, I want to describe this function by means of linguistic concepts, so I look for comparable phenomena within linguistics proper, and come upon the relation of *subordination*. Our order *I have to ask personnel with a short day to stay on for another forty-five minutes* contains a phrase *personnel with a short day* in which the modifier *with a short day* is subordinate to the noun *personnel*. It means that only the following combinations are possible

+noun + modifier (*I have to ask personnel with a short day to stay on*)
+noun - modifier (*I have to ask personnel to stay on*)

but not the odd one

-noun + modifier (*I have to ask with a short day to stay on*)

The relationship between noun and modifier looks like the relationship between order and action, and is normally described in terms of *subordination*, the modifier being subordinate or dependent upon the noun.

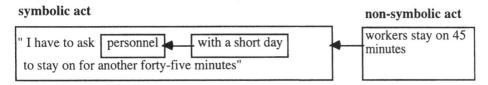

Fig. I.1.3. Subordination between symbolic and non-symbolic items.

I take this concept, which describes relations between symbolic items, extend it to cover relationships between symbolic and non-symbolic items, and define ordering as pairs of utterances and actions where the action is subordinate or dependent upon the utterance. The external relations of the utter-

---

[1] Labov & Fenshel 1977:78.

ance to its context are described by means of the same concepts as we use to describe the internal relations between its parts, as illustrated in the diagram above, where the arrow means *subordination* (Fig. I.1.3).

In this way, non-symbolic entities are introduced into the linguistic description, but *only as something having relations to linguistic entities.* I do not enter phenomena that have no relation to language; moreover, only those properties that are relevant for these relations are recorded[1].

It does *not* mean that the complexities of document processing or car repair can be exhaustively described in this way. The perspective on work is a very specific one since only those features that have functions in language are selected. I view work through the eyes of a linguist.

This will also be my general method when I have to treat subjects like organization analysis and programming, areas that have only been treated very superficially from semiotic viewpoints: I do not seek to give exhaustive accounts of these areas, but only to throw out some hooks from semiotics to those disciplines that have them as their proper subject matter, hooks that hopefully make it possible to establish some kind of collaboration between these disciplines.

I.1.3.2. Integrating the context in linguistic description

The importance of context is commonly accepted today, but in work language research this importance is increased by an order of magnitude. Short sentences or single words may convey a large payload of non-expressed contextual meanings.

Important components of work language contexts are roles, tasks, organization of work, social relations, and plant layout. If the researcher does the analysis on her own, she can collect information about these items and use it in the analysis. Another possibility is to do the analysis together with the speakers, thereby creating a new context, different from the work context, where normally non-expressed meanings are expressed.

A serious theoretical problem remains, however. How can one say that non-expressed meanings are conveyed? In the structuralist paradigm, the notion "non-expressed meanings" seems to be self-contradictory. The basic unit of language is the sign, and the sign is an association of something signified and something used to signify, but the signified does not exist "before" or "outside" the signifier, and conversely, the signifier does not

---

[1] The non-symbolic act associated to the symbolic act in this way bears some resemblance to Peirce's interpretant.

exist without its signified[1]. This should not be taken to mean that all thought is verbal, only that something special happens when thought is articulated by means of signs and turns into a signified content. The signified contents do not exist a priori to sign formation; what exists a priori is at most "thought-stuff" that is moulded into a content in the semiotic process.

The practical method for establishing units of signified and signifier is the *commutation test*. In order for two content units to be different, it is required that substituting one for the other entails a substitution of expression units. Content differences must be marked in the expression system. This principle is a sound one, in so far as it prevents setting up content units that cannot be empirically justified and it forces the researcher to describe what is actually said. To give a very striking example: in conversations aiming at distributing work, the content difference between first and second person is important since the question is: who is going to do it? Substituting the content unit /first person/ for /second person/entails a substitution of /jag, I/ for /du, *you*/, so

A: Rosa stansar *du* två sekunder? [A: Rosa, will *you* punch for two seconds?]

means something different from

A: Rosa stansar *jag* två sekunder? [A: Rosa, will *I* punch for two seconds?]

Thus, /jag/ and /du/ commute. However, in conversations aiming at teaching a new worker a task, the commutation has disappeared, since

A: Du har aldrig gjort det här förut? Först tar *du* ut checken, så kollar *du* att numret stämmer...att den är underskriven.
[A: You've never done this before? Well, first *you* remove the check, then *you* see whether it's all right... that it's been signed]

is for all practical purposes synonymous with

A: Du har aldrig gjort det här förut? Först tar *jag* ut checken, så kollar *jag* att numret stämmer...att den är underskriven.

---

[1] "Language can also be compared with a sheet of paper: thought is the front and the sound is the back; one cannot cut the front without cutting the back at the same time; likewise in language, one can neither divide sound from thought nor thought from sound; the division could be accomplished only abstractly, and the result would be either pure psychology or pure phonology. Linguistics then works in the borderland where the elements of sound and thought combine; *their combination produces a form, not a substance."* *Saussure 1963: 113*
"Expression [i.e. the signifier] and content [i.e. the signified] are solidary - they necessarily presuppose each other. An expression is expression only by virtue of being an expression of a content, and a content is content only by virtue of being a content of an expression. Therefore - except by an artificial isolation - there can be no content without an expression, or expressionless content.(...) If we think without speaking, the thought is not a linguistic content and not a functive for a sign function." *Hjelmslev 1963a: 48-49*

[A: You've never done this before? Well, first *I* remove the check, then *I* see
    whether it's all right.. that it's been signed]

The commutation test gives different results in different situations, implying
that the inventory of expression and content units is not stable, but varies
with situation type. In our case, the reason is that the work is single-person
work and the focus of the instruction conversation is on how to perform the
task, not on the worker doing it.

I view it as a methodological error to transfer the work distribution distinction between first and second person to the teaching situation, since we
would have stipulated content units in the teaching situation which we cannot prove to exist. Only the commutation test reveals the actual state of affairs.

However, my decision to stick to the commutation test gives me problems
with the context, since it presupposes that contents must be verbally expressed, and this presupposition makes it difficult to come to grips with the
fact that large amounts of shared knowledge among speakers may cause a
complex meaning to be communicated through simple short utterances.
Example 7, also aiming at distribution of work, illustrates the point[1]:

    S: They are short of people at cheque control. Can anyone go over there? (*Do I
        have the right to redistribute* one *of you two* to the cheque control *now?*)
    A: I was there last week (*You have no right to order me. According to the planned
        system for work circulation, the same person is not obliged to sit on the cheque
        control for two successive weeks*)
    B: I have to be at the dentist at eleven o'clock (*Ordering me does not make sense. I
        shall not be present since* I am to go to the dentist, *which is within my rights*)

The italicized parts are a paraphrase expressing contents that are implicit in
the original wording, but are understood by the participants because of their
knowledge of the rules governing work distribution. The implicit content
comes from the world of negotiations and agreements and includes content
units such as /right/, /order/, /sense/.

On the one hand, the paraphrase does express an important aspect of the
conversation, namely that the arguments obtain their validity in a legal universe consisting of agreements and rights, but, on the other hand, it is not
clear how the paraphrases can be justified scientifically, since the workers
would never use the bureaucratic terminology of the paraphrase, except perhaps in situations of severe conflict, and this again means that it is hard to
present arguments about the correctness of the paraphrase.

---

[1] Holmqvist 1986: 82.

The solution I shall use in this book is as follows. I accept the dialectical relation between content and expression (one not existing without the other), I accept the commutation test as the basic analytical tool, and I see the phenomenon of implicit meanings in the following way.

Imagine two types of situations. In situation A we observe experienced workers using short sentences, whereas in situation B one or more of the experienced workers are replaced by a non-experienced person, and we observe that longer paraphrases have been added to the short sentences. There is mutual exclusion between the skilled worker and the long paraphrases.

One linguistic analogy to this is the paradigmatic relations between elements of language. Elements that can substitute for each other in the same contexts are said to constitute a paradigm. Thus, the prepositions *on, under,* and *over* form a paradigm, since we can have

on	the roof
under	the roof
over	the roof

I again generalize the concept of paradigm, which describes relations between symbolic items, to cover relations between symbolic and non-symbolic phenomena, in this case between groups of persons and types of utterances. If we describe an experienced worker as one that can participate in a work process without being told everything in detail we will observe the following conversations:

(1)   experienced worker   + short sentences
(2)   explanations   + short sentences

In the first conversation, an experienced worker is present, and the conversation consists of short sentences, partly because it is possible, and partly because long-winded explanations may count as an outright insult to his professional qualifications. In the second one, there is no experienced addressee present (maybe because the addressee is a novice), and although the same sentences as before may be used, they are now supplemented with meticulous explanations. Thus, instead of an experienced addressee we observe the longer paraphrases.

Since we will not record conversations where an experienced worker is addressed by long explanations

experienced worker + explanations + short sentences

the conversation elements /experienced worker/ and /explanations/ are members of the same paradigm. Again, this does not mean that my analysis exhausts the subject of skills and knowledge. Disciplines like psychology, philosophy and economics can add other facets to the topic[1], but if linguists want to make a skilled contribution, they must focus on those aspects they have concepts for.

The general solution to the problem of contextual meaning is simply to state that categories of speakers enter into paradigms with types of utterances, so that if a certain type of speaker participates in a conversation, certain types of utterances are excluded. The latter are the implicit contextual meanings, and the implication is that if the situation had been another, with other speakers present, the implicit meanings could have been explicit. This analysis will justify some applications of the paraphrase techniques exemplified above, but not all.

Placing a competent worker outside the working situation and asking her to explain the goings-on to persons without knowledge (e.g. researchers) is a technique that can be justified, since what we do is to replace her normal (competent) colleagues, whose presence obviates the need for elaborate explanations, with persons that do not, and according to the theory, we expect the previously excluded contextual meanings to come forth.

Another technique, used by Wynn 1979, is that the researcher alone close-reads the transcripts; this method is more questionable, and can really only be defended if the researcher knows so much about the place of work that she herself can act as a competent worker.

I.1.3.3. Linking linguistic theory with a theory of organizations

The situational and organizational context influences language profoundly. In the preceding section, we saw that the context makes people interpret contents that are not explicitly expressed in the sentences, and the two cases in Section I.1.1 show that there exist relations between organizational types and communicative functions, since different functions were found in the small repair shop and the large bureaucracy of the Postal Giro. Many of the communicative functions of the repair shop were not verbalized at all, and some of them only on rare occasions. This is true of *ordering, work coordination, work distribution, priority ordering,* i.e. functions concerning the organization of work, and *control checking, supervision,* and *reporting,* i.e. the control functions. The overall organizational routines took care of this in the form of written schedules and internalized knowledge.

The relations between organization and language are not only a "natural" fact that can be discovered, but may even be the result of a conscious effort.

---

[1] See e.g. Dreyfus & Dreyfus 1986, which discusses skills from a psychological and philosophical point of view, and Masuch 1973, which treats them as economic entities.

To some degree, organizations are planned and changed by managers with a conscious view to theories of organizations; as a result, an understanding of the consequences of such changes must include knowledge about the organizational ideals aimed at. Since work language is part of wage labor, it is to some degree subject to the same forces of rationalization as are its non-communicative parts. Communication has a cost that must be paid by the employer, and reducing costs can be an incentive for the employer to remove "unnecessary" communication[1]. Therefore, work language must be expected to bear marks of the same organizational objectives as the non-communicative work it serves.

A link between organization theory and linguistics is needed, and I again look for linguistic concepts that can act as a bridge to other disciplines. Let me start by giving examples of the kind of organizational properties I want to describe.

The first task I set myself is to describe the difference between industrial, assembly-line organizations like the Postal Giro and small handicraft shops like the garage, since I hope to use this description to explain the communicative differences mentioned above.

In the Postal Giro, one worker performs few operations on many work objects (e.g. correcting 100 similar cards), whereas in the garage, one worker performs many operations on one object of work (replacing brakes, changing the oil, and mending the coolant system in the same car).

In the Postal Giro, the type of tasks depends upon the work place of the worker: if she is employed in the accounting section, she is allowed to do one set of tasks, whereas quite another set of tasks are the responsibility of personnel in special offices. In the garage, the situation is reversed: here, most mechanics have the same qualifications, so by knowing the worker, little is known about the tasks he performs. If we denote classes of workers by W_1, W_2, /.../W_n, work objects by WO_1, WO_2, /.../WO_n, and tasks by T_1, T_2, /.../T_n, then the typical work processes of assembly line and handicraft work can be symbolized:

Assembly line organization: $W_1WO_1T_1 - W_1WO_2T_1 - W_1WO_3T_1$
Handicraft organization: $W_1WO_1T_1 - W_1WO_1T_2 - W_1WO_1T_3$

---

[1] Transaction cost analysis (Ciborra 1981, 1985) presents an interesting possibility for analyzing communication from an economic point of view, and linking it with types of organizations. The organization is seen as a network of economic exchanges (e.g. wages for labor power); contracts are set up in order to control initiation, execution, and conclusion of these exchanges. The labor involved in this is mainly communicative, and incurs costs called transaction costs. Contracts are classified into types in order to explain the way the exchanges are organized and to predict changes in the organization, while organizations are classified according to their dominating type of contracts: markets, bureaucracies and clans.

In the first organization, the worker and task are closely linked, but work objects are exchanged freely, whereas in the latter, the work object and worker occur together for some time, while the tasks vary.

Phenomena like these also occur in language, where they are captured in the concepts of government and agreement. In the sentence *Ich fuhr aus der Stadt gestern,* the preposition *aus* governs the dative of the article *der* in the sense that if this preposition is chosen, then the dative must follow, whereas the accusative must be used if *aus* is replaced by *durch*. The preposition and its object are said to build a syntactic unit, held together by government.

In an analogous way, worker and task at the Postal Giro can be said to build a work unit, held together by government: if the worker is employed in the accounting section, her task is to code and correct paying-in slips, and if we replace her with a colleague from one of the special offices, the task changes to customer service.

The word *gestern* is outside the force of the government and forms a phrase by itself, since it can be exchanged with e.g. *Donnerstag* without effect on preposition and case, and vice versa. The work object plays a similar part, since it too can be (and in fact all the time is) exchanged without causing worker or task to be exchanged.

In handicraft work, the government is not between worker and task, but between worker and work object, and within this unit the tasks vary. A mechanic may spend a couple of hours on the same car, replacing the linings, mending the radiator, and adjusting the brakes.

In this first example, I have viewed the working process as analogous to a syntactic process, and I have extended concepts describing how words occur together in sentences to cover patterns in the parts of the work process. But not all properties of organizations can easily be formulated as rules for which items occur together in a work process, and this brings me to the second example.

One of the aims of the Postal Giro organizational change in 1986 was to ease the sharp division of labor, giving the employees in the accounting sections a certain amount of customer contact. An extremely simplified account of this change may be as follows: before the change, the staff was divided into two disjunct groups: group A would code and correct paying-in slips, and group B would take care of customer service. After the change, group A would still code and correct, but now also take care of parts of the customer service.

This change is essentially a change in the paradigm of tasks a person can perform. Before the change, the tasks of group A and B were disjunct: what one group could do, the other could not do and vice versa. After the change, group B's tasks are included in group A's. Again, parallels from linguistics are not hard to find, and the German prepositions will serve again. As is well known, some prepositions like *um* take only the accusative, while others like *aus* take only the dative. The case paradigms of these two classes are disjunct, like the Postal Giro organization before the change. However, there is a third class, including e.g. *auf*, that can take both accusative and dative; the case paradigm of the *um*-class is included in the *auf*-class, like the Postal Giro after the change. The change can be described as a change of the task paradigms, from one dominated by exclusive paradigms to one where some paradigms are included in others.

I should like to emphasize again that what I am doing here is not developing an organization theory, but rather projecting semiotic concepts on a subject outside its traditional research field, hoping to find compatible concepts in organizational theory that may connect to semiotic ones. Such a theory must have a functional view of organizations, not in the rationalist sense that organizations are established as means for attaining certain goals, but in the semiotic sense that members of an organization receive their identity by the functions of similarity and difference they contract to the other members. It must also be holistic in the sense that the "value" of a member is not only a property of her as a person, but a feature that emerges from the total organizational pattern of which she is a part[1].

I.1.3.4. The national language should not be taken as the sole basis of linguistic form

The structuralist tradition has always sought the constant behind the variable. As Hjelmslev puts it:

A linguistic theory (...) must seek a *constancy* which is not anchored in some "reality" outside language - a constancy that makes a language a language, whatever language it may be, and makes a particular language identical with itself in all its various manifestations.   *Hjelmslev 1963a: 8*

This constant is the form, the form being "the constant in a manifestation". The human ear can make uncountably many distinctions in the sound continuum, but only a score or two, defining the phonological form, are relevant to a language. In fact, sound as a substance is irrelevant to the language form, since the same small set of distinctions can be realized as marks on a

---

[1] Examples of organizational descriptions explicitly based on semiotics can be found in Barley 1983, 1986 and Gamberg 1986. Semiotic methods have also begun to be applied in design and marketing research, and the Research Center for Language and Semiotic Studies, Indiana University, is publishing a newsletter, "Marketing Signs", in this emerging discipline.

paper, or pixels on a screen. The constant sought therefore cannot be the physical substance, but must be this small set of distinctions.

The quest for the constant goes hand in hand with a drive to reduce the units recorded to the smallest possible number, the *invariants*[1]. In order to do this, Hjelmslev sets up a *principle of generalization* which allows him to describe two or more entities as variants of one and the same invariant. Invariants are entities that pass the commutation test, variants are entities that do not. /e/ and /i/ are invariants in English since exchanging /pet/ and /pit/ entails an exchange of content units, whereas the prevocalic consonantal /r/(*raw*) and the postvocalic vocalic /r/(*war*) are variants, since no context can be found where they commute. Hjelmslev formulates the principle of generalization in this way:

> If one object admits of a solution univocally, and another object admits of the same solution equivocally, then the solution is generalized to be valid for the equivocal object.   *Hjelmslev 1963: 69*

This principle is used in resolving *synchretism*s and doing *catalysis*.

A synchretism occurs when commutation is suspended between two elements that commute in other contexts. For example, first and second person commute in work distribution, but enter a synchretism in instruction. To resolve a synchretism means to take one of the elements from the context in which there is no synchretism, and insert it into the context with the synchretism. The principle of generalization says that this must be done if possible. In our case it means that we should take the content of *du*, viz. second person, from work distribution and insert it as the content of *du* in instruction although first and second person do not commute here.

Resolving a synchretism means that analyses from one part of the text are generalized to cover other parts of the text, and the same effect is produced by the technique of catalysis. Consider again the following utterance:

> B: higher up (towards you) - straight up - there, right there...(it has to be there) - there, right there

The utterances follow the pattern

> Movement in relation to the preceding one +
> Movement in relation to common system of orientation +
> Movement in relation to actor

---

[1] "Each analysis (...) in which functives are registered with a given function as basis of analysis shall be so made that it leads to the registration of the lowest possible number of elements."
                                                                    Hjelmslev 1963a: 61.

They lack imperative verbs found in other utterances, and catalysis means to insert the missing verb and object in so far as no meaning differences are produced. This would give:

> B: *move the nut* higher up (towards you) - *move the nut* straight up - *stop* there, *stop* right there...(it has to be there) - *stop* there, *stop* right there

Catalysis consists in replacing one entity (higher up towards you) with another (*move the nut* higher up towards you) which does not commute with the former and which contains it as a part.

The problem with these methods is not the generalization principle in itself: all things being equal, it is better to have few than many elements. The problem lies in that the scope and type of the text from which generalizations can be made is never specified, but I believe that the implicit assumption of the structuralist paradigm is that the smallest corpus of text that can be investigated is the national language, which in its intuitive sense simply is the linguistic habits that are characteristic of inhabitants of countries like England and Denmark[1].

However, this assumption cannot be accepted at its face value for several reasons:

- *Ontological*: a national language may not be sufficiently homogeneous to be usefully described as one and the same system.
- *Practical*: the purpose of the research may not be to gain insight into the national language, but only into a small part of it.

The ontological assumption is clearly the stronger: it asserts that the unity of a national language may be an illusion, national languages being artefacts constructed for keeping political units together. My conjecture is that the two sides of the sign are different in this respect: important parts of the expression plane, e.g. the phonemic system or the structure of syllables, may be common to speakers of a national language, while the content plane is so inhomogeneous that a simpler description is obtained by assuming that the national language consists of several subparts. It is very difficult to present convincing arguments about "what language really is", and in this book I simply accept the inhomogeneity assumption as a working hypothesis.

Still, this does not mean that the assumption does not have empirical consequences that cannot ultimately be tested.

---

[1] This intuitive sense cannot be used as a linguistic definition since inhabitants of the same country may speak different languages (Danish and Greenlandic in Denmark) and different countries may have the same language (English in England and USA). The concept of national languages is probably really a political, not linguistic, concept. In the end of this section I propose a definition that at least makes sense in the framework I build up in the following pages.

For example, the homogeneity assumption predicts that the class-subclass relationship will be an important meaning-relation: a word, such as *bachelor*, which can mean *unmarried adult male, young knight serving under the standard of another, a person having the academic degree conferred for completing four years of college,* and *young male seal when without a mate during the breeding time,*[1] should have a common semantic core in all its applications, and a concrete usage of the word should be a specialization of the common core.

In opposition to this, the inhomogeneity assumption would stress analogy and metaphor as the basic semantic structure: in principle, there is no a priori reason why a particular expression unit like *bachelor* occurring in different sublanguages should have any meanings in common, but if the same person speaks these sublanguages, one would expect him to use some situations as analogies for others, and therefore sometimes to use the sublanguage pertaining to one situation as a metaphor for another. The bachelor example favors the inhomogeneity assumption since the different senses only share the most general feature imaginable, namely *animate*, but of course this does not in itself disprove the homogeneity assumption.

The weaker assumption, i.e. that for practical reasons it is useful to refrain from generalizing over a whole national language, if the purpose is to gain insight into a small part of it, is easier to substantiate.

Suppose that I want to describe how work is controlled at the Postal Giro. In Section I.1.1 I said that few orders are found at the Postal Giro, since work is allocated to workers through written schedules, and the workers normally know what to do. Later I said that orders can be defined as utterances that are necessary preconditions for actions, so that the action would not have occurred if the utterance had not occurred. Since actions occur without utterances at the Postal Giro, they cannot be ordered, but would it not be possible to encatalyze an implicit order in these cases?

The only way we can do this is to extrapolate from data from other organizations which have explicit orders, or from previous times where explicit orders possibly might have been more frequent. But doing this would mean that we may underestimate an important characteristic of the Postal Giro, and for that matter many other places of work, namely that explicit order giving has become less frequent. This is an important historical fact connected with a change of management strategies from the classical Tayloristic methods to the Human Resources approach involving self-management within certain limits[2]. Encatalyzing implicit orders in this case blunts our tool of investiga-

---

[1] Katz & Fodor 1963, Katz 1972.
[2] Lund et al 1972.

tion so much that we would miss an interesting historical development and view all these strategies as basically the same phenomena with certain variants.

The example shows that there can be no general scope for generalizations. The scope depends upon the purpose of the research, so if we are interested in changes of management strategies, we may not use earlier language states or other organizations as a basis for catalysis and resolving synchretisms, whereas this is allowed if our topic is the general characteristics of work languages in this century.

In general, I would advocate a cautious application of catalysis in order to stress the unique and characteristic features of the object of research, and to avoid viewing the features prematurely as just surface variations of a more general phenomenon.

In this book I accept the ideal of generalization and constancy, but reject the implicit assumption that the national language is the unique basis for generalization.

Instead I use the situation type and its associated language, the register, as defining the scope within which sound generalizations can be made. Here I am in concordance with systemic theory:

> A fourth assumption of systemic theory is that language is functionally variable; any text belongs to some register or other.   *Halliday 1985: 9*

This quotation brings us directly to the subject of the next section: what is a register and a situation?

I.1.3.5. Situations and registers as the objects of research

Instead of the national language I choose situations and situation types as my basic object of research.

- A *situation* is a set of communicative and non-communicative acts that take place at a specific time and place. A situation is a social category, a "cultural unit" (cf. Eco 1977: 66). This means that it must be conceived as a unit by some community of speakers, have a special name, be marked at the boundaries, etc.

All the examples in Section I.1.1 are situations, and most of them include both communicative and non-communicative acts. The mounting of the rear lights includes for example both physical movements and conversation, and although it has no name, its boundaries are clearly marked verbally.

- A situation may belong to one or more *situation types*. A situation type is characterized by its participant *roles*, its *tasks* and *goals*, including *rules* for performing the tasks and the *objects* and *tools* it requires, the *organization* of activities, the *shared knowledge and norms,* and the *social relations* between the participants.

The notion of *situation types* is needed in order to account for some conflicts in situations: a situation can belong to two different types that make contradictory demands on the speakers, as when the mechanic is in doubt whether to stop working while chatting with the boss. It is also needed in order to explain the phenomenon of metaphorical language usage: phrases and language games can be transferred from one situation type to a situation of different type where they do not originally belong, as when two colleagues at the Postal Giro transfer verbal habits from family life to their work place (example 10).

The situation type defines the basic linguistic unit, the register.

- A *register* is the language used *in* a particular type of situation with the purpose of supporting or changing its activities.

The term *register* is borrowed from Halliday, who describes it in the following way:

> A register is:
>   what you are speaking (at the time)
>   determined by what you are doing (nature of social activity being engaged in), and
>   expressing diversity of social processes (social division of labour)
> So in principle registers are:
>   ways of saying different things
> and tend to differ in:
>   semantics (and hence in lexicogrammar and sometimes phonology, as realization of this)
>   /.../
> Typical instances:
>   occupational varieties (technical, semitechnical)
> Principal controlling variables:
>   field (type of social action); tenor (role relationships); mode (symbolic organization)
> Characterized by:
>   major distinctions of spoken/written: language in action/language in reflection)
> *Halliday 1978: 35*

The register is the largest linguistic unit in which generalizations can be made without more ado and therefore is the basis of linguistic content form, content invariants being defined within a register. This means for example that a word like *lining* is only described within the register of car repair, its meaning being determined by contrasting it to other words for spare parts (e.g. *drums*) used in car repair, and at this point, no reference is yet made to occurrences of the word outside this register (e.g. to the word senses pertaining to ships, books, and furnaces), just as an immanent description of Danish should not refer to English or German. In the next step, we will of course be interested in comparing two registers, for example if they are spoken by the same person or if similar words occur in them, but there will be no a priori assumption that they are part of a larger system. Maybe they are, maybe not.

My choice of the situation type, including both language and actions, and its registers as my basic units reflects an unproven axiomatic belief that language cannot be understood if isolated from our handling of the material world. From this perspective, the *work* situation also achieves an axiomatic importance, since it is the situation where we collectively and in a socially organized way influence the world by converting its raw materials into commodities. Since the topic of this book is computers and their use in work contexts, the work situation and its register, the work language, are also of more immediate practical interest:

- A *work situation* is a situation whose activities and roles are seen by the participants as belonging to the work they are paid to perform[1].
- A *work language* is the register of a work situation, supporting or changing the working process, the organization of work, the shared knowledge and values, and the social relations constituting the situation.

The notion of a work language neither coincides with a *language for special purposes* nor with a *sociolect*.

- A *language for special purpose* is a language defined by its special technical vocabulary. Of course, some work languages do include expressions that are specific to the profession, e.g. terms for tools, and in some cases these terms are codified in a lexicon.

It is true that on the one hand, many unskilled professions do not have specialized terms, but use terms from the respective national language to form non-standard concepts. These terms receive a special interpretation based on the specific work situation. In the Postal Giro Office for example, workers use a common concept like *brown envelopes* to denote a specific type of brown envelopes designed exclusively for accounting transactions. Also, terms from other types of work situations can be borrowed, reused, and reinterpreted in the present context of work. In the Postal Giro, the English term *reject* was used in various senses. In the data processing department, it means material that is rejected by the optical reader. But in the accounting department, it

---

[1] Note that the employer and employee may have different ideas of what is appropriate to a work situation. Here, I have used the conceptions of the employee.

came to mean materials coming back to the department at a specific time during the day.

On the other hand, the technical vocabulary of some professions is introduced into non-technical contexts, due to the prestige or power of the profession. The computer profession is one example of this. Therefore, merely compiling a dictionary will not characterize communication in a particular work situation. In particular, the dictionary compiler may be misled by the fact that some expressions also occur in standard language but are given a specific interpretation in the work situation.

A *sociolect* is a language variety that is characteristic of a particular social class. The Volvo plant in Gothenburg (cf. Andersson 1983) provides a good example of how boundaries between national languages and between sociolects may differ from those assigned to a work language. On the one hand, the Swedish workers in the plant share a lot of morphological, phonological, and lexical forms with other working class speakers in the city. On the other hand, more than 50% of the workers in the factory are immigrants from Finland, Yugoslavia, and other countries, and they hardly speak Swedish at all; still, they do communicate and make themselves understood in the working situation. In this case, the work language may comprise several different national languages, while the same sociolects are found in other professions.

Language used *about* the work situation, but *outside* it does not belong to work language proper, and should not be confused with it. Examples are: the teaching language of a profession, used during formal education, or the bargaining language used by union representatives negotiating with management. Awareness of differences between teaching language and work language is important when evaluating teaching materials: are the concepts presented useful in practice? Differences between negotiation language and work language are important to note for union representatives: are the demands relevant and understandable to the rank and file? Do negotiation situations create a new work language common to management and union representatives, far removed from the shop floor?

I propose the term *professional language* to denote these different types of registers:

- A *professional language* consists of registers used in work situations or in situations motivated by the work situation.

Since a work language is a register used in work situations, it is a subset of a professional language.

The Postal Giro provides an example illustrating the potential differences between negotiation language and work language. During the period in which the Postal Giro research was carried out, management and union representatives undertook several projects aiming at organizational and technical changes (Grip & Sundström 1984). When one glances at the documents reproduced in their book, the differences from the work language during the same period are evident: one is that the book tends to see a certain task as accounting, whereas the same task according to the view hidden in the work language is document handling. The documents seem to put greater emphasis upon results, abstract actions, and changes in the state of affairs, while the work language focuses upon the concrete actions that have to be done. The principle of getting all material done in one day was expressed in this way in a union document:

> Introduction of new technology may under no circumstances endanger the fulfillment for the demand of correct documentation to the customers within 24 hours.
>
> *Grip and Sundström 1984: 146*

On the shop floor, the same idea was worded in this way:

> Make sure those baskets get up here

A bird's eye view versus an ant's perspective. The workers do not describe what they are doing; they work in an already described reality and use language in order to get things done.

A similar example is provided in Andersson (1983: 99), although in this case the management, not the union, is involved. In the Volvo factories, the management launched a new designation for the employees, "bilbyggare" ("car builders"), in order to counteract their feeling of alienation. But the Volvo workers still preferred to call themselves "gubbar" (a colloquial Swedish expression for males) and rejected words like "car builders" or "operators", since these were not based upon their own experience and thus expressed an alien perspective on their work:

> Calling us "car builders" is odd. I just mount a couple of screws. I don't build a car.   *Andersson 1983: 99*

Bjerknes et al. 1985 provide good examples of the differences between the work language and teaching language of Norwegian nurses: in daily work, concepts such as "overall picture (of patient)" were important, although they did not exist in the theory that the nurses were taught. On the other hand, a textbook used words like "data collecting" that were not used in practice.

Choosing the situational language as my basis does not imply denying the existence of ideolects, sociolects and national languages.

An *ideolect* can be conceived as a set of situational languages used by the same person. This poses the problem of how the different situational languages are connected in one individual. Presumably they are related by the processes of analogy and metaphor: subsets of signs are transferred from one situation type to another, the content form being invested with a new substance.

A *sociolect* is defined as a set of situational languages used by a particular social class, the assumption being that a social class is characterized by living in and getting experience from a particular set of situation types.

A *national language* can be defined in two ways: either by means of the expression system that may well be similar for members of a particular nation, or as a set of registers common to the members. In the latter case we should look for situation types that most people participate in, e.g. eating, cooking, shopping, making love, etc.

I.1.3.6. Connect descriptions of language states and language changes

Work language and work communication often attract attention in periods of change. Changing an organization also entails a change of work communication, and conversely, organizational changes can be triggered by malfunction of communication.

This issue is particularly important when the organizational change involves introduction of computer systems. As in the Postal Giro case, computerization is often followed by organizational changes. In addition, computer systems are symbolic tools that are operated by interpreting and manipulating signs. The semiotic system inherent in the new technology interacts particularly strongly with the existing system of the work language: new concepts are introduced, old concepts disappear or are reinterpreted.

Therefore, a computer semiotics must have concepts for language change. This section describes various hypotheses about the causes and nature of language change. After this discussion, I forward the hypothesis that the situation type and its register defined in the previous section is an important locus of semantic changes which are most interesting in our connection.

However, we must first face our last theoretical problem caused by the fact that the structuralist paradigm builds upon a sharp division between descriptions of language change (diachrony) and descriptions of language states (synchrony), with an emphasis upon the latter.

Saussure himself considered the prime object of diachronic linguistics to be phonetics[1] and believed that phonetic changes only affect isolated aspects

---

[1] Saussure 1966: 140.

of the expression system[1], that they are fortuitous[2], and that the language users simply must take cognizance of the mess and make the best of it[3]. Language changes cause blind disturbances in the language state, and the task of the language users is to restore equilibrium. To Saussure, diachronic and synchronic facts have nothing to do with each other - they are facts of totally different types[4].

Although the initial disturbances may be outside the scope of structural linguistics, later research has shown that the subsequent adaptations of the system are not. One principle that has often been used to explain changes is the principle of vacant positions. If a language has two terms A and B that for some phonetic reason suddenly become pronounced identically so that A is identified with B, then A leaves behind it an empty semantic position that another word comes to occupy, changing its meaning accordingly. Latin *mulgere* (milk) and *molere* (grind) both were pronounced *moudre* in French, and therefore Latin *trahere* (draw) restricted its meaning and moved into the milk-position, becoming French *traire*[5].

Another principle is the principle of simplification. It asserts that changes are handled by speakers by adding new rules on top of old ones until a certain degree of complexity is reached: then all old rules are thrown away, and new ones invented that systematize the change[6].

Although Saussure himself seems to be rather categorical in distinguishing language states from language changes, there have been several attempts to construct connections. For example, in generative grammar, the phonological rules are ordered, and if language change consists in adding rules, thereby leaving older rules "under" or "before" the younger ones, the ordering can be interpreted as some kind of archaeological layer.

Others have hypothesized drifts of language change, the idea being that a language state itself has some immanent drive to change in a certain direction. For example, certain syntactical changes in the Germanic languages have been explained by the finite verb "striving" towards the second position in the sentence[7]. Immanent explanations like these presuppose that

---

[1] Saussure 1966: 95.

[2] Saussure 1966: 85.

[3] Saussure 1966: 85.

[4] "Language is a system whose parts can and must all be considered in their synchronic solidarity. Since changes never affect the system as a whole but rather one or another of its elements, they can be studied only outside the system. Each alteration doubtless has its countereffect on the system, but the initial fact affected only one point: there is no inner bond between the initial fact and the effect that it may subsequently produce on the whole system. The basic difference between successive terms and coexisting terms, between partial facts and facts that affect the system, *precludes making both classes of fact the subject matter of a single science.* [my italics]"   *Saussure 1963: 87.*

[5] Ullmann 1962: 200. Ch. 9 in his book gives more examples of this type.

[6] Lightfoot 1979.

[7] Haiman 1974.

there exist definable states of equilibrium towards which language must strive, and the work of Lehman[1] is a good example of this: he hypothesizes that there are only two stable language structures, one in which all modifiers precede heads (OV-languages, O(bjects) being classified as modifiers to the V(erb)), and one in which the opposite is the case (VO-languages). Languages that do not belong to these two ideal types tend to move towards the one or the other, and Lehman tries to show that the Indo-european languages have been moving from an older OV-type towards the new VO-type.

Although Saussure may be right in considering phonetic changes to be accidental, semantic changes seem to be easier to explain. Ullman[2] offers a good classification of causes for semantic changes that turns out to fit nicely into our description of a situation. The situation type itself is an important factor in language change, since words change meaning when they move from one situational register to another[3]. Change of the tasks or objects of a situation seems nearly automatically to cause corresponding language changes[4], and the same is true if beliefs change: the speakers can either keep the old words which then change their meaning or they can invent new ones. An example of the former is the term *humor*, which English took over from Old French. The term refers to the antique theory of the four chief body fluids which determine the person's temper. As this conception was abandoned, the term stayed but lost its reference to fluids.

Change of the social relations between the participants of the situation also causes language changes. Ullman has no examples here, but recent changes in the pronominal system of the Scandinavian languages caused by social changes give a very good example. The greater part of this century has been dominated by an ideology of equality, both socially and sexually. This meant that the old distinction between *De/Ni* [You] and *du* [you], marking differences in status and intimacy, was abandoned, and the Swedes in particular had difficulties in finding proper ways to address each other, since *du* was too intimate and *Ni* was too distant. At present, *du* has become the unmarked pronoun, and *De/Ni* is only used on rare formal occasions. The

---

[1] Lehman 1974.

[2] Ullmann 1967: Ch. 8.

[3] "When a word passes from ordinary language into a specialized nomenclature - the terminology of a trade, a craft, a profession or some other limited group - it tends to require a more restricted sense.(...)This has happened in French to a number of ordinary verbs when they passed into the language of the farm-yard. Latin *cubare* "to recline, to lie down" > French *couver* "to hatch."
                                                                                        Ullmann 1967: 200.

[4] "Whenever a new name is required to denote a new object or idea, we can do one of three things: form a new word from existing elements; borrow a term from a foreign language or some other source; lastly, alter the meaning of an old word. The need to find a new name is thus an extremely important cause of semantic change."   *Ullmann 1967: 210.*

disturbances caused by feminism have also had their effect on the pronouns. Previously, *han* was the unmarked member, denoting both male and female persons, and *hon* the marked member denoting only females. Language users have tried to change the paradigm in various ways, e.g. by making *hon* the unmarked member or by using the two pronouns as free variants.

I do not believe that the similarity between Ullman's classification and my description of the situation type is accidental, but see it as an indication of the importance of situation types and registers in language change. The content plane of language is intimately connected to the actions language users do, the objects they manipulate, the organizations they live in, the beliefs and values they share, and the social relations they enter into. It will be my working hypothesis that *the locus of semantic language change is the situation type and its associated register.*

Although in this way I stress the dependence of language on its physical and social context, I believe that dependencies can go in the opposite direction as well.

As an example of the first type of dependency, I would hypothesize that change of tasks, objects and tools will often cause change of lexical paradigms, since lexical paradigms presuppose certain tasks, objects and tools, and not the other way around. The fact that the boss in example 1 distinguishes between the noun phrases *linings* and *oversized linings* and between the verbs *mount* and *strip* is due to the existing technology for brake repair. If the technology changes so that brakes are repaired in a different way, his lexical paradigms would change, whereas change of his linguistic paradigms would not change the salient facts of brake repair.

Whereas the physical aspects of a situation are outside the direct control of language, its social aspects are to a large degree created and reproduced by language. The norm "problems are taken care of by somebody else" underlying the closing remark, *Piss on it*, in example 8 may change when workers and their superiors begin to say things like *you have got more responsibility now* and *if you don't take care of this, then you must handle your errors yourself, now everybody must begin to take responsibility* which they in fact did during the 1986 reorganization.

If we apply Saussure's ideas of language change to change of types of work situations and their associated registers we can say that he is right in asserting that the causes for change are external, since they are ultimately caused by economic and political forces and turn up at the work place as changed materials, tools and tasks. However, the changes are not predominantly phonetic, and in particular it is not correct that they are accidental and affect only isolated parts, since many organizational changes are carefully planned and affect large coherent parts of the working situation.

The systematic impact on language is even larger when the change involves large scale introduction of computer systems. Computer systems differ from other tools and raw materials in that they require the user to learn a certain linguistic register in order to be able to use them, since they are partly controlled by verbal means. Whether the boss calls his spare parts *overstør-relsesbelægning* or *oversized linings* has no consequences for his ability to mend brakes, whereas the secretary must learn the exact, often English, commands to be able to write letters on her word processor. In some sense, system development is like constructing a linguistic register: textbooks on the subject will often emphasize concept analysis and construction as important activities[1], and since the profession of computer scientists is based upon the register of mathematics, concepts from this professional language will often leave their mark on the system.

For example, in mathematics, and therefore also in computer science, there is a strong tendency to reduce the number of necessary concepts to achieve generality, for example by redefining one concept as a special instance of the other. Instead of having two different concepts, *something* and *nothing*, the former is defined as a set of elements, and the latter as a special set, namely the empty set to which all normal set operations can be applied. The same principle was applied in an editor I used, where creating a new text was described as adding something to the empty text.

The fact that there is a very clear tendency in the changes effected by computer systems may cause the linguist - and the layman - to see the absolute reversal of Saussure's conception of language change in system development and implementation: a whole foreign linguistic system seems in one fell swoop to be transplanted into an existing language[2]. Reality is different, however, and looks more like Saussure's fortuitous isolated phonetic changes than might be expected. What can be physically moved into the work place is not signs and meanings, but only expression units, screens that display letters and pictures. There is no natural law that says that these signs are adopted as signs by the users, and experience shows that many are not, and those that are accepted can be changed both phonetically and semantically. I believe that this process of assimilation can very well be described by the traditional notion of system adaptions of which some examples were given above. These adaptions may range from change of pronunciation and inflection, to semantic re-interpretation of the screen elements.

One of today's most important innovators of linguistic registers is probably the expanding and changing market of technological innovations and

---

[1] E.g. the entity action step in Jackson 1983.
[2] Josefson 1985 investigated the effects of computerization on the Swedish social insurance system, and found symptoms of a linguistic impoverishment.

commodities. New commodities create new types of situations, new types of situations make new distinctions relevant, thereby generating semantic changes, and new technology changes the work processes and thereby the work languages. These changes are not totally blind, natural, or unconscious.

These disturbances will engender internal, structural processes in the language; the language users will not assimilate the novelties as they spurt out of the economic system, but will change them according to the language and the experiences they possess, and accommodate their linguistic system to be able to hold them. From this point of view it is difficult to believe that the languages themselves should contain inner driving forces that determine the way they change; rather, the role of the language system in language development may be one of conserving: to insist on coherence and beauty, "to ensure a sense of tradition and continuity"[1].

I.1.3.7. A materialistic view of language[2]

The revisions of the structuralist paradigm described on the previous pages have partly been governed by the practical purpose of the book: to adapt and extend classical structuralist linguistics and semiotics, such that it becomes a coherent framework for understanding the semiotic aspects of computers and their use in work. Since the user works the computer system by means of signs and since the introduction of computers is often accompanied by organizational changes, I need a framework that allows me to understand and describe the interplay between work, organization, and language; and since a computer system is only used in specific types of work situations, the choice of the situational language instead of the national language is very well motivated from a practical point of view. For example, if I am designing a system for librarians, it is their work situation and their professional language I need to know, not the national language in its totality. But besides these practical considerations, my choices have also been governed by a materialistic philosophy of language, and I shall end this part by giving a short sketch of this philosophy.

To adopt a materialistic view of language means to see the structure and development of language as an answer to demands caused by the practical situations in the daily life of the language users, to explain linguistic features by the culture and society in which the language exists, and to prefer historical explanations over ontological ones.

---

[1] Ullmann 1962: 198.
[2] Bøgh Andersen 1977.

A materialistic linguistics sees the sign as the most important "fact of language", since by associating the signified with a signifier, the sign is our main vehicle for anchoring our consciousness in the material and social world in which it exists.

Of course, it is sometimes useful to abstract particular features of the sign for closer study. Phonology can focus on the signifier, without caring too much about the signified, and semantics can study meaning systems without special attention to the way they are expressed. Still, the basic fact is that ideas are never created and shared without a particular means of expression, and words are never perceived as pure sounds, devoid of meaning.

The materialistic point of view does not mean the people are passive victims of external social forces, but it does stress that creativity and imagination must exist within certain constraints. From a materialistic point of view, our consciousness is influenced by our position in the social division of labor, and since our work is an important link between ourselves and the society that gives us our identity and partly determines what we feel is relevant and right, important properties of our language should be explained by the communicative experiences in our work, and our work language should be counted as an important factor in our total language.

It does not mean, of course, that the work situation completely determines our communicative competence. We participate in communication in situations other than the work situation: in shops, in front of the TV, at parties, at the dinner table, in the sports club, in bed. The reason why I emphasize the work situation is that although work language contributes important properties to our total language, it is nearly absent in the empirical foundations of linguistics. It is very hard to find empirical investigations of language in the context of work, and in this book, I will try to give a more appropriate weight to our linguistic work experiences.

The materialistic point of view may also contribute to our general understanding of language. Why is language as it is? If there are universals of language, what are the reasons for them? Chomsky[1] believes that our cognitive apparatus determines the limits on possible language, and that, conversely, a study of language universals may be used to characterize the cognitive faculties of man. True as it may be, there are other explanations of language universals, namely that anything that functions as a human language must be able to perform certain functions[2]. Thus, universals of language do not necessarily express biological properties of the human brain, but may simply reflect basic constraints on human societies. For example, any society involves

---

[1] E.g. Chomsky 1968, section 3.
[2] See e.g. Halliday 1978.

some kind of division of labor, some kind of cooperation, some kind of commodity exchange, and some kind of reproduction. These activities are impossible without language, and conversely, any human language must be able to work in these activities.

If this line of thought is pursued to its conclusion, the content system of the national language no longer appears as an homogeneous entity, but as a conglomerate of possibly different sublanguages, variously influencing each other by the well-known processes of metaphor, similes, and borrowing. The reason is that in a society or organization based on a division of labor, the necessary communicative functions and semantic articulations will differ among subgroups, and although the means of expressions, be they sounds or letters, may be the same, the semantic system and communicative functions will differ. Since the sign is the basic building block of a language, it follows that a society or organization with a marked division of labor may have no common language, although its speakers may use the same means of expression, and therefore believe that they also mean the same thing.

The substance of this is not unfamiliar. After linguistics had succeeded in setting up a small set of basic elements, the phonemes and their distinctive features, from which the words and sentences of our language are built, it was believed that a similar procedure might be possible in the realm of meanings, but so far no one has succeeded in providing the requisite set of building blocks and a simple general structure for combining them.

From my point of view, the reason is that the task is impossible; it is impossible because the semantic system cannot be expected to be as homogeneous as the system of expression. For the botanist, the distinctive features of botany (e.g. the shape of leaves, the number of petals) and their systematical hierarchical arrangement, are a helpful articulation of the semantic field of plants in his job, since they are useful for classifying. However, very few people besides the botanist are engaged in classifying the trees or flowers in this way when they take a walk in the woods, and the layman's semantic field of plants may be structured in a quite different way, e.g. according to similarity to typical specimens[1]. Therefore a willow tree may belong to the class of trees in the semantic system of the botanist because it possesses the botanical distinctive features of trees, whereas to the layman it is seen as shrubbery, since its appearance is too different from typical trees like the beech and the spruce.

---

[1] See Folke Larsen 1981a and b.

I.2

Adapting and Extending Structuralist Methods

We have now looked at work language, the language variety that must be central to our concerns, and made a preliminary list of the descriptive shortcomings of classical structuralism with respect to this language type.

In the next, constructive sections I will describe those parts of the tradition I wish to keep, and propose changes in other parts that make the theory better suited for the purposes at hand. Although the next few sections are concerned with language proper, I shall append short indications of how the concepts described can be used to understand computer systems, so that readers primarily interested in computers may judge if reading on is still worth the effort.

After presenting the key concepts (Section I.2.1), I show in Section I.2.2 how they can be applied to analysis of work processes and organizations, in particular the car repair and the Postal Giro examples from I.1.

Section I.2.3 extends the framework further to deal with computer systems. Computer systems are interpreted as media for human communication, and as a consequence of this, the theoretical focus is shifted from the system itself to the relations between system and user (Section I.2.4).

I.2.1. Basic concepts for describing symbolic acts

One of the basic points of structuralism is that units of language are defined relationally.

> Instead of pre-existing ideas then, we find in all the foregoing examples *values* emanating from the system. When they are said to correspond to concepts, it is understood that the concepts are purely differential and defined not by their positive content but negatively by their relations with the other terms in the system. Their most precise characteristic is in being what the others are not. *Saussure 1966: 117*

I.2.1.1. Functions and functives

From a structuralist point of view, the important thing is not the stuff linguistic units are made of, but the dependencies between them: the units of language are nothing but end-points of dependencies. As an example, let us look at the Danish tones[1]. If we are interested in the stuff they are made of, we would say that there are two tones, of which one /⌐/ is falling and the other /´/ is non-falling, whereas a structural description is concerned with the dependencies between them, namely that /´/ cannot occur without /⌐/.

(English, too, has two tones, but uses them differently from Danish. The English reader will get at clear impression of the English tones by pronouncing enumerations like

In the room there was a ´table, a ´chair, a ´bed, and a `cupboard.

Table, chair, and *bed* have non-falling tones, while *cupboard* is pronounced with a falling tone.)

In Danish we can have

Han bliver ´glad hvis du kommer i `morgen (both occur)
[He will be ´happy, if you come `tomorrow]
Han bliver `glad (only "`" occurs)
[He will be `happy]

but if we hear

Han bliver ´glad (only "´" occurs)
[He will be ´happy]

with a non-falling tone, we expect something more to follow.

Behind the emphasis on dependencies lies a belief that it is the dependencies and not the way in which they are realized that makes language hang together. The Danish tones are used to establish a period, the smallest independent linguistic unit, but it is their particular dependency that does it and not the fact that they are manifested as differences in tone. In fact, written language also has "tones" in the functional sense, but these "tones" are manifested as written characters, namely as the comma and the period. The dependencies between these elements in normal prose are the same, the comma being unable to occur without a period, whereas a period does not require a comma. We can have

He will be happy, if you come tomorrow. (both occur)
He will be happy. (only "." occurs)

but if we read

He will be happy, (only "," occurs)

---

[1] The main points are based on Hjelmslev 1948-49-50.

we again expect something more, and if the text ends here, we are justified in believing that something is missing or that the writer was interrupted in mid-sentence.

This particular dependency is traditionally called subordination, the non-falling tone being subordinate to the falling. I used this term in the previous section, but now I would like to shift to Hjelmslev's terminology, in which subordination is called determination.

Hjelmslev 1963a:34 builds his theory upon three such dependencies, called *functions*: *interdependence, determination, and constellation*, which I will also use frequently.

The end-points of the function are called *functives*, and they occur in two types, *constants* and *variables*: the presence of constants is a necessary condition for the functive to which it has function, which is not true of variables. Thus, in our example, falling tone and period are constants, since they must occur, whereas non-falling tone and comma need not occur and consequently are variables. Interdependences are defined as functions with two constants, determinations are functions with one constant and one variable, and constellations are functions with only variables.

Let $\underline{a}$ denote absence of the element a, let $a.b$ denote a chain consisting of both a and b, and let $+a$ denote that the chain a has been recorded in the text we are working with. Two or more chains are said to *correspond* if their functives are the same or negatives of the same, and the three functions can be defined by different types of corresponding chains[1]:

Interdependence is defined as the corresponding chains (+a.b, -$\underline{a}$.b, -a.$\underline{b}$) , which I symbolize graphically as

$$\boxed{a} \longleftrightarrow \boxed{b}$$

Determination is (+a.b, +$\underline{a}$.b, -a.$\underline{b}$) and is symbolized

$$\boxed{a} \longrightarrow \boxed{b}$$

and constellation[2] reads (+a.b or -a.b, +$\underline{a}$.b, +a.$\underline{b}$) and is symbolized

$$\boxed{a} \longrightarrow \boxed{b}$$

In diagrams of this type, I symbolize functives as boxes and functions as arrows between the boxes. The whole diagram denotes a *functival field* that consists of a function and its functives.

---

[1] Uldall and Hjelmslev differ in the definitions and names of the glossematic functions, and both have separate terms to denote paradigmatic functions and syntagmatic functions. To avoid terminological disaster in this book, I mainly use Hjelmslev's definitions and terms, and furthermore use the same terms for paradigmatic and syntagmatic functions, hoping that the context will make the distinction clear.

[2] In the definition of constellation, I deviate from Hjelmslev and follow Uldall.

Our initial example, the Danish tones, generates the corresponding chains (+non-falling. falling, +<u>non-falling</u>. falling, -non-falling. <u>falling</u>), and their functival field looks like this in diagrammatic form:

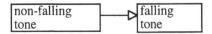

As an example of interdependence, I shall take the functival field defining sentences. In one analysis, a sentence always must contain a verbal morpheme like mood or tense plus a noun in the nominative. We can have

He (nominative) comes (present tense indicative mood)

but neither

Him (accusative) comes (present tense indicative mood)

which lacks nominative, nor

He (nominative) come (infinitive)

which lacks tense and mood. The diagrammatic representation of this functival field is:

There are exceptions that must be explained away. The imperative lacks a nominative

Come (imperative mood)

but a second person nominative pronoun can always be encatalysed:

Come (imperative mood) you (nominative)

Interdependence and determination share the property that they contain at least one constant, and I use the term *cohesion* as a general term for these functions.

These three functions can be seen as abstractions of the well-known linguistic concepts of nexus, subordination and co-ordination, but in glossematics they are not uniquely associated with language. For example, Uldall 1967 uses court ceremonials and greeting habits to exemplify these functions. In spite of their abstractness, they are known to be useful in linguistic description, and therefore they are of special interest in this book, since we are looking for concepts that can be used to characterize both symbolic behavior and its non-symbolic context, such as work tasks and work organization. In the next section, I shall present additional concepts for describing the special class of symbolic acts.

Hjelmslev's choice of terms is not always lucky. The terms *constellation* and *interdependence* are relatively easy to remember, but *determination* is a bad choice, since it often connotes the opposite meaning of its definition. When we say that an adjective determines its substantive, the meaning is that the adjective is the "weak" part that cannot do without the "strong" part, the substantive. However, non-technical usage of the terms unfortunately distributes the weak and strong roles oppositely, so saying that *Demand and supply determine market prices* means that *demand and supply* are the independent variables that influence the dependent price variable. Therefore I shall normally use *presuppose* instead of *determine*.

When the term is used about semantics, it has often the additional sense that the meaning of the subordinate phrase only affects its superordinate phrase. Thus, *little* in *A little boy crossed the street* only affects *boy*, but not *crossed* and *streets*. In these cases I shall use the term *modify*, saying that *"little" modifies "boy"*.

Application to computers

One possibility for using the three functions in interface design is to describe flexibility properties. Constellations are the most flexible, interdependences the least. Suppose we design data entry for a library system whose records contain document number, title, author, publisher, and year. If data entry is designed as a constellation, the user is free to choose the number (possibly zero) of fields to be entered, while if it is built as an interdependence, each field must be filled. In between lies the presupposition, which might make document number, title, and author obligatory, but publisher and year optional.

In general, the functions can be used to make structural descriptions of the man-machine interface, and I shall do that frequently. For example, certain types of menus (e.g. pop-up and pull-down menus) can be defined as presuppositions from the menu items to the menu headings, the items being the subordinate part of the menu.

I.2.1.2. *Form/substance, expression/content*

Symbolic acts and objects are double: when a symbolic act or object occurs, two entities occur: an expression and a content. To give an example, tossing a coin on the table may not be a symbolic act. If I just want to get rid of it, then only one act occurs: tossing the coin. However, this act can be used symbolically to settle a dispute. Then one side of the coin acquires the content "I win" and the other side "You win", and now two acts occur simultaneously: the coin is still tossed, but now accompanied by the element "you win". According to Hjelmslev, it is most appropriate to say that what occurs is not an object called a sign, but a sign *function*, which is a function between a *content* (the signified) and an *expression* (the signifier)[1]. Both expression and content must be present in a sign:

> If we think without speaking, the thought is not a linguistic content and not a functive for a sign function. If we speak without thinking, and in the form of series of sounds to which no content can be attached by any listener, such speech is an abracadabra, not a linguistic expression and not a functive for a sign function.
>
> *Hjelmslev 1963a: 48*

The expression substance of the symbolic acts we observe can be diverse: gestures, movements, sounds, dots on paper, pixels on a screen. In the very moment of symbolization this *substance* acquires a *form*. The substance is articulated in a new way, some expression features becoming distinctive in relation to the content, and content features becoming distinctive in relation to the expression.

In our example, the continuum of coin positions (expression substance) is articulated into two opposites: head up or tail up (expression form). Only these properties are distinctive, so it does not matter if the coin ends up in the middle of the table or at the edge, these properties being non-distinctive, with no content attached to the boundary between the two positions. If the coin ends up in a slanted position, it cannot be interpreted and the coin must be tossed again.

In the same operation, form is also introduced in the content substance. To exemplify this, let us elaborate our example a bit: an adult and a child are in the kitchen, discussing who is going to do the dishes. There are many possibilities: the adult does it, the child does it, the adult washes and the child dries, the adult does half, the child does the other half, etc., etc. Now we agree to use the coin to decide. At this moment, two things happen: 1. a field of actions is *selected* and segregated from all other acts so that only those involving one person are left. 2. This field is *articulated* into two halves: either the child does it, or the adult does it, and there is no compromise. The substance of possible dish-washing actions is articulated into a form.

We have seen how the sign has two parallel planes: the content plane and the expression plane, both of which possess a form that articulates a substance. In glossematics, the hypothetical non-articulated substance is called the *purport* of the sign. Thus the expression purport of our sign consists of

---

[1] A less abstract, but rather useful definition is given by Umberto Eco: a sign is "everything which can be used in order to lie" (Eco 1976: 7).

all conceivable positions of the coin, and the content purport consists of all conceivable ways for an adult and a child to do dishes.

The defining factor in sign functions is not the substance but the form: the important demand on our expressive system is not connected with the use of coins, but with objects that can end up in positions which the thrower can perceive as different. In fact, you don't need a coin at all. Any object which can be tossed and ends up in one of two positions can be used, and if you are out of coins a book of matches will do.

The articulation of acts into content and expression planes is dialectically connected with the introduction of the form/substance opposition in the purports of each plane. The category of signs is established by a functival field whose function is an interdependence and whose functives are the content and expression plane. But since content and expression are functives, they are elements of form and therefore by necessity induce an articulation in their respective purports.

In the structuralist concepts of form, four aspects can be discerned:

Classification: a form can be said to classify or articulate the purport. For example, the total set of coin positions is classified into three types: heads up, tails up, and anything else.

Difference: the core structure of a form consists of differences. The important thing in our example is that we have two different content units, each expressed by two different expression units. It is a matter of taste whether tails means "You do the dishes" or "I do the dishes". As long as we agree, one investment of substance works just as well as the other. An important corollary is that we can never have an isolated sign - what would it differ from? We must at least have two signs.

Pertinence: by form is meant a description of pertinent, distinctive properties. Two features belong to the expression form if and only if exchanging one for the other leads to exchange of contents. The location of the coin is not pertinent, since a coin ending at the edge does not have a different meaning from a coin ending at the middle of the table. Conversely, two features belong to the content form if and only if exchanging one for the other entails exchange of expressions. The time of the dish washing is not pertinent, since exchange of "You do the dishes now" with "You do the dishes in half an hour" does not entail an exchange of "Heads up" and "Tails up".

Portability: a form is portable in the sense that it can be used to articulate more than one purport. The reason is that the identity of the sign lies in the functions between content and expression form. The only demands on the purports are that they must be articulateable according to the form. For example, a book of matches can substitute for a coin as a means of expression, but not a ball. On the content plane, the content form of three-dimensional space can articulate the purport of social hierarchy (a *high* position), of states of mind (*high* spirits), of ethics (*high* morals), etc.

The form of a language is called the *linguistic schema*. It is the constant in its many manifestations whose variable features are called *linguistic usage*. The linguistic schema describes those functions and functives that must always occur when a given language is used, whereas the linguistic usage is a description of those features that may or may not occur.

To return to our coin example: *the linguistic schema* simply states that there are two sign-functions, which divide the expression substance into two parts, *A* and *B*, and the content substance into two parts *a* and *b*. We can further characterize these functions by the fact that *A* and *B* carry content directly (they are like words, not like letters).

The linguistic usage specifies how this schema is manifested: *A* and *B* are manifested by the two sides of a coin, but this is not necessary: a book of matches or dice could have been used. Furthermore, *a* and *b* are manifested in the purport of dish-washing actions, dividing them into two groups: "You do the dishes" vs. "I do the dishes". But again, the coin could have been used to settle all kinds of disputes, that is, it can articulate other kinds of purports: "You do the shopping" vs. "I do the shopping", "I empty the garbage can" vs. "You empty the garbage can", etc., etc.

In this book, I will adopt these concepts. However, in one respect I will differ from classical structuralism, namely in the question of the arbitrariness of the sign[1]. To Saussure and Hjelmslev, the articulation of the purport by the form was arbitrary, and there are no pre-existing general ideas that determine the content units of language.

> What determines its form is solely the functions of language, the sign function and the functions deducible therefrom. Purport remains, each time, substance for a new form, and has no possible existence except through being substance for one form or another.   *Hjelmslev 1963a: 52*

According to Hjelmslev, there is form without substance, but never substance without form. The function between form and substance, called *manifestation*, is of type presupposition, the form being the constant which must always be present, the substance being the variable, which may not occur.

I find myself in a position where I must both agree and disagree: since part of a register is determined by the situation type it is used in, I must agree that there exist no *universal* non-linguistic phenomena that determine the content form of language, but I strongly disagree in the assumption that particular properties of situation types will not influence it either.

---

[1] See Malmberg 1973, ch. 4 for a good discussion of this point.

I propose the following solution to this dilemma: it is true that the content units of language can only exist as contents of a sign function, associated with an expression. It is also true that the boundaries of the units are circumscribed by the form. Thus, language has an independent existence. But the form itself is not arbitrary, since some of the differences introduced in the content purport are motivated by the practical tasks of the situation. In our example, the task defining the situation is to do the dishes. The communicative function of our coin is work distribution: who is going to do it? The content articulation "You do the dishes" vs "I do the dishes" is clearly motivated by the task at hand and the conflicting interests, since in this situation, we would never think of creating signs that articulate the acts into e.g. "acts accompanied with music" vs. "acts not accompanied with music", a distinction which might be relevant in the work situation of a film director.

Application to computers

The concepts of expression and content, form and substance are the key concepts in semiotics, and therefore have a correspondingly broad range of applications in computer science. I shall just mention a few here.

On the expression plane, the form/substance dichotomy is useful for discussing various ways of manifesting the same expression element. Modern computers offer a wealth of expressive devices, both verbal and graphical representations, static and animated graphics, video and sound, so that choosing the right ones requires some systematic basis. The concepts allow us to say that the same element, e.g. selection of an object, can be manifested as graphical inversion, as movement, or as a beep.

It also allows us to distinguish between the essence of a program and its many manifestations on different machines, a distinction that has already shown its usefulness in practice.

Many programs include facilities for displaying views of different work objects, e.g. different sheets of paper, and each object can be presented in different subviews showing different properties and different details. In the present context, a collection of subviews can be understood as different content forms articulating the same substance - the same matter is viewed through different conceptual filters.

Finally the sign relation itself, the specific relation between content and expression, can be made the basis for aesthetic classifications. The dominant tradition in interface design seems to belong to the school of realism (the direct manipulation school) in advocating a similarity between expression and content forms, so that the interface disappears and the user can act as if the sign were identical to the object it signifies. The theoretical framework gives us concepts for discussing this issue and realizing that the equality relation is but one out of many possible.

1.2.1.3. The commutation test

As previously mentioned, the *commutation test* is the most important tool for the linguist. Hjelmslev describes commutation in the following rather obscure way:

> a correlation in one plane which...has relation to a correlation in the other plane of a
> language   *Hjelmslev 1963a: 73*

where *correlation* means: an either-or function, and *relation* means: a both-and function. What he means is simply that two expression units A and B commute if and only if exchanging A with B co-occurs with an exchange of content units, and vice versa.

The commutation test in the Hjelmslevian sense is designed to give information about relations between units, not about the units themselves. This accords with the view that a linguistic schema is defined by relations between terms, the terms themselves being just empty nodes. Let us look at our coin example again: we can apply the commutation test to our system by trying to replace the expression unit /tails up/ with /heads up/ and observe what changes ensue on the content plane. We record a change from /you do the dishes/ to /I do the dishes/. Thus we can state that replacing /tails up/ by /heads up/ causes /you do the dishes/ to be replaced by /I do the dishes/. That is all. Notice that we have not gathered any information about the terms themselves, only about their relations.

The commutation test is a method for finding *invariants*. Invariants are simply units that pass the commutation test. /tails up/ and /heads up/ are invariant, whereas /located in the middle of the table/ and /located at the edge of the table/ are *variants*. Exchanging one for the other does not entail a change of content.

The commutation test can be applied on both planes of language. If one wishes to describe the invariant phonemes of a language, one starts by guessing at possible candidates and then for each candidate one checks whether exchanging it with another produces some change of content. In English, *b, d,* and *g* are phonemes, since *breed* and *greed*, *grill* and *drill* have different meanings. In other cases, the decision is not so simple, since the data admits of different analyses. We might believe that the /ng/ sound is a phoneme different from /n/, since they commute in /sing/ *sing* and /sin/ *sin*. But in other cases, /ng/ is clearly a variant of /n/ before a velar, e.g. in the composite word *incline*, which can be pronounced /ing'klain/ as well as

/in'klain/. Nor do the two sounds commute in simplex words like /thingk/, since /n/ does not occur in /ng/'s position. It is not obvious whether /ng/ is a variant of /n/ or whether it is an invariant[1]

In theory, it is possible to apply the same procedure on the content plane. For example, many English words contain the units /male/ and /female/ since exchanging them causes the expression to be changed too: *he/she, man/woman, boy/girl,* etc.

However, from the point of view outlined in Section I.1.3, content analysis should not be conducted in the context of a national language, but inside a particular register, since we expect to find the content plane to be partitioned into many situation-specific compartments. To lump these compartments together will either bring about confusion, not clarity, or it will result in descriptions that are devoid of content.

To illustrate this, let us consider the vocabulary of situations where computer systems are constructed, and the vocabulary of situations where they are used. One will often find that terms from the construction situation have migrated into the use situation, partly because of the prestige of the terms, partly because screen text and manuals are written by the constructors. In a library system I investigated, it was possible to have the system execute both single commands and sequences of commands. The latter was called *stacking the commands* by the users, so in the use situation *stacking commands* is a member of the same paradigm as *entering single commands.*

The word *stack* is probably borrowed from computer science, where the situation is different. Here a *stack* is a data structure characterized by the fact that the last item entered is the first item removed, as contrasted to *queue,* in which the first item entered is the first item removed.

If we describe the two languages separately, we get two simple content structures, in which the members are united by a common element, and differentiated by simple features. In the use situation, *stacking commands* contrasts to *entering single commands* by a number feature (singular vs. plural) and the two expressions share the meaning of *entering commands.* In the construction situation, *stack* shares the meaning *data structure* with *queue,* and they differ in their methods of removing items (last out vs. first out). It is easy to relate the two fields to the tasks of their registers.

However, if we insist that both occurrences of *stack* belong to the same language, we must record that *stack* contrasts both to *queue* and *enter single commands.* The resulting field contains elements that have no common feature, and the contrasts are no longer simple: *stack* contrast to *queue* by

---

[1] I am indebted to Bent Preisler for the examples.

the method of entering and removing items, but to *enter single commands* by the number of items.

The principle of using registers as the scope of analysis can be used to solve the well-known problem of when to end a semantic analysis. The problem is sometimes formulated in terms of the concept of *distinguishers*[1]. Let us again look at the word *bachelor* with its four main senses:

(1)   unmarried adult male,
(2)   young knight serving under the standard of another,
(3)   a person having the academic degree conferred for completing the first four years of college,
(4)   young male seal without a mate during the breeding time.

From the point of view of structural linguistics, some of the distinctions, such as adult|child, human|animal, etc., belong to language, since they recur in many words, and recording these elements is in accordance with the goal of the analysis, which is to find a minimal set of semantic building blocks, in analogy with phonemes.

But what about *without a mate during the breeding time?* This element probably will not be found in any other word, since its internal structure is very complicated and specialized, so entering this element into the analysis will defeat its goal.

In the register-oriented approach, *without a mate during the breeding time* does not belong to language at all! According to Katz 1972:84, distinguishers "mark purely perceptual distinctions among the referents of conceptually identical sense", but these distinctions only come into existence at the linguist's desk when he compares all senses of a word, irrespective of the situation in which they are used. The alleged ambiguity of bachelor probably simply does not exist in real life situations. To see this, consider two situations:

1. University admission: a person applies for a grant to do academic studies that requires at least a master's degree, while the applicant has only a bachelor's degree. The important contrast in this situation is between bachelor and master, and seals and knights do not enter into the picture. There is no contrast between the academic sense of bachelor and the zoological sense.

2. Hunting: a couple of hunters are watching for prey and need to distinguish between different animals in so far as different weapons and tactics are needed. It is possible that it is important to distinguish between bachelors and mated seals, but it is quite certain that in this situation, academicians and

---

[1] Katz & Fodor 1963. Katz 1972.

knights will not be relevant. *Bachelor* will contrast with other prey, but the zoological sense will not contrast with the other senses.

Apart from its theoretical difficulties, the concept of a homogeneous national content system is to my mind psychologically implausible. A glance in a dictionary reveals that words may easily have 10 different senses, and if this is true of each word in a sentence with 10 words, the sentence can have 10^{10} different meanings. To compute all these meanings and select the right one will take such a long time that it is implausible that humans have to do it.

Combinatorial explosions like these have always pursued machine translation systems like a nightmare and within the field of AI given rise to concepts much similar to the approach advocated here[1]. The methodological fallacy consists in assuming that the language user has to single out an object from the total set of all existing objects in the world each time a noun is chosen, whereas he in reality uses a special register in a particular type of situation with a limited number of actions and objects and relatively few distinctions.

Although the register is my basis of analysis, the commutation test will still remain the fundamental analytical tool, but used only in a particular situation type, giving us the expression and content units that are *pertinent in this particular situation type*. I like to think that I take the Saussurian dictum "the value of each term results solely from the simultaneous presence of the others" at face value: the semantic value of a sign is identical to the contrasts it contracts in *real, recurrent situations of daily life*. Just as Saussure advocated an immanent analysis of national languages, I advocate immanent analysis of registers. And just as it is not allowed to add English meanings to a Danish word, just because they happen to be spelled in the same way, it is also forbidden to transfer meanings from one register to another, just because the same phonemic sequence occurs in both.

I.2.1.4. Parts and wholes

The glossematic school of linguistics views the text as a hierarchy of parts and wholes, which, superficially at least, resembles the immediate constituent structure of transformational grammar. A text consists of chapters which consist of periods which consist of sentences, etc. I shall not attempt to reproduce the glossematic procedure for analyzing texts into parts for the very good reason that I neither understand nor master it. The reason is that no systematic account of the procedure has ever been published, the only rea-

---

[1] I am thinking of the script concept of Schank & Abelson 1977 and the frame concept of Minsky 1975

sonably complete description being Hjelmslev's lecture notes[1]. Instead I shall briefly indicate what I have incorporated into my own analysis of computer systems in Part II and work processes in Part III.

I follow glossematics in that the initial partition of a text is that between expression and content plane, which are analyzed independently in the following steps, although of course we require all elements on both planes to enter the sign-function.

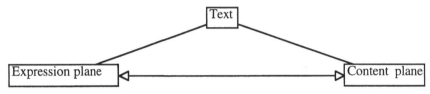

Fig. I.2.1. Expression and content plane.

Furthermore, I am not interested in any isolated piece of text, but only those that contract cohesions with other pieces. Metaphorically speaking, it means that I am always on the look-out for presuppositions and interdependencies as I cut the text into smaller and smaller pieces, and when I find one, I stop and record it.

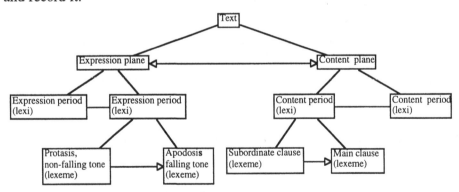

Fig. I.2.2. Main parts of a text.

In an analysis of the total set of Danish spoken texts on the expression plane, the first cohesion we encounter is the presupposition described above between a protasis with non-falling tone and apodosis with falling tone. On the content plane we find a similar presupposition between subordinate and main clauses, the former presupposing the latter. These parts are called *lexemes*, corresponding to the sentence, and their wholes are called *lexias*, corresponding to periods. Note that the two planes are not isomorphic since

---

[1] Hjelmslev 1942-43. Mortensen 1969 has reconstructed Hjelmslev's procedure, and I use his account in the following.

protasis and apodosis do not coincide with subordinate clause and main clause, respectively, since both main and subordinate clauses can be expressed as a protasis.

When I describe the units, I follow Hjelmslev in distinguishing between their functions vis-a-vis other units of the same rank (the analytical definition), and their internal structure (the synthetical definition).

For example, the analytical definition of a lexeme is that it is the first unit that cannot function as its superchain (the whole of which is is a part, viz. the period), since the subordinate clause presupposes the main clause. The synthetic definition of the unit, which Hjelmslev's analysis designates by a separate name (the *nexus)* consists of the interdependence between a nominative and the verbal morphemes described above.

The analytical procedure continues until no more cuts can be made in the text, and the atomic units we end up with are called *taxemes*. On the expression plane, they correspond to phonemes, on the content plane to roots, morphemes, and derivatives. Taxemes can again be classified according to the way they contrast with other taxemes. For example, the English phoneme /b/ differs from /p/ in the same way as /d/ differs from /t/, namely by being voiced, and the roots *boy* and *girl* differ in the same sex feature as *man* and *woman*. Units like these that do not occur as segments but as properties of segments are commonly called distinctive features: glossematics terms them *glossemes*.

Application to computers

If the first basic division of the "text" into a content and expression plane is transferred to computer systems, the expression plane will turn out to be those system properties that are under the most direct control of the programmer, while the content plane corresponds to the users' interpretation of the system. This does not mean that each plane can be treated separately; on the contrary, the form aspect of one cannot exist without the other, since identification of elements in one plane requires a successful outcome of the commutation test on the other.

The distinction between a lexia (the period) and its lexemes (the sentences) will in practice often correspond to a distinction between a task and its component actions known from the literature of human-computer interaction[1].

---

[1] See e.g. Norman 1986: 37.

1.2.1.5. System and process

The third participant in the dialectics of sign formation, besides expression/content and form/substance, is the articulation of an act in a *process* and a *system*. Signs exist because their two planes commute, but commutation presupposes that present units can be exchanged with non-present ones, if not in reality then in thought. By being used as a symbolic act, the process of tossing a coin is seen as options that can replace each other in a significant way. When we see the coin ending heads up, it must be possible for us simultaneously to imagine tails up.

Under the process aspect we describe functions between co-occurring entities (both-and), whereas the system aspect covers functions between entities that do not co-occur, but could have occurred in the same place (either-or). Process functions are traditionally called *syntagms,* whereas system functions are called *paradigms*. The notation for paradigms given in Uldall 1967 is nearly the same as for syntagms, except that round parentheses are replaced with sharp ones. The notation <+a +b -c> means that we have observed a context in which both *a* and *b* but not *c* can occur.

The descriptions presented in the previous section were all process descriptions, but the same functions can be used to describe relations between members of paradigms. As the syntagmatic functions were defined by corresponding chains, the paradigmatic functions are defined by corresponding paradigms which are called a *category of paradigms* in Uldall 1967: 58 ff[1]. Thus, a category of paradigms is a collection of paradigms with the same members. Categories are denoted by curly brackets. The notation {+<+a+b> +<+a-b> -<-a+b>} means that we have found contexts where both *a* and *b* and *a* alone can occur, while there are no contexts where *b* occurs alone. The category is therefore a presupposition.

Let me illustrate the difference between syntagmatic and paradigmatic functions with the German prepositions and cases.

In a process description we are interested in how prepositions and cases can occur together. For example, one can say that prepositions presuppose cases, since case endings can occur without prepositions (Das Auto meines Vaters), whereas prepositions - if we disregard proper names - require a case inflected noun (In der Stadt, Durch die Stadt).

In a system description, however, we want to know something about the elements of the case paradigm themselves, for example that some paradigms (as that generated by *auf*) contain both the a(ccusative) and d(ative) while other paradigms (e.g. that of *durch*) only contain accusative, and still others

---

[1] Although I am borrowing ideas from Uldall, I refrain from using his complicated notations in the analysis of sums and categories.

(e.g. that of *aus*) dative. We collect these paradigms and get the following category: {+<+a +d>+<+a -d>+<-a +d>}, which we, in analogy with the corresponding process concept, define as a constellation since both <+a -d> and <-a +d> occur. If the *aus*-paradigm had not been found, the category would have looked like this {+<+a +d>+<+a -d>-<-a +d>}and been a presupposition, accusative presupposing the dative, since then the dative would occur in all paradigms in which the accusative occurs, but not vice versa.

Application to computers

Many issues in design of the user interface of computer systems concern the structure of the system's syntagms and paradigms. For example, in the classical paper on the design of the Star user interface (Smith et al. 1983), the authors recommend a particular order between command and object, which later became very popular:

> Commands in Star take the form of noun-verb. You specify the object of interest (the "noun") and then invoke a command to manipulate it (the "verb").

This quotation is a recommendation to use a particular syntagm, object + verb, instead of the traditional verb + object, the advantage being that when the user has selected an object, the designer knows which actions are legal at this point. He can then remove illegal actions and thereby prevent user errors.

Other important issues concern the action paradigms of the system. An action paradigm specifies the set of actions available at a given point of time, and the paradigms offered by a system should match those needed by the user, so that he does not have to perform one action where he really wanted to do another. Presentation of action paradigms is also important, and a *menu* can be interpreted as a description of the paradigm available at the moment.

I.2.1.6. Systemic nets: combining process and system

In my attempts to use the glossematic concepts in practice, I have come across three notational difficulties.

1. Classes and members: the functions between categories are often different from the functions between their members. For example, the Danish verb must be inflected in voice (active/passive) and tense (present/past), so these two inflectional categories are interdependent. However, since the individual elements of one category can combine freely with elements in the other, e.g. active + present, active + past, etc., the function between the elements is a constellation. Sometimes I shall want to specify functions at this level of detail, but the functional diagrams give no elementary way of doing it.

2. System/process: I shall want to combine system and process aspects, since a more detailed description of syntagmatic functions often requires reference to paradigms. The tense inflection of Danish verbs presupposes the mood inflection, since they must always be specified with respect to mood, but not always with respect to tense. A natural description would be that only the indicative member of the mood paradigm can combine with tense inflection, but such descriptions mix system ("mood paradigm") and process ("combine") terms, and again the functional diagrams give no obvious way of saying that kind of thing.

3. Expression/content: in many cases, I should like to enter the sign-function in the description, indicating how content distinctions are expressed, or what expression distinctions mean.

I have found Halliday's systemic networks[1] to be very good tools for these purposes, and in the following I present a slightly modified version of them. As the name indicates, systemic networks primarily take the system view of language.

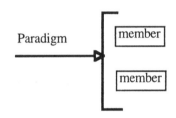

Language is described as a set of paradigms representing a set of choices open to the language user. A paradigm is represented as a label on a bold arrow pointing to a bracket enclosing the paradigm's members (above).

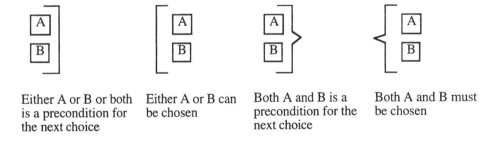

Either A or B or both is a precondition for the next choice

Either A or B can be chosen

Both A and B is a precondition for the next choice

Both A and B must be chosen

However, as said above, a particular choice in one paradigm may influence possible choices in other paradigms; this fact is not a system but a process fact, since it concerns the possibility of two elements co-occurring in the linguistic chain. Process functions like these are denoted by non-bold lines, and Halliday uses four types of process constraints as shown above.

---

[1] For a theoretical discussion, see e.g. Martin 1987.

The last graphical distinction is one between expression and content. A systemic net must have its point of departure in one of the two planes which it describes systematically, and from which it views the other plane. Halliday himself always locates himself in the content plane and looks into the expression plane, but I see no reason why the other direction should be excluded.

In the diagrams, I represent the sign-function by two connected boxes, of which the uppermost is the plane we are located in, and the lower one is the plane we are looking into.

The glossematic functions now turn out to be abstractions of systemic nets, describing properties of the latter. Each function can be realized in different ways in the nets, and below I give one example for each net.

The main facts in Danish verbal inflection are that voice and tense are interdependent, both presupposing mood:

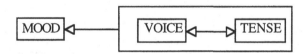

Fig. I.2.3. Functional description of mood, voice, and tense.

Presupposition between two paradigms can be due to the fact that the presupposing paradigms can only be chosen if a particular element from the presupposed one is chosen, as in the verbal example above, where voice can only be chosen if the mood is indicative:

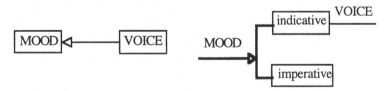

Fig. I.2.4. Functional and systemic representation of *presupposition*.

The diagram reads as follows: you have to choose *indicative* or *imperative* from the mood-paradigm. If you choose *indicative*, then you have to choose from the *voice* paradigm.

Interdependence can be exemplified by voice and tense, both presupposing the other.

Fig. I.2.5. Functional and systemic representation of *interdependence*.

The system diagram says that both voice and tense must be chosen. The two systemic nets can be combined:

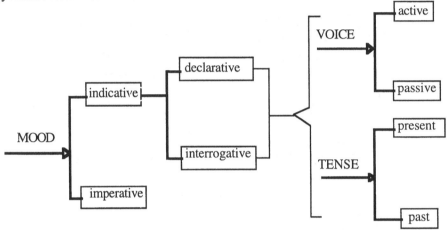

Fig. I.2.6. Systemic description of mood, voice, and tense.

and reads: you have to choose indicative or imperative in the mood paradigm. If you choose indicative, a further choice between declarative and interrogative must be made, and no matter which one is chosen, you must choose both the voice and the tense paradigm. In the voice paradigm, you must choose either active or passive, in the tense paradigm either present or past.

Since there are no constraints on the individual members of tense and voice, they form a constellation.

The last missing item is the sign function that correlates the content units to expression units. In treating this distinction I shall do my best to adhere strictly to the commutation test, and correlate every content distinction to an expression distinction. From this point of view, the distinction between imperative and indicative may only be entered if it correlates with an expressive distinction, which it in fact does, since yes-no imperatives are characterized by an empty thematic slot in the sentence. This brings me to the subject of syntactical order. Hjelmslev himself did not attribute much significance to word order, regarding it as belonging to language use. It is a little surprising for my generation that grew up with generative grammar, in which syntactical order often was a nuisance.

I shall treat word order as an expressive device in the manner advocated by Bazell 1949:

> For instance in the expressive chain *ab*, *a* and *b* are successive. But this succession of speech-units need not answer to anything in the system. To prove that it does we must show that the reverse sequence *ba* stands in distinctive contrast, i.e. that the reversal of phonemes is capable of calling forth a difference in content.
>
> *Bazell 1949: 77*

If word orders commute, they are invariants and belong to form, since they are functives in a sign function. Therefore, since *Jack gave Jill an apple* means something different from *Jill gave Jack an apple* and the only difference is the position of Jack and Jill, it follows that subject and object position must be expression units.

Besides the invariant word order properties, there will be bound variants. For example, the order object + adverbial is a bound variant, since we cannot have the reverse order with a different meaning:

Jack gave Jill an apple yesterday
*Jack gave Jill yesterday an apple

Thus, whereas subject and object commute and belong to the linguistic form, object and adverbial are bound variants and belong to linguistic usage.

Application to computers

In computer systems design, we can make a similar distinction between order belonging to form and order belonging to usage.

The Macintosh way of moving icons, e.g. folders, on the screen is a good example of the former. It consists of three steps: 1. press the mouse on the icon, 2. move the mouse, and 3. release the mouse.

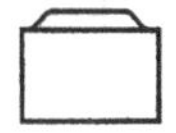

Fig. I.2.7a

Step (1) will invert the icon. If step (2) moves the mouse to the right and downwards, the inverted folder will follow, and when finally (3) the mouse is released, the folder will stay at its new location.

Fig. I.2.7b

Now, if we exchange step 1 and 3, pressing the mouse at the destination location, moving it upwards to the left, and releasing it on the icon, the result is that a selection rectangle is drawn, and when the mouse is released, the icon is selected.

Fig. I.2.7c

Thus, the order 1 + 2 + 3 expresses "moving the folder", whereas 3 + 2 + 1 expresses a different content, "selecting the folder". Positions (1) and (3) therefore commute and belong to the form of the Macintosh interface. As in language, the form of a system expresses its essence and changing the form means changing the identity of the system.

Systems can also possess order that does not contract a sign function, but is merely a standard way of doing things. A library system may require the user to enter the data in a particular order, for example author + title + year. A different sequence would not describe another book, so the sequence does not carry meaning. It is merely a bound variant.

A reasonable guide-line for design could be that the user should not be allowed to change order belonging to form, whereas bound variants should be tailorable if they turn out to be inconvenient.

Choice of specification tools is another issue where the difference between variant and invariant order is relevant. In Part II, I shall present methods for designing systems from a communicative perspective and in such methods we want to distinguish between specifications of the invariant properties that contribute to meaning and variant properties that implement the pertinent ones. Now, if sequence only sometimes carries meaning but not always, then we need specification tools that do not force us to describe sequence but allow an unspecified or concurrent order of events. That is the reason why I have chosen Petri-nets as formal description, and not e.g. flow charts.

I.2.2. Adapting and extending the concepts

In the preceding, I have presented concepts and methods for describing symbolic acts.

What can be said about non-symbolic acts themselves, and their relation to symbolic acts?

I will start by determining what can and what cannot be said about non-symbolic acts within the framework presented above. The first thing to notice is that the commutation test cannot be applied, since non-symbolic acts do not possess two planes. Therefore we have no method for determining invariants[1], which is a serious drawback, since it means that we have no method for defining the pertinent units of non-symbolic acts. On the other hand, we can retain the concept of function, we can divide the non-symbolic

---

[1] It is instructive to compare Hjelmslev's ideas to Uldall's (Uldall 1967). Uldall conceived of glossematics as a non-quantitative science, not particularly focused on language: it is significant that his presentation lacks precisely the invariant/variant distinction and the commutation test.

process into parts defined by the functions they contract with other parts, and we can set up the system corresponding to the process. It makes sense to talk about non-symbolic syntagms and paradigms, which I shall call *action syntagms* and *action paradigms*.

To solve the problem of defining the invariant units of non-symbolic acts, I use the fact that there are people that talk about the non-symbolic acts. They will always be the content substance of one or more languages. In large organizations like the Postal Giro, there exist many different languages whose content plane articulates the work processes of the organization and gives it a form, and in Section III.1 I will compare two such languages: the language of the workers and the language of management.

In this solution, the invariants of non-symbolic acts can only be defined with respect to some language:

Two units A and B of a non-symbolic act are invariants with respect to some language L if and only if they occur as content forms in L and therefore commute with respect to L.

This means that analyses of a work process can only be done within a definite register and from a definite perspective. Non-symbolic acts do not have an immanent form like symbolic acts do. This view will prove rather fruitful in Part III, where I treat work descriptions in connection with computerization.

I.2.2.1. The work process

A process consists of acts or objects that can occur together, and can be subjected to repeated analyses, partitioning the process into smaller and smaller parts. The parts are delimited and described by the functions they contract mutually and with other parts.

It is important to remember that sequence does not a priori belong to the glossematic concept of process (as it does to the string concept of generative grammar), but only in so far as it is a part of a sign function.

The following examples serve to illustrate the concepts, and to indicate their range of applicability.

Car repair revisited

Let us look at the work situation described in Section I.1.1, where two mechanics are fixing the rear lights of a car. It will be remembered that A wants to mount the rear lights of a car by means of a nut and bolt. The nut must be positioned over the hole from inside the car. Then the bolt is put through the hole from outside, and if it catches the nut, the rear light can be screwed on. It is not possible for one man to do this, so A gets hold of B, places himself in the car, and tries to move the nut over the hole; he cannot see the hole, but from the outside B can see when the nut is covering the hole, he directs A's movements, and finally inserts the bolt. The diagram below expresses an intuitive analysis of the work process, and in the following, I shall indicate how some of the units can be defined within our theoretical framework.

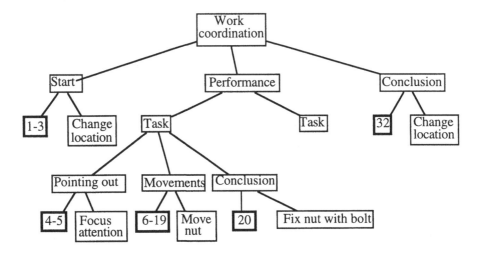

Fig. I.2.8. Analysis of car repair (= Fig. I.1.1).

The first partition of the process into three parts - Start, Performance and Conclusion - can be described by means of the function of *presupposition*. In the Start part, A requests B to help him and B walks from his place of work to B's. Functionally, we can record the following chains:

(+Start.Performance, +Start.<u>Performance</u>, -<u>Start</u>.Performance)

expressing that cooperation between A and B would probably not have started if A had not requested it (-<u>Start</u>.Performance), but B could have refused to help if he was busy with other things (+Start.<u>Performance)</u>. Thus, Performance is a variable that presupposes the Start part. Since the Conclusion is probably not obligatory, we have the following presuppositions:

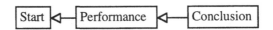

Fig. I.2.9. General structure of task.

The three parts also differ in their internal structure.

In the first part, only A has function[1] to the process, while in the Performance, both A and B are involved, and after the Conclusion, A is alone again, so in relation to this process, B presupposes A. This kind of presupposition can be taken to express a sense of "ownership" to the job: it is A's job, and his responsibility that it is completed, but he can call in colleagues to help in selected parts.

The performance part can be partitioned into two parts, called *tasks* in the diagram, that contract mere *constellations*, that is, the units combine freely with each other. Each task consists in moving a nut to the hole and fixing it with the bolt. Neither task presupposes the other, they can be permutated freely, their internal structure is similar, and each task can occur in the same contexts where their composition occurs, that is, a single Task can replace Task+Task in the context *Start - Conclusion*, and it would have if only one rear light were to be mounted[2].

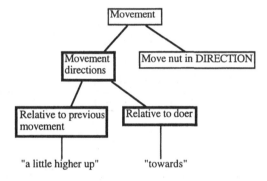

Fig. I.2.10. Utterance and actions (= Fig. I.1.2).

A characteristic feature of the task is that it establishes functions between worker, action, and work object. One nut and bolt belong to the first task, the other pair belong to the second task.

In this way, we can continue our analysis, looking for particular types of functions, and using them to define classes of process parts.

At some stages of this quest, we will be looking for symbolic acts and their functions to their non-symbolic environment of the same rank. In the beginning of the analysis, we found one such function, the symbolic Start part presupposed by the subsequent Performance.

---

[1] The phrase "has function to" may not be idiomatic English, but I use it since it is used in the English translation of Hjelmslev 1963a.

[2] The latter property is part of Hjelmslev's definition of periods as the smallest units that can occur in the same contexts as their superchains. The task thus turns out to correspond to the linguistic period.

If we look inside the Movement part (Fig. I.2.10), we find another sequence of utterance-action pairs. The movements of A and utterances of B occur simultaneously, the movements causing corrections to be uttered, and the corrections causing the movements to shift direction.

The utterances and movements are so intermingled that the most fitting description of their mutual function is *interdependence*. Utterances and movements presuppose each other.

The task concept is an example of work process units that correspond to units known from language, but we should be careful not to transfer linguistic concepts mechanically to work analysis, since work processes may have units not found in language, and vice versa.

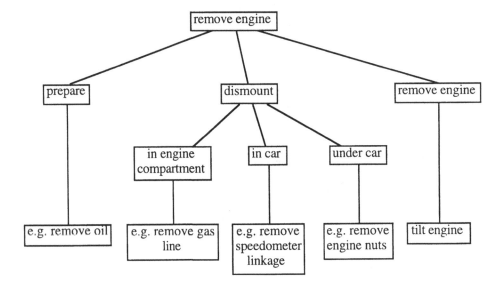

Fig. I.2.11. Engine removal.

The fragment in Fig. I.2.11 of the work process of removing the engine of a car exemplifies two new classes of process units that I have not come across in linguistic literature:

(1)   The *preparation*: some preparatory actions whose completion is outside the control of the mechanic are carried out before the work process, e.g. emptying the oil and water tanks. They run their course simultaneously with and independently of the rest of the mechanic's actions.

(2)   The *scene*: actions that are done in the same place are done consecutively, and form a whole, although they may not be "logically" related. For example, the gas line, choke linkage, and oil pressure detector are

all mounted in the engine area and are dismounted together. The boundaries of the scenes are marked by the mechanic's changing of position.

The parts comprising the preparation part can be characterized as lacking function to the worker, running their course independently. The scene can be described as having function to the location element of the action: all actions of a scene take place in the same location.

Application to computers

Some computer systems replace previous non-computerized tools and materials, and much can be learned from studying the way experienced workers organize the work process. Consider for example the principle of organizing car repair in scenes. The mechanic's reason for doing so is that on the one hand certain actions require him to be at a certain location (e.g. in the engine area), and by collecting all actions presupposing this location, he avoids making unnecessary movements. In a computer system, similar symbolic movements will also occur, partly because the worker needs to see the object he is working at and the screen cannot hold the whole object, partly because he needs to see it in a special way. I think that the mechanic's practical concept of scenes might be a good general way of structuring interfaces. As the car repair scene is defined by a particular location in relation to the car plus a certain repertoire of actions, so the computer-based scene may consist of a particular way of representing the work object plus a paradigm of operations appropriate for the scene, cf. the idea of "rooms" in Card & Henderson 1987.

Process units

I shall conclude this section by discussing units that can be used to analyze work processes.

As already mentioned, transferring semiotic methods to non-symbolic domains gives us the problem that there is no way to define the notion of invariant, since the commutation test that yields the invariants cannot be performed on non-symbolic material. Without the notion of invariants, a semiotic approach to the study of the work process amounts to nothing, since we would have no principled criteria to determine which units to choose as our basic units. The solution proposed is to refrain from studying the work process per se, but only see it as a topic of discourse, as content substance, always formed and articulated by some language.

Thus, we never look at a "naked work task", but always project a particular language onto it, and only see those units that can be spoken of in that language.

This does not entail work tasks having the same structure as a particular language. On the contrary, once we have determined the minimal units, we leave the language, and record dependencies between the work units qua work units. We now no longer describe relations between words, but between the referents of the words.

There are two immediate consequences of this methodology:

- We can only enter units into our description in so far as they are articulated in some language, causing tacit knowledge[1] to be outside the scope of our description, where tacit knowledge means: features of work that are not articulated in any language. Note that the language need not contain nouns that denote the feature, or adjectives that describe it. It is enough if the language in some systematic sense treats the features differently. To give an example, a language need not contain standard nouns denoting a certain role relationship in the work place (e.g. student/teacher, journeyman/boss); it is enough if the type of modality depends functionally upon the roles (weak modality like *might* or *could* presupposing the boss, strong modality like *must* and *have to* presupposing the journeyman).
- There will be as many analyses of a given work process as there are different sublanguages in the organization. The set of sublanguages existing in the organization will be our only point of entry, and there will be many entries in a large organization.

On the one hand, the description will be objective, since it rests upon observable verbal habits in the organization. On the other hand, each description will reflect the particular subjective perspective, purposes and interests of the "language owners". There will be no pure descriptions of the work process in itself.

Tasks and actions

I have already presented the concept of tasks, corresponding to the linguistic period, and defined a task as the smallest unit that can occur in the same places as the superchain of which it is a part. Since the task is the smallest unit satisfying these criteria, it follows that its parts, which I call actions and which correspond to sentences, cannot. The reason is that they contract functions different from those of their superchain.

Tasks and actions often have lexical designations. For example, the main activities in the Postal Giro in 1982 were called *granskning* [checking], *kodning* [coding], *rättning* [correction], and *inläggning* [putting in or entering].

---

[1] Dreyfus & Dreyfus 1986.

The size of a task in terms of the number of actions is an important property indicating the degree of complexity of the work. Task size can range from several years in managerial work to a few seconds in assembly line work.

Logical task structure: goals and and preconditions

The characteristic property of actions, the analogue to sentences, is that they contract functions to other actions. As an illustration, let us take the task of dish washing, from which the following examples can be extracted:

- *An action presupposes another action:* for example, washing a dish presupposes that it has been moved from the dinner table to the kitchen sink.
- *Two actions are interdependent:* grasping the dish with the left hand must occur simultaneously with the rotating movement of the sponge with the right hand.
- *An action presupposes an utterance:* the dish washing variant performed by children presupposes repeated and loud requests from the parents.
- *Two actions form a disjunct constellation:* dish washing and cooking are mutually exclusive since both require the use of the sink.

Dependencies of this kind are found in all tasks and the properties of the dependencies are important characteristics of tasks.

The above description is functional, and we may wish to make it a little more substantial by describing how these functions are manifested, for example psychologically. One way of doing this, which has been used in AI, is to attribute goals, side-effects and preconditions to actions. An action is done to achieve a certain goal, and possesses a set of preconditions that must be fulfilled in order to perform the action. Some of these preconditions may be identical to the goal of other actions, which themselves may have preconditions, etc.[1].

Let us reconsider the example of dishwashing. The *goal* of dishwashing is that the dishes no longer contain the remains of previous meals, and one of its *side-effects* is that the remains and detergents are led down into the sewer. The *action* itself consists of moving a brush or sponge over one or more dishes submerged in water. It requires certain *preconditions*: the dishes must be placed on the kitchen table, the sink must contain water with detergent, and a sponge must be available. Preparatory preconditions can be fulfilled by the person doing the dishes, but there are other *limiting* precondi-

---

[1] Similar concepts have been used for analyzing symbolic acts in e.g. Searle 1977, and for non-symbolic acts in Schank & Abelson 1977 and Sacerdoti 1977. See also Bøgh Andersen 1973, 1979.

tions that must be fulfilled but that lie beyond his power: for example, to manufacture detergent, and see to it that the faucets provide water. Finally, the action is *triggered* by events: in some cases, the trigger is simply finishing the dinner, in other cases orders must be given to the person washing the dishes in order to trigger his activities.

These parts can be characterized partly by the functions they contract with the actions, partly by means of their function to the actor. The goal pre-supposes the action, since the action can occur without the goal being achieved, whereas the existence of a certain state of affairs would not count as a goal if the action had not been performed. Similarly, the action presup-poses the preparations and the limiting preconditions, since both can occur without the action occurring. Finally, the triggering preconditions are inter-dependent with the action, since either both occur, or neither occur.

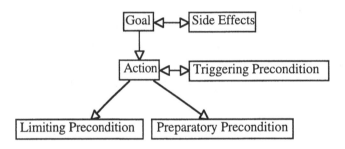

Fig. I.2.12. Actions as goal-directed behavior.

Analysis of the preconditions and preparations gives a good portrait of the possibilities of *self-management:* many triggering and limiting preconditions, and few preparatory ones yield a work situation where the worker is depen-dent upon the actions of other people, possibly to the extent of being a vic-tim of external factors over which he has no control.

Triggering and limiting preconditions can be at cross purposes: on the one hand it may be the responsibility of a secretary at a university department to send out the curriculum two weeks before classes start (triggering precondi-tion), on the other hand she has no right to put the curriculum together her-self since it must be done by the head of department (necessary precondition, not preparation). She *must* send out the curriculum, but if the head fails to produce the curriculum, she *cannot* send it out.

Two actions can have preconditions that are mutually exclusive, so that performing one action excludes the other. Shared resources are a good ex-ample. From the dishwashing example, we remember the sink as a shared re-source for dishwashing and cooking. One of the opportunities offered by computer systems is the removal of bottle-necks due to shared data resources by making instant screen or paper copies of an electronic representation available.

Application to computers

Concepts very similar to the ones described above are the basis of a practical system description method developed at the Norwegian Computing Center. The method is called WAND (Work Analysis and Design). The basic work unit of WAND consists of three parts, an initial state, a procedure, and a goal, corresponding to the preconditions, the action, and the goal. The procedure part can be broken down into smaller components yielding hierarchical structures like the ones shown above. A computer tool is available for drawing the diagrams and presenting them in various ways.

See Svendsen 1986, 1987a, 1987b.

Practical task structure: scenes and preparations

Since the goal of one action can be identical to the preparatory preconditions of another, we can get hierarchies of preparation/goal presuppositions, the "logical" task structure:

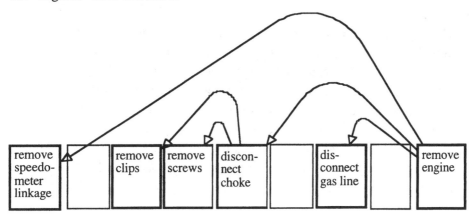

Fig. I.2.13. Logical task structure of engine removal.

This fragment of the engine removal task previously described expresses the fact that the mechanic removes clips and screws in order to disconnect the choke, and he disconnects choke, speedometer linkage and gas line in order to remove the engine.

In the diagram, I have placed the individual actions in the sequence in which they occurred in a particular process. Note that actions having the goal-preparation function to each other do not necessarily follow each other in time. The placement of actions in time not only depends on the functions, requiring preparations to occur earlier in time than goals: the actions also contract other kinds of functions that influence their position. I call this second structure the "practical" structure of the task.

For example, the mechanic's habit of organizing his work in *scenes* (cf. above) causes actions having function to the same location or tool to be performed consecutively, so when drums are dismounted, the mechanic first dismounts all wheels, and then all drums. He does not handle one wheel and its drum at a time. The reason is that dismounting wheels has function to a particular tool (a wrench) and he wants to avoid picking up and putting down that particular tool.

Another structure of this kind is the *preparation*, an initial work segment that contains tasks (e.g. emptying oil and water tanks) that once initiated can run their course without intervention from the mechanic.

Seen from the "logical" goal-preparation hierarchy, the "practical" functions create discontinuous constituents: units that belong together from this point of view are removed from each other.

The difference between "logical" and "practical" task structure can be found in many kinds of work. Take for example the everyday activity of cooking.

The task of making *potatoes au gratin* contains the action of placing a dish with potatoes, cheese, pieces of ham and cream into the oven, that in its turn presupposes two other actions: on the one hand peeling and slicing potatoes and on the other mixing cheese, ham and cream[1]. Although a cook must obey these "logical" cohesions if he wants to make potatoes au gratin, an experienced cook will introduce a preparation structure into his work. For example, if he is to use boiled potatoes in a dish, he will start with the potatoes because it takes half an hour to boil them properly, and he will interleave activities in a way that does not necessarily reflect their "logical" dependencies.

Application to computers

The second "practical" layer has recently attracted considerable attention in systems design, because it was neglected before at the expense of the "logical" layer of tasks and because systems work badly if attention is not payed to the "practical" layer.

Newman 1980 noticed for example that the "practical" activities of secretaries and typists in a typing pool differed, e.g. in the number of interruptions:

---

[1] Bøgh Andersen 1979.

Procedure interruption is also very frequent: few tasks run uninterrupted to completion.
                                                                                     Newman 1980: 8

a fact that ought to be reflected in the design of word processors. Card & Henderson 1987:53 list a series of factors that cause task-switching (digressing to do tasks that users are reminded of while performing another task, timesharing among concurrent demands, tasks with long waits, interruptions from outside, etc.) and uses the knowledge to design a particular way ("rooms") of organizing use of programs and data. Finally, Norman & Draper 1986:239 devote a whole section to the fact that

> People interleave their activities - and do so in many different ways. Real tasks can take hours, weeks, or even months to perform.

Invariant and variant structure in data-recording. An example

It is clearly useful to distinguish between the two kinds of structures, but how can they be related to the framework of this book?

The phenomenon is in fact well-known in linguistics. In generative grammar, we distinguish between deep and surface structure, the deep structure being an abstract representation of a sentence that - in some interpretations of transformational grammar - together with transformational rules serves to account for its similarities and dissimilarities to other sentences, in particular paraphrase relations. Thus, the two surface structures *Jack saw Bill* and *Bill was seen by Jack* can be said to have the same deep structure because they are paraphrases and systematically related by the passive transformation.

Halliday 1978:129 also assigns multiple structures to sentences, reflecting the fact that sentences must satisfy more than one type of constraints at the same time.

I propose to use the notions of *invariants* and *variants* to define the logical and practical layers of tasks.

On the "logical" level we describe the cohesions that must always be part of the task - that express the essence of the task. On the "practical" levels we describe cohesions that are not essential to the task, but are conditioned by special organizational circumstances. The structure recorded on the former level corresponds roughly to the schema concept in semiotics and I call it the *invariant task structure*. The structure recorded on lower levels, in special situations, is termed *variant task structure*:

- The *invariant task structure* of a task name consists of those cohesions that always must be present in a task with that name.
- The *variant task structure* is contextually conditioned cohesions that do not belong to the invariant structure.

In material work, the invariant task structure can be due to material and logical properties of the work objects and tools, and in social interaction the invariant task structure represents the constitutive parts of an interaction. For example, in a marriage ceremony, the questions from the clergyman and the answers from the couple are invariant, since if they did not occur, we could not call the event a marriage.

I conclude this section by analyzing a real work process in terms of invariant and variant structure, namely data entry in the PGP-system introduced at the Postal Giro in 1986. Since I shall use this task as an example several times in this book, I give here a fairly detailed description of it[1].

Before computerization, the task consisted of four subtasks, namely *granskning* [checking], *kodning* [coding], *rättning* [correction], and *inläggning* [putting in] that were organized in the following way: when the paying-in forms arrived at the department, the forms were taken out of the envelopes, sorted and checked *(granskning)*, and assembled in *buntar* [batches]. Most paying-in forms have hand-written information which was converted into machine-readable letters at the coding machines. Coding was a monotonous and noisy job, and the workers took turns at the machine, for example half an hour coding, then relaxing by checking, or correcting errors produced in the coding process. When checking, coding and correction were over, the material was sent to the data processing department in gray plastic *lådor* [boxes], where the actual accounting took place. In the afternoon, the material and statements of account came back to the department, were put into envelopes *(inläggning)*, and mailed to the payee.

After computerization, the old coding machines were replaced by OCR-machines that read the preprinted information of the paying-in-forms and store an electronic representation on a shared disk. From the disk, the card records go to six work stations, where the remaining data are input. The records are returned to the disk, and transmitted to a large IBM computer via a local network. The equipment also includes tape units and printers.

The diagram below gives an overview of the data flows entering and leaving the department (boldface means an electronic representation).

We see that payment orders and cards enter, and an electronic representation is added by the optical reader, which produces an electronic record of each card plus a film picture of the paper card. The film is used later to correct errors, and paper and data travel from the department to the computer department in boxes, *lådor*. Some of the forms *(C-kort)* are complete, since all information is machine readable, and should at least in principle not concern the workers.

---

[1] This is based upon Grip & Sundstrøm 1984, Holmqvist & Källgren 1986, and Holmqvist 1986.

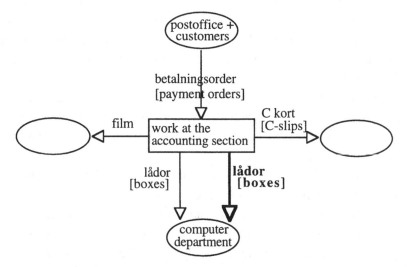

Fig. I.2.14. Main data flows in the accounting department at the Postal Giro.

After the paper cards have been fed into the optical reader and read, *jobs* [jobs] of paper cards (containing approximately 100 cards) are transported by hand from the reader to the work station tables, where the workers read the handwritten and other non-machine-readable information on the cards, and type the data into their electronic records. In the system, this work-process is called *komplettering* [completing].

The cards are grouped into *buntar* [batches], consisting of two item types: a *betalningsorder* [payment order, abbreviated BO], where the customer lists all the payments he wants to make at one time and their sum. The other items are *kort* [cards, slips, paying-in forms], cards that contain the individual payments of the batch. A batch will typically contain one payment-order and from one to ten cards.

The system checks whether the sum of the cards corresponds to the sum written on the payment-order. If not, it alerts the worker, goes into a new mode, and the worker tries to find the error. The system calls this work process *avstämning* [checking (off)].

If errors occur, the worker has a set of commands at her disposal.

If there are too many cards in the batch, the worker can use *Flytta Dok* [Move Document] to send the superfluous card into the *flygar fil* [flier file], from where colleagues who need this card can use the command *Hämta Dok* [Fetch Document] to fetch it. If the worker cannot correct the error, for example because she lacks a card that has not yet arrived at the flier file, she uses *Överge Bunt* [Abandon Batch] to make a *rött job* [red job]. Electronically, the batch is marked as incomplete, and stored for later processing. Physically, the paper cards are put aside with a red card attached to them (whence the name). Finally, a card may be faulty, e.g. the required signature may be missing, so that it must be sent back to the customer. Electronically, such cards are removed by issuing the *Ta bort Dok* [Take away Document].

When finished, the records are grouped in *lådor* [boxes] and sent to the large accounting machine in the computer department via the local network, and their paper equivalents are put into grey plastic boxes in which they leave the department.

The section takes care of other tasks, and the system has other functions. However, *komplettering* and *avstämning* are by far the most time-consuming tasks, and I will focus on them. We asked a worker (HK) to perform these tasks and to tell us what she did while we tape-recorded her comments.

Most of the work in the example consists of typing the non-machine-readable numbers of paying-in slips into the system, but HK also handles a couple of errors: a batch of slips without signature is *destroyed [macka]*, another batch lacks a card and since she cannot find it, the batch is *abandoned* - put aside to be resumed later on. Later she finds the card in a subsequent batch, and places it in the flier file - the shared file for misplaced cards. Another batch is abandoned because it too lacks a card that she cannot find in the file, and then the first run is finished. She *resumes the job [ta upp dom i jobb igen]*, and although she finds the first missing card she has herself placed in the flier file, the second one has still not come in, it not being retrieved until the third trial.

During all work, HK has the paper slips beside her on her table, leafing through them as she enters the handwritten data into the system.

The first step in the analysis is to find the work units coded in the work-language. The task itself has a special name, *registrering [data entry]*. In addition, the workers describe the concrete errors:

> Det där är felsummering [This is a an adding mistake]. Kort saknas [Missing card]...En sån här PKM greja, som misstämmer här på 1500 [One of these PKM things, which is out by 1500]. Titta här, 80, det misstämmer 492 och 70 [Hey look, 80, it is off by 492 and 70]....För det va ett sånt där konstigt kort [Because it was such a strange card]. Jag har här ett rött jobb, å så hittar jag inte kortet [I have a red job, and then I don't find the card]. När det är ett plus såhär [There is a plus here].

and the actions they take to remove them. They distinguish between 6 actions, each action taking care of a particular kind of error:

(1)   Macka, macka bort, makulera, ta bort [destroy, take away],
(2)   Leta, söka [look for, search],
(3)   Hämta [fetch],

(4)   Överge, göra rött job [abandon, give up],

(5)   Lämna in [hand in],

(6)   Skicka, göra, ta, flytta till flygare; lägga, sätta in i flygare [send, move to fliers].

They use no generic terms for the two subparts of the process, data entry (completing) and error-handling (checking).

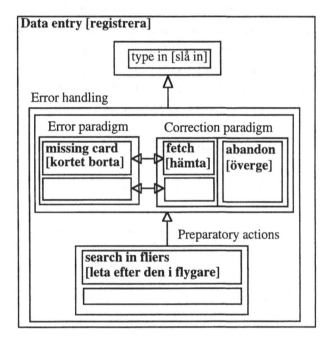

Fig. I.2.15. Invariant structure of the data entry task at the Postal Giro.

The closest we can get to error-handling is the noun and adjective *fel* [error], but this term is used about typing errors as well, and batch errors are most often described more concretely. *Slå in* [type in] can be used about the process of typing in the missing numbers of the card, but its meaning is broader, including all kinds of typing on the computer, e.g. entering date *(Jo vi kan slå in datumet* [Yes we can enter the date]) in opposition to writing on paper, which is called *skriva* [write].

After having recorded the work-units coded in the worklanguage, we leave the language and describe the functions between the units. First we look at the invariant task structure (Fig. I.2.15).

The task consists of a data entry part that will always occur, and a subordinate error handling part that may, but need not, occur. Error handling consists of an error paradigm and a correction paradigm, the members of the former governing members of the latter. For example, if a card is missing it must be fetched from the shared flier file. Occasionally, preparatory actions are needed; for example, if the worker does not know the serial number of the missing card, she has to open the flier file and search for it.

In the diagram, I have used boldface for the workers' own designations, and normal font for the work units constructed by me.

If we compare the analysis to the actual system they use, we immediately notice a difference in interpretation. The system itself distinguishes very clearly between the data-entry part and the error handling part, since they have separate names; data entry is called *komplettering [completing],* error handling *avstämning [checking off].* The workers themselves do not make this distinction, but see all operations as *registrering.*

The diagram above describes the invariant task structure, since violation of the description counts as an error. For example, if she *destroys* a batch with a missing card she is not performing the task correctly, since she should either *fetch* the missing card in the shared file, or *abandon* the batch and search for the card later.

Besides the invariant structure, the task has also a superimposed variant structure (Fig. I.2.16).

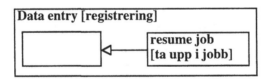

Fig. I.2.16. Variant structure of the data entry task at the Postal Giro.

If a worker either cannot or does not want to handle an error now, she can *abandon* the batch and resume it later on. This possibility creates a variant task structure consisting of a series of runs. The first run is special, since the job is defined here. Later runs only display the batches she has previously abandoned. In addition, the later runs have a special designation *ta upp dom i jobb igen [resume the job]*

The choice of abandoning and resuming jobs is left to the worker; she can do it if she wants, but need not.

One of the purposes of making analyses of this kind is to provide a basis for designing the interface so that it matches the worker's conception of the task. In II.1.2.4 I discuss how to use the two analyses above as a basis for design.

Cases

While goals and preconditions can be used for describing the relations between actions, the notion of *cases*[1] is useful for analyzing their internal structure.

The salient points in the linguistic theory of cases are that the constituents of a sentence fall into a small number of types, defined by their relationship to the verb. The exact number and definition of the cases may differ, but often include agent (the living being causing the action denoted by the verb), object (the entity directly affected by the action), instrument (the object used as an aid to perform the action), beneficiary (the living being that somehow is affected by the action), source and destination (the locations from where or to where something is moved), and time and location. Cases are normally expressed by

- Case-inflections: in *He hit her with them*, the agent *he* is nominative in contrast to the object *her* that is accusative.
- Prepositions: in the same sentence, the instrument *them* and the object *her* are both accusative, and are distinguished by the fact the instrument is governed by the preposition *with*.
- Word order: in *He showed the boy the president* word order signals the distinction between beneficiary *(the boy)* and object *(the president)*.

In the preceding sections, I have already used the concepts of worker (≈ agent), tool, machine (≈instrument), action (≈verb), object of work (≈object) to characterize work processes: handicraft work differs from assembly line work in that the worker and a work object are interdependent in the former (one worker - one object), whereas in the latter there is presupposition (one worker - many different objects). Tools are characterized by being interdependent with the worker (both worker and tool are necessary for an action to take place) whereas the worker presupposes the machine: the machine can do actions without the worker being present.

Time and location can be used in similar ways to characterize work processes: for example in assembly line work, actions and locations can often be *interdependent*, so that a location is always the scene of a particular action, which in turn is always performed at that location. This is the case in the Volvo factories:

The work one has is called one's balance. One is said to have a certain balance or to be standing on a certain balance. In this sense, the balance is a designation for work.

---

[1] Case theory is rather old, see e.g. Noreen 1904. The theory was revived by Charles Fillmore in Fillmore 1968 and 1977, and has by now become a respectable part of the linguistic toolkit.

In other cases, it can function as a designation for place, since the balance is always bound to a certain place/station (a certain number of meters of a track or by a certain machine).

Andersson 1982: 43

But the location can also *presuppose* the action in the sense that if actions occur at the location, it is always one particular action, but this action can also be performed on other locations. The location is specialized for one type of actions, which, however, can be done elsewhere. Typewriter tables are of this kind: they can only be used for typewriting, but it is possible to move the typewriter to other tables and work there.

Finally, there may be constellation: the location can be used for many different actions, and the actions can take place at different locations.

Time bindings are equally important: in some types of work, e.g. nursing, the tasks are bound to particular points of time, whereas other work types have no temporal connections.

The time/location units are of particular interest in connection with computerization, where on the one hand tasks are associated with one physical tool, the computer, but are dissociated from the space of the work place, since they can be performed anywhere the computer can be plugged in. The long range net effect is probably that tasks tend to lose their spatial anchorage[1], and the same may be true with respect to time, since computers on the one hand allow a delay between process parts that previously had to occur immediately after each other, and on the other hand may make previous sequencing unnecessary. Electronic mail is an example of the first, if we compare it to the telephone; whereas the telephone requires both sender and receiver of the message to be present, there can be delay between sending and receiving electronic mail[2]. Shared data often makes previous sequencing outdated; if tasks require access to the same paper document, they previously had to be queued, but with a shared electronic representation, screen or paper copies of the document are easy to obtain, and the tasks can then be performed concurrently[3].

Thus, the concept of cases is clearly relevant to task analysis, but unfortunately it is by no means clear how to understand and use the concept in a well-defined way. In my experience, the main problem with case theory is

that nobody working within the various versions of grammars with "cases" has come up with a principled way of defining the cases, or principled procedures for determining how many cases there are, or for determining when you are faced with two

---

[1] Krueger 1983.

[2] Severinson 1986.

[3] See Mathiassen & Bøgh Andersen 1984 for a discussion of the nurses' Kardex from this point of view.

cases that happen to have something in common as opposed to one case that has two
variants.   *Fillmore 1977: 70*

Thus, we may assert that the case (agent) of *John* in *John opened the door* is
different from that of *This key* (instrument) in *This key opened the door* even
though they form a syncretism here, because they are marked as different in
the expanded sentence *John opened the door with this key.* Nevertheless,
we have no way of determining if *The wind* is agent or instrument or something different in *The wind opened the door,* since the expanded version is
not possible here.

I believe that the reason for such problems is that cases are conceived as a
set of universal semantic relations, covering not only a national language but
all human languages. In the register-based approach of the present book, this
hypothesis would mean that the concrete roles of particular situations must
be viewed as specializations of the general set of roles. Charles J. Fillmore,
the reviver of case theory, is aware of these problems and has proposed another interpretation of case theory in Fillmore 1977, where he describes the
cases as a way of presenting types of scenes (corresponding to the situation
type) from a particular perspective. In a sales transaction, the roles are buyer,
seller, goods, and money, and if the perspective is that of the buyer, the
speaker may choose verbs like *spend* which classifies the buyer role as agent
and the money as the object *(I spent five dollars),* whereas if the perspective
is the seller's, *sell* may be chosen, classifying the seller as agent and the
goods as object *(He sold the book for five dollars).* I shall retain Fillmore's
idea of scenes, but prefer to start by stripping the cases of all semantic substance, and at least at the moment only view them as a content form that
serves to present situational categories from different perspectives, since it is
difficult for me to see that there is any substantial semantic similarity between
the relation of *hit* to *fence* in *I hit the fence with a stick* and that between
sell and *book* in *He sold the book for five dollars,* which case theory identifies as a verb-object relation[1].

The cases can be described as a set of sentential slots related by a set of
presuppositions and having definite positions in the sentence[2]. An informal
description along these lines[3] could say that the subject slot is interdepen-

---

[1] It is possible that cases *are* associated with more semantic substance, but I believe that this is better
viewed as a result of making analogies between situations; theoretically it means that the meaning of
a case cannot be viewed as the common meaning of its concrete manifestations, but rather consists of
a chain of similarities between concrete instances. The whole chain may be connected pairwise by
clear similarities, while the total set of case instances has no common properties.

[2] A related description can be found in relational grammar, e.g. in Comrie 1977, who sets up a partial order among the cases that by and large corresponds to that suggested below: subject > direct ob-
ject>indirect object>oblique objects.

[3] The following analysis is based on Diderichsen 1962.

dent with the verbal slot, and is used to present the situational items that are most important to the speaker. The object slot presupposes the subject slot and is itself presupposed by inner complements which case-theory labels instrument and beneficiary. Finally, the outer complement presupposes the subject, not the object. In addition, there is the general rule, that the constant slot in a presupposition represents more indispensable situational items than those represented in the variable slot, and that verbs have more or less fixed preferences as to which situational elements are salient.

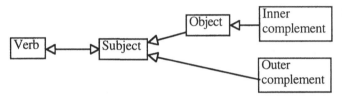

Fig. I.2.17. Functional definition of cases.

The criteria for salience depend upon one's role in the situation. Managers that are not responsible for the actual work may tend to focus on types of work objects and their general behavior, while persons are more important to workers. As an authentic illustration of this, a manager expresses the fact that some work objects are not processed by a particular machine called *B25* as *They never have to pass B25*, while one of the workers says *We never have to touch them.*

In the manager's formulation, work objects are put into the subject slot, while the workers demote them to the object slot. The object slot of the manager is filled with a machine designation, while the workers put a worker designation into their subject slot. I hasten to say that reality is not so simple as that - the example should only be taken as an illustration and no more.

The gist of this discussion is that *case theory can be used for analyzing actions into their constituent parts according to the saliency criteria of a particular register.*

There is no objective way of analyzing actions that I as a system developer can learn and apply. Rather, there are a number of different ways of articulating work that I can learn about by analyzing the relevant registers.

This means that when I enter a place of work I cannot assume that I know beforehand which items are tools and machines as I pretended in the analysis of the difference between tools and machines above - I even don't know if these categories are at all relevant units of work. I have to apply case analysis to the work language in order to find the important categories of work. The following example from the work done in the Volvo factory in track 6 shows how to use case-theory to analyze the internal structure of the individual actions. Part of a written operation description reads like this[1]:

mount	hood spring	on hood hinge
mount	hood hinge	with two screws
mount	fixture	on hood hinge
mount	hood	with crane
mount	hood	with two screws

Most sentences contain three parts: a verb, an object, and a complement, so initially we get two main paradigms of objects which are treated alike in the language.

The object paradigm contains designations for *parts of the object of work* (hood spring, hood hinge, fixture, hood), while the complement in the Swedish original distinguishes three subclasses by means of the prepositions *på* (hood hinge), *med* (two screws, crane), and *till* (hood spring).

Till and *på* seems to be variants, both meaning *on*, so the three paradigms can be reduced to two, *on* (hood hinge) denoting *parts of the work object,* and *with* (two screws, crane) containing *tools and means of fixture.*

The same work object part *hood hinge* occurs as an object and a complement, and if we compare the two sentences

| mount | hood spring | on hood hinge |
| mount | hood hinge | with two screws |

the difference is that in the former *hood hinge* is the immovable part on which a movable part *hood spring* is fixed, while in the latter it plays the role of a movable part that is mounted on something. Thus, the object and complement cases can be used to denote the difference between movable and immovable parts in the action of mounting something.

The analysis has given us the following classification of objects

1. parts of object of work
   1.1. immovable
   1.2. movable
2. tools and means

---

[1] The original Swedish examples are:

montera	huvfjäder	på huvgångjärn
montera	huvgångjärn	med två skruv
montera	fixtur	till huvgångjärn
hämta	huv	med lyftare
montera	huv	med två skruv

Montera = mount, *skruv* = screw, *huvfjäder* – hood spring, *huvgångjärn* = hood hinge, *lyftare* = crane, and *huv* = hood.

which is clearly relevant to the work of assembling cars and can be used as categories in a more detailed analysis of the work process. In addition, we obtained information about the perspective used in the descriptions from the case structure:

object	*complement*
movable	immovable
movable	means of fixture
movable	tool

where the movable parts are presented as the salient ones, while immovable parts, means of fixture and tools are circumstantial. A case-structure like this is probably characteristic of work that consists in mounting and dismounting parts. Workers in a chemical plant I interviewed described their work in sentences such as *you unscrew packings and put on new ones*, where the non-salient immovable parts are not expressed at all.

Application to computers

Case-theory has many applications in design of computer systems. It has been in use for a long time in AI as a good method for making formal descriptions of meaning[1], but here I shall mention other uses that are more in line with the general perspective of this book.

In designing a system, you need to arrange its objects along some scale of importance, important objects being present all the time and covering the largest space. The language of the users can be used as one basis for constructing this scale, since, as mentioned above, the case-structure of a language can be taken as a symptom of the salience criteria of its speakers. Differences of salience criteria in the stake-holders of a system can also be discovered in this way.

Design of the graphical user interface is another area where case theory is useful. If we assume that users spontaneously analyze and describe their actions by means of a particular case-structure, then the users' possibilities for understanding and communicating about their system would be enhanced if the layout clearly indicates which case roles the screen items can play, and if the actions themselves have a clear case structure.

The first requirement is in fact often fulfilled with respect to instruments and objects: instruments (tools) are placed on a special palette, and objects (work material) are represented by windows or parts of windows.

However, modification of instruments, like choosing between a line with no, one or two arrowheads, often presents difficulties to me if it is coded in

---

[1] Schank & Abelson 1977.

the same way as selection of an instrument, namely as a palette with different kinds of arrows. The designer's intention is that I have to choose the line instrument first, then the arrow-modification; the modification has no effect if no instrument is chosen. I on my part believe that I *have* chosen an instrument when I select a line modification, and cannot understand why the system will not let me draw with the arrow-headed line I have selected. The cause of the confusion is an unclear case-structure.

I.2.2.2. Perspectives - selection, articulation and role

Hjelmslev and Uldall do not spend much time on the problem of how to select processes for study. The reason is probably that they always had the written text, where the process is already selected, in the back of their mind, but when we visit work places as field workers, we see no ready-made processes to take home for analysis. Several hundred people may simultaneously be engaged in different work tasks, conversations start, end, and are resumed, work objects move from one table to another, manuals and memos litter the desks, and the text and pictures of computer screens are changing all the time.

Overwhelming confusion is the immediate reaction, realization of the absolute impossibility of recording and analyzing all these processes is the next. What one takes home is bits and pieces collected where possible: tape recordings of spontaneous conversations, written material, screen dumps, talk-aloud recordings, etc. Maybe you are guided by some principles, like not recording conversations in breaks, maybe you are just desperate and collect anything you can get hold of and carry away. Whatever the case may be, a very strong *selection* takes place.

The next step is to divide the material into manageable chunks with some common properties. There are many possibilities: you can pick out one person, and collect all data with some relation to her, or select all data concerning a particular work process, or follow a typical work object through the production process, or you can organize snapshots, grouping together all data occurring at the same time. In this manner, the researcher picks out some property and *articulates* the material according to this property: involving a particular person, work process, work object or occurring at a particular time or location.

These processes of selection and articulation may ring a bell, and we have in fact met them before in Section I.2.1 in our little example with the coin. The processes are the two basic processes of sign formation: a part of the content purport is *selected* and the rest ignored, and the selected part is *ar-*

ticulated by the content form of the sign system. The process of selecting and analyzing processes is itself a semiotic process.

To see our own activity as a semiotic activity has two practical consequences.

- The language we are creating is a register suited for use in particular types of situations. The way we select and articulate must therefore be evaluated in relation to roles, intentions and tasks in these situations. What is it going to be used for? Who is going to use it? A selection and articulation that is related to definite roles and tasks in an organization or society is what I will call a *perspective*[1].

- Since signs obtain important parts of their meaning by the contrasts they enter into, it is important to write *parallel*, viz. different, but related descriptions of the same subject. Monolithic descriptions employing the same simple set of concepts will produce a meagre understanding of the organization, simply because the signs of the text do not contrast with sufficiently many signs.

I shall illustrate these concepts by an example that is a simplification of the research I did at the Postal Giro. Suppose I return from my field work with the following kind of data[2]:

Anna is coding card 1	Berit is having lunch
Anna is coding card 3	Berit is correcting card 1
Anna is doing nothing	Berit is correcting card 2
Anna is doing nothing	Berit is correcting card 3
Christina is phoning a customer	Christina is stopping card 3
Berit is coding card 4	Anna is having lunch
Berit is coding card 5	Anna is having lunch
Berit is coding card 6	Anna is correcting card 4
Berit is doing nothing	Anna is correcting card 5
Berit is doing nothing	Anna is correcting card 6

The first thing to do is to select items to form a process which I want to analyze, and the criteria for selecting items cannot come from other sources than

---

[1] The definition of perspective is borrowed from Andersson & Furberg 1974. The importance of the perspective concept in informatics is emphasized in Nygaard & Sørgaard 1987. On the use of perspectives in systems development, see Andersen et al 1986.

[2] The terms are translations of the following Swedish terms:
Granskning: checking and preparing paying-in slips for coding.
Kodning: coding the non-machine readable parts of paying-in slips.
Rättning: correction of coding errors.
Inläggning: putting slips and statements of account in envelopes.
Hejda: stopping payments because of a deficit in the customer's account.

the purpose I want to achieve. Let us consider three such goals and see the different solutions they give rise to:

(1)   I want to build a computer system in which electronic representations of the cards are processed
(2)   I want to investigate the work environment: e.g. is work monotonous or varied?
(3)   I want to effect changes in the work organization.

Building a computer system

If my goal is to *build a computer system*, I need to know what is done to the cards and therefore see the work from "the perspective of the data"[1]. To do this, I select a sample of cards e.g. cards 1, 2 and 3, and then select all those events which have function to that card, giving me one process for each card:

Card 1   Anna is coding card 1, Berit is correcting card 1
Card 2   Berit is correcting card 2
Card 3   Anna is coding card 3, Berit is correcting card 3,
            Christina is stopping card 3

In this selection, I have cut away every event that does not involve cards, e.g. workers having lunch, being idle or phoning customers.

For each process, I set up a paradigm of actions done to the card. This gives me three paradigms:

Card 1   <+coding, +correcting, -stopping>
Card 2   <-coding, +correcting, -stopping>
Card 3   <+coding, +correcting, +stopping>

Card 1 is a normal card where some information is written by hand, and has to be coded in machine-readable form. The amount of the card is added together with the amount of the other cards to give a check-sum, and since the customer has made no errors, nothing has been changed. Since card 2 has all of its information preprinted, it is not coded. The payment of card 3 turns out to be too large for the customer's account, and therefore is stopped.

In order to provide an overview of the different combinations of operations applied to different card types, I write down the *category* of the paradigms, that is, a collection of paradigms having the same members[2]:

{+<+coding +correcting -stopping>

---

1 DeMarco 1978.
2 Cf. section "System and Process" in Section I.2.1.

+<-coding +correcting -stopping>
+<+coding +correcting +stopping>}

and describe it: for example, I note that *correcting* occurs in all paradigms, whereas *coding* and *stopping* are optional. Thus, coding and stopping presuppose correcting:

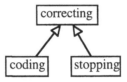

Fig. I.2.18. Data centered task analysis.

I may also be interested in obtaining an overview of all operations that are applied to cards at all. This is provided by the *sum* of the paradigms[1] (which in logical terms can be described as an *or*-operation):

<+coding +correcting +stopping>

Thus, sums of paradigms describe the full range of actions applicable to a member of a class of objects, while categories of paradigms divide the class into sub-classes according to the particular combination of actions applied to it.

If I am to use an object-oriented programming style to build the system such information is very useful. Object-oriented programming means that I design the system as a structure of "objects" consisting of a set of properties and actions applicable to those properties. The "objects" will typically designate real objects.

A paper card will be described by a data object containing descriptions of properties of the real card (e.g. the customer name) and of actions that can be done to the card (e.g. stopping the card). The sum of paradigms described above yields precisely this set of actions.

Investigating working conditions

Let us now select processes that enable us to say something about *working conditions*. The most sensible selection seems to be to make a typical sample of workers, and for each worker to select events having function to her. Finally, these events are arranged in temporal sequence, corresponding to a working day. This gives us:

---

[1] "By the *sum* of two or more corresponding paradigms is understood the totality of their assertions".
Uldall 1967: 58

Anna:

Anna is coding card 1

Anna is coding card 3

Anna is doing nothing

Anna is having lunch

Anna is correcting card 4

Anna is correcting card 5

Anna is correcting card 6

Berit:

Berit is having lunch

Berit is correcting card 1

Berit is correcting card 2

Berit is correcting card 3

Berit is coding card 4

Berit is coding card 5

Berit is coding card 6

Berit is doing nothing

In the following analysis, I use the working day as a unit, so that two actions occur together if they occur in the same working day. Anna's and Berit's working day consists of four interdependent activities that always occur: having lunch, doing nothing, correcting, and coding, with *coding* and *correcting* having function to an object of work. Since each action has function to many objects of work, I can say that there is interdependence between correcting/coding and the class of cards, while there is presupposition between the individual card, e.g. card 3, and correcting/coding, since I have

+correcting/coding card 3

+correcting/coding <u>card 3</u>

-<u>correcting/coding</u> card 3

+<u>correcting/coding</u> <u>card 3</u>

I recognize the typical form of assembly line work: interdependence between worker and a small set of actions, and presupposition between individual work objects and the actions. One work day resembles the other, but within a day, the worker shifts between several tasks, and there is no stable bond between worker and work object.

Note how the functions registered depend upon the way I selected the processes. When I take the working day of one worker as the unit in which actions are registered as occurring together, there is in fact presupposition between the four activities, since they always occur together during a day. However, if I choose a smaller time interval, e.g. half an hour, I would register a disjunct constellation between the tasks: at eleven o'clock Anna is coding, but at half past eleven she is correcting cards.

I.2.2.3. Organizational change

A process description is a description of both-and functions between parts of a chain, and makes us view working and speaking as a temporal succession of acts and states. Therefore, the process aspect is well suited for describing the working day of an employee or the flow of work material from process to process, from machine to machine.

A system description is different in being a description of either-or functions between members of paradigms, or between paradigms, and makes us see activities as a set of choices or possibilities in which temporal order is no prerequisite:

> The speaker of a language, like a person engaged in any kind of culturally determined behavior, can be regarded as carrying out, simultaneously and successively, a number of distinct choices. At any given moment, in the environment of the selections made up to that time, a certain range of further choices is available. It is the system that formalizes the notion of choice in language.   *Halliday 1976: 3*

The last task I set myself in the preceding section, to describe organizations and organizational change, seems to be easier to do within the system aspect, since organizations are characterized by divisions of labour and modes of cooperation, which can straightforwardly be understood as differences in the possibilities of action available to organizational groups.

Let us put ourselves in the shoes of the organizational consultant. The Postal Giro has hired him to change the work organization, from the assembly line work we saw above, to a more modern type. The first thing I am interested in is an overview of the existing division of labour, not only in Anna and Berit's departments, but in principle in the organization as a whole. It means that I add Christina's work to Anna's and Berit's:

> Christina is phoning a customer
> Christina is stopping card 3

In this case, I am not particularly interested in describing the process itself. Rather I want a good description of the system underlying it, that is: of paradigms and relations between paradigms. Also, I ignore those parts of the working day that have no function to the work objects; that is, I leave out *having lunch* and *doing nothing*.

I set up two large types of paradigms: one containing workers and one containing tasks, and record which paradigms of workers occur with which paradigms of tasks:

> <+Anna +Berit -Christina>.<+coding +correcting -phoning -stopping>
> <-Anna -Berit +Christina>.<-coding -correcting +phoning +stopping>

This gives us two categories of paradigms, one category containing workers,

> {+<+Anna +Berit -Christina> +<-Anna -Berit +Christina>}

and one containing tasks:

{+<+coding +correcting -phoning -stopping>
+<-coding -correcting +phoning +stopping>}

Both categories are *disjunct constellations*, containing a paradigm and its inverse, and as such characteristic of a strong division of labour. What Anna and Berit can do, Christina cannot do, and conversely.

If the consultant placed some parts of the customer contact in Anna and Berit's departments, the resulting work system would look like this

{+<+Anna +Berit -Christina>+<+Anna +Berit +Christina>}

{+<+coding +correcting -phoning -stopping>
+<+coding +correcting +phoning +stopping>}

Now both categories are *presuppositions*, Anna and Berit occurring in both paradigms, but Christina only occurring in one. This is typical of an all-purpose organization with specialized departments.

The three examples show

- there is no general way of selecting processes. The selection depends upon the practical purposes of the selector. Therefore: make the purpose of the description explicit!
- the selection to a large degree determines the functions that emerge from the analysis. Therefore: make the selection criteria explicit!

I.2.2.4. Functions between work context and language

Types of functions

The functival fields set up in the preceding sections are *homogeneous* in the sense that they contain either symbolic material only or non-symbolic material only. Conversely, the fields describing the relationships between symbolic and non-symbolic acts must be *heterogeneous*. Adding heterogeneous paradigms to the theoretical framework will be my main method for describing relations between symbolic and non-symbolic acts, between language and its context of usage, and constitutes probably my most basic deviation from immanent linguistics.

In this section I will set up a framework for describing functions between symbolic and non-symbolic acts, beginning with a brief sketch of Halliday's views on the relation between situation and language. According to Halliday, there are three main functions in the adult language:

- *Ideational* (language as content and interpretation): e.g. grammatical roles, types of verbs ("Aktionsart"), and tense.

- *Interpersonal* (language as action and participation): e.g. mood, modality.
- *Textual* (language as texture and organization): e.g. theme/rheme, given/new, text cohesion.

These functions are metafunctions, and can be used to characterize and group the more concrete functions we observe in actual situations. The types of functions we find are explained by the types of situations language is used in and the needs that must be met in these situations. Since we have to characterize the situation in order to understand the functions of language, we need

- a set of concepts describing situations
- a linkage between these concepts, and the linguistic functions.

Halliday (Halliday 1978: 221 ff) offers the following:

- *Field*: the nature of the activity, and subject matter. [Functions between actions. The specific tasks of the work situation, and the means of production: tools and raw materials]
- *Tenor*: the role relationships among the participants. [Functions between persons and actions/utterances. The work organization, the social relations, and the roles of the work situation]
- *Mode*: the channel, and the part played by language in the total event. [Functions between utterances]

and postulates the following close linkages:

Field - ideational
Tenor - interpersonal
Mode - textual

giving us definite ideas of how the work situation influences work language.

This means e.g. that the field, the type of activity, has the most direct influence on the ideational part.

Thus, in example 1, the workers are mounting a light on a car (field), and therefore their sentences contain many directional and locative cases (ideational function): "It should be a bit *further towards you*" , "I think it's *there*".

They cooperate: one person is moving a nut and the other one is watching the movements and correcting the former (tenor). Therefore the conversation consists of requests, either imperatives or modalized, followed by feedback in the form of repetitions or yes/no grunts (interpersonal function): "Try and hold it. Yes". Furthermore, after the cooperation has been established (tenor), there are no politeness markers (interpersonal function). Finally, the utterances are intermingled with and dependent upon non-linguistic work and they are oral (mode). Therefore, they have very little internal cohesion, their structure being derived from the physical work. The theme of the utterances is often implicit, only the rheme being explicit (textual function):"Higher up towards you" can be expanded into "The nut should be higher up towards you".

In the example I have given, the most reasonable guess seems to be that the functions between linguistic and situational items consist in linguistic paradigms presupposing the situational ones. In the first example, the particular case-paradigm consisting of direction and locative owes its existence to the fact that the work, like the Volvo example, consists in mounting a movable part (the nut) to an immovable part (the hole in the car), implying that if the field paradigm had been otherwise, the case paradigm also would be different.

The second example has a similar structure. If a shift from non-cooperation to cooperation had not been a part of the tenor, then the interpersonal part of the linguistic paradigms would not need to include a distinction between polite and non-polite forms of address.

Similar types of functions are described in Berry 1987.

I believe the framework is basically sound, but it is a problem that Halliday seems to take the utterance as his unit of analysis, although the linguistic functive that relates directly to non-verbal phenomena is not the utterance, but a unit I call the *language game*, and which can consist of several utterances. We can have long conversations (e.g. meetings) in which utterances relate to each other as e.g. question and answer, proposal and rejection, but not to non-verbal actions. Often only the whole meeting as a unit can (under lucky circumstances when decisions are made) relate to non-verbal actions. As a concrete example, let us look again at example 7.

The work distribution example

In Section I.1.3, I suggested that communicative functions like requesting or reporting can be defined as particular functival fields involving utterances and actions.

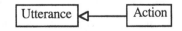

Fig. I.2.19. Functional description of requests.

Requests, for example, can be defined as utterances entering in a field like

(+utterance.action, +utterance.<u>action</u>, -<u>utterance</u>.action)

that is a presupposition from action to utterance (Fig. I.2.19).

Variants of requests can also be described in this fashion: work distribution, for instance, focuses on the allocation of workers to tasks (who should do it?) and allows e.g. the following combination:

+utterance.worker.task

since if a request is followed by association of a worker with a task, it succeeds and clearly counts as work distribution. If this association could have been made without the occurrence of the utterance, then the utterance cannot count as work distribution,

-<u>utterance</u>.worker.task

and in the cases where the task is not associated with the worker (the task may be performed by another worker, or the worker is doing another task) the utterance can still qualify as work distribution, although it failed to be obeyed.

+utterance.<u>worker</u>.task
+utterance.worker.<u>task</u>

Thus, work distribution can be described as an interdependence between worker and task presupposing an utterance (Fig. I.2.20). However, in real life, work distribution is not done by a single utterance, but often by several, since the persons involved may object and present counter-arguments which again may be countered.

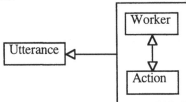

Fig. I.2.20. Functional description of work distribution.

In example 7, the initial request is countered by two arguments to the effect that the addressees are unable to comply. The function between request and the counter is probably interdependence since the request requires an answer, no reply counting as an impolite accept, and conversely, the refusals could not occur without the request. If the conversation had ended here, the requester would have lost, but she argues that one of the persons is in fact able to do as asked, and wins the game. My point is that the subsequent binding of the unfortunate worker to the task is not a function of the individual utterances, but of the whole game.

While the initial examples showed presuppositions from non-symbolic to symbolic paradigms, showing how aspects of language are dependent upon the situation, this example exhibits presuppositions in the opposite direction, from non-symbolic syntagms to symbolic ones, illustrating how other aspects of language create or change the situation.

In fact, within this framework, we can define functions by combining the following factors:

> *Function type*: interdependence, presupposition
> *Functive type:* symbolic act, non-symbolic act
> *Aspect*: System(paradigms), Process(syntagms)

Besides the two combinations already treated (system presupposition from symbolic acts to non-symbolic acts, process presupposition from non-symbolic acts to symbolic acts), one can imagine other combinations like presuppositions from processes of non-symbolic acts to systems of symbolic acts describing the influence of ideology on action pattern by asserting that certain types of actions owe their existence to certain symbolic paradigms.

At the Postal Giro, the general rule was that the workers were female while most of the higher positions were occupied by males. The female workers used the paradigm of sex <boy(kille), girl(flicka)> instead of the worker/superior paradigm to describe the organization, and this choice also influenced their tactics for handling conflicts with superiors[1].

Presuppositions from systems of symbolic or non-symbolic acts to processes of symbolic acts are also interesting, since they assert that features of a semiotic process can influence system features of semiotic and non-semiotic phenomena. For example, utterances may change the linguistic choices later in the conversation or the action possibilities after the conversation. The next section gives examples of this.

Opening, constraining, and closing functions

It is well-known that questions can be classified along a scale according to the number of possible answers, closed questions of the yes/no type allowing only two (and sometimes only one) answers, open questions of the wh-type allowing large paradigms of nouns or verbs. Thus, the teacher's question *Do you really think that Stockholm is the capital of Denmark* allows only one answer, while *What did you do in your vacation* sets very few limits on accepted answers. Since the distinction between open and closed questions to

---

[1] Berit Holmqvist, personal communication.

some degree can be described as structural process properties, closed questions having inverted word order and lacking wh-elements which are part of open questions, the question-answer relation is a good example of a function between paradigms (possible answers) and preceding syntagmatic structures (inverted word order), the former presupposing the latter.

Some discourse processes can be formulated in this way as functions between verbal syntagms and non-verbal paradigms, e.g. courses of action.

Meetings will initially often contain utterances containing conjunctions or disjunctions like *and, or,* and *but,* that serve to articulate a paradigm. If a course of action is discussed, the participants may start with an un-articulated nebulous paradigm that is successively articulated in different ways of tackling the problem. I shall say that paradigms are *opened.*

Additional paradigms may enter the discussion, and dependencies may be set up between them. For example, a paradigm of possible conditions may be related to the paradigm of actions by means of constructions like *if X is the case, then we should do Y, but if Z is true, then W should be done*:

What happens in this case is that choices in one paradigm are made to depend upon choices in another one. This is a syntagmatic process function which I shall call *constraining*[1].

After some time, the theme of discussion changes, the goal now being to select one course of action out of the paradigm created. I shall say that the paradigm is *closed.*

The notion of opening and closing functions is not new in itself. Language has developed special syntagms for opening (e.g. *Pardon me* or *Hello* in telephone openings) and closing (*O.K. + Bye* in closing a telephone conversation) linguistic paradigms, and a number of studies have been made in this area[2]. What is new is only the idea that besides opening and closing of linguistic paradigms, verbal control of non-linguistic action paradigms is also a proper subject for linguistics.

In Section III.2, I use these concepts for classifying language games. Here I show how they can be used to describe the problem solving in example 2.

The first part of the conversation is a *problem definition*, performed by the mechanics and aiming at defining the problem at hand:

E: Oh hell, they are damned bad, the other side is just as worn

A: Yes, I can see that

---

[1] With a literary analogy, the opening functions can be said to provide the setting of the plot, the type of universe in which we move, while the constraining functions determine a set of possible plots.

[2] See Clark & Clark 1977: ch. 6 for references.

E: Damn it, it has worn the lining clean off one of the shoes. There are only the rivets left.

B: It must have new drums, there is nothing else to do

B: Well, in the rear things are better

and the next part, which can be called *rule construction*, is performed by the boss and aims at setting up the possible courses of action:

Because if they can strip them, then they must mount oversized linings themselves, you know, but if they can't strip them, then we'll see, then we will have to take one pair of linings home, and then hope that they have the bits over there.

Repairing linings consists of three main parts:

(A)   dismounting the wheels and inspecting linings and drums,
(B)   exchanging linings,
(C)   mounting the wheels again.

and when the first conversation is uttered, the mechanic has just finished (A), and the boss is now trying to figure out what to do. Normally, linings can be exchanged in three different ways, depending upon the condition of the drums:

(1)   mount ordinary linings
(2)   make a specialized garage turn the drums and mount oversized linings
(3)   buy new drums and mount ordinary linings

Since 1-3 can all occur after part A and exclude each other, they form an *action paradigm* which can be called "exchanging linings".

The utterances of the boss have opening and constraining functions. The two main clauses *Because...you know, but...there* set up an action paradigm containing two main courses of action, namely (2) *mount oversized linings* and (3) *mount ordinary linings*, while the subordinate constructions *if...then* establish functions between this paradigm and a paradigm of drums states *(the drums can be stripped* vs. *the drums cannot be stripped)*. The paradigms will be *closed* later at the specialized garage.

Application to computers

The scheme used above to classify relations between signs and their non-symbolic context can also be applied to computer systems and their components viewed as a special type of signs. From a product-oriented viewpoint it is important to specify the kinds of data coming into and out of systems and system modules, but descriptions of this type do not say anything about the function and use of inputs and outputs. Very symptomatically, the data flow

diagrams of DeMarco 1978 call the destination of output data flows for *sinks*
- bottomless holes of no concern to the designer.

However, if our concern is not the internal workings of the system, but its
use in the organization, the concepts of input and output must be replaced
with concepts that describe the functions between events and actions in the
organization and the data, now conceived as signs. Instead of the term *output* (which views data from the computer system's perspective) I shall talk
about acts or utterances presupposed by computer-based signs, thereby
shifting my perspective from the system to the relation between system and
organization. Computer-based signs of this type all perform directive communicative functions like ordering, work distribution, and work coordination,
and dominate in administrative case handling, control room, and production
control systems, all serving to elicit actions or sentences from their users.

The term *input* is also replaced by a relational concept, namely computer-
based signs that are presupposed by acts or events. Signs of this type count
as assertions about a state of affairs or course of events. A good example is
inventory control systems that serve to keep track of a stock of objects.
Addition or removal of an object may cause a new name to be entered in the
system's record or some number to be increased or decreased. In some cases,
the function between acts and signs is manifested by users typing a description of the event into the system, but it can also be maintained by the system
itself, as in control room systems that are connected to gauges in the machinery.

Not only the system itself can be characterized functionally, it turns out
that some types of computer-based signs can be defined in this way. This is
true of the *menu*, whose function is to make the user aware of a set of action
possibilities and therefore is specialized to perform the *opening* communicative function mentioned above. The menu can be defined as a computer-
based sign that is presupposed by an action paradigm.

Communication

I am now in a position to describe the notion of communication as a special kind of function between symbolic and non-symbolic acts:

- *Communication* is a presupposition from an act or set of acts, whether
  symbolic or non-symbolic, to a symbolic act or object, based on a semiotic schema.

Communication takes place whenever an utterance or action would not
have occurred, had another utterance not occurred, if the relationship between the two is a manifestation of an underlying semiotic schema. This
definition makes many of the functions described in the preceding commu-

nicative functions, for example work distribution, opening, closing, and constraining functions.

The description is in no way an exhaustive description of communication, but is intended to view utterances and other sign tokens as acts that serve to change reality, and not primarily as true representations of it, a perspective that is clearly motivated by my basis in work language, and one which may not be appropriate in other linguistic varieties.

The description is not a variant of the behavioristic account of communication, consisting of stimuli and responses, since the presupposed utterance cannot be interpreted as a cause whose effect is a verbal or non-verbal response. The function may very well be manifested as no action at all, but, since a semiotic schema underlies the event, in this case "no action" is not equal to "nothing", but it is a marked absence.

For example, if I hear a street vendor crying "Ten tomatoes for a dollar," communication takes place even if I continue my walk and buy nothing, since in this case, "doing nothing" is significant, it is an absence, an empty place, the cry counting as a request, which in turn is a presupposition from action to utterance.

Empty places are different from no places in that it makes sense to ask why the action was not performed, which is odd if the place did not exist. Thus, my companion may ask "Why didn't you buy tomatoes?" after the cry, and I may answer "They were too expensive", whereas the same question would be out of place if no request was made.

The description is structuralist in the sense that it shifts the focus from the objects and persons themselves to their interrelations, the communicative situation itself being established by a network of expectations and contracts. The persons involved are described by means of positions they occupy in this network. For example, the sender of a message is one or more persons who are presupposed by it - it would not have occurred without the sender(s), while the receivers are persons whose utterances or acts presuppose the message. This definition of sender- and receiver-roles is useful when a team of communicators have collaborated to produce the message (which is typically the case in mass-communication) and, as we shall see in the next section, it is also a good way of conceiving sender- and receiver-roles in connection with computer systems. In these cases, it is often not sensible to define the sender of a message as the person that physically produces it, since this person is just a part of a larger division of labor and acts on instructions from other members of the team.

Although some positions are transitory, valid only for that particular occasion, other positions are more permanent. For example, there exist stable in terdependences between paradigms of communicative functions and paradigms of persons, only certain kinds of persons being able to perform certain kinds of acts. Performative acts like appointing an employee to a position or firing an employee can only be done by a manager in charge, sentencing a prisoner only by a judge, and marrying couples only by a clergyman.

I.2.3. Computer systems

After having discussed the possibilities of extending the basic structuralist framework to cover functions between language and actions, the next task is to find a sound semiological way of interpreting computer systems. One possibility adopted by AI is to view the computer system as analogous to a semiotic sign system and grant the computer some kind of language faculty. However, the following comparison of system concepts from computer science and linguistics shows that although there are some resemblances, the concepts cannot be considered identical, and therefore computers cannot play the role of participant in a communicative process. Instead, they are assigned the role of a medium for communication between human users. A computer system is described as a calculus of empty expression units, some of which can be part of the sign system that *emerges* when the system is used and interpreted by humans. What can be designed is only the substance in which this sign system is manifested, not the sign system itself.

I shall start by discussing the concept of system in linguistics.

I.2.3.1. The concept of system in linguistics

Since the birth of structuralism, a recurrent question has been: to what degree is our praxis as human beings governed by underlying "systems" and "structures"? Are humans just media through which structures are manifested? - or as Lévi-Strauss has it: humans do not think in myths, myths think in humans, and without their knowledge.[1]

The growth of bureaucracy during the 20th century may have furnished some of the material motivation for such conceptions, since, to a large degree, the daily life of the ordinary wage earner is governed by large, unintelligible structures such as the state and the company that make decisions behind his back, decisions over which he has very little influence.

The spread of computers in public and private organizations further nourished the idea of autonomous systems governing our life. We receive letters

---

[1] Lévi-Strauss 1964: 20.

untouched by human hand, decisions about our financial affairs are made by computers in the tax department, and the stream of raw materials and tools in factories is controlled by complicated production control systems. The computer is seen as the incarnation of the impersonal system that functions without human intervention.

Linked to these historical developments is the growth of the conviction that systems can be planned and constructed. Scientific management and its assembly line was based upon the assumption that the physical work process itself could be decomposed, changed and reassembled, implying that the work practice of humans can be constructed. The emergent discipline of cognitive science and its piece of machinery, the computer, tries to do the same thing to intellectual work: the communicative and reasoning abilities of humans are dissected, formalized, assembled in the shape of a program, and "put into the computer".

The issues involved are not just philosophical but have practical implications in management and computer science.

If it is true that the systems are the real things and humans only manifestations of them, then the most sensible way to build a computer system is to begin by constructing the system, without regard to whether processes are performed by human or computer. These decisions are postponed to the implementation phase. Conceptually it makes sense to use the same words about acts humans and computers do; on the one hand, humans *retrieve, process* and *store* information as computers, and on the other hand, computers *think, know, understand,* and *speak* like human beings.

But if "systems" are not seen as some hidden controlling agency that can be constructed, but rather as a post hoc description of regularities of praxis, then it makes no sense to "construct" systems. Instead, the sensible strategy will be to develop new practices by experimenting, recording the regularities underlying the new practices, and designing the system to support those regularities that are desirable.

As was mentioned in the beginning of Section I.2.1, the linguistics of Saussure and Hjelmslev show a strong tendency to posit the structure as the real existing entity. In Hjelmslev's universe[1], linguistic usage is clearly subordinate to the linguistic schema[2].

A linguistic schema is a form, and linguistic usage is a substance that manifests a linguistic schema. This can mean two things:

---

[1] See e.g. his La stratification du language. In Hjelmslev 1971: 44-77. For a good discussion of the schema/usage distinction, see Fischer-Jørgensen 1966.

[2] Hjelmslev has replaced Saussure's term *system* by *schema*, reserving *system* for the paradigmatic aspects of the *schema*. Systemicists like Halliday have adopted Hjelmslev's terms, as shall I.

- The weak version: one linguistic schema can be manifested by more than one usage
- The strong version: a linguistic schema can exist without usage

The weak interpretation is uncontroversial and very useful: the schema of the Danish language can be manifested e.g. in sounds, on paper, or on screen pixels. What defines a given language as Danish is not the sounds, the ink-marks, or the pixel pattern, but the common way in which these substances are articulated into graphemes and phonemes, the rules for building syllables and words, and the meaning attached to these entities.

However, the strong interpretation was adopted by Hjelmslev, his reason for doing so being that in his view schemas are theoretical constructs, produced by the linguist using a linguistic calculus:

> All possibilities must here be foreseen, including those that are virtual in the world of experience, or remain without a "natural" or "actual" manifestation.
>
> *Hjelmslev 1963a: 106*

and therefore there will be constructed schemas that accidentally are not the schemas of any existing usage, so that the category of usages presupposes the category of schemas.

In other places, he describes a schema as the result of an analysis of a text, and since this is also my understanding of the term, the strong version becomes to me untenable: if no text exists, how can the schema be constructed?

As indicated in the discussion of form and substance in Section I.2.1, I accept the weak version above, but reject the strong one. Consequently, there will exist interdependence between the categories of linguistic schemata and language usages, since neither can exist without the other, but presupposition from a particular usage to a particular schema. This standpoint is no mere academic question, but has influenced most pages in this book; for example, it is the reason why empirical data plays so large a role.

Since I will not only be concerned with verbal signs in the following, I will replace the linguistic schema with semiotic schema in the following definition that expresses my view of the schema concept:

> A *semiotic schema* is a description of the *invariant* features of the sign usage that is *socially* possible in a specified *situation type* by a specified *community* of sign users. A semiotic schema describes a form which is a *semiotic*, a semiotic being a system and a process, each of which can be divided into two planes, an expression and a content plane, whose elements commute.

In non-symbolic work I will use the terms *work schema* and *work practice* as analogues to semiotic schema and semiotic usage.

My definition, which is very similar to the one used in systemic theory, differs from Hjelmslev's in being bound to specific situation types. The schema represents the *socially given* aspect of sign usage that is not invented, but must be learned by the individual speakers. Since the schema includes a description of possibilities, it describes the actual sign tokens by describing which other sign types could have been produced instead, and the differences it would have resulted in.

Sign usage is viewed as production of sign tokens. The tokens are always produced against a background of the semiotic schema, and are motivated by demands and concerns of the use situation. Schema and usage are interdependent: there will be no sign usage without a common schema, since individual sign usage gets its meaning from the social semiotic schema by conforming to or deviating from it. On the other hand, there will be no schema without sign usage, since the schema is the invariant features of sign usage.

The distinction between schema and usage can only be made relative to particular situation types and a particular community of speakers. If we add more situation types and speakers in our description, some properties will no longer be invariant, and consequently will belong to sign usage. Conversely, if we exclude situation types, some of the features of sign usage will be promoted to the sign system, because they are invariant in the restricted domain.

I.2.3.2. The concept of system in computer science

After having described a linguistic variant of the system concept, I shall consider its use in the register of computer science. My main question will be: are there sound analogies between computers and humans? Are computer systems similar to the systems that underlie our language? Are human and programming language entities of the same kind? I am afraid that the following pages will have to be very abstract, but the arguments are crucial to the purpose of this book, since they serve to make clear how semiotic and computer-science concepts correspond, and indicate how semiotics can be applied to the field of computer systems in a theoretically sound way.

As I see it, there are two possible communicative roles the computer may be assigned to: it may replace humans in the roles of sender and receiver, or it may replace paper or sound as a medium of communication. The first solution is adopted by AI, but I shall argue against this and for the second solution.

Since the system concept has as many variants in computer science as in linguistics, I choose to concentrate on one variant that I am well acquainted with, namely the system concept used in the development of programming languages like Simula and Beta, and system description languages such as Delta[1].

The Delta report (Holbæk-Hanssen et al. 1977) presents a diagram of systems, descriptions, and languages (Fig. I.2.21).

The *referent system* is a part of the world that the *system reporter* has chosen to view as a system, and the *system description* is a description of the referent system produced by the system reporter. The system description and the language in which it is written are used by the *system generator* to make a *model system* of the referent system. If the language is a programming language, the referent system may be a set of administrative routines, the system description is a program modelling these routines, the system generator is a computer, and the model system it generates is a program execution.

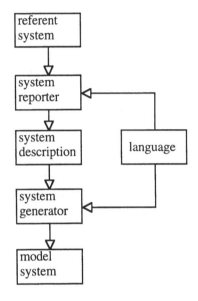

Fig. I.2.21. Systems development in the Delta report.

Three features of this conception of systems are relevant to my thematic question for this chapter:

The model system should be similar to the referent system. Thus, the basic relation between program executions and reality is *similarity* (Holbæk-Hanssen et al. 1977: 19). If models are analogous to signs or representations, this statement is in glaring opposition to the basic assumption of structural linguistics, namely that the sign relation is arbitrary.

The model system is generated from the system description. Since there may be system descriptions that are not read by any system generator, system descriptions can occur without model systems, whereas model systems must be described by a system description. Therefore, *model systems presuppose system descriptions.* This assumption motivates a negative answer to our thematic question, "are there sound analogies between computers and

---

[1] My sources are Birthwistle et al. 1973, Holbæk-Hanssen 1977, Håndlykken 1977, Bratteteig 1983, Nygård & Sørgård 1986. In addition, I have had several personal discussions with the "authors" of the concept, and I have used the Simula language in practice.
The system concept developed in these texts is not the only one found in computer science. Mathiassen 1981 for example, has redefined the concept so that it corresponds more closely to the structuralist concept presented in this book.

humans" for the following reason: if program executions correspond to language usage, there is a difference between the system and usage concepts of informatics and linguistics, since in informatics, usage presupposes a system description, whereas in the linguistic variant I use, usage is of course possible without system descriptions: computers cannot do anything without descriptions, but people can.

Computers and humans are treated as entities of the same kind. For example, the system generator may also be a theatrical ensemble, the system description a play, the language a natural language, and the model system a performance of the play (Holbæk-Hanssen et al. 1977: 24). If these analogies hold, the thematic question must be answered in the affirmative: then computers participate in man/machine interaction in the same manner as humans do, they can be said to master a language, to know and understand things, and a good system must be one that does these things in way that resembles human performance most closely.

But we have not yet learned what a system can be in computer science:

A *system* is a part of the world that a person (or group of persons) - during some time interval and for some reason - *chooses* to regard as a whole consisting of *components*, each component characterized by *properties* that are selected as being relevant and by *actions* relating to these properties and those of other components.

Nygård & Sørgård 1986: 381

No part of the world *is* a system, but any part can be viewed as a system for some particular reason, e.g. if one wants to build a computer system. To describe something as a system is to apply a particular perspective and in linguistic terms corresponds to a particular content form.

A system consists of two main parts: a *structure* that delimits the possible *processes* it can undergo. To view a phenomenon as a system is to characterize it by means of properties we see as stable. The system concept is a tool for describing the framework of the process. The structure controls the set of states in which a process can be.

Since the system structure consists of the stable properties of a process, it resembles the linguistic schema concept, the system process being analogous to linguistic usage, to substance. This translation is supported by the way Nygård & Sørgård describe the distinction between processes and structures:

A *process* is a development of a part of the world through transformations during a time interval. *Structure* of a process is limitations on its set of possible states (and thus on its possible sequences of states). In most programming languages, the transformations are prescribed by *imperatives* (and thought of as *actions*) in structure descriptions called *programs*.

Nygård & Sørgård 1986: 380

In the process concept above we recognize the notion of a substance that is articulated by a form. The similarity between the linguistic usage concept and the computer science process concept is even more clear in the next quotation:

The three qualities of an *information process* are:

• its *substance*, the physical matter of which it consists,
• *measurable properties* of its substance,
• *transformations* of its substance and thus its properties.

Nygård & Sørgård 1986: 380

The part of the world can change in uncountably many ways. There is a continuum of possible changes, but when we see the process as part of a system, we articulate the set of changes by imposing limitations upon it and in order to do that we must articulate the process into distinct properties, the measurable properties and their transformations.

From the above arguments I conclude that the following translations between computer science and linguistics are theoretically sound:

Computer science	*Linguistics*
Substance of process	Substance
Measurable properties of process	Distinctive features
System structure	Schema
System process	Usage, Text
Referent system	Content

The substance concept is here identified with the semiological substance concept, and its measurable properties and possible transformations correspond to the distinctions a form creates in a substance.

The system structure focuses on the stable, invariant part of the process, and in this respect resembles the schema concept from linguistics, while the process itself corresponds to linguistic usage. The system structure comprises both the system (either-or) aspect and the process (both-and) aspect of semiotics.

To describe these phenomena computer science uses system descriptions written in some suitable system description or programming language. Since a system description is a description of a (part of a) semiotic system, its linguistic correspondent is a linguistic description of some language, for example a grammar of English. Such descriptions can be defined as *meta-semiotics* whose content plane is an *object-semiotic* - they are texts that refer to other texts (cf. Hjelmslev 1963:119).

Finally, there are texts that define system description languages. Their linguistic analogues are textbooks on how to write grammars.

These can be called meta-meta-semiotics, but in order to avoid such cumbersome nomenclature I follow Hjelmslev in calling a meta-semiotic a *semiology*, which makes a meta-meta-semiotic a *meta-semiology*.

In spite of the apparent complexity and abstractness of the terminology, it will later turn out to be of very practical use in discussing program structure:

Computer science	Linguistics
Computer science	*Linguistics*
System description	Semiology
System description definition	Meta-semiology

The diagram in Fig. I.2.22 summarizes the relation between the three levels.

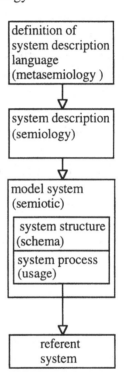

A system description (e.g. a program) describes a system, and since the system itself corresponds to a semiotic, the system description corresponds to a semiology that refers to an object semiotic. Finally, a definition of a programming or system description language is a meta-semiology. This gives us a hierarchy of three texts where the higher texts describe the lower ones: definitions of programming languages and systems description languages specify programming and system description languages that describe model systems that in their turn describe referent systems. Hierarchies of this kind are characteristic of computer science in the sense that they are necessary: a system cannot exist without a system description, e.g. a program, and a programmer cannot write a program without a specification of the programming language. I shall later argue that an important difference between the system concepts of linguistics and computer science lies precisely in their relations to descriptions.

Fig. I.2.22. Hierarchy of signs in computer systems.

I.2.3.3. Differences between the informatic and linguistic concept of system

In spite of the analogies, there are also differences between the concepts:

The content/expression distinction

Although both system structure and schema involve invariant, stable features articulating some continuum, the informatic concept lacks the content/expression distinction. This distinction is avoided by assuming that the same form, e.g. the system perspective, can be applied on both planes. Thus, the system concept is not only a possible expression form articulating the possible state changes of the computer, it is also implicitly assumed to be the content form.

The content and expression planes are seen as homomorphic, since the program itself is structured as a system, and the part of reality it signifies is assumed also to be structured as a system. In systems descriptions this homomorphism shows up in a systematic ambiguity in systems descriptions: it is difficult to determine whether they describe the referent system, e.g. a set of administrative routines performed by clerical workers, or the model system, e.g. an administrative system to be used in these routines. The following example refers to both referent system and model system, but an elegant use of comments has merged the two "texts" into one:

```
COMPONENT PATTERN POSITION:
  BEGIN
   SCALE OF PAY:INTEGER gives the scale of pay which the
     position belongs to
   . . .
  END POSITION
```
Håndlykken 1977: appendix 3.A, my translation

The upper-case words belong to the formal system description language called Delta, and can be used as a basis for writing programs, the underlined words being reserved words, the non-underlined upper-case words names. The lower-case text is not part of Delta, but comments that explain the meaning of the other words to the human reader. There are really two texts: a formal description in Delta (consisting of upper-case words) that is easily interpreted as a description of a computer system:

```
COMPONENT PATTERN POSITION:
   BEGIN
   SCALE OF PAY: INTEGER
   . . .
   END POSITION
```

and an informal description consisting of non-underlined words in Norwegian

```
POSITION:

  SCALE OF PAY: gives the scale of pay which the
    position belongs to

  . . .

POSITION
```

whose interpretation is the administrative referent system. This blending of the computer system and the referent system is not particular to the Delta language, but can also be found in Jackson 1983.

In the Delta report, the model system is clearly described as a representation or portrayal of selected aspects of the referent system, so it must be viewed as a collection of signs whose content is the referent system. Since model and referent system are structured similarly and are difficult to distinguish in the system description, then either we must say that the system description describes a semiotic schema in which content and expression planes are homomorphic, or we may choose to see it as a description of only one part of the sign, the expression plane.

I shall adopt the latter solution, but before I can give my reasons I need the following concepts:

- *System processes:* all possible computer processes allowed by the system structure.
- *Computer-based sign:* a sign whose expression plane is manifested in the processes changing the substance of the input and output media of the computer (screen, loudspeaker, keyboard, mouse, printer, etc.).
- *Interface:* a collection of computer-based signs, viz. all parts of system processes that are seen or heard, used, and interpreted by a community of users.

The important thing in this definition of interface is that it denotes a *relation* between the perceptible parts of a computer system and its users. The system processes are substances that can be turned into expressions of computer-based signs in an interpretative process that simultaneously establishes their content. The definition is one more example of a structuralist shift from focus on objects to their interrelation. The definition clearly differs from those found in older textbooks on interaction that describe the interface as a system part,

> the part of the program that determines how the user and the computer communicate
> *Newman & Sproull 1979: 443*

However, the shift I propose has been made by other authors, e.g. by Bødker 1987 who describes the interface as preconditions for operations done by the user:

> The conditions for the operational aspects which are given by the computer applica-
> tion will be called the *user interface*. The user interface is the artifact-bound conditions
> for *how* actions can be done.   *Bødker 1987: 38*

One consequence of this shift is that the same system may have many interfaces, since it may have many user groups, each viewing different parts of the
system and interpreting it differently because of different registers. Also it
does not make sense to say that a system in isolation has an interface; interfaces "emerge" when the system is used.

Let us now look at a large corpus, consisting of sequences of screen and
input-output operations from many different use sessions. What is the nature
of the schema underlying this corpus? The first answer might be that it must
be identical to the system structure, but a little reflection shows that this cannot be true. Although any screen sequence must be generated by the system
structure, not every system process is represented in the corpus. Users will
develop special ways of doing things, preferring some system processes and
rejecting others. In addition, there will be processes that are allowed by the
system, but do not make sense in terms of task semantics, and therefore are
not used by users:

> To bridge the gap between the functions of the DP [data processing, my comment]
> system and their actual work-tasks, user communities develop practices that can be
> described as "fitting" system functions to actual needs, "enhancing" system functions
> by manual practices, "working around" inadequate system functions in order to
> achieve human work-goals.   *Floyd 1987: 200*

This means that the schema behind an interface will contain functions that
are absent in the system structure. To give a very simple example, consider
the *save* command in an operative system. The command is used to store
modifications made to a file on the disc, and in most Macintosh applications
it belongs to the same paradigm as commands that create a new file or open
an existing one. However, even if it is possible to perform *save* immediately
after having created a new file, and to perform two save commands after
each other, this will not happen in work practice since in these cases there
will be no modifications to save. In the schema underlying work practice,
saving will presuppose typing operations or similar modifications, a syntagmatic dependency that does not exist in the system structure.

The example shows that work practice introduces structures into the system processes that are absent in the system structure.

Since content and interface are not properties that can be assigned to the
system in itself, but are a relation between system and use, it follows that the
system should not be viewed as a semiotic schema in which content and expression planes are homomorphic, but rather as a mechanism for generating

the expression substance for one or more interfaces. Umberto Eco's description of books as "machines for generating interpretations" fits very nicely onto computer systems too.

Therefore, I choose to see computer systems as expression systems, and restrict the usage of the computer science term "system" to mean the expression form of a semiotic schema, whose content plane is generated by the users, and which is a part of a larger semiotic schema, namely the register belonging to the work situations in which the system is intended to be used[1].

In spite of the abstract wording, the theoretical position described in the preceding paragraph is of very practical importance, since it is from that position we can treat computer systems as media, an approach that will dominate the rest of the book. Seeing the computer system as an empty expression system means that we see it as consisting of a "palette" of expressive devices that designer and user invest with meanings.

However, to say that the computer system itself is an empty expression system is only a half truth: by relating it to other semiotic systems, e.g. the existing work language, the designer can strongly invite certain interpretations and a certain content system.

I will say that the computer system generates *sign candidates,* reflecting the view and intentions of the designers. Some candidates win and become full-time members of the human semiotic system, other candidates lose, and are soon forgotten, while still others are reinterpreted and used for purposes that the designer may not even have dreamt about.

The revised translation from computer science to linguistics will then look like this:

Computer science	*Linguistics*
Substance of process	Expression substance
Measurable properties	Expression features
System structure	Expression schema
System process	Expression plane of text

There is one final problem in this translation I must comment on. On the one hand the problem is both theoretically and practically relevant, on the other hand I can propose no nice solution to it. The problem is that in the transla-

---

[1] Incidentally, this also seems to be the interpretation adopted by Hjelmslev when he writes about other formal sign systems:
"The logistic theory of signs finds its starting-point in the meta-mathematics of Hilbert, whose idea was to consider the system of meta-mathematical symbols as a system of expression-figuræ with complete disregard of their content, and to describe its transformation rules in the same way as one can describe rules of a game, without considering possible interpretations. This method is...brought to its conclusion by Carnap in a sign-theory where, in principle, *any semiotic is considered as a mere expression system without regard for the content."* *Hjelmslev 1963a: 110.*

tion, I treat the expression plane in isolation, but this cannot be done in linguistics that views the two planes of the linguistic sign as interdependent. Expression and content invariants are established in one dialectical process. Saying that some element belongs to the expression form presupposes that it commutes with respect to some content. Then how can I say that the system structure describes the expression form without specifying the other part of the sign? I cannot know whether an element is an invariant before I have made the commutation test, and the following example clearly shows that the system structure may contain expressive elements that do not commute.

Suppose I design a system in which I need two kinds of buttons, e.g. one type I use to navigate, and another type used for affecting some work object. I want to code the difference so that it is easy for the user to interpret the button signs, and therefore I distinguish the two button types in three ways: one is white, the other grey, one is a rectangle, the other a rounded rectangle, and one has a thin border, the other a thick one.

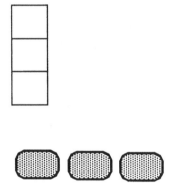

Fig. I.2.23. Variants and invariants.

The system description of my buttons may contain the following piece

```
Class button
  Shape: (Rectangle, RoundedRectangle)
  Color: (White, Grey)
  Border: (Thin, Fat)
```

However, none of the six values commute separately since a change of shape is always accompanied by changes of color and border. Therefore we can only demonstrate that two invariants, A and B, exist, which are manifested in three variants, A = Rectangle + White + Thin, B = RoundedRectangle + Grey + Fat.

Before analysis, we may have believed that the system contains six expression taxemes, but the analysis proves that there are only two. We are often in the same situation in linguistic analysis. Consider for example the two Danish sounds [g] and [γ]. The first one is a stop, the second one a spirant, so with respect to pronunciation they are clearly distinct. However, they never commute, since [γ] is a variant of [g] in syllable-final position, and the two must be regarded as variants of the same /g/ phoneme. Hjelmslev uses the prefix *pre-* to denote linguistic units whose status is as yet unclear. Thus [g] and [γ] are pre-taxemes, since on the one hand they are candidates for being taxemes because they are clearly distinct, but on the other hand we do not yet know whether they in fact are.

A more correct translation of *system structure* would be *expression pre-units,* and our six values above would probably be classified as pre-taxemes, which turn out to be variants of only two real taxemes. This analysis says that the designer who builds the system structure does not design the semi-otic schema, but only its pre-taxemes. He does not design signs, but only sign candidates. Which signs in fact come to exist and which pre-taxemes turn out to be invariants can first be determined a posteriori by an analysis of the way users actually use and interpret the system.

In this interpretation, it makes no sense to say that computers possess or understand language. What they possess is the ability to process the expression plane of a language, to manipulate "expression-figuræ with complete disregard of their content".

This does not mean that it is not possible to construct interfaces where the two planes come close to being isomorphic, so that there are few functions on the content plane that do not have counterparts on the expression plane.

A formal system can be defined as a monoplanar schema where expression and content plane are isomorphic and need not be distinguished.

Let me give an example of what the above definition means by consider-ing the question-answer relation. In the English exchange,

(1)   Where is the annual report?
(2)   It is in drawer 4.

we have a composite sign on the content plane consisting of two relationally defined signs, question and answer, sentence 2 counting as an answer to sentence 1. However, we have no expression units of the same size as the two content units with a similar dependency between them. Suppose now we build a question-answering system with rudimentary reasoning abilities and implement transformational rules like R1 and R2:

R1   Where is NP_1 + NP_1 is in NP_2 ->   It is in NP_2
R2 NP_1 is in NP_2 + NP_2 is in NP_3 -> NP_1 is in NP_3

The rules are of the form A -> B reading: if a text contains a string x matching A, then x can be replaced by y, a string constructed from x and B.

R1 gives a rule for answering questions like *Where is the annual report,* and R2 allows the system to collapse descriptions of location, producing *the annual report is in drawer 4* from *the annual report is in file 102* and *file 102 is in drawer 4,* expressing that the content of *in* is a transitive relation. To illustrate this, suppose we start by giving our system the text:

Where is (the annual report) + (the annual report) is in (file 102) + (file 102) is in (drawer 4)

By mechanically applying rule R1 we get

Where is (the annual report) + (the annual report) is in (drawer 4)

and by rule R2 we get

It is in (drawer 4)

which is an answer to the question.

Now the system via R1 provides expression structure for the composite question-answer sign as a whole, since it precisely describes how the expression of the question and the answer should be related in order to count as a question-answer pair. Just as natural languages have rules governing the structure of syllables like "any syllable must contain a vowel, and may contain initial and final consonants", our system has rules governing the expression structure of question-answer pairs.

This analysis is representative for the way I view AI in this book. I shall try to avoid metaphysical phrases like "Knowledge-based systems", "Intelligent programs", since I find that the above description accounts for the known facts without major changes of epistemological paradigms.

Oppositions and relations versus classification and decomposition

Most computer systems are built according to a part/whole relation, large objects being decomposed into parts that are again decomposed into subparts. Modern programming languages support *decomposition* by means of the procedure concept, and programming methods include decomposition as an important part.

Some languages, e.g. SIMULA and Smalltalk, add the feature of *classification*. It is possible to define subclasses of a superclass, the former inheriting the properties of the latter and possibly adding new properties. Classification and decomposition are found in some linguistic theories, but they are not essential in the classical structuralist version I use in this book.

Instead, the basic semiotic concepts are relations and differences. The units of linguistic form are defined in relation to each other, they mutually delimit and circumscribe each other, keeping each other in check in an equilibrium, and if one position in this equilibrium is changed, it may have repercussions throughout the system.

In this perspective, it makes no sense to describe a sign in isolation, which is a perfectly legitimate and recommended activity in systems design, and in semiotic analytical methodology, systematic *comparison* takes the place of decomposition. For example, the commutation test in Section I.2.1 consists of *comparing* two expression forms to see if their contents are *identical* or *different*.

Construction versus development

In the sense in which I use the concept of schema, semiotic schemata are normally not constructed, but the usage that gives rise to them has evolved through the ages, whereas computer systems are artifacts that are constructed by certain persons at a certain time.

The fact that computer systems are constructed means that they are nearly always a result of a division of labor, so that the decomposition of computer systems into subsystems often corresponds to a division of labor in the construction process. Computer systems are layered and fall into several parts with different authors, the higher levels using components from the lower levels. For example, an application program may use a compiler, while the compiler may use the operative system and a graphical library. Of course, a similar clear-cut partitioning cannot be found in natural semiotic systems.

This difference in the mode of existence also shows up in the mode of change. The computer system develops stepwise and not continuously, and the development is planned and not spontaneous. In fact, this mode of development is often a major problem since it makes the system inflexible and unable to accommodate new developments in its surroundings.

The "labor" involved in changing the semiotic system is not organized in this way. Natural semiotic systems develop continuously, anarchistically and partly unconsciously, the dialectics between daily usage and change being one of the most important factors in this development.

Prescriptions versus abstractions of usage

The expression plane of any computer-based sign must always be described by one or more system descriptions, e.g. programs, and there must be a physical causal connection from the expression plane of the metasign to that of the object sign. It must be possible to convert the system description into a form so that it physically can "determine the set of states in which a process can be".

To give a simple example, suppose my program execution contains a rectangle denoting a file cabinet. Then

- my program must contain a complete description of the rectangle, e.g. a command *DrawRect(l,t,r,b)*.

- there must be a causal chain from the bits representing the letters
  d r a w r e c t (l , t , r , b), through the compiler and graphical library to
  the actual bit pattern representing the rectangle.

Complete descriptions of natural semiotic systems rarely exist, and in any
event their expressions cannot generate the object signs through a causal
chain, although folklore has often dreamed of that kind of signs: they are
called *spells*.

Summary

The differences between a computer system and a human linguistic schema can be summarized as shown in Fig. I.2.24.

Computer systems presuppose a system description, because no system can exist without a system description, whereas the opposite is clearly possible, since there may be programs that are never run on a computer. In my interpretation, human semiotic schemata can and do exist without any description, since they are invariants of usage, and therefore a linguistic description presupposes a schema, but not vice versa.

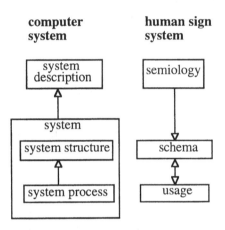

Fig. I.2.24. Difference between computer systems and linguistic schemas.

There are also differences in the relation between structure/schema and process/usage.

In human sign systems, usage cannot be conceived of without a socially accepted schema, but neither can a schema, viewed as invariants of and constraints on usage, exist without usage.

However, the structure of a computer system may well exist without any processes, since the patterns of all system objects, their properties and actions, may be declared in the program, without any actual action taking place, and therefore the system process may be said to presuppose the structure.

These differences between the categories of the two sciences correspond to real differences in the two objects of research. The human sign system has only two levels that are dialectically related: the schema imposes limitations on sign usage, but sign usage can change the system, and sign usage need not conform to the rules of the system, whereas computer systems *are* normally constructed in such a way that executions do not change the system structure, and any process *must* stay within the limitations of the structure.

In computer systems, the dialectics between system and usage is much weaker, since production and modifications of the system normally involve other knowledge and skills than those required to use the system.

Why (present-day) machines can't talk or think: a functional analysis

In the preceding, I have rejected the AI hypothesis in various places by pointing out that computer systems and human linguistic schemata are still so different that only confusion will result if we use the same designation for both. I have nothing against the idea that machines may think, talk, feel, and reason, I just believe that what they do today is too different from what humans do.

A strict functional analysis of what happens when machines seems to exhibit intelligence or master a language, will give the result that it is really the designer or programmer that shows his faculties through the machine. Program executions with the property of language mastery presuppose a program text: without program text, no intelligence, and similarly, the program text presupposes a team of programmers and designers. A physical machine contracts only constellation with language mastery, since the program can be run on other machines, and the machine can run programs that are not intelligent. Therefore, the physical machine has no relation to a faculty of language, and saying that a machine is intelligent is totally unmotivated.

This conclusion is inevitable when we compare it to the language faculty of humans. Here the faculty does not presuppose a description, since people can speak even if no written grammar exists, and the linguistic schema does not presuppose identifiable authors, since natural languages are not constructed but have evolved. Instead there is interdependence between an ideolect and an individual. The individual cannot exist without speaking, and his language does not exist without the individual. It is true that there are cases where this interdependence does not hold, for example when a person A repeats the words of another person B - but in precisely these cases we would tend to say that the sender of the message is really not A, it is B that speaks through A's mouth. Present-day programmers and designers speak through the mouth of their machines.

But this line of argument also yields criteria for when it is sensible to say that machines can speak, namely in cases where the machine contracts the same functions as the human does. The language faculty must be interdependent with a particular machine or class of machines, and neither program nor programmer necessarily exists. Research inspired by biological concepts (as e.g. the theory of cellular automata[1], the concept of neural nets, and the logical theory of self-reproduction[2]) may possibly produce this kind of machine in the future, but then the notion of a "machine" will have changed so radically that it may have little to do with what we call machines today.

I.2.4. Interface and register

We now have some concepts for describing and understanding human language, and I have presented one framework for constructing and understanding computer systems. The next thing to consider is what happens when a computer system is inserted into a human symbolic environment, as for example when computers replace typewriters in an office.

The corpus of signs we are investigating includes both signs generated by a computer system and signs belonging to a human work register. I call this a computer-based register:

- *Computer-based register:* the union of an interface and a work language.

I have chosen the computer-based register - and not the interface - as the basic unit of analysis because (1) we normally do not observe interface and human speech separately, since people talk in connection with their work, and (2) in the structuralist framework, the individual signs are established and delimited by the whole they are part of (cf. the Saussure quotation in the beginning of Section I.2.1).

The important question of fitting the system to its use context can now be reframed as a question of how this computer-based register is structured. Does it fall into two parts, the computer part and the task part - with nothing in common or can its words and phrases be used for interpreting and relating both sides of work? Are the structural principles of the computer interface so different from those of the original work register that no merge is possible and users either refuse or are unable to learn the new symbol system? If a merge takes place, will the computer-based signs influence the original work register so that tasks are now interpreted as computational processes, or conversely, will the original work register dominate and its words be extended to describe computers? These are important questions which to a large degree can be empirically investigated with linguistic methods and I shall start by looking at the content of the signs.

---

[1] Lindenmayer 1968, Burks 1970.
[2] Löfgren 1968.

1.2.4.1. Formal and real meaning

The content form of the interface signs can be manifested in two different substances, since they can be interpreted as designating computational processes and objects in the computer and as designating actions and objects in the program's application area. The former I call its *formal meaning*, the latter its *real meaning*. The formal meaning is clearly relevant to the tasks of the system developers, whereas the real meaning is just as relevant to the users' activities, but the balance between the two variants is by no means clear.

The two major positions (described in Floyd 1987) differ in the weight they assign to the two types of meanings. The *product-oriented perspective* regards programs as formal mathematical objects whose meaning is defined by their formal semantics as given in their specification and derived from semantic atoms in the documents by applying semantic rules, whereas the *process-oriented perspective* views programs as working environments for people. The meaning of the programs must be seen in connection with the intentions of the authors, and relates to the totality of possible program uses.

Some recent textbooks in interface design clearly have come to emphasize the real meaning of computer-based signs. Shneiderman 1986, for example, distinguishes between task and computer concepts:

> The semantic knowledge is separated into task concepts (objects and actions) and computer concepts (objects and actions). A person can be an expert in the computer concepts, but a novice in the task, and vice versa. *Shneiderman 1986: 43*

and in many places advocates use of task concepts, e.g. in menu design. Hutchins, Holland & Draper 1986 define the concept of semantic distance, which is the difference between the concepts offered by the computer system and the concepts of the users' work language, and advocate semantic directness:

> Is it possible to say what one wants to say in this language. That is, does the language support the user's conception of the task domain?
> *Hutchins, Holland & Draper 1986: 100*

which the designer can achieve by constructing

> ...higher-order and specialized languages that move toward the user, making the semantics of the input and output languages match that of the user
> *Hutchins, Holland & Draper 1986: 103*

Given that we actually want to create some cohesion between formal and real meaning, the designer can follow one of two main principles (roughly corresponding to Floyd's two positions):

- *Product-oriented:* Use the work language as a metaphor and disguise of a formal meaning that has already been defined by other means, or
- *Process-oriented:* Use the work language as the main basis for creating the formal meaning variants of the interface.

Our preference will of course depend upon the perspective we work in, but probably also on the type of system we design. The first strategy may be the best one when the system denotes a topic where no skills and knowledge, and therefore no professional language, exist at the moment, whereas the second should be preferred when the system is to be a tool in a work process where knowledge, experience and skill already exist and are couched in the professional language of the work. In this case, the language provides a gold-mine of good concepts.

In the following, I shall illustrate both methods.

Formal meaning primary

In the first strategy, the designer writes a formal description of the system processes in the professional language of computer science, and then tries to add a suitable metaphor from situations that many users will know about. In the following example, I shall imagine I am given a description of a simple file system in some formal notation, and I want to create a new description that the users can understand and use.

I shall use a variant of Petri-nets[1] as the specification language. From a semiotic point of view, specification languages can be treated as special kinds of human languages in which part of the semiotic schema is described in explicit rules.

The *content form* of the notation includes three distinct kinds of mathematical units

$S = \{s_1,...s_n\}$ is a finite set of states or *places,*
$T = \{t_1,...t_n\}$ is a finite set of *transitions*

F is a *flow relation* between places and transitions, where $(S \times T) \cup (T \times S) \supset F$.

S and T are disjoint, and the union of S and T is nonempty.

A net is *marked* by assigning a nonnegative integer N to each place. We shall say that N *tokens* occupy that place, where a token is an undefined concept. A place p is said to be an *input place* of a transition t if F contains (p,t), and an *output place* of t if F contains (t,p).

The expression form is isomorphic to the content form, and is often manifested in a graphical substance. The three content units - places, transitions,

---

[1] Peterson 1981.

and flows - are expressed by three *expression units* - the ellipse, the box, and the arrow - the *sign function* being: ellipse ~ place, box ~ transition, and arrow ~ flow. Tokens are expressed by dots placed on the places.

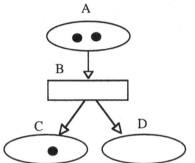

Fig. I.2.25. Petri-net. Start configuration.   Fig. I.2.26. Petri-net. Next configuration.

In Fig. I.2.25, A is an input place of B and C and D are output places. A contains two tokens and C contains one.

A transition t can fire if and only if it can remove one token from each input place. A transition need not fire when it can, but when it does, it removes the tokens from its output places, and places one token on each output place.

In Fig. I.2.25, B can fire, and when it does, it removes a token from A and places one token in D and one token in C, yielding Fig. I.2.26.

Petri-nets have been used for describing different kinds of contents, e.g. a physical production process, computer hardware and software, administrative procedures, or flow of paper in an organization. All these purports will be articulated in the same way, since they will be seen as events (described by transitions) that have certain preconditions (input places), and cause other conditions to hold (output places).

In the product-oriented tradition, concepts like these will also be the basic semantic units expressed by the interface signs, although they become disguised by some a posteriori metaphor.

Although this book is clearly within the process-oriented tradition, I shall occasionally use formal specifications also, and since I am particularly interested in formal properties of the interface, I shall add a few new elements to the basic Petri-net language. Besides transitions, places, flows, and tokens, I want to introduce the concept of regions, denoting a collection of objects belonging together, and to distinguish between visible versus invisible, and machine- versus user-controlled transitions and places.

This enhanced schema includes sign tokens like the following:

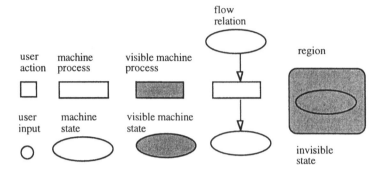

Fig. I.2.27. Petri-net. Graphical conventions.

In addition, I shall use a double arrow as shorthand for two opposite arrows with the same source and destinations. Double arrows between a place and a transition mean that the transition needs to "read" the material in the place and thus occupies the resources for some time, but it does not change anything.

After this digression, I proceed to build my little file system by specifying an abstract version in the Petri-net notation:

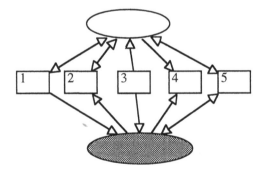

Fig. I.2.28. Petri-net description of toy file system.

There are two places, an invisible one denoting the disc, and a visible one denoting working memory, including the part controlling the screen. When files are not processed they reside only in the invisible place, but when the user wants to work on a file, parts of it are transferred to working memory and made visible.

I plan to implement five operations to handle the data flows between disc and memory. (1) takes a file from the invisible place (the disc), places parts of it on the visible place (memory and screen), and returns the file to the invisible place. (2) takes the visible and invisible representation of a file, updates the invisible part, and returns it to the invisible place. (3) places a new file on the visible and the invisible place, (4) removes a file from both places, and (5) takes the invisible and visible representation, updates the invisible version to match the visible one, and returns both items.

This is an abstract description of a set of system processes, articulated by the content form of Petri-nets, that will later be detailed and used as a basis for programming the system. However, I am afraid the concepts will be too strange for users to employ, and before I invest money in implementing the system, I want to ensure that a suitable metaphor can be constructed, so I look for a register with a content form so close to that of the Petri-net that it can be moved from its original content substance to the new substance of computational processes.

The first thing I do is to describe the formal content form that consists of the functions the five commands contract to other signs. Since it is a formal description, content and expression planes are largely isomorphic and therefore the content can be described by enumerating expression features.

I choose to characterize the five commands by their arrows. The first dimension concerns the direction of the arrows: an arrow can lead to, from or both to and from a command. The second dimension describes the other endpoint of the arrow, which can be the invisible or the visible place. Combining these differences gives a 3X3 paradigm into which the individual commands can be plotted:

The invisible place

		Double	One to	One from
The visible place	Double	5		
	One to	1	3	
	One from	2		4

Fig. I.2.29. Semantic field analysis of file system.

Now I look for a register with a similar paradigm. This task is not as easy as it seems, but at last I hit upon the kitchen, where at least four commands have analogues: I have eaten, and some of the food remains. Should I (2) *put* it *aside* in the freezer so that I can (1) *take* it *out* next week, thereby avoiding (3) *creating* a new dish? Or should I (4) *discard* it by throwing it in to the garbage bin?

I set up a paradigm with two dimensions. One distinguishes the words according to type of action: do the words denote beginnings (Ingressives), endings (Cessatives) or continuations (Perduratives)[1]. The other classifies the words according to the process denoted: is it the existence of the objects that begins, ceases, or continues, or is it the focus of attention of a human perceiver?

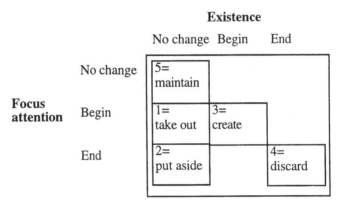

Fig. I.2.30. Metaphor for file system.

Thus, whereas *taking out* left-overs from the refrigerator means that the cook focuses his attention on them, but their existence is unchanged, *discarding* left-overs means that they cease to exist as food, and that the cook loses interest in them.

Finally, I map distinctions from the Petri-net description onto the cooking distinctions in the following way:

Cooking	*File system*
Existence	The invisible place
Focus of attention	The visible place
No change I begin I end	Double I one to I one from

The semantic mapping should be such that it enables the user to use experiences in the kitchen to make correct predictions about his actions in the file system. Thus, the invisible disc representation is mapped onto existence because the changes to the file must be recorded on the disc in order to persist from session to session, while the visible place is made to correspond to the focus of attention, since the parts of the file must be moved to working memory in order to be perceived.

I have deliberately postponed commenting on the fifth member, *maintain,* translating command 5. Number 5 is necessary in the file system, since my system does not automatically update the disc representation of the file, but its properties (no change of existence nor focus of attention) have no good

---

[1] Noreen 1904.

correspondent in the kitchen. The reason is of course that food does not live the double life of a file, partly in the visible, partly in the invisible place, therefore there is no need to update two versions of a potato soup, and therefore no word has been created to denote this process. Thus, the two paradigms are not completely alike, since the Petri-net paradigm fills a place that is vacant in the kitchen paradigm.

Such discrepancies are unavoidable, and we should not expect to find a complete match when we look for metaphors. Apart from lexical mismatches like the one above, we should expect that many meaning distinctions from one area have no mapping in the other, or that distinctions collapse when we move from one area to another. For example, if we use a spatial metaphor to denote social rank (a high/low position), the left-right dimension has no correspondent, and the depth dimension collapses with the vertical (he is on his way down = he is falling behind).

Real meaning primary

After having illustrated the first method, I shall now turn to the second one. In this case, I shall not start with a formal specification but with a specific professional language that I shall analyze with traditional linguistic methods as illustrated in the following example[1], where I want to redesign the part of a library system that allows users to navigate between its main modules.

Collecting a corpus

The corpus I shall use is based on tape recordings of three one- to two-hour conversations with employees at a Danish library: two librarians, and one clerical worker. The three employees were working in the circulation department, at the circulation desk, and the catalogue department. During each conversation one of the employees was sitting in front of a terminal with us. The employee was asked to show us some typical tasks involving use of the present computer system, and as she went along, to tell us what she did. To stimulate the conversation, we asked questions like "what does this mean?" or "what was it called before computerization?"

It turned out that like many other users these employees use a spatial metaphor (which was not exploited in the actual system they used).

They can go into the system,

så kunne jeg *gå ind* og lave sikkerhedskopier, og lægge nogen magnetbånd *ind på* systemet [then I could *go in* and make back-up copies, and place some magnetic tapes *on* the system]

---

[1] This section is based upon Bøgh Andersen & Halskov Madsen 1987.

and when they have entered the room they may call forth the system they want to use,

og jeg kan også *gå ind* og kalde udlånssystemet *frem* [and I can also *go in* and *call forth* the circulation control system]

There are two alternatives, the circulation control system and the information retrieval system. In the information retrieval system they can move between several databases,

så *skal* jeg *tilbage* til ALIS-basen [then I have to *get back* to the ALIS-base]

and move objects from one base to another,

det er vi *flytter* en søgning *mellem* baserne [that is we *move* a search *between* the bases]

Analysis of the underlying linguistic schema

The design method I want to illustrate consists in setting up lexical paradigms, and using the glossemes that structure these paradigms as a basis for design. In order to set up the paradigms, it is necessary to make a grammatical analysis of the corpus. The analysis results in three main sentence types that are syntactically similar[1].

I. Actions without object

Subj	FinV	Adv	InfV	Time	Rel	Abs
jeg [I	kunne could		gå go		ind in]	
jeg	skal				tilbage	til ALIS-basen
[I	have to get				back	to the A-LIS base]

II. Actions with an object

Subj	FinV	Adv	InfV	Obj	Rel	Abs
jeg	kunne		lægge	nogle magnet-bånd	ind	på sys-temet
[I	could		place	some magnetic tapes		on the system]

---

[1] Subj = subject, FinV = finite verb, Obj = object, Adv = adverbial, InfV = infinite verb. Rel and Abs are two parts of the Danish prepositional phrase. Rel describes the action relative to previous locations of a moving object while Abs describes the end-point of the action in relation to another object.

vi	flytter			en søgning		mellem baserne
[we	move			a search		between the bases]
man	bærer	lissom		bestillin-gen	rundt	mellem nogle forskellige kartoteker
[you	carry	as it were		the order	around	between different card files]

III. Relations without an object

Subj	*FinV*	*Adv*	*InfV*	*Rel*	*Abs*
jeg	er			inde	i det
[I	am				in it]

The preliminary sentence analysis shows us which elements are treated as belonging together and it makes it possible for us to set up paradigms of contrasting words:

- *Action* (subsets of FinV and InfV): flytte(move), gå(go), bære(carry), køre(run,drive), komme(come), skifte(shift), lægge(place), kalde(call)
- *Transport and location:* flytte(move), gå(go),komme(come), bære(carry), køre(run,drive), lægge(place), sidde(sit), ligge(lie), befinde sig (be located).
- *Relation*(subsets of FinV and InfV): sidde(sit), ligge(lie), befinde sig(be located).
- *Modality*(subset of FinV): kunne(could), kan(can), skal(has to, wants)
- *Adverbs of direction and place*(subset of Rel): ind(in), tilbage(back), over(over), frem(forward), rundt(around), ned(down), inde(within).
- *Prepositions of direction and place*(subset of Abs): til(to), i(in, into), fra(from), på(on), mellem(between).

A first shot at the interface

After having constructed the paradigms, I have a go at the interface by transferring the underlined members to a command language and giving them a formal meaning variant. The real meaning of the system is described as a space, and that of the commands is physical movements in the space.

1. Outside the system

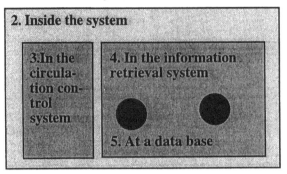

Fig. I.2.31. Sketch of library system.

There will be commands corresponding to type I, e.g.

> *Go in*
> *Go out*
> *Go back*
> *Go into the circulation control system*
> *Go over into the information retrieval system*
> *Go back to the information retrival system*
> *Go to base 1*

and feedbacks corresponding to type III, e.g.

> *You are now in the information retrieval system*

Examples of commands corresponding to type II are

> *Move search profile to base 2*
> *Move reference to the circulation control system*

Searching the lexical material of corpus for good ideas

By comparing the first primitive command language with the corpus we can get many more ideas of functionality than came to mind in the first trial.

Consider for example the adverbs of place and direction[1]. *Into* and *out* occur in the interface (*go into the circulation control system, go out*) but in no place can a particular computational difference be assigned to them, since they are always positional variants, *into* occurring with locations and *out* always occurring alone. Therefore they have no formal meaning, but it is not difficult to imagine data processing facilities that will give *Go into the circulation control system* a formal meaning that is different from *Go out into the*

---

[1] *ind(in), frem(forward), tilbage(back), over(over), rundt(around), ned(down), inde(within).*

circulation control system: For example, a space can be allowed to have the same name as one of its subspaces. The name of the room may be X, we are placed in one of X's subspaces called Y, and Y has itself a subspace called X. If we are placed in Y, *Go out into X* will bring us out into the largest space, whereas *Go into X* will bring us into the smallest space.We could also make the system issue error messages telling us that we have a wrong conception of our position in the system. For example, we are placed in space B, which is a subspace of space A. We write *Go into A,* and the system writes back: *You have a wrong conception of your position. Room A is outside room B.*

The verb paradigm of transport and location[1], used by the library staff as a part of the metaphor for their system, gives further ideas for formal meanings.

In non-metaphorical usage, *go* and *come* differ in the orientation of the movement in relation to a point of reference, often the place of speaking. Although both verbs signify a movement from an initial to a final position, they differ in that with *go,* the default initial position is identical to the point of reference, often the place of speaking, whereas with *come,* the point of reference is the default value of the final position. *He goes* can mean "He removes himself from the place of speaking".

A point of reference meaning "here", where I place the objects I work on, might be a good idea to include in the system. To issue the command *come* to an object would move it inside the workspace, and *go* would throw it out into the outer darkness.

Differences between formal and real meaning

However, a formal meaning is no prerequisite for including words in the command language, since their real meaning may help users to maintain the metaphor, so although the purpose is to assign a formal variant to some of the words of our corpus, the principles for doing this are by no means clear.

Designers of many programming languages, like Pascal and LISP, seem to prefer that each real meaning distinction has a formal correspondent. This amounts to a principle saying that *the content form of the real and formal meaning variants should be identical.*

The advantage is that most distinctions carry a formal meaning, making the language simple and terse. The draw-back is that the texts may be difficult to read for a human reader, since they can only to a limited degree be organized from his point of view.

Other languages give the user the opportunity to choose between expressions that are formally synonymous but whose real meanings are different.

---

[1] *komme (come), flytte (move), bære (carry), hente (fetch), køre (run,drive), gå (go), lægge (place), sidde (sit), ligge (lie), befinde sig (be located).*

The Hypercard system marketed by Apple is a good example. Hypercard is a programming environment intended for non-professional users; it has become popular because it provides many and good built-in tools for designing interfaces, and its own interface allows novices to build applications that at least look impressive. Its programming language, Hypertalk, is closer to English than other programming languages, and one consequence of this is that the same formal meaning can have several synonyms. The user can then choose the term that has the appropriate real meaning.

For example, equality can be denoted either = or *is*. Although the expressions *A = empty* and *A is empty* are formally synonymous, = and *is* have different real meanings, = denoting equality and *is* denoting either attribution or identity. In this case, distinctions in the real meaning are canceled in their formal variants and thus form a *synchretism* (on the concept of synchretism, see the discussion in Section I.1.3).

Although the possibility of writing *A is empty* instead of *A = empty* connotes a real meaning that makes it easier to interpret the program, it can be difficult for the user to remember which expressions are synonymous and which not.

As mentioned above, synchretisms such as the above are usual in metaphorical usage. For example, in the spatial world, there is a speed difference between *go* and *run*, but this difference has disappeared in the world of data processing, where they both mean "start a program's execution". *Run* is not faster than *go*, and thus they are mere variants.

Searching the morphological material of corpus for good ideas

I have now given examples from the domain of lexical paradigms, but morphological paradigms can also provide a basis for design choices, as the next examples will show.

Most languages offer *mood* choices between declarative, interrogative, and imperative mood. A simple analysis of a mood system was given in "Systemic Nets" in Section I.2.1. In the corpus, most sentences are declarative. The user obviously talks to us *about* the work - she tells us about what *she or we do*, whereas I have chosen imperative mood with empty subject in the command language, since I want to create the illusion that the user moves a thing or person around in space by commanding them to move. Compared to the corpus, the command language is defective, since it lacks two of the three members of the mood paradigm.

Normally, command languages are imperative, and this means that the subject is left out and that the user addresses the system and tells it what it must do. But if more persons are working together, it may be important to be able to distinguish between different subjects in the command language: I am doing this, and you are doing this. Even if it is hard to notice, we do have a mood choice: a request to the computer about what it should do *versus* a description of who is doing what with the computer now.

A similar choice is known from recent developments in programming languages, where traditional imperative languages such as Pascal have been supplemented with declarative languages like Prolog. The idea is that the user should only need to state the problem, not specify the exact algorithmic steps that solve it.

Besides the mood system, the corpus contains a *tense* system with a present and a past tense. The tense system has a time interpretation, but can also express other semantic dimensions, e.g. the difference between the actual and the potential.

Most verbs in our corpus are in the present tense, but there are two examples of *kunne(could)* in the past tense and their meaning is not temporal but potential: *jeg kunne lægge nogen magnetbånd ind på systemet (I could place some magnetic tapes on the system).* In the commands, tense is not used, since I have chosen imperative mood, and imperatives cannot be tensed, but one possibility would be to use past or perfect tense in questions about commands that have just been executed: *Where was I before* or *Have I come into the circulation control system?*

The next function to consider is *modality*. Again, although many sentences in the corpus are modalized, modality is not exploited in the interface.

The main modality distinction in the corpus is between what it is possible to do (weak commitment, expressed by the Danish verb *kunne(could, might))* and what I intend to do (strong commitment, expressed by the verb *skulle (should, must[1]))*. In the command language, weak modality may be exploited in advanced "undo"-facilities that make it possible to check if an operation is possible or feasible without committing oneself to doing it, e.g. because it might have undesirable irrevocable consequences.

I.2.4.2. Comparing interface and work language

In the preceding section, the design strategies were described in close relation to the computer-based register. One of its two sign systems, the interface, was designed and evaluated in relation to the other, the work register. Design methods of this type presuppose methods for comparing two sign systems and for assessing their mutual compatibility, some of which will be presented in the following.

---

[1] The translations are only approximate, the Danish and English modality systems being rather different.

I shall only present concepts for the relations between interface and work register that are theoretically motivated in the glossematic conception of signs used in this book although I know that much more can be said on the subject. However, my intention is not to be exhaustive, but to explore the descriptive power of the theory.

As mentioned in Section I.2.1, the glossematic sign is described along two orthogonal dimensions[1]: in the first dimension, the *manifestation* dimension, we distinguish between form and substance, and in the second one, the *semiotic* dimension, between content and expression:

Semiotic relation

	Content Form	Expression Form
Manifestation relation	Content Substance	Expression Substance

Fig. I.2.32. Sign dimensions.

If we have two signs or collections of signs we want to compare, not all comparisons make sense. The signs must be compared along the same dimensions.

The manifestation dimension

In this dimension, we investigate how the same expression or content forms are manifested in different substances; both expression and content plane are important in describing a computer-based register. In the former case we are interested in whether the screen expressions are actually adopted into the users' language or whether they are only manifested on the screen. The latter case may be the more interesting of the two, since computer-based signs often have two meaning variants, the formal and the real one, and, as illustrated in the two small design exercises, an important aspect of design is simply to create new formal or real variants. Thus, a complete account of a particular sign's role in the register requires a 2X2 matrix (Fig. I.2.33.).

A complete integration of interface and work register requires all four variant types to occur. The sign occurs both on screen and in language, and it is used for denoting both computational and non-computational processes. In the 1986-Postal Giro project, we collected data on an emerging computer-based register, and in the following I give a few specimens of signs as they

---

[1] Hjelmslev 1954 (1971: 53) speaks of two relations, the *semiotic* relation between content and expression, and the *manifestation* relation between form and substance.

appeared in our tape recordings. The task is the data entry process described in Section I.2.2. A more detailed treatment is given in Part III.

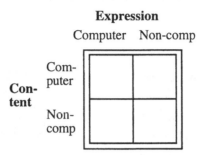

Expression
Computer
Non-comp
Content
Com-puter
Non-comp

Fig. I.2.33. Manifestation variants.

The first is *hämta*[fetch], which occurred in contexts like the following:

"Fetch dok"[on screen about data operation], the zeros can fetch missiv [a special kind of documents] for the new technology - well, now I have to go and fetch somebody - now I have to go to fetch the C-slips [verbal, about physical action] - I could have fetched too [verbal, about data operation]

Expression
Computer
Non-comp
Content
Com-puter
Non-comp

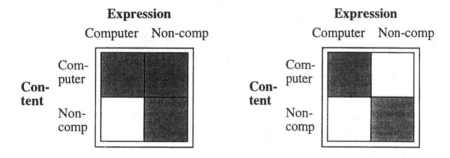

Fig. I.2.34. Integrated computer based sign.

Expression
Computer
Non-comp
Content
Com-puter
Non-comp

Fig. I.2.35. Non-integrated computer based signs.

The command "Hämta Dok" is an operation that moves a record from the common disc to the work station, and in verbal language, *hämta* denotes "fetching" both paper cards and their electronic representation, as well as getting hold of persons. The word comes close to full integration (Fig. I.2.34).

In other cases, the work register used other words than proposed by the designers. The screen calls the work process *produktion* [production], while the work language designation is *registrering* [registering] (Fig. I.2.35.).

However, the structure is not always so simple, and we recorded some examples of the phenomenon of *participation*, a variant configuration where one term can cover the whole substance while the other can cover only a part, and a quite common structure in natural language.

For example, the work register had two words denoting search, *leta* [look for] and *söka* [search].

Söka can only be used about searching in the system, while *leta* can also denote searching through paper cards. The restricted use of *söka* is probably due to the command "Sök Dok" that searches a file for a document with particular account numbers or amounts. Fig. I.2.36 shows the structure typical of participation.

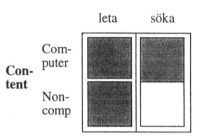

Fig. I.2.36. Participation.

As noted, the phenomenon is common, and the pronoun system before feminism gives a good example of this. In those days, the masculine pronoun could cover the whole field of both genders, whereas the female pronoun is used only for the female gender. As the example shows, variant structure can be ideologically important since it is a symptom of a particular world view. In the pronominal system, the male case was seen as the unmarked case, male representing the totality of mankind, whereas language treated the female case as the marked one - a special instance. In addition, the pronouns exemplify the phenomenon of *insistence*. It turns out that although *he* sometimes covers the whole field, sometimes only the male part, in every variation *he* must cover the male field, and therefore is said to *insist* on this field. I denote the place insisted upon by a bold line.

The phenomena of participation and insistence can also be used as indicators of dominance in a computer-based register: is the computer seen as the dominating unmarked case and non-computer items as the special instance, or is it the other way around? In my own language, the computer seems to have gotten the upper hand in my usage of the word *document*. I can use it about about data (open a document) or in a general way about texts without distinguishing between paper and data (a long document), but not about the paper version alone, which I have to call *paper document* or *printout*.

Besides being an indicator of a particular point of view, the concept of insistence can be used to describe metaphors which have become increasingly important in the design of computer systems. In both design exercises I used a metaphor to present the system. In the first case, I first made a formal specification and afterwards developed a metaphor for presenting it to the users, while in the latter case I started in an existing user metaphor, and extracted formal meanings from it. One successful type of operative system, the desktop type invented by Xerox for the Xerox Star machine[1] and later adopted by Apple (Macintosh) and Commodore (Amiga), consciously presents the file system as a desktop littered with documents and folders.

Apart from being usable in constructing the product, metaphors can also be employed in the design process as a technique for getting new ideas by viewing the subject matter as something else[2].

Metaphorical usage consists in moving a content form to a new substance which it has not been used to articulate before, while still keeping the old substance in mind. The new substance is the metaphorical meaning, the old one the literal meaning. Metaphorical usage is a common and important source of language innovations. When new objects or situations appear, people use known situations as a metaphor for the new ones in order to use old experience to cope with the new, as when conversations are used as a metaphor for understanding the situation of using a computer. Like two people talking, user and system can ask and answer questions and request actions of each other. In other cases, metaphors are used to see a (partially) known phenomenon in a new way. This is not uncommon in scientific research (a famous example is Bohr's model of the atom, which uses the planetary system as a metaphor) but also occurs in everyday language, where for example financial transactions (investing one's feelings) or warfare terminology (siege and conquer someone) has served as (somewhat misleading) metaphors for emotional relations.

Language is full of dead metaphors, sediments of past endeavors of language users to cope with new situations by using conceptual structures known to be useful in old and familiar ones.

Often metaphorical usage momentarily cancels distinctions that belong to the linguistic schema, creating a transient linguistic break-down, and it is mostly this kind of metaphors that are treated in classical rhetorics. For example, abstract concepts presented as living persons (Thou blind *fool, love,* what dost thou to mine eyes[3]) exemplifies the rhetorical figure of personification, and animation, the preferred rhetorical device of romanticism, cancels the distinction between animate and non-animates (Now, ere the *sun* advance his burning *eye*[4]).

In the present framework, I define a metaphorical usage as one in which a content form is manifested in two meanings[5] at the same time (the literal and

---

[1] Smith et al 1983.

[2] Halskov Madsen 1988.

[3] W. Shakespeare: Sonnet 137.

[4] W. Shakespeare: Romeo and Juliet, Act II, Scene III.

[5] I use meaning here as synonymous with content substance, a slight departure from Hjelmslev's terminology.

the metaphorical meaning). The meanings are normally kept apart in the linguistic schema, and the metaphor insists on the literal meaning. Another way of putting the same idea is that the metaphorical meaning presupposes the literal one.

The system introduced at the Postal Giro consciously uses "old Giro words" to denote system parts. A good example is the word *låda* [box]. It has a literal meaning both before and after computerization, namely grey plastic boxes used to transport finished paper cards away from the accounting department. With the system, it also came to denote the electronic file containing the cards in a plastic box. Thus, paper was used as a metaphor for the computer medium, a very common metaphor that makes technological change easier to handle for the employees by presenting the system in analogy with the well-known paper.

Although *låda* works as a real metaphor initially, like other metaphors it is bound to die, since the sign sooner or later stops insisting on its literal sense and just ends up with two separate content variants. Graphically this life cycle can be illustrated as follows:

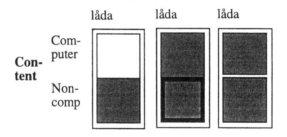

Fig. I.2.37. Death of a metaphor.

In the beginning, the substance is articulated into two parts, computer and non-computer (=paper), and *låda* can only occupy the paper position (the grey part).

Next, metaphorical usage brings momentary disorder in the system, since now the word can both be applied to the paper alone (the area marked with a bold line, the literal usage) and paper and computer at the same time (the grey area, the metaphorical usage). Finally, the word acquires two different variants of meaning, one referring to paper, the other to the computer, that no longer exist simultaneously: in one context one is chosen, in another the other. The paradigm is re-established, the both-and relation relapsing into an either-or relation. The metaphor dies. The net effect of the process is to add formal meaning variants to words that previously had only a real meaning. In this way it contributes to creating a homogeneous computer-based register.

It is by no means clear what computer-based registers should look like, but one idea that has been tacitly assumed in the preceding is that there should be one! Thus a general piece of design advice would simply read: *Design interfaces that make it possible for the users to create at least one computer-based register!*

The interface and work language should belong to the same semiotic schema, and not to two separate ones. Work with computers should employ concepts that are compatible with those used in other aspects of the work situation, so that screen work and other tasks are interpreted as parts of the same work situation.

The opposite situation would be one in which the simplest description of the interface and work language consists of two independent schemas, so that the user interprets the work situation as divided into two sub-situations, screen work and other work, with little in common.

My proposal has the merit of relating directly to the theoretically basic question about the identity of a given language, thereby placing the practical construction of interfaces in an interesting theoretical context. The proposal does not give any constructive advice on how to proceed, but it offers the whole arsenal of linguistic methodology for analyzing a use situation where the interface is used in practice in order to determine whether the goal has been attained. I do not regard this as a flaw but rather as a consequence of one of the basic properties of human languages: they cannot be designed and their development is difficult to predict. However, after the change has occurred it is possible to give a systematical account of what has happened and educated guesses about why. In this context, interface design must be conducted as a trial-and-error process, where proposals are designed, used, and evaluated iteratively.

The recommendation of Smith et al. 1983 to use so-called universal commands

> Star has a few commands that can be used throughout the system: MOVE, COPY, SHOW PROPERTIES, COPY PROPERTIES, AGAIN, UNDO AND HELP. Each performs the same way regardless of the type of object selected. Thus we call them "universal" or "generic" commands.   *D.C. Smith et al. 1983: 307*

can be interpreted as an implicit recommendation to create a coherent computer-based register by not introducing distinctions into an interface that only have meaning in the formal, but not the real meaning variant. If copying texts, paper, tables, movies, and program modules have the same designation in work language and the same function in work, then the interface should also present the tasks as the same, even if the implementations may be widely different.

It is worth noticing that I do not say that the work language and the interface, considered separately, should be similar or identical. What I am saying is that if they are put together then the simplest way of describing this composition is to set up one semiotic schema, the computer-based register.

This means that it is quite possible for the interface to be completely different from the work language considered in isolation, and still be able to constitute a homogeneous computer-based register when combined with a work language. The easiest way to illustrate this is to apply the commutation test to the verbal means of expression in an interface. Although the file command *close* at first glance looks as if it is composed of five graphemes, c l o s e, as long as we restrict our attention to the system, the commutation test will not allow such an analysis. Suppose for example that we want to prove that *s* is a grapheme. This is true if exchanging *s* with e.g. *n* produces a meaning difference, viz. if *close* means something different from *clone*. The problem is that this word does not occur in the interface, and so the commutation test fails. However, in English, where the word comes from, the test will give positive results since *clone* is an English word different from *close* and thereby establishes *s* and *n* as two different graphemes in English.

The commutation test reveals to us that although these verbal signs resemble normal verbal signs, they are in fact different. The graphical shape *close* should probably be analyzed as one whole form, and the individual letters should be considered variants, not invariants as in English. Thus, considered separately, the interface and the register of English that surrounds it are completely different semiotic systems. The interface has only a superficial resemblance to English, but note that if we plug this interface into an office, and consider the composite computer-based register, then with respect to spelling they form one homogeneous schema, since the computer-based sign happens to follow the same graphotactical schema as English. This is the case *precisely because the interface was parasitic upon the system of English spelling*.

The lesson to be learned is that interfaces should not be thought of as *being* a language, but as being able to *fit into* an already existing language. It is easy to come up with one or two letter command languages that do not obey this rule, using combinations like GT, EQ, LT that violate all word formation rules and which therefore may only exist on screen and never enter the work register. Although abbreviations like these are useful devices, I think that designers should use them cautiously. Remember that workers not only work, they also need to talk about their work, and in the particular case of computer systems, designing the tool is also designing the conditions for talking about it. Although the ESC button on the work stations at the Postal Giro can be pronounced in Swedish and therefore is adopted as a verb in the work register (*eska*) this verb is not particularly well suited for telling inter-esting things about work.

It is important to note that our maxim does not require the interface to adapt to an immobile work language, it only asserts that the result of the *in-teraction* of interface and work language should be one computer-based register. The interface may very well be intended as an opportunity for changing the work register, and this is relevant to the choice of metaphor. Suppose we have made a system in which one office sends data to another via a local network. Since the receiving office may sometimes use its machine for other purposes than receiving, it wants a facility for advising the senders that they may not send data at the moment.

One metaphor would be to describe the network as water pipes with valves that can be closed and opened, and this was in fact done in the Postal Giro system. The valve was called *data valve (datakomb ventil)*, and opera-tions for opening and closing it were defined. The metaphor was adopted by the users who would use expressions like *sända (iväg) lådan, lådan går iväg* [send the box, the box leaves] and use the valve and pipe metaphor to explain malfunction *dom har ingen kontakt, den tar inte emot, du får ut den på linjen* [they have no contact, it doesn't receive, you get it out on the line], and wonder what happens to the boxes if they are sent but not receiv-ed - do they remain in the valves?

Now, although the concepts of valves and pipes are used in other situa-tions users know of, they are not used in the working situation of the office, and will therefore only be used about the system's behavior, contrary to our intention.

Instead we should choose concepts that are useful for understanding phe-nomena that are relevant to the working situation. Since data exchange is probably a symptom of some kind of cooperation between the two offices, and since this cooperation is a real and important part of the work (which in addition may not be transparent to the workers, if the organization is built upon a strong division of labor), the designer should use this aspect of the working situation as a metaphor, for example describing the nonavailability of data exchange as due to the fact that the receiving machine is a shared re-source that colleagues have occupied at the moment. From this point of view, interface concepts should be chosen according to the following prin-ciples:

- does the existing work language already have concepts that could be given a formal variant?

- if not, we should choose concepts that are able to acquire a real meaning, viz. be useful for understanding phenomena outside the computer, as well.

The semiotic dimension

Whereas the manifestation dimension concerns the meaning variants of signs and the media in which they are used, the semiotic dimension can be used to describe differences of form - which I believe to be the most important.

The first thing to note is that although meaning distinctions can appear or disappear when signs travel from one content substance to another, the simplest description can very well be one in which we keep the same form and describe the differences as contextually bound variants. In the *go/run* example above the speed difference that separates them in their literal meaning is canceled when they are transferred to computational processes and they become synonymous.

The Hypercard example *is* vs *equals* is also of this type. The diagram illustrates how the content form of *is* and *equals* introduces a distinction in non-computer matters, namely that between attribution and identity, which is canceled in the substance of computational processes.

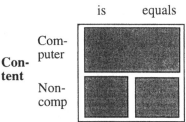

Fig. I.2.38. Synchretism.

This is an example of the synchretism we meet when real meanings are given a formal counterpart, cf. above. Another type of difference of form is the case where members of a paradigm are simply missing under certain circumstances. The *defective* mood paradigm of command languages that only allows imperative is a good example.

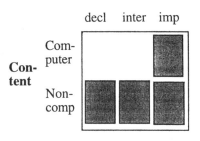

Fig. I.2.39. Defective paradigm.

In both types of cases, the idea of one form that undergoes contextually conditioned modifications gives a simple description of the relevant facts, but it is not difficult to find examples where we have to stipulate two different forms, one for the interface and one for the work register. These cases are symptoms of more deep-seated differences between the two symbol systems that may prevent a common computer-based register from being formed, since they reflect basic differences in outlook.

The PGP-system at the Postal Giro provides a good example. The interface of the system divides the work process into two main parts, *komplettering* [completing, entering data], and *avstämning* [checking off, balancing].

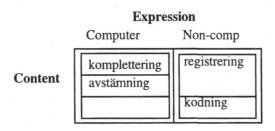

Expression

Computer   Non-comp

Content   komplettering   registrering

avstämning

kodning

Fig. I.2.40. Different content forms.

In the first part, the workers enter missing data into the system, whereas in the second part they correct the data entered.

However, the workers themselves do not classify their work by means of logical properties like these, but use time and location as distinctive features. Work at the work stations is called *registrering* [registering data] and on the one hand contrasts to work at the old mechanical coding machines, called *kodning* [coding], on the other hand to work at the optical reader, called *stå* or *köra* [stand or run]. In this case, the very principles for structuring paradigms seem to be different, and the interface terms cannot be described as variants of the work language terms. They belong to two different linguistic schemas.

It is obviously useful for us to know whether a set of terms we want to use in the interface conform to the linguistic schema of the work register or whether they constitute a different semiotic schema. This issue can be described in terms of the traditional notion of *accidental gaps*. Accidental gaps are signs or sign combinations that do not occur in a given language, but conform to its linguistic schema. There are no structural reasons for the absence of the signs - it just happens that nobody has needed them yet.

In a children's book by the Swedish author Astrid Lindgren, the heroine called Pippi Longstocking invents a new word called *spunk*, which she assigns her own private meaning. The word conforms to the phonotactical rules of Swedish, so although nobody has used it before, it is just an accidental gap, and Pippi Longstocking and her playmates have no difficulty in using it. However, if Pippi had proposed a new word like *vlk* (which means *wolf* in Czech), her success as a linguistic innovator would have been limited since this word is not an accidental gap in Swedish but violates a basic rule for syllable structure, namely that a syllable must contain one vowel.

The design lesson to be learned from Pippi is to try to exploit accidental gaps in the work register. However, the principle should be applied differently to the two planes of the sign, since, if the code is graphical, it does not make sense to use it on the expression plane, although it may still be a useful guide for interpreting the content plane.

Example: the Macintosh way of throwing documents away is to press the mouse while the cursor is on the document, moving the mouse to the waste basket icon, and then releasing the mouse button. The meaning of this action can be paraphrased as *throwing away the document* or *moving the document into the waste basket.* The expression plane of the sign is composed of at least three distinct expression units which we can call *MouseDown, MouseMove,* and *MouseUp.* In addition, the location of the cursor is an invariant element, since it must be placed on the document icon when the mouse is pressed down, and on the waste basket icon when it is released. A preliminary analysis of the expression plane of the sign will decompose it into three sequential parts, the first part consisting of a simultaneous occurrence of a MouseDown on the document, the second one of movement of mouse, and the third part of a MouseUp action on the waste basket:

Graphical expression:
MouseDown+document icon/ MouseMove/
MouseUp + waste basket icon

This structure is completely different from the phonological structure of the spoken description of the event which in my language would be "Throw away the document".

The spoken version is structured in words and syllables, and contains units like stress, tones, and phonemes. The schema behind the utterance is the English phonological schema containing combinatorial rules for e.g. stress (primary stress is presupposed by secondary stress) and phonemes (vowels are presupposed by consonants).

There is also a schema behind the graphical interface, but the units and functions have of course nothing whatsoever to do with English phonology, which is illustrated by the following specimens of "phonological rules" for the Macintosh graphical interface:

- The units MouseUp and MouseDown form an interdependence, since neither can occur without the other.
- Although the two elements can be separated by a MouseMove in a drag action (MouseDown + MouseMove + MouseUp), it is normally

possible to describe them as bound variants of one invariant, namely the Click. Dragging will then contain two "phonemes", Click + MouseMove.

- The Click itself can either occur alone or together with another Click in a construction called DoubleClick.

However, since expression and content plane are not necessarily isomorphic, the contents of the two signs can perfectly well belong to the same semiotic schema, and in fact do so here and in many other graphical interfaces that distinguish between actions and objects and assign the objects to cases very much like those found in language, as illustrated in the following analysis.

The content plane of our graphical sign can be analyzed as three units, an action (move), an object (document) and a direction (waste basket).

Graphical content:
Action: move/ Object: document/ Direction: waste basket

Although my verbal paraphrase, *throwing away the document,* uses a more compact synthetical phrasing, with another verb (throw) and directional case (away), and adds morphological inflexions like mood, number, and definiteness,

Verbal content
Action:throw+imperative/ Object: document+definite+singular/ Direction: away

the categories are sufficiently similar to belong to the same schema. The contents of the computer-based sign are a subset of the verbal sign.

Let me conclude this section with additional examples from a concrete system, namely the mail system Intermail.

The content of its interface is different from my work register in at least one respect. When I read my morning mail, the distinction between *read whole text* and *read heading* is important, because it helps me to avoid being drowned in the flood of official administrative garbage I receive. However, this paradigm does not exist in the interface, although it is relevant to me when the sender has appended a file to his letter. In this case, I interpret the letter as a heading, and the file as the "whole text" that I may not want to read.

Reading the heading is expressed by doubleclicking a letter in the list of letters, giving me the screen in Fig. I.2.41.

The menu in the bottom allows me to reply (besvara), send a copy to someone (kopia till), print (skriv ut), save (spara text), and remove (ta bort), but there is no sign for *reading the whole text*, so if I want to read the appended file, I must first press the *file*-button whereupon the system invites me to *save* the text.

Fig. I.2.41. Different content forms.

After pressing a *save* button, and *closing* the mail system, the file is now located on my desktop, and at last I can *open* and *read* the text.

My two-member paradigm of ways of reading text does not exist in Intermail, since I have to pick out four operations from four different paradigms in order to express the content *read whole text*.

The reason for this difference is that the designers of Intermail have seen my activity in a different way than I do. They are not concerned about reading or not reading whole texts, only with reading letters, and to them, my "whole text" is an appended file, and their only responsibility is to enable me to store it. Reading it is outside their universe, since it consists in running another product than theirs, namely the word processor in which the file is written.

This discrepancy between the interface and my work register could easily be remedied by exchanging the *file* button for one named *Whole document* that would launch the word processing program belonging to the document, allow me to use it, and return control to the mail system when I quit the program.

I.2.4.3. Design as language politics

The setting in which interface design should be understood is not merely a matter of semiotic technicalities, but also of language politics, as has rightly been stressed by Kristen Nygaard[1], who points out that many professions lack a suitable vocabulary for discussing information technology:

Much of a profession's culture and world view is reflected in its language. People are to an important extent socialized into their professions by learning its language through education and practical work.

The professions' languages have always been reflecting changing technologies and social structures by changes in these languages. In fact, a stagnant professional language may in our technology oriented societies imply a stagnant and dying profession.

The invasion of information systems in a large number of professions today is, however, taking place with a rapidity, commercial thrust and restructuring force which should cause serious concerns with these professions. *Nygaard 1984: 5*

He submits the following proposal:

(1) A careful examination of a profession's language followed by *the extension of that language by a POL[2] built upon generally applicable concepts* for understanding and relating to information processing (independent of any particular software package, programming language or any commercial organization).

(2) *The introduction of this POL in the education of the profession's members,* and the description of the various software products in terms of the POL. This should lead us to the use of the terms and concept of the POL in the design and presentation of the new systems developed by the suppliers in the software market. (The italics are mine.)

Although I agree with his description of the problem, I am skeptical about the solution, since in Nygaard's formulation (my italics), a professional language seems to be modifiable in nearly the same way as we change a programming language, and since it is not clear *who* chooses the concepts relating to information processing, *how* it is done, and what *actions* the concepts are to be used for.

We have already seen that computer systems and linguistic schemata are different precisely with respect to their mode of development. Computer systems can be manipulated since they are *physical* facts, but the schema underlying a human language cannot be constructed and modified directly since it is a *social* fact, consisting of regularities of language used by speakers, and mainly develops when changes of *concrete* elements of language use engender changes of the system.

---

[1] Nygaard 1984. This section owes many ideas to discussions in working group 2 of the Scandinavian SYDPOL project.

[2] P(*rofession*) O(*riented*) L(*anguage*).

In Section I.1, I argued that professional languages are deeply dependent upon the working context, which among other items contains computer systems. If the concepts of education are at cross purposes with the concepts presented by the systems of the working context, the latter will win. Therefore, I believe that the problem Nygaard raises should be reframed from being a question of language development to being a matter of design principles: interface design is language politics, since designing interfaces is to influence professional languages.

I agree with Nygaard that users need new concepts, both in order to gain influence on the technological politics of their work place, to participate in systems development, and to tailor their system according to their needs. But I am not sure that the concepts of computer science are the right ones to use, and I doubt if anyone is able to come up with a set that is obviously well suited.

I think that the necessary concepts, whatever they may turn out to be, should do what concepts usually do, namely evolve from practice, and the first step in a language politics of interface design could be to remove some of the existing obstacles for this. One such obstacle is that designers of systems normally do not construct the systems in a way that permits the user to learn how they work, this being of no concern to the users. Most systems do not create knowledge that can be used for modifying them, since the contents of the object-signs (the program execution) and the meta-sign (the program text) used to change the object signs are so different that one has to learn a completely new language and acquire new skills in order to modify the program. Apart from making it difficult for users to generalize their work experience into being useful for more general purposes, this is also a practical problem, since it prevents small-scale tailoring of the systems.

In my view, this situation is not a natural law, but only a symptom of a historical schism between system executions and system descriptions, deriving from organizational rather than technical[1] reasons and mirroring a traditional division of labor between planning and operative functions. The following guide-line might be a good point of departure for changing this state of affairs: *Experiences gained from using the system should be applicable for modifying and changing it*[2].

Besides helping to accumulate knowledge about technology, systems designed according to this principle will also be commercially interesting, since they make it easier for users to expand their repertoire of actions through using the system, enabling them to tailor and redesign larger and larger parts

---

[1] Andersen & Nielsby 1981.
[2] Andersen & Kjær 1982: 332.

of it. However, such systems require a radical rethinking of what a computer system is.

One possibility is to use the same content form for object- (system processes) and meta-sign (system description) - only the purport articulated would be different. The object sign denotes work processes and work objects, the meta-sign program executions, and concepts from the application area are used as a metaphor for understanding the technical properties of the system. Thus, the workings of a library system should be described like the working of a library, the workings of a control room system as a control room.

Although this strategy should be tried out, I believe that the metaphorical concepts are bound to break down. After all, they did not evolve to support technical work on computer systems, and I believe there to be good reasons why the professional language of computer science differs from other registers.

The second solution would be to retain a difference between object- and meta-signs, but constructing the system in levels, so that it is possible to move gradually from using to developing systems. This is the strategy of the Hypercard system, which contains five levels: *browsing* (reading), *typing* (writing text into card fields), *painting* (modifying the background of cards), *authoring* (building new systems by reusing old ones and a set of simple operations), and *scripting* (building new systems by programming).

The real meaning of the system is a stack of cards, and on the first levels, this meaning dominates. The system can be understood as a *stack* of *cards*, each card containing writeable *fields* and *buttons* that can be pushed. For example, on the typing level, the user needs to know the concepts stack, card, button and field. Besides pushing buttons, he can only read and write in the fields. At this level, his semiotic schema may look like this:

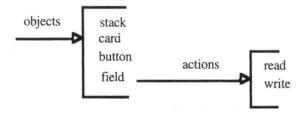

Fig. I.2.42. Semiotic schema at browsing level.

In ascending from browsing to scripting, the concepts of the user are gradually changed. As he progresses towards the script level, three things happen:

- the old paradigms acquire new members
- new paradigms are added
- the syntagmatic restrictions are loosened, so that actions are generalized to apply to more objects.

and the real meaning slowly gives way to a formal meaning. A fragment of the final semiotic schema may look like this:

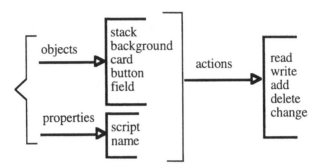

Fig. I.2.43. Semiotic schema at scripting level.

We see that the object paradigm has acquired a new member, the *background*. A new paradigm named *properties* has appeared, and the action paradigm has three new members, *add*, *delete* and *change*. Furthermore, it is now possible to perform actions on all members of the two paradigms, whereas reading and writing could previously only be done to one member, the field. These processes mean that the content form of the words changes, since - as we should remember - it is identical to the functions it contracts with other words. For example, at the typing level, the content of *card* is very much like that of an ordinary paper card, being readable and writeable. At the scripting level, the card concept has turned into the informatic *object* concept, since it contains properties that can be changed and a script that specifies processes it can perform.

Apart from taking pains to facilitate the shift from a real to a formal meaning, designers should also in other ways change their view of what a computer system is. According to Floyd 1986, they must stop viewing the purpose of software development as producing a single system, one that is basically stable but may need some maintenance, and instead apply the following perspective:

Software development aims at a sequence of related versions of a software system. "Maintenance" is rejected as meaningless in connection with software. The tasks associated with maintenance are mapped onto the development of versions.

Floyd 1986: 201

In this view, what the user buys is akin to a house built of Lego toy bricks: the house can immediately be used for some purpose, but it clearly shows how it is constructed, can be torn apart, and easily be used for new buildings, since the rules for putting the bricks together are simple. There will be no formal specifications of such systems, since their mode of operation will be more easily understood by a historical narrative recording how and why it was rebuilt.

I.2.5. Computers as media

This concluding section summarizes some of the points made in the preceding sections, and assigns the computer a particular role in communicative processes, namely that of a medium comparable to books, films, theaters, telephones, letters, and sound.

In Section I.2.2.4, I defined communication in the following way:

- *Communication* is a presupposition from an act or set of acts, whether symbolic or non-symbolic, to a symbolic act or object, based on a semiotic schema,

senders of communication being the person or persons that are presupposed by the symbolic acts or object, receivers being persons whose acts or utterances presuppose the symbols. In Section I.2.3.3, a strict functional analysis indicated that computers could not (yet) be said to possess anything analogous to a human language and consequently could neither be sender nor receiver of communication. Rather, the designers of the system should play these roles. Therefore, the communication model of user-computer interaction[1] where the computer acts as a communication partner may be a good metaphor, but it cannot be used as a basis for a more systematic understanding of computer systems.

Now, since computer-human interaction clearly involves communication and employs signs, an application of the maxim of Sherlock Holmes, "when the impossible is eliminated, what remains, however improbable, is the truth", results in assigning the role of medium to the computer system.

In some kinds of applications, this role is unproblematic. For example, in mail applications many screen elements are clearly messages with a human sender that are transmitted to another human using the mail system as a channel. But even in such clear-cut cases the computer system features properties of its own. Not all the signs I see on the screen are messages sent

---

[1] See e.g. Gaines & Shaw 1984.

by me and my colleague: the screen also contains menus of buttons that neither of us has created. For example, in the Intermail screen, we find a menu with five members, whose communicative function is to open an action paradigm in much the same way as the boss did in Section I.2.2.4. In addition, we can see that somebody has taken pains to indicate this function to us. It is expressed by two elements, *style* and *rectangle form*, their style being *bold* as opposed to the *non-bold* style in the upper part of the screen, and their framing rectangle having *rounded* corners as opposed to the other *non-rounded* boxes. If we replace bold style with non-bold, the "button" meaning disappears, and since in this way we get positive results from the commutation test, the button is a sign type in the semiotic schema of the Intermail interface.

These signs are clearly made for communicative purposes, and the people that did it are the designers of the system, Nick Holt and Steve Ullman.

This observation can be generalized as a characteristic of computer-based signs: apart from the normal senders and receivers, a third party is always involved in computer-based communication, namely the designer. He or she sets the limits for communication and creates a stock of signs that users may activate but not produce themselves in the same sense as they produce words.

The actual sign usage, as expressed in the system processes, partly presupposes the users, partly presupposes the system structure, which again presupposes the designer.

According to the definition of a sender given above, the designer is a sender, but, except for help facilities, only indirectly, by creating the structure for processes in which the interface is manifested.

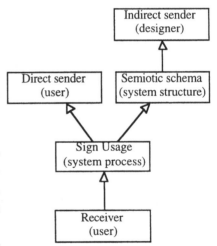

Fig. I.2.44. Functional analysis of the computer medium.

The diagram is easy to apply to a mail system like Intermail, but in fact can be taken as a general communication model for computer systems. Many systems in reality perform communicative functions, but since they were not conceived of as tools for communication by their designers, the communication is disguised or hidden. For example in a conventional transaction-oriented system, transactions typically draw on information provided by others and supply information to be used by others later.

Although a system may not be designed nor experienced as a medium, important properties can be revealed by applying the media perspective (Bøgh Andersen & Mathiassen 1984), and redesigning it as a channel of communication may give ideas for making the system work better. For example, it can be difficult to use information in a database since important parts of the context for interpretation are often missing, such as: *who* provided the piece of information, for what *purpose*, and *when*? Nurminen 1988, who notices the problems with implementing hidden or disguised communicative and cooperative processes, describes an ideal type of systems where only providers of information are allowed to use and change it without special permissions:

> the basic premise is that all the functions performed by the system (storing, processing and transmission of data) are carried out by human beings /.../ We further stipulate in this model that the actor /.../ must be a clearly specified individual; in this respect, a shared database or joint act of processing do not constitute meaningful concepts.   *Nurminen 1988: 125*

and Sandström 1985 proposes to make information about senders and receivers explicit in data bases.

When we have assigned the role of medium to a computer system, we have a sound theoretical basis for transferring methods for analyzing and creating other media products to computer science: literary analysis, picture analysis, dramaturgy, choreography, etc. These methods again require a change of point of view of the type recommended by Floyd 1987, from "The product-oriented perspective [that] regards software as a product standing on its own" and focuses on the internal components of the system and their relations, to a "process-oriented view [that] views software in connection with human learning and communication".

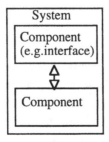

Fig. I.2.45. Object-oriented view of computers.

In the system concept described in Section I.2.3.2, the basic components of a system are objects that have certain properties and can perform certain actions on their own properties and properties of other objects (Fig. I.2.45).

This definition lies within the product-oriented paradigm, since it does not define objects in their relation to the use context. I will keep the notion of objects, since it is clearly useful in programming, but redefine it as a sign.

This means that the system objects are seen as the expression plane of signs whose content is generated in the work context.

Objects are no longer self-sufficient entities, but merely endpoints of functions between system and user, and the functions, not their functives, are the important concepts (Fig. I.2.46).

Therefore, we have to give traditional concepts a relational redefinition.

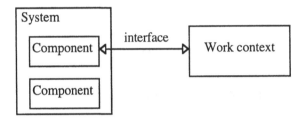

Fig. I.2.46. Media view of the computer.

We have already met some examples of this type. For example, the interface can no longer be viewed as a component of the system, but must be seen as a relation between system processes and the users' interpretation, and input and output viewed as data types must be replaced by the communicative functions they perform.

In the next sections of the book, more redefinitions of this kind are to come.

Furthermore, programming is no longer mainly seen as engineering, but rather as an activity of sign creation, comparable to writing, directing, or painting, whose goal is to create meanings.

Along with these general perspectives, I have sketched possible concrete uses of the concepts as they were introduced.

The three *glossematic functions* for example can describe the flexibility of the interface, *constellation* giving the most flexible kind.

The *case* concept has several applications; it can be used to discover saliency criteria in users' language which again may decide which items are made most prominent in the interface, and it can act as a guide for classifying and arranging interface items in graphical interfaces. Techniques for semantic analysis were given, and the distinction between *formal and real* meaning variants introduced. A couple of guidelines were offered, which all aimed at maintaining a coherent work language, for example to attribute formal meanings to words already existing in the work language, or - where this is not possible - to introduce new words that can be given a real meaning that is relevant to work and organization.

In the task domain, I used the concepts of *schema and usage* to introduced the distinction between *variant and invariant task structure*, and argued that designers should not only pay attention to the former, but also to the latter, cf. the "rooms" example.

The relationship between the semiotic schema and usage are different from that of their computer analogues, *system and process,* since usage of a language causes changes in its underlying schema whereas program executions normally do not change the program structure. Since the difference between the natural (language) and constructed (computer application) system is by no means ontological, I suggested that the computer concepts were made more similar to the semiotic ones, making it easier to make experiences from usage relevant for changing - or at least tailoring - the system structure.

However, all this has mostly been mere hints, and the next two parts of the book elaborate these and other ideas in more detail: how to apply the framework to analysis and design of computer system (Part II), and how to make analyses of the use context that are useful for designing and correcting computer systems (Part III).

PART II. COMPUTERS

Introduction

The first part of the book ended with a sketch of the computer system as a medium, and the purpose of this second part is to turn this sketch into a more detailed portrait. What are important properties of computer systems from this perspective, and how should systems be structured?

It should come as no surprise that the *interface*, defined in Section I.2.3.3 as a collection of computer-based signs, and its functions relative to the linguistic environment and working context reign supreme in this approach. The basic function of a system is to generate processes in which an interface can be expressed, just as the only reason for having the costumes and wings in a theater is the experience they may contribute to giving the audience. Although this view on design is relatively new in computer science, it exists under the name of *user centered design.*

This view makes it difficult to maintain the tradition of separating *functionality* from the interface. Traditionally, functionality is what can be done with the system, while the interface is the manner in which it is done. Thus, two word processors have different functionality if one allows the user to make an automatic table of contents while the other does not. They have the same interface if operations are done in the same way, for example if text is selected by dragging the mouse over the desired piece of text, whereas their interface is different if one uses the mouse while the other requires the user to type line and character numbers in to select text.

However, like Bødker 1987: 38 I find it impossible to maintain that distinction here, since aspects of the functionality contribute to the interpretation of the computer-based signs. Suppose for example that a pencil icon appears on my screen. If I can use the mouse to draw with the icon, I interpret it as some kind of tool, whereas I see it as a signpost if I cannot manipulate it but only interpret it as information meaning that I have write access to the file it appears with. This difference is clearly a difference in functionality, but since it determines my interpretation, it must be incorporated in my notion of interface.

However, not all aspects of functionality belong to the interface. For example, in a drawing program, there may be differences in the algorithms implementing the drawing actions of a pencil tool that make one algorithm more slow and inaccurate than another, but if these differences do not influence my classification of the actions, both being labeled *drawing*, they are not part of the interface, but only expression variants. However, we cannot say in advance that a particular part of the system structure is irrelevant to the interface, since this can only be ascertained by applying the commutation test when the system is used. For example, it may turn out that one algorithm for drawing is so slow that users interpret the slowness as a system error, and no longer regard themselves as "drawing".

Because of the supremacy of the interface and its functions regarding the work context, a good system structure is one that makes it easy for the designer to experiment with different effects for achieving a given communicative purpose, and makes visible the role of the different system parts in the creation of meaning.

However, this method of structuring systems is neither common, nor unproblematic. In fact, we have seen a quite different view of system architecture in I.2.3, where the computer system was viewed as a model of reality, a model system that somehow was supposed to be similar or correspond to its referent system. This view is not uncommon, being e.g. the basis of Jackson's System Development, a well-known system development method:

> JSD development starts ... by building a model of the real world which provides the subject matter of the system and in which it is imbedded. The model is a realization, in the computer, of an abstract description of the real world; in a sense, it is a simulation.
>
> The functions of the system are then added to the model. The system can produce a visible display of the state of the model (and hence of the state of the real world); it can produce outputs when particular circumstances occur, and these outputs can be used for information or for control purposes.   *Jackson 1983: 15*

The designer in this method is like a play writer that first describes the plot of the play without regard to its theatrical effects, and then later puts selected episodes on the stage.

The main argument in favor of this method is that the model is more stable than its communicative functions, and therefore the system is easier to maintain. However, precisely because the referent system is focused at the expense of the use context, the practical usefulness of the system can be endangered, and the product may turn out to be neither particularly economical nor very usable:

> ...In order to ensure that it will be a useful tool, it is necessary to pay much attention to the work in question. Since this work may be rather complex, focussing on the [referent system] and the [computer system] instead of the work, may not solve real problems.   *Håndlykken 1983: 103*

From my point of view, the designer should not see herself as a natural or social scientist describing real objects or persons. Instead she should compare herself to the more humble position of a play writer or stage director -

people that basically do not describe or create real persons or events, but only painted canvas, fake uniforms, and would-be dramas that the *audience* in lucky circumstances may use to create real emotions and insights. The system structure only specifies cardboard actors on the puppet theater of the computer screen.

In the following sections I shall explore this idea in greater detail[1].

---

[1] My examples include the following systems:

Large administrative text-based systems: here I use the PGP-system developed and implemented at the Postal Giro in Stockholm. The purpose of the part of the system I refer to is to support manual input of non-machine-readable data on paying-in forms, and correction of errors. Part III will describe the interplay between this system, work process and work language.

Single user, tool-like graphical systems: my examples are the advanced word processing program Word 3 (Microsoft Corporation, 1987), the Design program Design (Meta Software Corp., 1987), the painting program Fullpaint (Ann Arbor Software, 1986), and the database Fourth Dimension. I have chosen them because I use most of them in my daily work.

Programming environments: although I have used many programming environments myself, I have chosen Hypercard (Apple Computer, 1987) as my main example, not because it is typical, but because it can be seen as a practical implementation of some of the theoretical ideas of this book.

Games: I use a simple game, Breakout, as the general example. In addition, I shall take examples from my son Jeppe's large collection of professional games. Games are particularly relevant to interface design, because they are nothing but interface which then has to be good if the game is to sell at all.

II.1

The Basic Means of Expression

II.1.1. Computer-based signs

I start my investigation of computer-based signs from the viewpoint of the expression plane[1], partly because the computer's means of expression are different from other media, partly because the history of linguistics tells us that expression analysis is easier than content analysis. What are the characteristic features of computer-based signs, and in which respects do they differ from other kinds of signs we know?

II.1.1.1. Handling, transient, and permanent features

The prototypical computer-based sign is composed of three classes of features:

- A *handling feature* of a computer-based sign is produced by the user and includes key-press, mouse and joystick movements that cause electrical signals to be sent to the processor. Handling features articulate user actions.
- A *permanent feature* of a computer-based sign is generated by the computer. It is a property of the sign that remains constant throughout the lifetime of a sign token, serving to identify the sign by contrasting it to other signs. Permanent features articulate system states into parts.
- A *transient feature* of a computer-based sign is also generated by the computer, but unlike permanent features, it changes as the sign token is used. It does not contrast primarily to other signs, but only internally in the same sign, symbolizing the different states in which the sign referent can be. Transient features articulate system transformations.

As our first example, let us look at a version of the game *Breakout*.

The system displays a paddle, a ball and a brick wall. The ball bounces back and forth, and the player must hit it with the paddle. If the ball hits the

---

[1] In the following I draw mainly on Newman & Sproull 1973.

wall, a brick disappears. The game is won when the whole wall has disappeared:

Fig. II.1.1.The Breakout game, version 1.

Its *handling* features are very simple and consist in moving the mouse back and forth, causing the paddle to move down and up on the screen. Most professional games use the joystick, which can be moved in eight directions, and contain one or two buttons that can be pressed.

In Breakout and many action games, the handling features are like words in that they have a fixed meaning in the game. So when I move the mouse in Breakout, it *means* that I move the paddle (even though there is no paddle), and when I move the joystick forward in Fist II, it means that the Karate master delivers a blow.

However, in other applications the handling features are more like letters that have no or little meaning in themselves, but are used to spell signs with meaning. For example, the Macintosh handling system articulates the continuum of possible movements in three distinctive parts: press mouse, release mouse, move mouse. From these elements, composite units are built, e.g. *click = press + release* which often means "select", *double click = click + click* which means "open", and *drag = press + move + release* meaning "moving something".

But in general, there is a clear tendency to avoid completely arbitrary sign-functions in computer systems. They tend to have a closer relationship between expression and content than languages like English and Danish, and some authors recommend this as good design practice.

Whereas handling features articulate the movements of the user, the permanent and transient features are properties of the screen[1]. The former consists of patterns of pixels, the latter of changes of pixel patterns.

In the following I shall give a brief outline of the graphical facilities of the computer with an emphasis on how substance properties of the computer medium influence the expressive possibilities we have at our disposal, and consequently the computer-based signs we can create.

Permanent sign properties are known from paper, and transient ones from theater and film, but compared to these media, the screen has two important physical properties: it is discrete and manipulable.

Discrete

The smallest graphical elements of the screen are pixels, small spots of light that can be in one of a limited number of states. In black-white systems, the pixel can simply be on or off, while color screens offer a larger set of states.

Compared to paper, the discreteness of the screen severely limits the kind of *permanent* features that can be exploited.

The most obvious point is that there is a limit to how small graphical elements can be, and to how delicate lines can be. Furthermore, lines and curves will always have to be rough approximations to the geometrical shapes. As the illustration shows, a slanted line really consists of an arrangement of small horizontal lines.

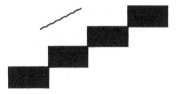

Fig. II.1.2. Screen displays are only approximations to geometrical shapes.

Also, discreteness makes it difficult to distinguish the graphical dimensions of shade and texture, since shade can only be represented as a particular pattern of pixels. The two greys shown opposite differ in both color and texture.

Fig. II.1.3. Shade and texture are difficult to distinguish.

---

[1] I disregard sound since systematic use of sound is so new that no fixed practice has been established yet.

Manipulable

Although discreteness creates limitations, it also opens up possibilities that
we do not have on paper, adding *transient* features to our repertoire of expressions. The pixels can be manipulated by a program, enabling the designer
to use changes of pixel patterns as a means of expression. Icons can move,
documents can open and close, text can appear or disappear.

The exact possibilities of manipulation depend upon the way in which the
graphical shapes are represented. There are essentially two ways of doing it,
the motivated representation and the arbitrary representation.

In the *motivated* representation, the screen pixels are represented by a so-
called *bitmap*. A bitmap is a part of the internal storage consisting of a collection of bits. In the simplest case, there is exactly one bit per pixel. If the bit
is 1, the corresponding pixel is on, if it is 0, the pixel is off. Thus there is a
one-to-one correspondence between the bitmap and the screen, while a
fixed routine continually refreshes and updates the screen so that it mirrors
the bitmap, and the screen is simply manipulated by manipulating the bitmap.

The *arbitrary* representation contains data describing the graphical
shapes. Special languages like Postscript has been developed for this purpose. The data are processed by drawing routines that produce the actual
image. In most modern systems, there is both arbitrary and motivated representation, since the drawing routines do not directly influence the cathode
tube rays, but manipulate the bitmap. The descriptive data need not have any
likeness to the final graphical shapes, since they are input to different drawing routines; from the programmer's point of view, the arbitrary representation is interpreted as a description of the motivated representation.

Let me give some examples, first a textual one:

(1)   **Kilroy** was *here*

The font of the text is geneva, its size is 13, the first word is boldface, and the
last italic. Suppose we want a representation that allows us to change both
font, size, and style.

```
001110
000110
000110
000110
000110
001111
```

(2). Fig. II.1.4. Homomorphic representation of an "l".

With a *homomorphic* representation of the "l" on the bitmap like (2), it will
be extremely difficult to write routines that treat the bitpattern as a "l". To

the machine, (2) is nothing but a jumble of bits, and identifying the "l" and changing the font from e.g. geneva to times or the size from 13 to 18 points, or making it italic, would require it to perform complex pattern recognition algorithms that will make the task so slow as to be impossible for all practical purposes.

Therefore, a text processing program will contain an *arbitrary* representation of the "l" written in a suitable notation, in which the relevant information is explicitly represented. (1) above could be represented as a string of characters, e.g.:

(3)   [s13 [g [b Kilroy]b was [i here]i]g]s13

where s13 = size13, g = geneva(font), b = bold, and i = italic, and additional drawing routines will take (3) as input and draw (1). All text manipulation is done on (3), e.g. replacing s13 with s18, g with t(imes) and removing [i]i yielding

(4)   [s18 [t [b Kilroy]b was here]t]s18

with the visual result

(5)   **Kilroy** was here

The same trick can be done with graphical signs, and the general rule is that an arbitrary representation is necessary if the screen element is to be manipulated in a systematic way.

The distinction between motivated and arbitrary representation is semiotically relevant in that some of the properties described in the arbitrary representation are considered as strong candidates for taxemes in the interface because they are easy to manipulate. Properties that in a natural language are perceived as a whole and can only be isolated by phonematic or graphematic analysis have here acquired independent existence and can be manipulated in the arbitrary representation. For example, if a graphical toolbox offers routines for drawing circles and rectangles, the wise programmer will naturally choose these elements to express himself, referring to these concepts when input is received (did the user click on rectangle no. 12?) and when response is given (the user requests a new circle with radius 100 and center 100,100 to be drawn).

The two ways of representation invite a separation of form and substance, and offer new possibilities for presenting the same data in different substances: as pixels on a screen, as drawings on a paper, or as sounds from a loudspeaker. Suppose for example that we have an English text, and assume for the sake of the argument that only the identity of the letters belongs to form, whereas font or size are variants:

here = here = here = **here**

Given an arbitrary representation, like *[s13 [g here]g]s13*, it is easy to strip away the properties that belong to the graphical manifestation, namely [s13 [g]g]s13, and use the invariants /here/ as inputs to a routine that will manifest it as sound.

Arbitrary representations tend to give signs a particular internal structure, in semiotics often treated under the heading of *manner of articulation.* When we split up a composite sign into components, the components may or may not be meaning bearing. If we can decompose a sign into components that have meaning, the code is said to have a *first articulation.* Furthermore, if we can continue decomposition and end up with components that have no meaning in themselves, but only serve to distinguish meaning, then the code is said to have a *second articulation.*

In the framework of the book, the manner of articulation concerns the degree of parallelism between content and expression plane. If content and expression taxemes are not identical, the latter being smaller than the former, a second articulation exists. If the content plane itself can be divided, a first articulation exists.

Natural language has both articulations: a text can be split up into content taxemes, stems and morphemes that have meaning. The stems and morphemes are composed of smaller expression taxemes, namely phonemes or graphemes. Thus, *He throws the stones* consists of six minimal content taxemes: *He throw s the stone s.* Each of these signs can be split up in graphemes, for example *throw* = t h r o w.

There are codes that have only the first articulation: an arithmetical expression like 2 + 3 = 5 can be split up into five stems, 2,3,5,+,= each having a definite meaning. But these signs are identical to the expression taxemes, so the language of arithmetical expressions only has the first articulation.

Most graphical codes have only the first articulation since most pictures can be divided into smaller meaning-bearing signs, but normally there are no standard recurrent expression elements, corresponding to phonemes, of which a picture is composed. However, a few graphical codes do have both, and computer-based pictures that have an arbitrary representation tend to belong to the latter category, and are therefore more language-like than other pictures. As an example, consider the following picture in Fig. II.1.5, which is a simplified version of the Macintosh window. It is built of two elements, the rectangle and the line. The Macintosh toolbox contains routines to draw rectangles, lines and other shapes that are used in most of the programs running on the machine.

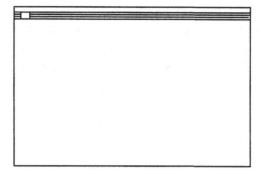

Fig. II.1.5. Simplified Macintosh window.

Many graphical signs will be built from these elements, and the individual element, e.g. the rectangle, being a part of many larger signs but not having a content of its own, will be a meaning-differentiating graphical taxeme.

In the preceding, we have seen that the permanent features of computer-based signs are constrained by their substance, which is different from paper: we cannot draw delicate lines, it is difficult to distinguish shade and texture, and graphical signs tend to fall in two classes: free-hand drawings with one articulation that cannot be systematically manipulated, and schematic pictures with two articulations that can.

The same is true of the *transient* features that are not like those in films or cartoons. For example, most games use overlapping, not geometrical perspective. The scene consists of a flat background, which can change continually as we move around, and a foreground consisting of small figures (sometimes called *sprites*) moving in relation to the background. However, the reason why geometrical perspective is rather rare is not an aesthetic one, but is simply due to the limited capacity of the computer to perform the extensive trigonometric calculations and updating required to simulate movements in geometrical space.

The lesson to be learned from the preceding is that we should not treat the screen as a piece of paper or a strip of celluloid but as a medium in its own right. Computer aesthetics should not develop by trying to mimic paper or film, because the constraints of the new medium are such that the copy will be of poorer quality than the original.

Instead it should exploit the unique feature of the computer medium, namely the possibility of constructing signs consisting of all three types of feature: handling, transient, and permanent. Although the distinction between the three types of feature is analytically useful, the three components are experienced as a whole by the user, and it is this whole that creates the enjoyment and fascination. Moving a mouse is in itself no fun, and neither is the contemplation of a black rectangle moving up and down or a square moving left to right on the screen. But if a mouse movement is immediately accompanied by a movement of the rectangle, and if contact between rectangle and square makes the square change its direction, then something new happens, the three features are assembled into signs that are interpreted as paddle and ball, and I feel I am wielding the paddle and hitting the ball. The study of how such interpretations emerge should be the heart of computer aesthetics.

When we analyze the three essential features of computer-based signs, we should take pains to maintain the distinction between manifestation and form known from other types of signs, since it is this distinction that separates the system processes from the interface. The system processes can be controlled by the programmer and are the content of system descriptions like program texts, while the interface emerges during use and manifests its expression plane in the system processes. The system processes can be planned a priori while the interface can in principle only be analyzed a posteriori. Although a skilled programmer can be said to have full control over the computational processes that manifest the interface, he can only partially control which of its features the user exploits in his interpretation and how he exploits them.

This basic uncertainty can be elucidated by the hierarchy of symbol systems introduced in Section I.2.3.2: the *object semiotic*, the *semiology*, viz. a description of the object-semiotic, and the *meta-semiology* that describes the semiology. In addition, the hierarchy can give definite guidelines for structuring programs so that it becomes easier for the programmer to direct his attention towards the interpretation of the computational processes - to work more directly with the interface.

Let me first give a concrete example to show the relation between the three symbol systems: the phoneme sequence /bæk/ (back) is a part of the English language. English can be made the object (become an object-semiotic) of a phonological description (which is then a semiology). This description may contain statements like

(1)   /b/, /k/, and /æ/ are different phonemes in English. The former two are consonants, the latter is a vowel. The two classes are defined by the fact that consonants presuppose vowels, since we can have syllables with only a vowel, whereas consonants alone cannot build syllables.

The statements address the invariant features of English syllables. It describes form since it does not say anything about how the three units are manifested (e.g. that /b/ is voiced while /k/ is unvoiced, or that both are pronounced with an oral constriction, which the vowel is not). These sound properties do not belong to the essence of English, since English can also be manifested as written text which contains none of these properties.

However, it is possible to write a text that treats (1) as a symbol system and analyzes its elements. Since (1) is a semiology, the new text will be a meta-semiology and may contain statements like:

(2)　There are three words in text (1), /b/, /k/, and /æ/. The meaning of /b/ and /k/ differs in that /b/ can denote a voiced stop while /k/ can denote an unvoiced one. /æ/ differs from the former two in that it can denote a sound without oral constriction.

The example shows that *a meta-semiology will contain a description of the substance of the object-semiotic,* so that the expression and content variants of the object semiotic, which are left out in the semiology, become content elements in the meta-semiology. A semiology is concerned with the invariants and the ultimate variants of its object semiotic and stops when all variants have been recorded and assigned to their proper invariants. It cannot talk about the variants themselves, since then it would no longer talk about its object semiotic, whereas the meta-semiology can talk about them qua meaning distinctions in the semiology; what are primitive unanalyzable terms in the semiology are objects for further study in the meta-semiology.

Let us now transfer this line of reasoning to computer-based semiotic systems.

In Part I, I defined an interface as "a collection of computer-based signs, viz. all parts of system processes that are seen or heard, used, and interpreted by a community of users", and the interface was classified as a semiotic whose expression plane is manifested in system processes. These processes must be described in a program text that (partially) specifies how the processes are manifested. Therefore the program text must at least play the role of a meta-semiology that specifies the variants of the interface, its object-semiotic.

To give a concrete example, consider for example the program text that specifies the Breakout system. If we view it as a text programmers read and interpret, the commutation test tells us that the Pascal assignment *color :=* *LightGrey* means something different from *color := DarkGrey.* Thus, in the program text, the two colors are content invariants. However, content invariants in this meta-semiological text may well turn out to be expression variants in the object-semiotic, viz. the game. In fact, as the following semiological analysis of Breakout will show, it turns out that the two particular shades of grey are just accidental variants that do not belong to the essentials of the game.

In general, although we can use invariants in the program text as indications that the programmer intends to signify something different, we cannot know if this is in fact true before we have applied the commutation test to the system process itself. It is perfectly possible that the content invariants of the program text turn out to be mere expression variants in the interface.

It might be a good idea to design programs so that it is easier to see what is what, and in the next sections I suggest therefore that the distinction between a semiology and a meta-semiology be transferred to the program text, so that parts of the text primarily address the interface form, i.e. those features that are operative in the interpretation of the system, while other parts are primarily concerned with the detailed implementation of the form elements.

In this way the programmer can better concentrate on the essentials of the communication he wishes to accomplish, and - temporarily - disregard the details of hardware and software. In fact, distinctions similar to, although not identical to, the form-substance opposition are well-known in computer science. A software engineer is interested in separating the machine-independent parts of the program from the parts that are specific for a particular machine, since this makes it easier to transfer the system from one machine to another. Similarly, different types of knowledge are recognized in human-computer research; although Shneiderman 1987 uses a different framework, his distinction between syntactic and semantic knowledge can to a certain degree be compared to the form-substance opposition.

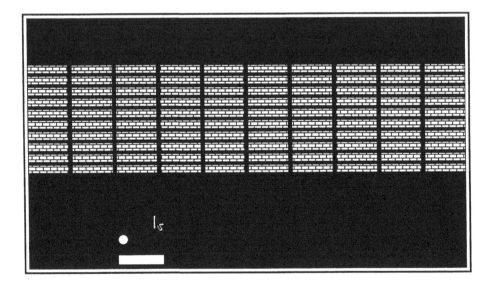

Fig. II.1.6. The Breakout game, version 2.

I shall start by illustrating what a semiological analysis of a computer system might look like, and my examples will still be the paddle, the ball, the brick, and the border from the simple game of Breakout. The purpose of the analysis is to find the invariants of the game, viz. the features that cannot be exchanged without changing the meaning of the game, and in order to do this, I must use the commutation test. Although it can be performed in imagination, it helps to have another different version of the same game exemplifying some of the variants, and I shall use the following version in Fig. II.1.6 as comparison.

We first look for their *permanent* features. As the definition says, these are found by comparing all signs, looking for features that are constant throughout the lifetime of a sign, and serve to distinguish the individual signs from the rest in the collection. A preliminary survey of the screen shown in the beginning of this section results in the following paradigms of pre-taxemes:

Gestalt: figure | ground
Color: light grey | dark grey | black
Size: small | large
Shape: square | rectangle | line

For example the ball is characterized as a black figure (against the "air" which is ground and light grey), small (against the bricks which are larger), and square (against the paddle which is rectangular).

The next important part of the analysis consists in determining which of these features pass the commutation test and are invariants in the small semiotic schema of the game. For example, are all three colors really distinctive? The answer is yes, since if we replace the dark grey of the bricks with black, then the whole wall will be black and the meaning would change from "a wall composed of bricks" to "a homogeneous wall". Similarly, we cannot replace the light grey with dark grey, without getting a meaning change, since then the wall will look as if it has holes in it:

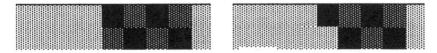

Fig. II.1.7. Light and dark grey commute.

Therefore three colors pass the commutation test, and are expression invariants. However, the particular shade of the colors does not matter since colors are used as phonemes here in that they only serve to distinguish meaning, not to convey meaning. This is evident if we compare it to the second version of the game. This version also has three colors, but they are black (corresponding to light grey), patterned (roughly corresponding to dark grey) and white (black).

So much for the colors. Now, what about the Shape dimension that in the first version serves to distinguish paddle from ball: the paddle is a rectangle, the ball is a square. If we look at the second version of the game, the square | rectangle distinction is replaced by a circle | rectangle opposition and therefore must be considered a (rather clumsy) variant of a more abstract invariant. This invariant could be size, since in both cases the ball is smaller than the paddle, but it is also possible that shape is not relevant at all, since the difference between paddle and ball is not primarily signified by shape, but by the occurrence of handling features and the functions between the two signs. If we had not experienced that the rectangle moved up and down when the mouse is rolled back and forth, we would never guess that the shape means a paddle, the essentials of a paddle being to function as a tool you can control, and if the black square had not changed direction when in contact with the paddle, it would not have been interpreted as a ball. The active handling features partake in sign formation just as much as the passive permanent or transient features.

The same line of argument can be applied to the *transient* features. According to the definition, they are differences of the same sign token that signify different properties of its reference. The transient features of the ball include the direction in which it moves and the objects with which it is in contact. The direction paradigm contains at least two members, *left* and *right*, and the Contact paradigm at least two members, the *paddle* and the *bricks*.

To show this, let us look at the manner in which three events of the game are expressed; *the ball flies, the player hits the ball with the paddle*, and *the ball smashes a brick.*

The first one, *The ball flies,* can be "spelled"[1]

(Direction: left) + (Direction: left)

that is, two consecutive states in which the direction is the same. If we replace *left* with *right* in the last state, yielding

(Direction: left) + (Direction: right)

we also get a different content, namely "the ball hits something". For example, the event "The paddle hits the ball" is spelled

---

[1] I use "." to denote glossematic co-occurrence with no sequence implied, while "+" denotes co-occurrence in which sequence is significant. Thus, A.B = B.A while A+B ≠ B+A. In the notation (A: B), A denotes a paradigm, and B one of its members. Thus, *(Direction: left)* denotes the element *left* of the direction paradigm.

(Direction: left).(Contact with: paddle) +
(Direction: right).(Contact with: <u>paddle</u>)

This proves that Direction in some way or another is an invariant. In a similar way we can see that Contact is an invariant, since if we replace *paddle* with *brick* in the above expression, the meaning changes from "The paddle hits the ball" to something like "The ball smashes the brick". The latter event is fully expressed by the ball first having the Direction feature *right* and the Contact feature *brick*, while the brick has the Color feature *dark grey*, and in the next moment the ball changes to having Direction *left* and no Contact with a brick, while the brick changes Color to *light grey*, thereby merging with the light grey of the background.

Besides the directions *left* and *right*, we also have the *up* and *down* movements of the ball when it hits the upper and lower border, and of the paddle when the mouse is moved. However, a closer scrutiny of these features will show that the four elements *left*, *right*, *up* and *down* in themselves are not invariants, but variants of more abstract invariants that can be labeled *continuity of direction* vs *change of direction*. For example, although *left* and *right*, and *up* and *down* commute pair-wise, signifying the difference between "hitting" and "missing, flying free", *left* and *up* never commute. We may say that *left+right*, *right+left*, *up+down*, and *down+up* are variants that spell the same content unit, namely "hit", while *left+left*, *right+right*, and *up+up* all spell "miss". A glance at the second version of the game corroborates this analysis: this version is rotated so that the paddle moves horizontally, while the ball moves vertically. What is constant in the two games is not the particular directions of ball and paddle, but the way the opposition *change of direction | continuity of direction* is exploited.

A semiological analysis like the preceding is only concerned with the expression features that have function to meaning, and if we want to focus on the communicative aspects of computer systems, it is clearly a good idea to incorporate some version of semiological analysis into software development.

But we also have to write code that manifests the signs we wish to communicate, and the next question is therefore: how does interface analysis relate to programming - or in more theoretical terms: how is a semiology related to its meta-semiology? I cannot answer these questions in an exhaustive way, but the next section offers some preliminary ideas. It presents a perspective on programming I call *Sign-oriented programming* that views programming as a sign-creating activity, in analogy with play-writing and stage directing, and a program execution in analogy with a performance of a play.

II.1.1.2. Objects as signs

(This section, together with Section II.1.3, can be skipped by readers that are not interested in programming. The purpose of the two sections is to compare the sign concept of semiotics to the object concept of computer science, and to illustrate concretely how the program texts would look if they are built on the form-substance distinction.)

Although the example game in the preceding section is trivial, I consider the *type* of observations made above essential in a semiotic approach to programming and program analysis and start by extracting a few principles from it:

1. Perceptibility. The default requirement for a sign is that a human interpreter must be able to perceive it. Without expression, no content. In special circumstances, however, signs can be invisible, conveying their meaning through their effects on other signs, but even so, invisible signs presuppose visible ones.

2. Sign morphology. Computer-based signs consist of structures of permanent, transient, and handling features. We will typically want to be able to group combinations of these features into wholes that will produce the intended interpretation. For example, we want to assign both permanent, transient, and handling features to the paddle-sign to create an interpretation of a tool the user may wield, while the ball should not possess handling features, since it is to play the role of the unpredictable, and only partly controllable, factor in the game.

3. Actions belong to signs. Signs can perform actions that influence themselves and other signs. In the normal interpretation of the Breakout game, the player assigns the action of flying and smashing bricks to the ball, while hitting the ball is not an action of the ball itself, but of the player using the paddle as instrument. We want to be able to express that an action belongs to one sign and not to another.

4. Signs classes should be defined by their combinatorics. Since the purpose of programming is to create signs, the most natural classification of primitive computer-based signs is their ability to combine into complex signs, for example those denoting actions or events. The three game elements are clearly different in this respect. The bricks cannot alone denote an event, only together with the ball *(smash)*. The ball in turn can denote the event of *flying* alone, but can also combine with the paddle to signify the action of *hitting*. Finally, paddle and ball are different in that the paddle, with or without ball, can denote actions performed by the player *(moving, hitting)*, while the ball in isolation can only signify events. I shall later give names to these classes: the paddle is classified as an *interactive sign*, the ball as an *actor*, and the bricks as *object signs*. This method of classification is well known in linguistics, and a very good example is shown in Section I.2.1, where the two Danish tones are defined by their mutual combinatorics, the falling tone being the one that can occur alone, while the non-falling tone requires the presence of the falling one. In addition, the tones are distinguished from accents in that tones can establish sentences, which accents cannot.

Another example that comes closer to the Breakout example is the theory of cases described in Section I.2.2.1, where the traditional cases of subject, object, instrument, beneficiary, location and time are described combinatorially: the subject is the case that must be present, while objects, location and time presuppose the subject, instrument and beneficiary presuppose the object, and location and time form a constellation. Cases are interesting because cases and the computer-based sign types described above seem to play comparable roles. Both are defined by their abilities to enter into sentences or actions and events, respectively, and their meaning variants seem also to overlap. When the game is paraphrased in verbal language, the paddle is naturally described as an instrument (I hit the ball *with* the paddle), the ball as a subject (*The ball* flies, *the ball* smashes the brick), the brick as an object, and the border as a location (The ball bounces *against the border*).

5. Form and substance. The programming perspective must allow two levels of description, the form and the substance, corresponding to a semiology and a meta-semiology. Since I have chosen to see the ultimate purpose of programming as creation of meaning, I want to be able to separate those properties that are immediately relevant to this purpose from those that are connected to particular ways of achieving the purpose.

6. Concepts are relational. Concepts of form are relational concepts, not defined by their absolute values, but by their differences and similarities to other concepts. For example, it turned out that the important thing in Breakout is that three colors must be available, not their particular shade. Similarly, the important thing in the actions of the game is not the actual directions (left, right) of the movements, but opposition between the same and different directions.

Which existing view on programming is easiest to combine with these ideas? Lehrman Madsen & Møller Pedersen 1988 lists four main perspectives for understanding programming:

Procedural programming. A program execution is regarded as a (partially ordered) sequence of procedure calls manipulating data structures.

Functional programming. A program is regarded as a mathematical function, describing a relation between input and output.

Constraint oriented (logic) programming. A program is regarded as a set of equations describing relations between input and output.

Object-oriented programming. A program execution is regarded as a physical model, simulating the behavior of either a real or imaginary part of the world.
Lehrman Madsen & Møller-Pedersen 1988: 2-3

and it seems to me that the last perspective is the one that comes closest to the above requirements, although some minor and major modifications must be made.

The quotation defines object-oriented programming as a way of viewing a program execution, namely as a physical model that simulates the behavior of a part of the world. A physical model is composed of *objects* that are described in the following way:

A physical model consists of *objects*, each object characterized by *attributes* and a sequence of *actions*. Objects organize the substance aspect of phenomena, and transformations on substance are reflected by objects executing actions. Objects may have part-objects. An attribute may be a reference to a part object or to a separate object. Some attributes represent measurable properties of the object. The *state* of an object at a given moment is expressed by its substance, its measurable properties and the action going on then. The state of the whole model is the states of the objects in the model.
Lehrman Madsen & Møller-Pedersen 1988: 5

The notion of *cohering attributes and actions* fits nicely to requirements 2 and 3, and analogies to 5, the distinction between form and substance, can also be found in object-oriented programming languages like Simula, where the external aspects of a procedure can be declared and used in a superclass without explicating the details of its internal structure. These details can be given later in subclasses of the superclass, so that the "same" procedure can be "manifested" differently in different subclasses.

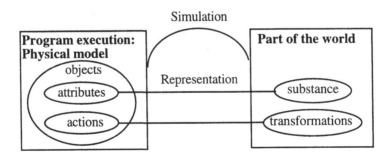

Fig. II.1.8. Computer systems as physical models.

The real difference lies in requirements 1, 4, and 6, and is due to incompatible conceptions of the relation between program execution and its context. The Physical Model interpretation is that the program execution simulates a real world system, "reflects reality in a natural way", and that components in the model represent real world phenomena, objects the substance, and actions transformations of the substance (Fig. II.1.8).

It is this "naturalness" that is questioned and made problematic by a sign-oriented perspective on programming. Linguists know that different languages and language varieties articulate the "parts of the world" in rather different ways, and are very careful when postulating "natural" ways of doing this[1]. Although there may be universals that depend upon the physical nature of reality and the sensory and cognitive apparatus of human beings, other important properties depend upon the culture in which the language develops and the practical tasks language must fulfil.

Theoretically, the problem is that the Physical Model mixes up a meta-semiology and an object-semiotic, assuming that the content units of the former automatically are expression units or even content units of the latter. However, as the next example shows, there is no automatic connection between the concepts expressed in the program text and those emerging in the interface. The most obvious interpretation of the picture below is that it depicts four columns, but this is a complete coincidence from the program's point of view.

Fig. II.1.9. Rectangles that look like columns.

The program that drew the picture did not express any concepts for columns, but only contained a recursive definition of rectangles, since it simply draws rectangles within rectangles. A closer look at the picture will reveal the rectangles and the system after which they are drawn, but this articulation of the picture is completely different from that of the interface.

---

[1] Whorf 1970.

The weakness in the Physical Model view is that it implicitly assumes that the ideas expressed by the programmer in the program texts are communicated to the user through the program execution, but the example shows that this is not a necessity.

The un-problematic relations of simulation and representation between program execution and the real world must be made more realistic and problematic by inserting the uncontrollable interface between program executions and the "part of the world". In creating the interface, the users in one dialectical movement articulate both the program processes and "the part of the world", and neither interpretation need coincide with that made by the program text. We note a change of direction of the Ball because it means hitting and smashing, and at the same time we see hitting and smashing because these actions are denoted by changes of direction.

The semiological analysis of the Breakout game given above can give an idea of what sign-oriented programming might be like. The main points of the analysis can be summarized in the Petri-net below.

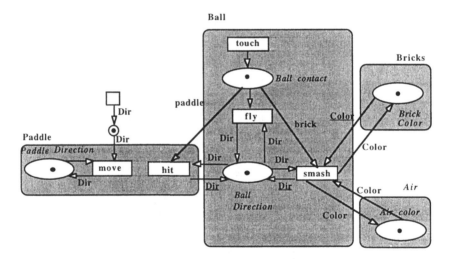

Fig. II.1.10. Semiological analysis of the Breakout game.

The actions of the signs are described by transitions (boxes), the paradigms of handling and transient features are symbolized by places (ovals), and the tokens (black dots) are the individual features. The flows of the diagram (arrows) are decorated with conditions that the tokens must satisfy. *Hit*, for example, removes a *Direction* token from the *Ball Direction* place and returns the opposite token to it.

The diagram describes form since it does not mention any absolute values of Direction or Color, but only relational notions like "different from" or "identical to": for example, *fly* is expressed by identical consecutive directions of the ball, while *hit* and *smash* are signified by changing the direction to a different one (from Dir to <u>Dir</u>), and Color works in the same way: a brick is smashed by changing its Color from different to identical to the Color of the air (from <u>Color</u> to Color).

In the program text, I would like to have one part, the semiology, in which only these essentials are written, for example in the following way[1]:

```
Object Paddle
Permanent
 Color = DifferentFrom(Air.color)
 Size = LargerThan(Ball)
Transient
 Direction: {X, X̲}
Handling
 Mouse: {Y, Y̲}
Actions
 Action hit
  Precondition: Ball.Contact = me
  Method:
  Ball.Direction := Opposite(Ball.Direction)
 End hit
 Action move
  Precondition: none
  Method:
  Direction := Mouse. Direction
 End move
End Paddle

Object Ball
Permanent
 Color = DifferentFrom(Air.Color)
 Size = SmallerThan(Paddle)
Transient
 Contact: {Paddle, Brick, none}
 Direction: {X, X̲}
Actions
 Action Fly
  Precondition: Contact = none
  Method:
  Direction := Direction
 End Fly
 Action Smash
  Precondition: Contact = brick
  Method:
  Direction := Opposite(Direction)
  Contact.color := Air.color
 End Smash
End Ball
```

---

[1] The notation is partly borrowed from the programming language Pascal. {} enclose a set of expression units. A: {B,C} means that A can take the values B and C, "A = B" means that A permanently gets the value B, while "A :=B" means that A temporarily is assigned the value B. If B is a sign and C is a feature of the sign, then "B.C" means B's C. For example, *Ball.Direction* means the ball's direction.

```
Object Brick
Permanent
 Shape = rectangular
Transient
 Color: {Air.color, DifferentFrom(Air.color)}
End Brick
```

Note the relational concepts. The size of ball and paddle is not given in pixels but the former is only required to be smaller than the latter (Size = LargerThan(Ball)). The possible colors of the brick are not described as grey or light grey, but only as different and the same as the color of the air (Color: {Air.color, DifferentFrom(Air.color)}). The actions are specified in the same way: the resulting direction of the *hit* action of the ball is only required to give the ball the opposite direction (Ball.Direction := Opposite(Ball. Direction)), and the *smash* action of the ball only to make the color of the brick identical to that of the air (Contact.color := Air.color).

In the hypothetical syntax of the language, I have made the terms *permanent, transient, handling* and *action* formal categories that are accessible to a classification facility since these elements are important indicators of the combinatorics of the individual signs. For example, if a sign, like the border, has no transient features, it cannot participate in events as instrument or object, but only as location, and if handling features are missing, it cannot function as instrument. If the action component is absent, the sign cannot participate alone in an event, but always requires one that possesses actions.

Since the program describes manifestation of signs, the objects must by default have visual or auditory properties at every stage in the specification process. Invisible objects should be the exception. This means that the system must be able to select default visual or auditory representations that satisfy the constraints described so far. In the beginning, the only requirement is that the color of ball, paddle, and bricks is different from the air, so the system may choose the maximal contrast, making the air black and the objects white. If the programmer is not satisfied, new constraints may be added to the objects, e.g. requiring the ball and paddle to be lighter than the bricks, which again must be lighter than the air. A part of the programming would simply consist in adding more and more constraints to the program, making the set of possible default values smaller and smaller.

Although my example has been a game, the principle of designing objects according to their role on the stage of the screen can be extended to all interactive programs in which the interface is important. If we abstract away all features that are peculiar to the game, we will have a representation like the following, which only describes the roles of the signs on the stage of the screen.

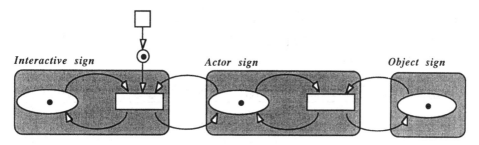

Fig. II.1.11. General sign structure of the Breakout game.

The paddle has been reduced to its class, the interactive sign, which possesses all three features and contains actions that influence other signs. These properties are sufficient to enable it to act as instrument in an action that also contains an object or actor, and to constitute an action alone. The ball in turn has become the prototypical actor, which alone or together with object signs can signify an event, and together with an interactive sign can establish an action performed by the user.

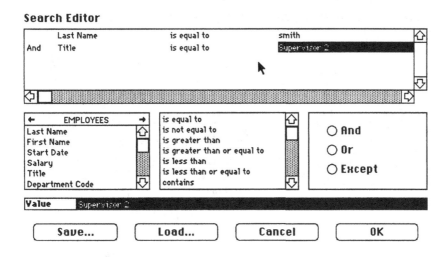

Fig. II.1.12. The Fourth Dimension data base system.

Sign classes like these and their possibilities of combination can be found in many other applications than games. Above is shown one example from the Fourth Dimension data base system. It contains a complex interactive sign that allows the user to formulate queries about a data base. In the example, the user asks: "Which employees have a last name equal to "Smith" and a title equal to "Supervisor 2"?

Pressing the OK-button causes the system to initiate an automatic search process in its data base of employees, and finally produce the result of the search, in this case one person:

Last Name	First Name	Start Date	Salary	Title
Smith	Sally	ons 5 feb 1986	<<<<	Supervisor 2

EMPLOYEES: 1 of 25

Fig. II.1.13.The Fourth Dimension data base system.

Although this program is certainly no game, we can recognize the sign structure: an interactive sign (the query, corresponding to the paddle) that interacts with an actor sign[1], outside the control of the user (the invisible search process, corresponding to the ball). This actor in turn manipulates two signs that in this connection are object signs (the data base and the answer, corresponding to the bricks). In fact, the Fourth Dimension is even more game-like than that, because both answer and data base are really not object signs, but interactive signs, since they can be manipulated in other tasks:

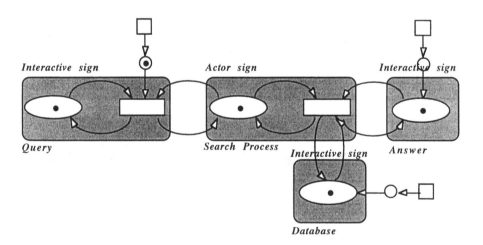

Fig. II.1.14. General sign structure of the Fourth Dimension data base system.

---

[1] The reader may rightly object that invisible signs cannot be signs at all. In fact, the search process is not an actor at all in the typology set up in Section II.1.2.1, but a ghost sign. Ghost signs are defined as signs that have no visible shape themselves, but influence other signs in a meaningful way. Thus, although the search process itself cannot be seen directly, it can be observed indirectly in its effect on how answers are tied to questions.

I shall conclude this section with a definition of the concept of sign-oriented programming that shows the similarities to and differences from object-oriented programming.

Sign-oriented programming. A program execution is regarded as a manifestation of a play that aims at giving its audience experience of and insight into either a real or imaginary part of the world.

A computer-based play consists of *signs*, each sign characterized by *attributes* and a sequence of *actions,* most of which the audience can hear or see but some of which it must infer. Signs organize the expression substance generated by a program execution, and transformations on substance are reflected by signs executing actions. Attributes and actions are described on two main levels: the semiology specifies their *form,* viz. their invariant features relevant to meaning, while the meta-semiology describes the substance, viz. how the particular *variants* are implemented and manifested in a particular environment on a particular machine. Attributes fall into three main classes, *permanent, transient* and *handling* features. An attribute may be a property of the sign itself or a reference to a part or to a separate sign.

The definition is modelled over the definition of object-oriented programming in order to emphasize the similarities and differences.

From an object-oriented point of view one can say that sign-oriented programming classifies a certain type of objects as computer-based signs, namely those possessing visual or auditory properties that have function relative to the meaning of the program execution.

In addition, it recommends a particular program architecture. All things equal, the system should be structured as a collection of computer-based signs, and the specification of each sign should contain at least two main parts: a semiology that describes those parts of the sign that are pertinent to the interpretation of the system processes, and a meta-semiology that describes how the semiology is in fact implemented. Section II.1.3 presents a concrete example of this kind of architecture.

In the next section, I shall elaborate the classification of computer-based signs presented above.

II.1.2 Analysis of computer-based signs

The purpose of the following classification of computer-based signs is to describe computer-based signs according to the roles they can play in the interface, thereby giving a principled framework for using the interface as the main point of reference for designing computer systems.

II.1.2.1. A typology of computer-based signs

The classification is based upon the combination of features possessed by the sign and whether the sign can perform actions with function to features of other signs.

		+action		-action
		+handling	-handling	
+permanent	+transient	Interactive	Actor	Object
	-transient	Button	Controller	Layout
-permanent		Ghost		

Fig. II.1.15. Classification of computer-based signs.

As a supplement to the verbal description of the sign classes, I shall include a graphical Petri-net representation which gives a very general formal characterization of the classes.

Other classifications are of course possible, for example Peirce's distinction between index, icon, and symbol. A footprint is an *index*; it signifies a human being by means of a natural connection between expression (footprint) and content (human being). In general, the interpretation of indices are based on spatial, temporal, or causal contiguities between expression and content. The cursor is a typical index, since it gets its meaning from the items spatially "under" it. In opposition, the meaning of *icons* (which are commonly used in graphical interfaces) emerges from a likeness between expression and content, whereas this relation is arbitrary in *symbols*, and based on a convention. The reason I do not use this classification is that it is not sensitive to the characteristics of computer-based signs, namely that they can be handled and interacted with.

Interactive signs

These signs are unique to the computer medium. They exploit features from all three dimensions. The sign token is distinguished from the other signs on its level by permanent features like e.g. size and shape, and during its lifetime it can change transient properties like e.g. location and color, these changes being functionally dependent upon its handling features. In most cases it can perform actions that change transient features in other signs.

We have already met many interactive signs. In Breakout the paddle belongs to this category, since it has a definite shape and color (rectangular and black), it can move up and down on the screen, its movements having function to the reader's mouse manipulation, and when the ball hits the paddle, it influences the trajectory of the ball.

The heroes of video games, like the lonely soldier penetrating the enemy camp in the action game Commando (Elite, no year), are nearly always signified by interactive signs which provide a very strong identification for the "reader".

The hero of Dark Castle (Silicon Beach Software Inc.,1986) is a very impressive example. He is able to change shape to simulate walking, fighting, throwing, jumping, climbing, falling, etc., and within the individual actions like jumping there are several varieties:

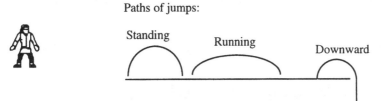

Besides changing his own features, he can act on the enemy signs: kill rats, bats and vultures with stones, hit a henchman with a mace, etc.

The general Petri-net schema for interactive signs looks like this:

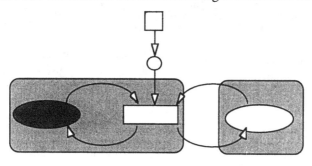

Fig. II.1.16. The interactive sign.

The transitions of the sign require two or three inputs: one from the user, one from its own and/or other's transient features. The result of the transition is a change in these features.

In tool-applications, the semantic relationship between an interactive sign and the sign it affects is often that of instrument to object or locative, as in Fullpaint, where I can paint the "paper"(object) *with* the brush (instrument). In video games the interactive sign signifies a human 1st person agent (viz.

the reader) pitted against hostile agents denoted by actor signs, and in data bases, the interactive query is interpreted as a question that elicits an answer.

Thus, although the properties of the signs are the same, the semantic relations they contract are different in the three genres. We could never exchange the case relations of the Dark Castle fiction with the those of Fullpaint : saying "I defeated the Black Knight with the hero" instead of "I (or the hero) defeated the Black Knight" is just as odd as saying "The brush painted a picture" instead of "I painted the picture with the brush". This means that no general content can be assigned to the sign types; however, within the individual genre, a particular interpretation seems to prevail.

Although the most striking examples of interactive signs comes from the graphical variety, they can also be found in text based systems like Word 3. In a strict sense, only the mouse and text cursor are interactive signs in the Word 3 screens.

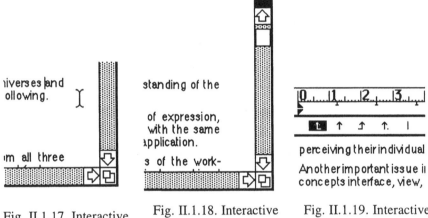

Fig. II.1.17. Interactive signs: the text cursor.

Fig. II.1.18. Interactive signs: the scrollbar box.

Fig. II.1.19. Interactive signs: the margin triangles.

The mouse cursor (the I-beam) can change position when the mouse is moved, and it affects the position of the text cursor (I). The text cursor itself can be handled through the alpha-numeric keys, and changes the "paper" by leaving a stream of letters behind, pushing the rest of the line to the right (Fig. II.1.17).

However, often the effect on the other sign is not dependent upon the mouse cursor, but upon an intermediary sign manipulated by the cursor, causing us to feel that the intermediary sign, and not the cursor, is the tool we handle. For example, the box in the scrollbar can be moved by means of the mouse cursor, and in its turn makes the "paper" move in the opposite direction (Fig. II.1.18). Similarly, the margin signs (the small triangles at the top of the tabulator) can be moved by the mouse cursor, changing the margin of the "paper" (Fig. II.1.19). In these cases, the changes of the object sign do not depend upon the mouse cursor, but on the intermediate sign. Therefore, we may ignore the cursor, and classify the intermediary signs as interactive signs also.

In some interactive signs, the transient features are very simple. A very common type are *buttons* that only show a short inversion when they are clicked. It is still true that these signs are interactive signs, but their transient features are so simple that they call for a special designation.

Actor signs

Another common type lacks the handling features, but still has some action associated to them. They are able to change position and/or shape on the screen and to influence other signs, but they cannot be influenced directly by the reader, although they may adapt their behavior according to the way the reader manipulates his interactive signs. I call them *actor signs*.

In Breakout the ball is an actor sign. It has color and shape (square and black), it can move horizontally, but it is not directly under the control of the reader, who needs the interactive paddle to influence its behavior. In the action game Commando, all the enemy soldiers are expressed by actor signs: they can move but cannot be controlled by the player, and Dark Castle presents the following horrifying cast of bad guys:

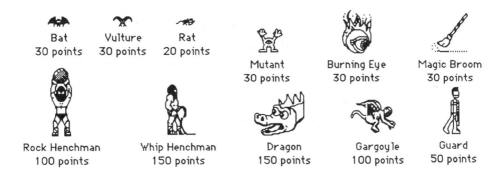

Fig. II.1.20. Actor signs: bad guys in Dark Castle.

Each exhibits its own pattern of behavior, carefully contrasted to the others. While bats start by hanging a moment in the ceiling and then flap irregularly down towards the hero, the vultures attack him in one streamlined dive.

In line with its ideology, the Macintosh system contains very few pure actors (at the moment I can only come up with the clock, but there are probably more, cleverly disguised). However, there is a class of signs that resemble actors in that although their processes can by initiated by handling features, they cannot be interfered with once started. Examples from Word 3 includes the *Repaginate* command that inserts new page numbers in the document, the *Index* that produces a list of indexed terms, complete with the number of the pages on which they occur, the *Table of Contents* that generates an automatic table of contents, and *Sort,* which sorts lines in alphabetic order.

When we for example activate *Table of Contents* above, the following signs appear:

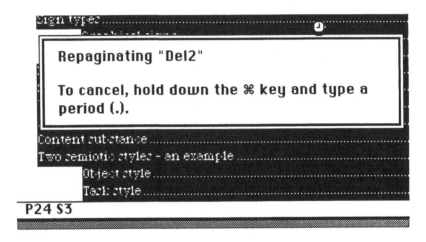

Fig. II.1.21. Actor signs: "table of contents" facility in Microsoft Word.

The permanent clock icon is the standard sign for actors, meaning that the machine is busy and cannot be interfered with. In addition, this particular actor also has its own permanent and transient features: the verbal sign ("Repaginating...") informs us which operation is going on, and the transient features, the numbers in the bottom line, change all the time to show us which page the machine is processing at the moment. When the process is finished, the resulting state of the work object, viz. the new table of contents, is shown in reverse.

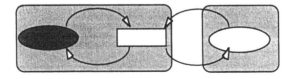

Fig. II.1.22. The actor sign.

The command *Table of Contents* is a button that sets an actor in motion, just like the paddle changes the direction of the ball. However, once awakened, the Table of Content Maker cannot be handled by the user (although it can be stopped), it has its own permanent and transient features (the clock, the verbal sign, and the changing numbers), and it changes the document in two ways: by repaginating it and producing a new table of contents.

The Petri-net description of actors is similar to those of interactive signs, except that handling features are missing (Fig. II.1.22).

Controller signs

Some signs change other signs although they do not change their own visual appearance. The actions belonging to them are presented indirectly by clearly influencing the behavior of other signs. Controller signs are signs that only change properties of other objects, not of themselves.

Non-fiction applications like Word use controllers to divide the screen into work areas, which influence the mouse cursor. The rectangle enclosing the "paper" is a controller, since it changes the cursor when it moves across the border.

It follows from the definition that controllers are only fully realized in connection with another sign, in this case the interactive cursor.

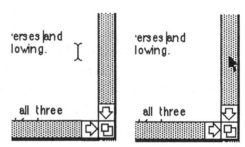

Fig. II.1.23. Controllers: window borders.

Their permanent features can always be seen, but the actions associated with them are only perceived through the transient features of the interactive sign.

The same use of controllers can be seen in Fullpaint. In Fig. II.1.24, there are three work areas. In the paper area, the cursor sign is a drawing tool that puts marks on the paper (1), in the movement areas, it is a cross that can change the location of the menus contained in the area (2), and in the rest of the screen, it is an arrow that can be used to click and drag signs (3). When the cursor moves from one area to another, it changes shape and functionality.

In Breakout, the bottom and top borders of the screen are controller signs, since they make the ball change its trajectory, but do not change their own appearance. In Commando, trees and walls inhibit the movements of other icons, and the screen is littered with dangerous controller signs: for example, if the protagonist moves into blue areas denoting water or black areas denoting trenches, he dies.

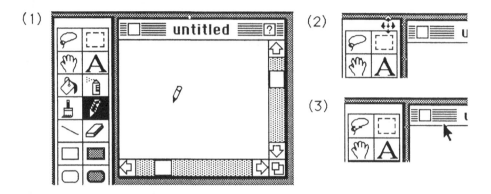

Fig. II.1.24. Effects of controllers on the cursor.

Dark Castle exploits controller signs in a very brilliant way. Its scenes depict caves in a castle, and express three modalities: obstacles that *prevent* movement, paths that *allow* reader/player controlled movement, and abysses *forcing* movements without reader control. One can say that abysses change an interactive sign to an actor by removing reader control. Obstacles and paths are solid matter, abysses air, and paths are often further articulated according to the repertoire of movements allowed.

To give an impression of a refined use of controllers, let us look at the scene termed Trouble 1:

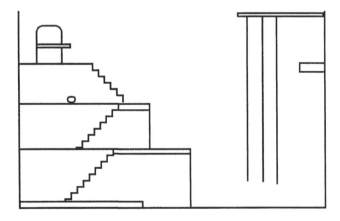

Fig. II.1.25. Controllers in Dark Castle.

The scene depicts three staircases to the left, and three ropes to the right. The reader enters the top floor and has to descend the staircases, avoiding or killing bats coming from the ceiling, rats running on the third floor, and guards marching on the ground. He must walk to the ropes (avoiding rats on the floor), climb the ropes (still avoiding rats coming down), and enter the little shelf to the right. That's the task.

The floors are *paths* where the reader can go left, right and jump (besides doing other things like shooting, picking up things, etc). On the staircases the reader can can go up and down, and at the bottom, there is a step that can only be passed by jumping. The left and right sides of the picture are *obstacles* that cannot be entered. If the reader tries, he gets "concussed". Finally, the space is an *abyss*: if the reader walks into the air from a landing, he drops down.

A preliminary Petri-net of controllers would look like this:

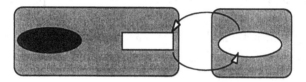

Fig. II.1.26. Controllers.

It follows from the definition that although their permanent features can always be seen, the process properties associated with them are only perceived through the transient features of the interactive sign; but then, how can we argue that the process itself belongs to the controller, and not to the interactive sign?

The question is interesting since it concerns the principles we use to build larger signs out of smaller ones, to "parse" the computer-based signs. Let us look at the Dark Castle case.

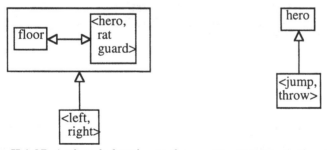

Fig. II.1.27. Actions belonging to the floor controller.

Fig. II.1.28. Actions belonging to the interactive sign.

If the hero is on a floor, he can move left, move right, jump and throw stones, but he cannot move up and down. Let us call this paradigm of actions P. Thus P = <left, right, jump, throw>. It now turns out that a subparadigm, namely Q = <left, right>, is closely connected to the floor controller, since rats and guards also can move left and right on floors (Fig. II.1.27), while another subparadigm R= <jump, throw> belongs to the hero, since only he and neither rats nor guards can perform them (Fig. II.1.28).

It seem reasonable to associate those actions with the controller that all signs can do when in contact with the controller. In functional terms, the actions that are associated with a controller presuppose an interdependence between the controller and a paradigm of those signs that actually do the actions. In the example, the characters in the game can be on the floor without moving left or right, but if they do it, they must be on the floor and not on the staircase (Fig. II.1.27). Other controllers have other action paradigms associated with them. For example, the staircases are presupposed by the paradigm <up, down> .

The paradigm of actions that are particular to the hero and do not require the presence of the floor, only presuppose the actor and therefore do not cohere with the controller (Fig. II.1.28).

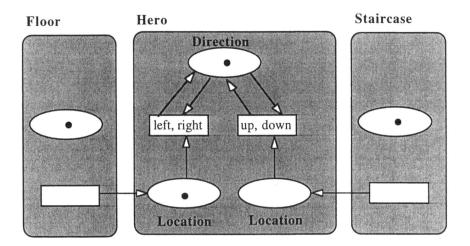

Fig. II.1.29. Petri-net description of the interplay between controllers and interactive signs.

In the Petri-net notation we can incorporate this analysis by saying that the other sign has more than one repertoire of actions, and the controller controls which one is in effect. In this analysis the location of the hero is described by two places. When a token is placed leftmost, the hero can move right and left, and when placed rightmost, he can move up and down. The tokens of the former place are supplied by the floor, those of the latter by the staircase.

In the present case, it is most natural to say that the actions are performed by the hero, but controlled by the controller, but in other cases, not only control but the actions themselves should be assigned to the controller, although they are still manifested in transient features of the hero. For example, the wall is an obstacle preventing locomotion, and the most natural paraphrase of the event of stopping the hero's movements attributes it to the wall and not to the hero. We will say *the wall stopped the hero and gave him a concussion* and not *The hero stopped himself at the wall and used it to create a concussion.* The reason for this seems to be the particular structure of cases involved. The wall plays the role of cause and the hero the role of experiencer/recipient. Since "stop" and "get concussion" is not something the hero intends, we do not attribute these processes to the hero, but to the wall.

The point of this example is that we should recognize two ways of parsing complex signs. The first one consists of a functional analysis, and assigns the actions of moving left and right to the floor, the action of throwing a stone to the hero, and the action of stopping something to the wall.

The second one can be formulated as a case analysis, and reflects our everyday experiences, our "naive physics"[1]. In this method, the three actions, *the hero throws a stone, the hero walks left on the floor,* and *the wall stopped the hero,* could be analyzed as follows:

Agent: The hero, Action: throws, Object: a stone
Agent: The hero, Action:walks, Locative: left on the floor
Cause: The wall, Action: stopped, Object: the hero

As the second example shows, the two analyses need not coincide. The functional analysis sees moving left and right as belonging to the floor, while our naive physics ascribes it to the human agent. The two parsing methods differ in their relation to the illusion: the case analysis accepts the illusion, and describes its structure, while the functional analysis disregards it, and tries to explain how it is created.

Object signs

Object signs possess permanent and transient features, but no handling features: they cannot influence other signs, but can themselves be influenced. Often the user handles an interactive sign denoting a tool to influence an object sign denoting a work object. The "paper" in Word 3 is an example: it is an object sign that can be modified by means of the interactive text cursor whose permanent features include shape(|) and whose transient features include location (Fig. II.1.30).

The text cursor is handled by pressing a key, causing the rest of the text to be pushed one character to the right and leaving a new character in the available space.

---

[1] On the importance of naive physics, see Owen 1986: 187-201.

ıt ACTION1 determines an inter
the paradigm members seem no
on the floor, since we discover
oors.
ıRIZONTAL

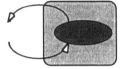

Fig. II.1.30. Object signs: text in
Microsoft Word.

Fig. II.1.31. The object sign.

The Petri-net diagram is shown in Fig. II.1.31. As the diagram suggests, object signs often combine with interactive signs. Both change, but the process is ascribed to the interactive sign, not to the object sign. Consider for example the paper and the pencil in the Fullpaint system:

Fig. II.1.32. The Fullpaint system.

We see an icon signifying a pencil. The icon can be moved across a white space signifying a piece of paper by moving the mouse. Thus, the icon is an interactive sign, containing all three kinds of features. Finally, as long as the mouse button is pressed, a black trace in the form of a one-pixel line is left on the paper.

How should these features be assembled into signs? In the controller case we saw that there were two ways of segmenting signs: on the one hand we can rely on our "naive physics" and assign the computer-based signs to cases in a manner we know from everyday life, and on the other hand we can do a functional analysis that sometimes accords with our naive physics, sometimes contradicts it. In the present case, a "naive physics" analysis would be:

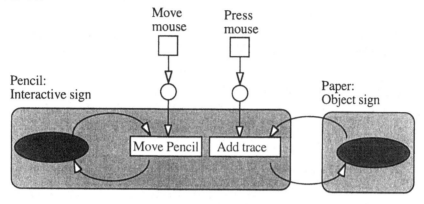

Fig. II.1.33. Pencil and paper: analysis 1.

The pencil-sign is an interactive sign represented by a small pencil icon, which can be moved across the screen by moving the mouse, and in addition it can be used to draw a line on the paper by pressing the button.

The paper-sign is a layout sign represented by a white space which can do nothing.

All processes belong to the pencil-sign, the paper consists only of permanent features. Although this way of segmenting the signs is clearly favoured by our everyday experience of real pencils and paper, there is a possible alternative analysis, where the handling features of pressing the mouse and the transient feature of adding a trace are assigned to the paper, which then has turned into an interactive sign too:

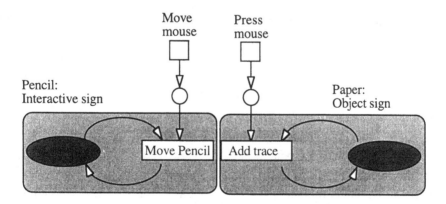

Fig. II.1.34. Pencil and paper: analysis 2.

The functionality is exactly the same, only the sign boundaries have shifted.

Although analysis 1 may seem to be the only possible analysis, the apparent naturalness is easily upset, and has in fact disappeared in the so-called hypertext and spread-sheet systems.

These former contain signs denoting "text" and "pictures", only their type is not objects but also button signs, since parts of a text or picture can be clicked and cause another piece of text or picture to appear.

The illustration is taken from the Guide system and looks like an ordinary text; however, as the cursor shape indicates, the phrase "click here" is a button that causes a new piece of text to appear.

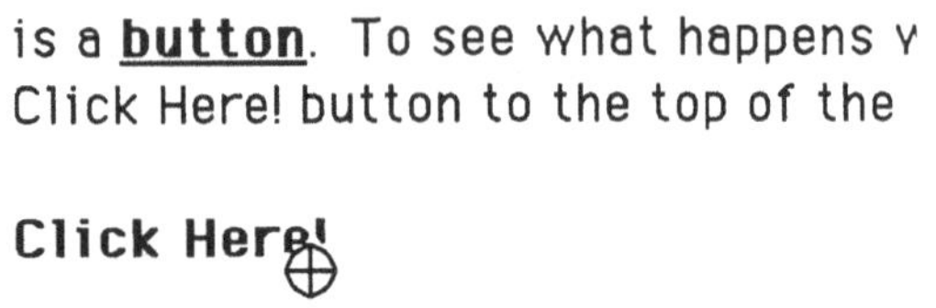

is a **button**. To see what happens ∨
Click Here! button to the top of the

Click Here! ⊕

Fig. II.1.35. The Guide system: interactive text.

Spread-sheets, the second example, are represented as large pieces of "paper", consisting of rectangular cells. If I change the value of one of the cells, the other cells are recalculated and change their own value. The process of changing the number in the cell is clearly experienced as belonging to the individual cell. Since the processes of the individual cell are not initiated by myself, but occur automatically when I change another cell, the cell, which is a part of my paper, is an actor, not an object sign.

So relying on our pre-understanding of the natural world will not suffice in the strange universe of computers. Although analysis 2 seems somehow unnatural, there are other computer-based signs where this analysis is the "natural" one.

In the future, the connotations to non-computerized media will probably lose some of their present importance, and thus the typical case may well be that of the hypertext or the spread-sheet, rather than of the paper and pencil, and in that situation we will not benefit much from a "naive physics" approach, but will be on much safer ground using the functional analysis exemplified in the controller case.

Thus, the reason why analysis 1 should be preferred in the present case is not that it accords with our naive physics, but that it is supported by a functional analysis. In a functional analysis, the reason why the trace leaving should be assigned to the pencil, brush or spray can, and not the the paper, is that the properties of the trace depend upon the tool and not upon the paper. If the pencil is replaced by the spray can or brush, the trace acquires a new property, namely a pattern, and if the brush is chosen, the additional property of size is added.

The reader may think that the preceding discussion is really to make a fuss about nothing. Does it really matter whether walking left and right is a property of the hero or the floor, or whether drawing is an action attributed to pencil or paper? Although the particular analytical alternatives may be without consequence, the principles behind them - relying on a naive physics or relying on functional analysis - are quite important. The first principle means that we implicitly accept the aesthetics of realism and regard the system as a mirror of reality, while the second principle implies that we see the system as an artifact that produces meanings by means of calculated aesthetic devices. I shall treat this question more thoroughly in Section II.2.2.3.

Layout signs

Layout signs lack transient and handling features, and have no function vis-à-vis other signs. They serve as mere decoration and are quite similar to conventional paper based signs.

In the action game Fist II only horizontal movement is possible, and no graphical elements denoting things behind or in front of the actors have any influence on the game. They are mere decorations describing the scene of the combat: trees, leaves, rock, mountains and flower pots.

Fig. II.1.36. The Layout sign.

Ghost signs

Ghost signs are signs that lack both permanent and transient features. They are not represented by icons or other identifiable graphical element, and they cannot be manipulated directly. However, they do have function to other signs. Like controller signs they show their existence by influencing the behavior of other non-ghost signs.

Breakout has no ghost signs, but they are common in other games, where they are used aesthetically. For example, some maze games have hidden traps: they cannot be seen, but they cause the protagonist to fall down if he steps on them.

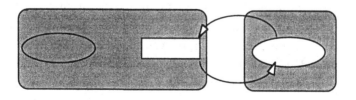

Fig. II.1.37. The Ghost sign.

II.1.2.2. Genres

Our typology is based on expression features, but within a particular genre of computer applications there is a correspondence between the sign types and the possible contents they can be assigned. It is possible to group applications into genres characterized by a common content system ("a universe of discourse"), and *within* such types one finds relatively stable mappings from the sign types to the content units.

Let us look at adventure games first. The main semantic distinction is between animate and inanimate entities. Animateness is coded by presence, inanimateness by absence of transient features. One the one hand, we have the *hero* and the *villains* coded as interactive and actor signs, on the other the *tools, nourishments, valuables, paths, obstacles* and *abysses* that are often all coded as controller signs. Semantically, hero and villains differ in person, since the hero is first person "I", and villains third persons, "they". The person distinction is coded by presence and absence of handling features.

As mentioned above, many inanimates are coded as controllers, and the different subtypes can be distinguished according to the nature of the features they influence. *Spaces* have function to the locomotion of hero and villains, and can be divided into *paths* that enable locomotion, *obstacles* that prevent it, and *abysses* that make a certain locomotion mandatory. In the Dungeons and Dragons variety, cave walls are obstacles and tunnels are paths.

The non-spatial controllers include *tools, weapons, nourishment* and *valuables*. Tools or weapons can be defined as signs affecting the villains, and in many games there are functions between the individual weapon and the enemy, for example, swords may kill ghosts but not skeletons. Nourishments have function to the hero and his properties, e.g. vitality. They need not be edible, but can also be magical items. Finally there are valuables like money or jewels, which do not affect enemies or protagonist, but control the score at the end of the game.

Ghost signs are used to code traps. They cannot be seen, but influence the hero's vitality; in fact they often kill him. Finally, most games have layout signs that have no function to other signs, but are merely decoration.

The next example is the Macintosh universe. In many respects, the Macintosh world is the reverse of the video games' universe. It is friendly and takes pains to remove any sign of weirdness. The interactive sign\actor sign distinction does not signify the lonely ego pitted against the rest of the world, but is used to denote tools in opposition to automatic processes.

It is instructive to compare how tools are expressed in the two universes: in most games, when a weapon is grabbed, the mere possession influences the hero's abilities. The weapon itself may not be visible at all, and it seldom changes itself or other signs as a part of its use: it is a controller. In the Macintosh world, tools are always denoted by interactive signs changing shape and/or position as an integral part of their use, and they effect changes in a work object which, unlike the bad guys of the game, cannot do anything by itself.

The Macintosh space is also articulated in a different way - it contains no ghost signs denoting traps, but has spatial controllers that, beside obstacles, include special subspaces that influence the tool. When the cursor is in one subspace, it may be a pencil that can draw, but moved to other areas of the screen it turns into an arrow that can be used to click and drag things.

Which factors govern our interpretation of computer-based signs? Why, for example, do we come to interpret interactive signs as tools, and actors as automatic machines, and not conversely? One important reason is probably that the real tools and machines and their computer-based counterparts contract similar functions to action and worker.

In non-computerized production, actions presuppose something else, either a worker, a tool, or a machine, but tools and machines differ in their relation to the worker. Tools are means of production that require a worker to wield them in order to get work done, whereas machines can be defined as means of production that only sometimes, but not always, require a worker in order to operate.

We can express this difference[1] by saying that actions either presuppose an interdependence between a worker and a tool (Fig. II.1.38), or they presuppose a presupposition between a worker and a machine, the worker being functionally subordinate to the machine (Fig. II.1.39.).

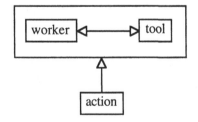

Fig. II.1.38. Functional characteristics of tools.

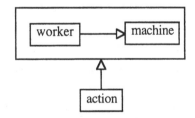

Fig. II.1.39. Functional characteristics of machines.

Interactive signs contract the same functions to worker and action as the physical tool, whereas the functions of the actor sign are similar to the automatic machine.

---

[1] On the notion of tools, see Ehn 1988, Ehn & Kyng 1985, and Bødker 1987.

The choice between tool-like and machine-like functions may be one of the most basic design choices that are made at all: is an expert system planned as a tool for an expert that will not produce any results without him, or is it conceived of as a reasoning engine that is just activated by a push-button?

II.1.2.3. Direction and scenography of computer-based signs

In the preceding, I have tacitly assumed that the linguistic framework set up in part I can directly be applied to computer-based signs. This is not true because computer-based signs are different from verbal signs, and I shall illustrate the problem with a very basic concept of linguistics, namely the notion of a *chain*.

The fact that computer-based signs contain transient features that change over time and permanent features that are constant over time makes it necessary to revise the chain concept. The words and morphemes of the linguistic chain do not change through their lifetime, and it makes no sense to say that the same sign token occurs in more than one place in the chain. It is of course possible to refer to the same content units in different places, but we have to employ different sign tokens to do this, for example using a noun like *my car* the first time and a pronoun *it* the second time.

However, in computer interaction the *same* sign can occur in more than one place in a chain. Here the same icon, whose identity may be given given by its shape and location, can change color, sometimes be grey, sometimes black, and at one point of time it can be part of an action that moves it from one place to another, while at another point in time it belongs to an action that opens it and displays its content. One can say that in contradistinction to the verbal sign, the computer-based sign is a two dimensional object that is always a part of two different types of chains. On the one hand, it has function to signs that are present on the screen at the same time, on the other hand, it also builds syntagms together with sign elements that precede or follow it. The former kind of chains I call concurrent chains, the second kind sequential chains.

- A *concurrent chain* consists of signs or sign parts that occur together at the same point in time.
- A *sequential chain* consists of signs or sign parts that occur after each other at different points in time.

The concurrent chains represent the static working environment of the system: the work objects, the tools and machinery available, the way they are grouped in terms of similarity and dissimilarity, the conceptual structure behind the system, and (not to be forgotten) the general atmosphere.

Sequential chains on the other hand embody the dynamic aspects of the system, the action possibilities and the action patterns.

These properties are crucial to any interactive system, but since there is no tradition in linguistics for treating these two kinds of chains, I shall start by looking at dance and theater, where they are of the same importance as in computer systems.

Dance

A dance instructor or a writer of textbooks on dance has the same problems as a designer of computer systems, since dancers, like computer-based signs, participate in two kinds of chains: they move in time, and they enter varying concurrent constellations with each other. The dance instructor must teach the dancers both how to move in time, how to coordinate their movements with their partner, how to hold each other, and how to establish collective patterns. In the following I shall briefly describe how an author of a textbook on folk dance[1] has solved these problems.

The first thing to note is that he treats the two chains separately, the sequential one being described in most detail. The author invents a notation for describing the atomic movements of which any dance is composed. The atomic units, the "dance taxemes", consist of two main features, the orientation of the dancer, and the movements of the feet. Below are shown three examples: in the first, the dancer moves the right foot to the right, in the second he puts it back, and in the third the left foot is brought together with the right foot.

Fig. II.1.40. Notation for steps.

These taxemes are composed into larger sequences defining particular steps like waltz and polka. Some of these involve only one dancer, but a few are only defined for couples. This is true of waltz that is described as shown in Fig. II.1.41.

The waltz step is composed of two times three dance taxemes, the first three steps of one dancer being identical to the last three steps of the partner. Although the main syntagm is *sequential* (the horizontal boxes) the dance

---

[1] Jørgensen 1979.

steps require a particular *concurrent* syntagm (the vertical boxes), namely the *couple*.

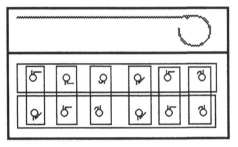

Fig. II.1.41. Waltz.

There must be exactly two dancers, and they must hold each other in a particular way. In addition, the movements of the couple enter a concurrent government function.When one dancer puts her right foot to the right, her partner must bring his left foot back, and when she brings her left foot together with her right, her partner must bring his right foot together with his left[1].

In folk dance there are two main concurrent syntagms, the chain and the couple:

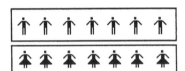

Fig. II.1.42. Chains.   Fig. II.1.43. Couples.

In Danish dances it seems as if the category of chains presupposes that of couples, since some dances involve only couples, others both couples and chains, whereas few (if any) involve only chains.

The basic syntagms can be further classified. For example, couples are sometimes established by an interdependence between two individuals (the same persons dance with each other), sometimes merely by constellation between individuals, but an interdependence between the paradigms of male and female dancers, so that a male always dances with a female, but partners can change throughout the dance.

---

[1] Note that the complex step may have properties that are not found in its part. For example, *turning*, indicated above the steps, cannot be found as a property of the six individual steps, but only emerges as a property of the composite units. The whole is not equal to the sum of its parts.

We see that the abstract concepts of sequential and concurrent chains have very straightforward interpretations in dance: the sequential chains represent the movements of the dancers, and the concurrent ones the particular groupings they enter. The different types of steps are sequential syntagms, while standard groupings like chains versus couple are concurrent syntagms.

Theater

Theater plays and films can put even more meat on our abstract bones.

All theatrical signs, in particular the actors themselves[1], are part of both concurrent and sequential chains. On the one hand, the collection of actors present on the stage at the same time forms an important type of concurrent chain that in classical theater was used to segment the play into scenes. There is a new scene each time a new constellation of actors is formed. On the other hand, the individual actor normally goes through some kind of change during the play. In the beginning, Hamlet is shy and indecisive, but during the play he matures and succeeds in revenging his father in the ending. Actions not only form sequential chains (beginning-middle-ending), they also enter into concurrent chains with set-pieces and props, which must be motivated and significant in relation to the actions. The line "Alas! poor Yorick. I knew him, Horatio..." in Act V scene I of Hamlet requires the presence of a skull, which again must be motivated by the graveyard set-pieces of the scene, which in turn would be out of place if not required by the dialogue. Here a whole collection of actions and utterances is interdependent with a particular set-piece, but we can also see functions between individual actions and props, as when entrance and exit of actors require the presence of a door.

As in dance, the process and system views can be applied to both sequential and concurrent chains, giving us four types of structures:

Concurrent syntagms: functions between elements that occur together in a concurrent chain. The most obvious are the syntagms formed by props and wings that communicate a global atmosphere to the audience and indicate the location where the action takes place; however, actors also enter concurrent syntagms. For example, an auxiliary character may only appear on stage when a certain main character is present. The auxiliary character then presupposes the main one, the former having dramatic function only through the latter.

Concurrent paradigms: all the elements that can replace each other in the same place in a concurrent chain. The settings of the play may consist of a

---

[1] From a semiotic point of view, all elements on a stage or screen are signs. The actor playing Hamlet is not really the prince of Denmark but only signifies him, he does not really slay Polonius, and the castle of Elsinore is not present on the scene but only a painted canvas.

main set-piece, with different props marking different locations within the main piece, e.g. a bed signifying bedroom, a table the drawing room, and a tree an outside location. Since bed, table and tree can be interchanged in the same context, effecting a change of meaning in the whole setting, they form a perfectly normal concurrent paradigm.

Characters can also form paradigms: in one of Brecht's plays, *The Good Woman of Setzuan,* the heroine splits herself up into two characters in order to survive in a hard and unjust world: an unselfish woman, whose good heart brings her into one difficulty after the other, and a selfish man that uses the ways of the world to get her out again. The two egos never appear together on stage, but enter into identical person constellations, and therefore constitute a concurrent paradigm. On the other hand, the alter egos act completely differently, and never enter into the same sequential syntagms. Therefore they do not form sequential paradigms.

The example demonstrates how the two chains can be exploited artistically. A basic rule of modern art is that its message should not be postulated verbally, but must be shown and demonstrated by using the special effects of the theater. Brecht's message is that goodness and self-preservation cannot be reconciled in our society, and he demonstrates this very skilfully by letting the two egos of the protagonist enter into a concurrent paradigm. When one aspect of the heroine is present on the stage, the other is excluded.

Sequential syntagms: functions between elements that occur together in a sequential chain. These syntagms range from very general dramatic patterns, like Ibsen's illusion-disillusion pattern, to functions between individual lines, like question-answer, offer-accept.

Sequential paradigms: all the elements that can replace each other in the same place in a sequential chain. In Ibsen's case, the outcome of the disillusionment would constitute a sequential paradigm, consisting of e.g. Nora's leaving the home *(A Doll's House),* and Hedvig's death *(The Wild Duck),* each expressing different views on the value of disclosing the truth.

Computer systems

Computer systems possess some of the features exemplified in dance and theater. They too have analogies to steps and groupings, to set-pieces and dramatic episodes[1].

I shall start with a very simple example, a fragment of a panel controlling a video recorder. It consists of three buttons, an *on/off* button, a *play* button, and a *rewind* button placed in a rectangle. In the beginning, only the *on* button is visible (1). When it is clicked, the two other buttons appear under-

---

[1] See Laurel 1986.

neath, and the *on* button turns into an *off* button (2). Each of these can be clicked: if clicked, they invert and stay inverted as long as their process runs (3,4). The system is closed by clicking the *off* button that toggles and again turns into the *on* button.

A possible system process, consisting of five states, would look like this:

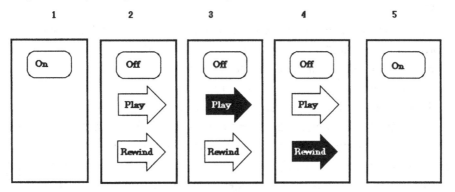

Fig. II.1.44. Video recorder panel.

What are sequential and concurrent chains in this small system, and what do they signify?

The sequential chains come into existence when you read the figure from left to right, and the concurrent ones when you read it from top to bottom. However, we are not interested in merely any chain, only in those that have meaning and function as signs. Thus, although we have *On* in state 1 and *Play* in state 2, *On + Play* is not a sequential chain since this sequence does not express any content and is not marked as a constituent on the screen, whereas the sequence *Play + Play, inverted + Play* in 2,3 and 4 is a relevant chain, since it expresses the content "playing the video recorder" and is marked as a unit because it involves the same sign (same letters, same location) with different properties (inverted-non-inverted). In the same way, On + Off is a chain consisting of two signs with the same location signifying changes in the video recorder: on or off.

The video panel exemplifies the four types of structures in the following way:

Concurrent syntagms: the chains (On. <u>Rewind.Play</u>) and (Off. Rewind.Play) give rise to a three member syntagm, whose first slot is filled with *On* or *Off* and whose second and third slots are occupied by *Rewind* and *Play*. The syntagm should be interpreted as meaning that the actions of the signs whose permanent features fill its slot are available to the user. In this case it signifies that the last two actions depend upon the first one. Only if the recorder is turned on, can it be played and rewound. Syntactically, the last two slots presuppose the first one, since the first slot is always filled, while the last ones may be empty. In general, computer systems use concurrent syntagms much in the same way as the theater: they represent the scene in which action is taking place with work objects and tools, a scene which is often used to communicate a particular feeling: *this is fun* or *this is serious work*!

Concurrent paradigms: if we look at the upper part of the rectangle and record which elements can replace each other in this context, we get the chains (Rectangle.On) and (Rectangle.Off), giving us a concurrent paradigm of two members, <+On, +Off>. Concurrent paradigms can be used to signify that its members are similar but antonyms or mutually exclusive. Thus, *On* and *Off* both concern the state of the video recorder, but they are antonyms, one reversing the action of the other, and they are also mutually exclusive: when *On* is possible, *Off* is impossible, and vice versa. This type of paradigm is so common that it has its own name, a *toggle* (toggle switch). In general, concurrent paradigms can be used to mark objects or actions as having similar function.

Sequential syntagms: the chains *Play + Play, inverted + Play* and *Rewind + Rewind, inverted + Rewind* means that the operations Play and Rewind are executed, and are examples of a very common three member sequential syntagm $X + X, Y + X$, where X is the permanent features of a sign and Y one of its transient features. The meaning of the syntagm is "execution of action X". Sequential syntagms in computer systems are like those of the theater and the dance: they represent action patterns.

Sequential paradigms: if we look at state 2 in which neither Play nor Rewind is inverted, and record the possible actions that can follow, we end up with three possibilities, namely 3 (play), 4 (rewind), or 5 (close). State 2 thus generates a sequential paradigm of three actions, <+play, +rewind, +close>, representing the action possibilities in this state. In general, sequential paradigms represent action possibilities. In theater and film they are one of the main sources of excitement: what happens next, while in computer systems they represent the action possibilities of the user: the interactive range[1].

This simple example demonstrates that like the props and wings on the theatrical scene, the concurrent syntagms of the scene of the screen tell us where we are and what can be done, and the concurrent paradigms tell us which items are similar. The sequential syntagms describe patterns of actions, and the sequential paradigms represent the choices available to us.

---

[1] Laurel 1986.

Graphical aspects of concurrent chains

In later sections, I shall describe in detail the structure of sequential syntagms. In this section I shall confine myself to some short remarks on how to build concurrent syntagms.

The main point to be made is that on modern machines with advanced graphical facilities, concurrent syntagms are created by a mixture of pictorial and verbal codes.

Let us first look at the pictorial codes. In pictorial codes[1], *closure, proximity, similarity* and *order* are important means for building composite signs, and the Fullpaint screen shown above uses all of them: all items from the same panel are enclosed in rectangles (closure) and positioned close to each other (proximity). For example, the pencil belongs to the same menu as the brush and therefore the pencil is placed near to it, and not to e.g. the black paint. Also, the items of the submenu concerned with the same type of drawing (free hand vs geometrical) are similar in shape, and differ from the other items of the same panel (similarity).

If the screen image is to be unambiguous, the composite signs should be expressed by all three means of expression: its components should be near to each other, they should be similar, and enclosed by some regular contour. In the first picture below, the sign formation is very clear, since all three conditions are fulfilled: there are two composite signs enclosed in a rounded rectangle; their parts are close to each other and similar to each other with respect to color and shape.

Fig. II.1.45. Unambiguous composite sign.

In the next example, all three features contradict each other, and the result is ambiguous. It is not clear which parts belong together and where the boundaries between the signs should be:

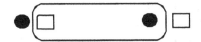

Fig. II.1.46. Ambiguous composite sign.

---

[1] This paragraph is based upon Hansson et al 1974.

Ambiguous pictures should be avoided in non-fiction systems that must tell the user which actions he can do or has done, but are indispensable in artistic pictures.

The last feature, sequence, is also important in building composite signs. Like word order in verbal language, the order of graphical signs can commute and therefore contract a sign function, as becomes clear by comparing the two pictures below. The only difference is that the man and woman have been flipped horizontally, yet the meaning of the first picture, "a man meets a woman", is different from that of the second one which may be paraphrased "a man helps a child down from a wall".

Fig. II.1.47. Graphical sequence.

Note also that pictorial elements can have different functions to the net content of the picture[1]. In the first picture, the boy is not necessary for the message, whereas both man and woman must be present. With respect to the interpretation, man and woman form an interdependence that is modified by the boy, who is mere decoration. The situation is reversed in the second picture: here man and boy are interdependent with respect to the given interpretation, while it does not matter whether the woman occurs or not.

Verbal codes can of course also be used to create concurrent syntagms by designing the syntagm as a sentence or a phrase, but normally pictorial effects are used to support the verbal syntagms. The form in Fig. II.1.48 is a form from Word 3 (slightly modified in order to show the point more clearly) for specifying page layout.

In order to show that the individual choices hang together, it is constructed as one sentence "Pages (subject) are numbered (verb), 1.3 from top (and) 1.4 cm from right (locative) using "1 2 3" or "A B C" or "I II III" or "i

---

[1] Since pictorial codes are looser than verbal ones, a picture may have more than one possible "net content", and it is necessary to select one of them when analyzing the picture in this manner.

ii iii" and starting at number 1 (appositions)", whose parts can be selected or specified.

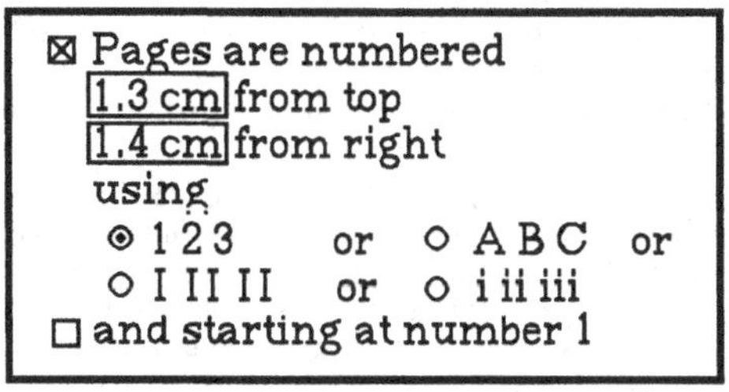

```
┌─────────────────────────────┐
│ ☒ Pages are numbered        │
│   [1.3 cm] from top         │
│   [1.4 cm] from right       │
│   using                     │
│     ⊙ 1 2 3    or  ○ A B C  or │
│     ○ I II II  or  ○ i ii iii │
│   □ and starting at number 1 │
└─────────────────────────────┘
```

Fig. II.1.48. Mixing verbal and graphical codes.

Some of the contents, however, are not coded by verbal but by pictorial elements: the box means "yes or no", the circle denotes one of a limited set of alternatives, and the boxed text can contain many different alternatives that are to be entered by the user. In addition, the verbal syntagms are underlined by pictorial ones: the sentences are enclosed by a rectangle, and parallel sentence parts align horizontally or vertically.

II.1.2.4. Using the concepts

From the stand-point of classical structural linguistics, the interface analysis above is the most obvious to come up with. It uses the basic concepts of syntagms and paradigms, and the only modification made to theory is the doubling of the concepts into concurrent and sequential varieties. So the analysis is clearly theoretically motivated, but which practical uses can it be put to?

I shall give three examples of possible uses: the concepts can be used as a method for abstracting useful features from complex descriptions, for designing systems with a basis in work practice, and as a framework for formulating interaction styles.

Means of abstraction

Like all other systems specifications, interface specifications easily get extremely messy, threatening to drown the essentials in details. As an example, consider the simple operation of copying, cutting and pasting text in the Macintosh version of Word 3. The text itself is presented as shown below:

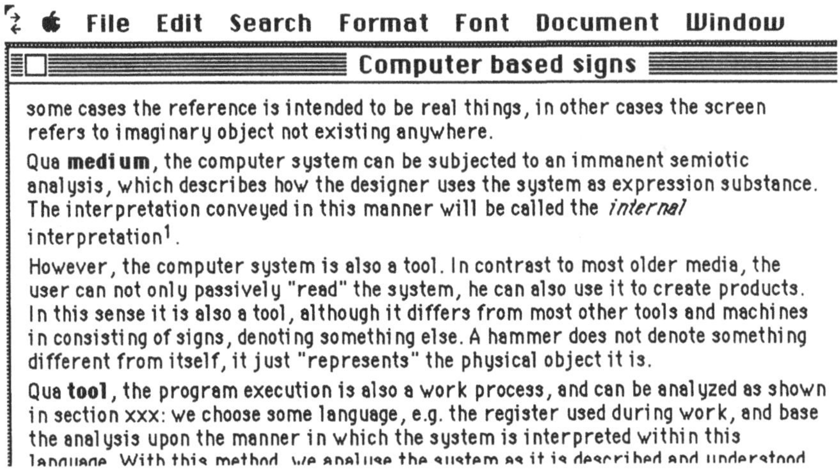

File   Edit   Search   Format   Font   Document   Window

Computer based signs

some cases the reference is intended to be real things, in other cases the screen refers to imaginary object not existing anywhere.

Qua **medium**, the computer system can be subjected to an immanent semiotic analysis, which describes how the designer uses the system as expression substance. The interpretation conveyed in this manner will be called the *internal* interpretation[1].

However, the computer system is also a tool. In contrast to most older media, the user can not only passively "read" the system, he can also use it to create products. In this sense it is also a tool, although it differs from most other tools and machines in consisting of signs, denoting something else. A hammer does not denote something different from itself, it just "represents" the physical object it is.

Qua **tool**, the program execution is also a work process, and can be analyzed as shown in section xxx: we choose some language, e.g. the register used during work, and base the analysis upon the manner in which the system is interpreted within this language. With this method, we analyse the system as it is described and understood

Fig. II.1.49. Text in Microsoft Word.

Editing text is done by pulling down the Edit menu in the menu bar, and selecting one of its items. Let us look a little closer at one of these, namely cutting a piece of text.

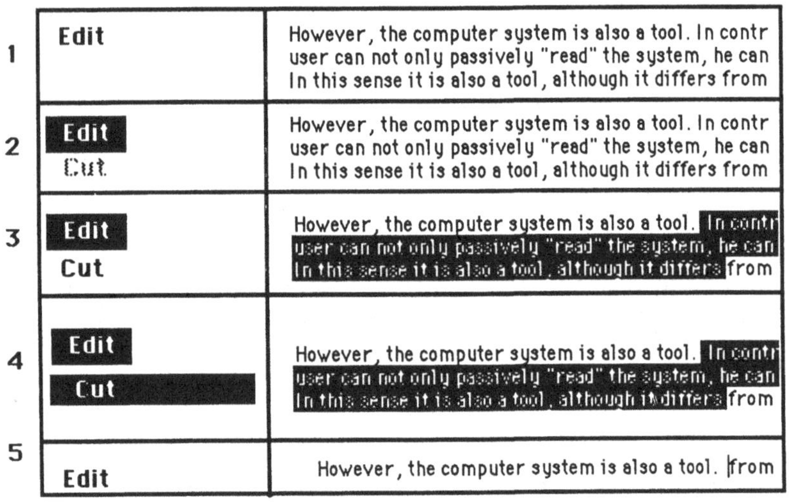

1	**Edit**	However, the computer system is also a tool. In contr user can not only passively "read" the system, he can In this sense it is also a tool, although it differs from
2	**Edit** Cut	However, the computer system is also a tool. In contr user can not only passively "read" the system, he can In this sense it is also a tool, although it differs from
3	**Edit** Cut	However, the computer system is also a tool. In contr user can not only passively "read" the system, he can In this sense it is also a tool, although it differs from
4	**Edit** **Cut**	However, the computer system is also a tool. In contr user can not only passively "read" the system, he can In this sense it is also a tool, although it differs from
5	**Edit**	However, the computer system is also a tool. from

Fig. II.1.50. Cutting text in Microsoft Word.

In the beginning the screen looks like (1), and when we pull down the "Edit"-menu, the word "Cut" has a grey color (2). However, we can select a piece of text by dragging the cursor over it, and now "Cut" has become black (3). If we select the "Cut"-operation (marked by inversion, cf. 4), the selected piece of text and the pulldown menu disappear, and we end in situation (5).

These events can of course be described in a Petri-net, but even an incomplete net-description of this simple event already tends to become messy - imagine what a complete description of the total Word system would look like! The problem with formal descriptions is not a lack of precision, but rather vastness, confusion and the danger of getting lost in details, so methods for abstracting useful concepts out of such descriptions are welcome. Let us see what we can do with the four concepts:

Concurrent syntagms: Before we pull down the Edit menu, we record

Edit. <u>Cut. Copy. Paste</u>

and after we have

Edit. Cut. Copy. Paste

These two chains can be described as a two member concurrent syntagm, in which the first slot is occupied by the menu heading that is presupposed by the second slot with the menu items.

In general, pulldown and pop-up menus can be defined as two member concurrent syntagms in which the permanent features of menu items presuppose those of the menu heading.

Fig. II.1.51. Menu and menu items.

But there are other syntagms to be discovered. One important type is *government* between transient and handling features.

I shall later define government (in Section II.2.1.2, where I analyze complex computer-based actions), but for now suffice to say that it is a syntagmatic function between members in two paradigms, so that choice of a member in one paradigm influences the choice in the other one.

Let us take the cut-action again. We first record the other features that can co-occur with the "c u t" letters of the cut-action, constructing the concurrent paradigm of its transient features. The letters can have two different colors, black and grey, and the black version can be inverted or non-inverted. There are two paradigms (or systems, in Halliday's terminology), a Color paradigm that is presupposed by an Inversion paradigm (Fig. II.1.52).

The text representation cannot change color, but contains the same Inversion paradigm as the commands, and the Inversion of the text governs the Color of the commands (Fig. II.1.53). Government can not only obtain between transient features as above, but also between handling and transient features.

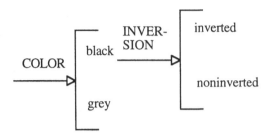

Fig. II.1.52. The transient features of color and inversion.

The handling features of the mouse include two main elements, pressing and releasing the mouse button, with government obtaining between the handling and the inversion paradigms of the individual signs (Fig. II.1.54); releasing the mouse requires the sign to be inverted, and pressing requires it to be non-inverted.

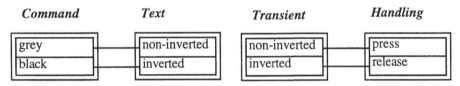

Fig. II.1.53. Government between   Fig. II.1.54. Government between
transient features of commands and text.   transient and handling features.

We shall later see that government and the related concept of agreement are good abstractions, since they account for many ways in which simple computer-based signs are combined to denote composite signs. In addition, the concepts are not peculiar to computer-based signs, but can (and for many centuries have been) used to describe human language. For example, the verbal morphemes can contract functions of both agreement and government. Agreement is found in *He saw me after I came* where both verbs must agree in tense (also known as consecutio temporum) - we cannot have **He sees me after I came* or **He saw me after I come,* and the force that, according to the analysis in Part I, establishes the sentence is a government between tense and case, namely an interdependence between a tense morpheme and a nominative case.

Concurrent paradigms: We have already met one type of important concurrent paradigm, namely the handling and transient features of the individual signs, e.g. Color (black, grey) or Inversion (inverted, non-inverted) or the handling possibilities (pressing, releasing, or moving the mouse). Black and grey are members of the same concurrent paradigm, since they occur in the same context (e.g. with the letters "c u t"), but never together, whereas

Inversion and Color are two different paradigms because their members are not mutually exclusive. A command can be both black and inverted.

Sequential syntagms: Sequential syntagms can be parts of each other, the smaller syntagm filling a particular slot in the larger one.

If we start at the bottom, we note recurrent patterns like *pressing mouse button + releasing mouse button* ("clicking") and *pressing mouse button + moving mouse + releasing mouse button* ("dragging"). If we only look at these two, we record an interdependence between pressing and releasing, while moving presupposes this muscular syntagm, since it may or may not occur.

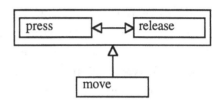

Fig. II.1.55. The syntagm of mouse handling.

Elements like *press, release* and *move* are in this example below the level of meaning, and correspond to phonemes, while the units they form correspond to syllables. Design of syntagms like these therefore lies on the borders of semiotics, and substance considerations like rhythm and ease of movement should play a major role.

When we ascend one level and transcend the barrier of meaning, we arrive at the level of actions (which later turn out to be analogous to sentences). Their internal structure follows the syntagms above, so that the action of selecting text is expressed by pressing, moving and releasing the mouse, but they also mutually contract functions. For example, it turns out that actions can only be selected when an object has been chosen, while objects can be chosen without actions.

Thus, the composite action of cutting a text consists of two slots, object selection presupposed by action selection.

Fig. II.1.56. The syntagm of object and action selection.

This pattern has become popular in recent years, but it is worth noticing that it is just a convention, and that other syntagms are perfectly possible.

Continuing our ascent, we arrive at the next level, where task-related actions begin to emerge: copying, cutting and pasting are all constructed according the previous syntagm, but again contract new dependencies among themselves.

For example, *pasting* presupposes *copying* or *cutting*, since one of these operations must have filled the buffer with something.

Fig. II.1.57. Action syntagms.

Sequential paradigms: "Cutting a piece of text" forms a sequential paradigm together with "copying a piece of text" and "pasting a piece of text", provided that the text is already selected: at a given point of time, we can choose between all three actions. Sequential action paradigms like these to a large degree determine how well the system fits to a given work process, since they express which actions are available at a given point of time.

With this little list of examples I have shown that the four concepts can be used as a systematic basis for abstracting concepts from the interface that are commonly recognized as important and useful. In the next paragraphs I shall demonstrate how they can support particular design methods.

Design methods

In Section I.2.3.3, I summed up the difference between the system concepts in computer science and linguistics in the following way: in computer systems, we cannot have processes without a structure, while the opposite is possible, so that processes are subordinate to structures. We must first make the structure, before we can have processes. In opposition to this, the usage and schema of human language (and other kinds of behavior) are interdependent: schema emerges from usage and is changed by it, but usage in its turn requires an underlying schema to count as a particular kind of social behavior, e.g. language usage. Since the raison d'etre of computer systems is the interface they manifest and the work schemas they can support, and since neither can be constructed but must emerge as patterns of usage, a good design strategy seems to be to start with usage and then abstract recurrent patterns from this usage[1].

Thus, we want to gather data on the tasks users want to do and then analyze this data in order to construct a computer system. To use the theatrical analogy once more: before we build the stage setting, we want to rehearse the various parts of the play we are staging, and make notes of necessary props and set-pieces as we go along. Having done this, we want to bring these bits and pieces together to a total conception of the stage layout that will support the performance. Classical structuralist linguistics supports this design method because it is descriptive and analytic. Its methods presuppose

---

[1] Ehn & Kyng 1987, Bødker 1987, ch. 5, Ehn 1988 ch. 15.

that some kind of corpus exists, and aim at finding regularities in the corpus. In the following, I shall give three small examples of this technique.

The first example is taken from a small research project on cooperative design[1]. The purpose of the project is to investigate user-designer dialogues in design situations, and the concrete exercise in question aimed at designing useful tools for researchers that write books. Besides the actual texts they write, the researchers use notes, literature references, and some kind of conceptual classification system. The first prototype implemented turned out to be unusable since it focused too much on the auxiliary documents and too little on the purpose of the work process, namely the texts; moreover, it contained a wrong conceptualization, and did not allow the users to do frequent tasks in an easy way.

Since I had spent a lot of time programming a fancy interface for the prototype, I felt rather dejected. In order to circumvent the paradox of design - that if users are to develop an interface, system processes must be available to them, which again requires a lot of possibly wasted work with programming the system structure - I made a little system without any functionality, in which users could make and handle dummy screen signs. The simulator consisted of a palette of screen signs (menus, cards, texts) that could be dragged into the simulated screen when needed.

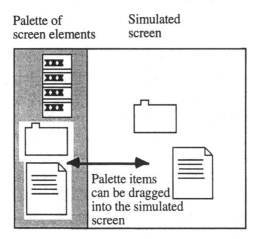

Fig. II.1.58. Simplified screen image of simulator.

By pressing a key, I could obtain snapshots of the screen plus the handling events that had occurred since the last snapshot, and I tried to have the users

---

[1] The project is a part of a larger research effort "Computer support for cooperative design and communication", described in Bøgh Andersen et al 1987.

segment their work by making them type a new name into the system when they felt they were doing a new and different task.

In one of the early sessions, data of the following kind was obtained:

1. Write. The session starts with the user writing a paper called "Perspective and work" to be published in a new Scandinavian journal. Only the text is necessary.

> *Screen snapshot:*   text
> *Preceding actions:*   none

2. Add reference. She has been told by the publisher to consult another paper called "The perspective concept in informatics" on the subject, and wants to add a reference showing that she has been obedient to their wishes. To accomplish this, she adds the index card with the reference, and imagines that she can transfer the reference to her text by clicking on the text where she wants the reference, then clicking the index card of the reference.

> *Screen snapshot:*   text, index card
> *Preceding actions:*   click text, click index card

3. Make a note. Now that she has the reference, she wants to make a note of the way she has used it and how she has interpreted it. Therefore she adds yet another prop, a note, which she fills in and connects to the index card by clicking the card and the note.

> *Screen snapshot:*   text, index card, note
> *Preceding actions:*   click index card, click note

4 . Add concept. The reason why the publisher asked her to consult the paper was that it treated the same concept as she does, namely "perspective". The concept is so familiar to her that she has not entered it into her conceptual system. However, she wants to do so now, so that she will be able to find the index card and notes by means of the concept. According to the protocol, she seems to have invented the following method: select the word, possibly in the text, and click at the concept list, whereupon the word is entered.

> *Screen snapshot:*   text, index card, note, concept list
> *Preceding actions:*   click concept list

She continues her simulated work in this way, indexing her notes, searching her notes for particular topics, making reference lists, and inventing props, e.g. menus, when necessary.

When finished, the user has simulated a possible task during which she has created the settings she wants. The data available to the designer consists of the snapshot's concurrent chains of work objects plus sequential chains of the actions that preceded the snapshot. The task is now to discover patterns in these chains, and design a system structure that will accommodate these and other practices.

The most conspicuous feature is that the text is present in all concurrent chains, while index cards, menus, notes and concept list come and go, so that the text is presupposed by all other documents. The reason for this is that the latter are only means for the former, which is the end. The means only obtain meaning in relation to the end, which must be present in order to judge their usefulness. Had I realized this from the beginning, I would have saved many hours of pointless programming.

A glance at the concurrent paradigms generated by the four sign types

concept list.	<index card, text, note, menu, <u>concept list</u>>
menu.	<index card, text, note, <u>menu</u>, concept list>
index card.	<index card, text , note, menu, concept list>
note.	<index card, text, note, menu, concept list>

reveals that

(1) menu and concept list differ from index card and note in that the screen only contains one specimen of the former, but can hold more than one example of the latter, but
(2) apart from this restriction, all signs combine freely.

(1) seems to reflect a real difference, since concept list and menu are similar in that they are used for retrieving index cards, notes and texts, and we may wish to underline this similarity by giving them similar visual appearance.

If (2) is accepted at face value, the analysis can be summarized by saying that they all form a concurrent constellation. However, a closer inspection indicates that we may have to encatalyze a menu in action 2 (add reference), where she gets hold of an index card and 3 (make a note), where she generates a new note. At this point of the session, she has not thought about how to get hold of these items, and just provides them by hand, but in a real system she will need some way of specifying the type of document she wants. Encatalyzing a menu in all actions changes its concurrent functions, since now the menu acts as a tool for getting hold of concept list, notes and index cards and is therefore presupposed by them.

I shall stop here, but the design process goes on by enacting new "plots" and abstracting new patterns of behavior from them. The preliminary result for "stage" layout can be summarized in the diagram shown on the next page.

The superordinate sign is the text which is always present. Sometimes a menu can be called forth and be used for retrieving or creating arbitrary combinations of index cards, notes and concept list.

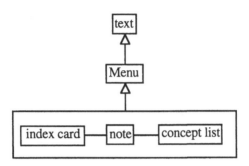

Fig. II.1.59. Functions between screen elements obtained by analysis of task simulations.

The example illustrates how program executions can be viewed as a "text" that can be analyzed with traditional linguistic methods and concepts, and in addition shows the benefits of doing it: namely that the system structure can be constructed from usage.

In this example, the task structure is almost identical to the structure of the interface because each task uses only one primitive interface component. However, normally the tasks will be expressed by several components, and therefore the structure of the components may well be different from the task structure. The next example illustrates how to use a task structure to discover the structure of its primitive interface components.

Suppose I am to design a word processor in which three actions should be possible: reading, writing, and scrolling. From task analysis I know that writing and scrolling form a constellation that presupposes reading. I always want to read, and sometimes to write or scroll. I have also decided to express the three actions in the following way:

Read: text
Write: text + I-beam cursor
Scroll: text + arrow cursor + scrollbar

Now, which functions should obtain between text, I-beam cursor, arrow cursor, and scrollbar? This can be seen from a table in which the rows represent possible action sequences, and the columns the occurrence or non-occurrence of our four screen elements.

	text cursor	I-beam cursor	arrow	scrollbar
read	+	-	-	-
read+write	+	+	-	-
read+write+scroll	+	+	+	+
read+scroll	+	-	+	+

We immediately see that arrow cursor and scrollbar are interdependent and together with the I-beam cursor they form a constellation that presupposes the text.

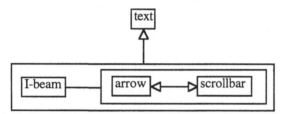

Fig. II.1.60. Functions between screen elements in simple text editing.

Thus, the screen will always present the text, and sometimes the I-beam cursor alone, the arrow cursor and scrollbar alone, or all together. This again means that the I-cursor should only be placed in the text at the request of the user, since it is irrelevant and disturbing if he only wants to read, and the scrollbar should not be present all the time, but could be made to pop up when the user moves his cursor into the margin of the text.

The last example is the data-recording task at the Postal Giro whose structure was described in Section I.2.2.1. The actual interface was textual, but how would a graphical interface to the same task look like?

Let us look at the three actions *fetch*, *destroy* and *send to fliers*.

All three actions can be signified by means of three-part structure

selection in list + dragging + deselection in list.

that is used to express movements of a work object, either a card or a batch, from one pile of paper (the source list) to another pile of paper (the destination list).

I need three signs to express actions of this type: the cursor, the source list (which must be open if I am to select the wanted work object), and the destination list (which can be closed). To express the three actions, three lists are needed, namely my own *current batch [bunt],* and the files shared with the department, *the fliers [flygare]* and the *destroyed cards [borttagna kort].*

In addition to these actions, I have to support the variant task structure, allowing the worker to postpone error handling (*abandon* the batch). In order to show the special status of the *abandon* operation, I choose to use a push-button instead of having one more list called *abandoned batches.*

Now I know how to "spell" the actions, and the next step is to look at the
task structure in Section I.2.2.1 in order to find out which syntactic relations
should obtain between these signs in order to be able to express the tasks in
a convenient way. I look at the diagram, record which actions occur together, and note the signs necessary to express the actions.

	closed batch	*open batch*	*abandon button*	*closed fliers*	*open fliers*	*destroyed cards*
card missing + fetch or abandon	+	+	+	-	+	-
superfluous card + send or abandon	-	+	+	+	-	-
no signature + de-stroy or abandon	-	+	+	-	-	+

The table tells us that the *open batch* and the *abandon button* must always
be present and that the three rightmost elements (*closed fliers, open fliers,*
and *destroyed cards*) form a paradigm, since they mutually exclude each
other. However, since one of these elements is always present, the paradigm
itself is interdependent with the batch list and the abandon button.

The error scene will then have the following structure

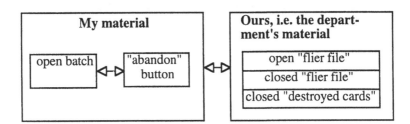

Fig. II.1.61. Functions between screen elements in error handling, based on task
analysis.

Its basic element is an interdependence between the worker's current batch
list and the abandon button. To this skeleton must be added one member of
the paradigm of the department's lists (the fliers or abandoned batches), governed by the error paradigm.

According to the analysis, the screen configuration used to fetch a missing
card from the fliers (open batch, open flier file, abandon button) could look
like this:

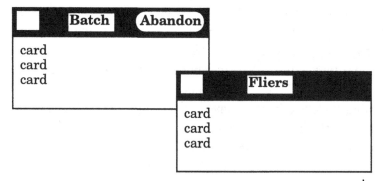

Fig. II.1.62. A possible implementation of the functions in Fig. II.1.61.

Interaction styles

In a very general way, the scenography of a play presupposes its plot and direction. We do not mainly go to the theater to enjoy the beautiful set-pieces, but to engage in the characters' actions, and the scenography is supposed to support the experience of the plot, not vice versa. Although we can imagine plays with no set-pieces and props, we cannot have one with a beautiful scenography without action.

I think the same is true of computer systems, and since concurrent chains are mainly relevant to scenography while sequential chains concern the direction and plot, it follows that concurrent chains should be designed to make the sequential ones possible and understandable.

This poses the question of how the two kinds of chains should be related. One general way of relating the two chains is simply to exchange the paradigmatical and syntagmatical dimensions:

- *The rule of inversion:* Signs constituting a sequential paradigm should form a concurrent syntagm, and those constituting a sequential syntagm should form a concurrent paradigm.

As has appeared from the preceding analyses, all kinds of menus and buttons are subsumed under the first part of the guide-line.

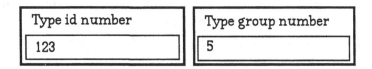

Fig. II.1.63. Prompt driven log-in procedure.

The second part recommends that sequences of prompts and responses occur in the same place of the screen, as in the following example (Fig. II.1.63) from a multi-user system, where the log-in procedure consists of long sequences of pairs, the first of which is a system-generated prompt, while the second one is characters typed by the user.

The system first writes "Type id number" and the user writes "123", then the system prompts "Type group number" and the user types "5". The two system prompts clearly form a sequential syntagm, and the same is true of the user actions. In the design above, the members of these syntagms simultaneously form concurrent paradigms, since they occur in the same place, but never together. "123" and "5" occur in the same box, but at different times.

The rule of inversion is clearly a sensible one, since on the one hand, it informs the user of which actions are possible by presenting parts of them to him, and on the other hand it tells him which operations belong together by displaying them on the same place of the screen.

But what kind of rule is it? Is it some kind of psychological law that psychologists can find out by experiments? From a semiotic point of view, this view is misguided. Good and exciting symbolic products, like the paintings of the impressionists, the plays of Ibsen, or the films of Bergman are not developed by assessing and improving existing products, but by breaking and re-negotiating a contract with the public or audience.

Scenography is a good example. Basically, all items on the scene are incomplete replicas of real things, but the audience and the director have entered a specific contract: the audience has agreed to disregard the faults for a couple of hours provided certain demands are fulfilled. In the beginning of naturalist theater, the audience demanded a complete furnished drawing room with suitably dressed actors, and in exchange agreed to ignore the space outside it. However, this contract was broken and re-negotiated several times later. Some directors got rid of superfluous furniture and only kept the bare necessities, others removed all wings, and placed the scene in the middle of the audience, and still others dressed the actors in the same outfit, thereby removing the code of clothing from the stage. The sequential plot of the play is the same, but the concurrent chains changed dramatically.

My point is that there is no objective way of measuring which stage setting is the "best" one, since choice of setting depends upon the director's theory of theater and his outlook on life, and its success upon the experiences and expectations of the audience. The "Rule of inversion" is therefore not a scientific hypothesis about which screen-layout is the best one, but rather a proposal of a contract with an audience.

II.1.3. Semiotic aspects of programming

In Section II.1.1, I described sign-oriented programming as a programming perspective that sees a program execution as a play, manifesting computer-based signs that aim at giving its audience experience of and insight into either a real or imaginary part of the world.

II.1.3.1. Programming as a meta-semiology

The computer-based signs articulate the expression substance generated by a program execution. Since program texts prescribe program executions, this means that they must contain meta-semiologies, analyzing the expression substance of the computer-based signs.

This statement implies that although a component of a system may not be visible to the user and therefore not directly be a sign, its ultimate justification is that it contributes to sign formation. For example, the search processes of data bases are normally not seen by the users, but they still contribute to establishing the most important part of data base systems, namely the composite query-answer sign. The search process defines which responses can count as answers to which queries, so although it does not appear as a visible sign in the interface, it certainly appears as a relation between visible signs.

However, this does not mean that the sign concept must dominate in all activities of programming. An analogy to a meta-semiology of natural language, phonology, will be helpful. Phonology is concerned with the physical substance (sound) and production of speech (manner of articulation), in much the same way as programming is concerned with physical states and state changes of the computer system, and it needs concepts like *voiced* and *aspirated* that can describe that substance. In the same way, programming needs concepts like list, number, character, record, object, loop, condition, etc. that are good for describing the particular expression substance of computer systems.

But the interest of phonology is always guided by the linguistic system, so if a phonologist is to describe the /b/ and /p/ sounds of Danish, the voice properties will not be interesting, since they play no role in distinguishing the two sounds, whereas they will become interesting in English because there they are distinctive. In the same way, the substance of computer-based signs should also be described with a bias to their communicative function, even if few programming languages support this type of descriptions.

Most traditional programming languages are concerned with the invisible system structure and pay very little attention to the fact that the system processes must be interpreted by users. The core definition of Pascal[1], for example, offers a rich variety of invisible data types: scalars (including integers, reals, booleans, and characters), arrays, records, powersets, files, classes, and pointers, but no special operations for presenting this treasure to users, since the screen and keyboard are treated as if they were the same kind of entities as the files in storage. However, particular implementations can of course add new standard functions to this core that address the interface.

The situation is just as inconvenient with regard to the concepts they offer to describe program executions. Of the four perspectives described in Section II.1.1, only object-oriented programming explicitly looks at program executions as signifying something outside the machine. Functional programming (LISP) regards a program execution as evaluations of mathematical functions, logic programming (Prolog) sees it as a proof of a logical formula by means of other logical formulas, and procedural programming (e.g. Pascal) sees it as a hierarchical structure of procedure calls.

As appears from the above, the languages of mathematics and logic have traditionally provided the main concepts for articulating system processes. In view of this, it is important to state that *computers in themselves do not contain any numbers*. They contain a huge mass of bits that many programming languages have chosen to interpret and treat as numbers, but the same configuration of bits can sometimes be interpreted as a string of characters, sometimes as numbers, and sometimes as a picture of Mickey Mouse. The mathematical interpretation of computers is only an interpretation, a fact which is important, since it can then be replaced by something else if it does not suit our purposes.

In sign-oriented programming mathematical concepts are not a priori suitable. In general, a good program text is one that articulates the system process in such a way that on the one hand, it makes allowance for the special characteristics of the computer, and on the other hand enables the programmer to orient his description towards the form elements of the interface. Sometimes mathematics can be helpful, sometimes not.

The following concrete example illustrates how two implementations of the same form element can be at very different distances to the element they aim at manifesting. My example is the movement of the paddle in the Breakout game. It will be remembered that the pertinent feature is a agreement between mouse and paddle movements. When the mouse moves upwards, so does the paddle. In our fictitious programming language, I expressed this agreement by the command

```
Direction := Mouse. Direction
```

---

[1] Wirth 1971.

but an even better solution would be to have agreement as a primitive in the language. A command like

```
Agree(Location, Mouse)
```

where the first parameter denotes the paradigm that establishes the agreement, and the second one the other sign that enters the agreement, would see to it that the location property of paddle and mouse agree at all times.

The Hypertalk language designed for Macintosh by Bill Atkinson allows us to write something that is very close to the ideal:

```
on mousewithin
 repeat
  get the loc of me
  put the MouseV into item 2 of it
  set the loc of me to it
 end repeat
end mousewithin
```

The *loc* is a primitive function and denotes the location of the paddle sign, while the *MouseV* denotes the vertical location of the mouse cursor. The three lines retrieve the location of the paddle, replace the vertical component of it with that of the mouse, and store it again.

This simplicity is no coincidence, since Hypertalk is the first language I have seen that consciously articulates system processes as expression substance for signs. Its universe of discourse does not consist of numbers, logical formulas, or complex data structures, but of objects that are important means of expression in the interface. The language supports "object-like programming", which means that it contains some but not all ideas of object-oriented programming. Its basic objects are signs that appear on the screen: buttons, fields, cards, and backgrounds. These objects have standard properties that are normally used as means of expression: they can have a style, a location, an icon, a size (defined by a rectangle), and can be highlighted, made visible or invisible, etc. The system offers advanced graphical operations for drawing on card and background.

It is no coincidence that agreement is easy to describe in Hypertalk. The same symptom of the similarity between sign-oriented programming and Hypertalk can be seen in the ease with which the 6 sign types from Section II.1.2 can be defined.

Of its two main objects, buttons are mainly intended for implementing interactive signs while the typical use of fields is for object signs.

The properties of the objects can be used to manifest transient and permanent features. Since most properties can be manipulated, they can nearly all be used as *transient features*. In a particular system, only those that are in fact changed function in this way, the rest are used as *permanent features* that identify a particular sign. Each object has a special property, the script, in which the *actions* of the signs are written. Some of these are called handlers and execute if the object receives a particular message. A subset of these messages reflects user actions with keyboard and mouse. To give a few examples, if the user presses the tab key, the system generates a *TabKey* message, and pressing the mouse button gives a *MouseDown* message. These messages are good for implementing the *handling features* of the objects.

As a contrast to this, let us take a look at an implementation in Pascal. The piece of code below gets the mouse location, calculates the new rectangle defining the paddle plus the part of the old paddle that must be erased, draws the new paddle and erases a part of the old.

```
procedure MovePd;
var
 d, s : Rect;
 h, v : integer;
begin
 Mouse location
 GetMouse(h, v);
 Restrict paddle to screen locations from 0 to 270
 if v < 0 then
  v := 0
 else if v > 270 then
  v := 270;
 Create new paddle Location
 if v <> Pd1.top then
 Mouse and Paddle locations are different
 begin
  Pd1 := Pd;
  Set Pd to new paddle location
  SetRect(Pd, 5, v, 10, v + 50);
  Calculate paddle part d to be erased
  if not SectRect(Pd1, Pd, s) then
   d := Pd1
  else if Pd1.top > Pd.top then
  Paddle moves down
  begin
   d.top := s.bottom;
   d.left := 5;
   d.botRight := Pd1.botRight;
  end
  else
  begin
   Paddle moves up
   d.topLeft := Pd1.topLeft;
   d.bottom := s.top;
   d.right := 10;
  end;
  Paint the new paddle rectangle
  PaintRect(Pd);
  Erase part of the old paddle rectangle
  FillRect(d, ltGray);
```

```
 end;
end;
```

The view expressed in this program is basically mathematical. The screen is seen as a coordinate system on which geometrical figures can be defined and drawn and the paddle itself is represented as a rectangle by the variable Pd that is defined as a record of four integers describing the four coordinates of the rectangle. Most of the concepts directly relevant to the interface do not belong to Pascal at all, but are procedures defined in a graphical tool-box. This is for example true of GetMouse(h,v), which reads the coordinates of the mouse, PaintRect(Pd), which paints the outlines of a rectangle, and FillRect(d, ltGray), which fills it with color.

These features make the Pascal code longer and more difficult to relate to the form elements it manifests, viz. the agreement between paddle and mouse locations.

Advocates of Pascal may say that the Hypercard version can also be implemented in Pascal, since it contains tools for building the necessary procedures and functions. This is true, but totally beside the point. What is at stake is different views on programming and program executions which certainly can be debated, but once a particular perspective is selected, its adherents must judge programming languages on whether their basic concepts are similar to those of the perspective. The burden of work should not lie on the programmer, but on the designer of the programming language.

These problems are well known in computer science, and have resulted in the so-called fourth generation languages that provide facilities for expressing concepts in a particular domain, for example document handling, in a more direct way. However, this does not make these languages particularly well suited for sign-oriented programming. What is required of such a language is that it is based on a set of minimal expression units, computer taxemes, and basically views computational processes as consisting of structures of these taxemes, much in the same way as Prolog views computation as inferences on a set of propositions. A precondition for constructing such a language would be to establish a set a of taxemes through an analysis of existing computer based signs. This is no easy task; it is for example clear that the Hypertalk primitives do not form the required inventory of taxemes, since a host of external commands and functions, bypassing the Hypercard universe, are being published and circulated at the time of writing.

II.1.3.2. Levels of description: handling features

Although programs should in principle, directly or indirectly, be relatable to the interface, some parts will be closer than others, as we will recognize from the distinction between phonology and phonetics. Some kind of layering of the text is possible, and since layering is known to be a good programming principle in other programming styles, it should also be recommended here.

From a theoretical point of view, the structuring principle of the layers should be the distance between the description and the form elements of the interface.

The top layers will be similar to a semiology and contain descriptions that directly relate to the pre-taxemes of the interface, corresponding to phonological descriptions of the sounds, their distinctive features, and their combinatorics.

The bottom layer will be a meta-semiology that describes how the elements of the semiology are manifested in the machine. It may very well employ quite different concepts, since its purpose is to relate the form elements to physical processes that can actually run on the machine. In this respect it resembles physical and articulatory phonetics that address the physical properties of sounds, e.g. their length, frequency, and pitch, and the manner in which the vocal organs actually produce the sounds. At this level the languages of mathematics and physics are appropriate.

In the last part of this section I shall give a simple example of layering, namely a Hypercard implementation of a simplified small part of a direct manipulation operative system. I shall focus on the handling features in order to show in detail how these features can be treated like all other expression units. For my own part, at least, it has been difficult to understand how my own hand movements can be treated analogously to well-known expressive elements like graphemes, phonemes, and pictorial elements. It turns out that when we get down to details, the same type of articulation takes place in all cases.

The toy system represents a document as a small icon that can be handled in three different ways. If it is *clicked*, it inverts and becomes part of the set of objects selected for some operation. If it is *double-clicked* it "opens", that is, the application belonging to it is launched, using the document as its data. Finally, it can be *dragged* across the screen.

In the top-level description, we want to treat the three handling taxemes as unanalyzable units and concentrate on their function in the interface.

Form-related description: semiology

```
Icon

on mouseDown
  Analyze
end mouseDown

on DoubleClick
Transient features:
  hide me
Action on text : open the text
  set the loc of cd fld the short name of me to the loc of
  me
The text has the same name as the icon, so "cd fld the
short name of me" denotes the text object with the same
name as the icon
  show cd fld the short name of me
end DoubleClick

on SingleClick
Transient features: hilite icon
    set the hilite of me to not(the hilite of me)
end SingleClick

on Drag
Transient features: drag icon
  set the hilite of me to true
  repeat until the mouse is up
    set the loc of me to the mouseloc
  end repeat
  set the hilite of me to false
end drag
```

The description is form-related in several respects. It says that the icon can combine with both click, doubleclick and dragging, and the handler for each describes what happens, but the program text does not define the three handling features.

           non-hilited   *hilited*

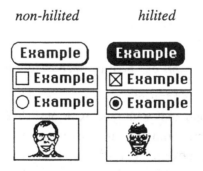

Fig. II.1.64. Bound variants of the hilite invariant.

Another example is the term "hilite", which in Hypertalk is a transient feature of texts and buttons. The term itself denotes a form element with at least three bound variants: inversion with icons and rectangles, a cross with the check box, and a black circle with radio buttons. These variants do not show up in the program text, but are automatically generated.

Substance-related description: meta-semiology

Since neither Click, Drag, or DoubleClick are provided in the Hypertalk language, they have to be constructed by means of concepts that are in fact provided, and we must create another level on which we specify how to manifest these three form elements.

In the present example, as soon as a MouseDown message is received, each sign sends a message down to this level requesting it to analyze the user action. A handler here receives this request, and analyzes the movements according to the following system:

1. Mouse movements occur before the next MouseUp: the taxeme is *Drag*.
2. Mouse movements do not occur before the next MouseUp:

     2.1. A MouseUp occurs within 15 ticks after the previous MouseUp: the taxeme is *DoubleClick*

     2.1. A MouseUp does not occur within 15 ticks after the previous MouseUp: the taxeme is *SingleClick*

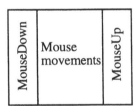

Fig. II.1.65.
Manifestation of *Drag*.

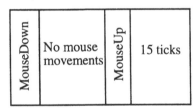

Fig. II.1.66. Manifestation of *SingleClick*.

The three types of segments can be illustrated as follows:

- *Drag* starts with a MouseDown, continues with at least one movement of the mouse, and ends with the next MouseUp (Fig. II.1.65).
- *SingleClick* starts with a MouseDown, there then follows an inactive period without movements lasting until the next MouseUp is encountered. After this, a period of 15 ticks must follow in which no MouseUp is recorded (Fig. II.1.66).

- *DoubleClick* starts like the SingleClick, but ends with a MouseUp within the 15 tick period (Fig. II.1.67).

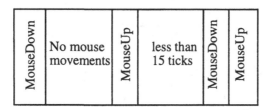

Fig. II.1.67. Manifestation of *DoubleClick*.

After having classified the action, the substance handler sends the result back to the form handler, which responds in the appropriate way.

One way of writing the substance handler could be:

```
on Analyze
  put the MouseLoc into PrevLoc
  repeat until the Mouse is Up
   if the MouseLoc is not PrevLoc then
     send "Drag" to the target
     exit Analyze
   end if
   put the MouseLoc into PrevLoc
  end repeat
  wait 15 Ticks
  if the MouseClick then
    send "DoubleClick" to the target
  else
    send "SingleClick" to the target
  end if
end Analyze
```

The handler first records the location of the mouse. Then it enters a loop which is exited at the first following MouseUp. If the mouse has moved within this loop, the action is classified as dragging. If not, it must be clicking or double clicking. The latter is the case if a mouse click occurs within 15 ticks, otherwise the action is classified as a single click.

Note that elements that do not belong to the expression form of the interface have appeared at this level, for example *time*. The handler sets a limits of 15 ticks of the internal clock of the machine. If no additional mouse operation has been received in this space of time, the user action is classified as a SingleClick. However, the exact length of this period is not a form element, since it does not commute in the interface. We can replace 15 by 10 or 20 and still get the same meaning expressed there.

This is a characteristic of a meta-semiology whose content invariants are variants of its object-semiotic: although the command *wait 15 Ticks* means something different than e.g. *wait 20 Ticks*, this content distinction is a mere expression variant in the interface semiotic.

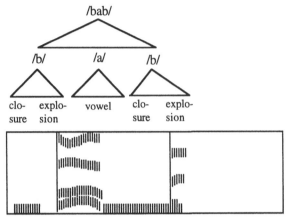

Fig. II.1.68. Sound manifestation of the syllable /bab/.

The type of articulation I have described above is completely analogous to that found in speech-segmentation studied in phonetics. Fluent speech is not articulated in itself, but contains certain clues that are used by speakers and hearers to segment and classify the sound chain.

Above is shown a spectrogram of the syllable *bab*.

We see that the b consists of a closure followed by a sudden explosion (the vertical bars), while the /a/ is manifested as four main formants.

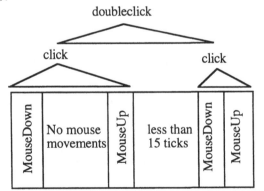

Fig. II.1.69. Kinetic manifestation of the DoubleClick.

The formal similarity to the mouse handler is very obvious. The double click corresponds to the syllable /bab/. Both signs are composed of smaller tax-emes, the DoubleClick of SingleClick + SingleClick, the syllable of /b/+/a/+/b/. These taxemes can be further segmented into units that are not semiologically relevant, since they do not commute. As the /b/ can be decomposed into a pause + explosion, the click can be analyzed as two "explosions" (MouseUp and MouseDown) separated by a pause.

I contend that these similarities are not fortuitous but are due to the fact that the same semiological process takes place: a substance is analyzed by a form. The only difference is that instead of frequencies of sound, the programmer is articulating the hand movements of the users.

II.2

Composite Computer-based Signs

In the previous part, I described the basic properties of computer-based signs. They have three main kinds of features (permanent, transient and handling features) and are organized in two main chains (concurrent and sequential). In this part, I shall treat composite computer-based signs. How are smaller computer-based signs combined to form larger signs?

It is very clear that complex signs corresponding to linguistic concepts like phrases, sentences, and periods exist. The player of video games will experience long nerve-racking combat episodes involving the hero and one or more enemies, and the user of a word processor will engage in major tasks like proof-reading a manuscript or reorganizing the composition of a text, involving extensive handling of tools and text. Since these larger activities are manifested in system processes, they must be considered signs also, and since they contain smaller recurrent elements with meaning (the hero and enemy, the tools and texts), they are composite signs.

Although the three main features of computer-based signs have been treated in detail, I have not yet said much of the analytical consequences of the fact that computer-based signs participate in two different chains.

I shall continue using the textbook on folk-dance from Section II.1.2, since a dance instructor or a writer of textbooks on dance faces problems similar to those facing a designer of computer systems. Like the designer prescribing the sequence of computer-based actions and the stage of the screen, the dance instructor must teach the dancers how to move in time on the floor, how to coordinate their movements with their partner, how to hold each other, and how to establish collective patterns.

In general, his strategy is to analyze each chain separately and define the individual dance as a specific combination of sequential and concurrent syntagms. In specific cases he makes notes of the fact that the combination of the two syntagms is not totally free. For example, the concurrent syntagms of holding each other have function to the main syntagms of couple and chain, since a dancer has to connect to two persons in chains, but only one in a couple. Similarly, there are functions between concurrent and sequential syntagms, since some steps like the waltz are only possible in couples, while other movement patterns, like hopping around in a circle, require a chain.

Disregarding these cases, the general principle I shall use can be formulated as follows:

> Analyze sequential and concurrent chains separately, and describe the individual "dances" as particular combinations of these two kinds of elements.

If this is added to the basic division into content and expression, we get four kinds of chains to analyze in computer-based signs:

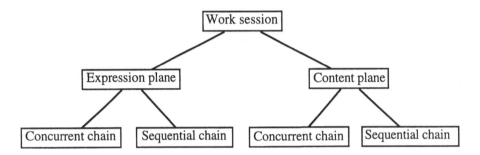

Fig. II.2.1. The four chains of computer-based signs.

However, it must be borne in mind that these divisions are only analytical. The analysis gives us a tool-box of units that will be combined in actual computer-based signs.

The functions between the elements of the two levels are different. The resultants of the first division into content and expression are interdependent, whereas the sequential chains are more important than the concurrent chains, both in computer-based signs, and in the dance and theater metaphors I have used. We can have sequential chains without concurrent ones in both computers (e.g. old-fashioned textual interaction), dance and theater, but not conversely. A dance without motion is no longer a dance, but a charade. Because of this, I shall mainly concentrate on sequential syntagms in the following, and concurrent syntagms will be included in the description when necessary.

II.2.1. The structure of composite computer-based signs

The Petri-net notation makes it easy to describe how signs are put together, since Petri-nets can be composed by identifying places and transitions from the partial nets. For example, the interactive scrollbar sign and the paper object sign of Word can be composed to a sign meaning "I am scrolling the text" in the following manner:

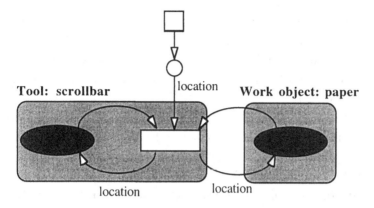

Fig. II.2.2. The composite sign "I am scrolling the text".

and the interactive hero and a villain actor from Dark Castle combine to a sign meaning "I am fighting the henchman" in the following net, where both influence their own and their opponent's transient features:

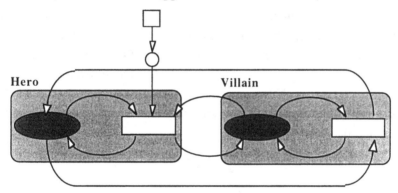

Fig. II.2.3. The composite sign "I am fighting the henchman".

Although some characteristics of the expression plane can be captured by means of Petri-nets, it is not clear whether they can be used to describe the contents of the signs, since in that case we would have to view semantics as consisting of events that have certain preconditions and cause other preconditions to hold. In addition, important properties of processes are not shown directly but must be calculated from the nets by various techniques. In the next sections I shall therefore present classical linguistic analytical procedures that hopefully provide good abstractions of both the content and expression plane of the signs.

Since the computer system is a symbolic tool that is used to accomplish practical tasks, composite sequential computer-based signs can be labelled symbolic *actions* and *tasks*, but it is possible to place the emphasis differently in the phrase "symbolic action". In the psychologically dominated tradition of human-computer interaction research, the emphasis has been on the "action" aspect, and complex signs have been described in terms of goals, intentions, and methods. The concepts involved are very similar to those described in Part I.2.2.1.

For example, in Norman 1986: 37 tasks are characterized by certain *goals* and *intentions* the user wishes to carry out via an *action sequence* that is constructed by a mapping from psychological goals and intentions. In order to do this, the user must be able on the one hand to *interpret* the system state in terms of his goals, and on the other hand to map actions of the system's control mechanisms onto the system state. Finally, the outcome must be *evaluated*.

The point of departure in Bødker 1987 is also psychological, but she stresses that important aspects of actions are not conscious in practice. The basic unit of action here is the *activity*. Activities are conscious, they are bound to an object that is to be manipulated, a person one wishes to talk to, and/or a goal to accomplish, and consist of similarly conscious *actions*. But besides being characterized by intentions (What ought to be done?), it has also *operational* aspects: How is it done? Operations are not consciously planned, but are triggered by the meeting with the actual material conditions. Finally, the difference between actions and operations is not absolute. Actions can be operationalized through exercise and operations conceptualized if something goes wrong.

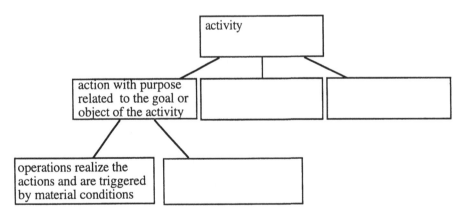

Fig. II.2.4. Activities and operations.

From a linguistic point of view, these descriptions are descriptions of sign usage, but it is a basic axiom of structural linguistics that a language or any other semiotic behavior cannot be fully understood alone through its individual uses and this underlying system also has an independent existence that exists before the individual enters the stage, defines the range of possibilities of usage, and only slowly changes. This is true of natural semiotic systems, and it is also for all practical purposes true of computer systems. Therefore, the subject of the following analysis is not the user's cognitive state or her work practice, but rather the computer system itself in the special capacity of manifesting a semiotic schema, of setting the limits for human symbolic practice. I do not see this description as an alternative, but as a supplement to descriptions of usage.

II.2.1.1. The glossematic analytical procedure

The purpose of the following sections is to present a method of analyzing the "text" generated during usage of the computer system. This text consists of computer-based signs, and is itself a composite computer-based sign. I present the method in two steps; first I give an informal exposition based on a concrete example. In a following section I repeat the same procedure, but now worded in glossematic terminology. Some readers may want to may skip this section.

Informal description of the analytical procedure

Let us look at the activities of a person painting with the Fullpaint system described in Section II.1.2.

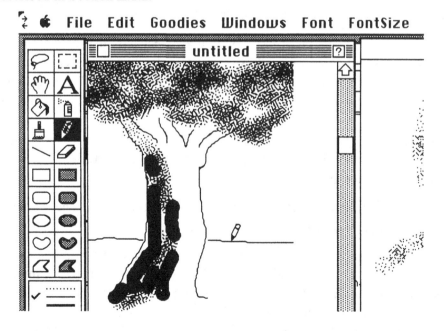

Fig. II.2.5. The Fullpaint system (= Fig. II.1.32).

Here are some actions we might observe:

> Select rectangle tool + draw rectangle + select pencil tool + draw free-
> hand + select airbrush tool + make shadows.

We want to analyze this activity into parts that are functionally different, since from a structuralist view it is not the "things" that are important, but the relations between the "things"; therefore the parts are not defined by means of their internal properties, but by the functions they contract, the "magnetic field" between them.

The largest parts we call *tasks*. The intuitive concept of a task is the smallest independent part of the activity, corresponding to the linguistic period, and we try to capture this intuition in the following definition:

Tasks are the smallest elements that alone can function as the wholes of which they are parts without any catalysis.

Where are the tasks? Is

(1)   Select rectangle tool + draw rectangle + select pencil tool + draw free-
       hand

a task? No, because (1) can be cut into two parts, e.g. "select rectangle tool + draw rectangle", each of which can occur in the same context as (1) does itself.

So we try with a smaller piece,

(2)   Select pencil tool + draw freehand

and discover that this piece has a part "draw freehand" that depends upon the first part "select pencil tool", so that "draw freehand" cannot occur immediately after "draw rectangle". Therefore "draw freehand" cannot function as (2) - the whole of which it is a part - and so (2) must be the smallest element that can do it.

In the same operation where we found our task, we also find the *action*. The intuitive concept of an action, corresponding to the sentence, is the first piece of behavior that is not independent.

- *Actions* are the first elements that cannot function as the whole of which they are parts without catalysis.

Since tasks and actions are different in that the former can combine freely whereas the latter are dependent upon other units, this difference is immediately relevant to the *flexibility* of an interface. Large tasks mean that many actions cohere, and if these cohesions are forced upon the user by the system, it means that the system controls the user's work. The larger the system-defined tasks, the smaller the degree of freedom.

But actions can be further subdivided into smaller signs. For example, the action "draw freehand" consists in applying the interactive pencil sign to the paper sign (type object). The action itself requires of course movement of pencil on paper, but both pencil and paper alone can be used to signify a drawing action, provided the interpreter adds something himself. The pencil sign alone for example means "now you can draw". In this way, the pencil icon has the same function as words, since words can also be used as a complete period, provided the reader encatalyzes something. *Water!* can mean *Give me water!,* with *give me* encatalyzed. I have not come across a good HCI-term for this kind of sign, so I have to invent one. I called them *indicators*, since their function in interfaces are to indicate what can be done and what has been done.

- *Indicators* are the last elements that alone can function as tasks, provided they are catalyzed.

Indicators are also relevant to interface design. They can be interpreted as the smallest units from which a larger context of tasks can be inferred, and if the resting states of a computer system contain many and clear indicators, it becomes easier for the user to infer or remember which tasks are completed, under way, or can be initiated. Thus the concept is relevant to *understandability*.

We continue cutting the activities into smaller pieces, and the smallest ones, corresponding to phonemes and graphemes, are called *taxemes*, again in want of a standard HCI equivalent:

- *Taxemes* are the elements yielded in the last division of the text, based on syntagmatic cohesions

Computer taxemes include common semantic oppositions like *possible\impossible,* and *selected\not selected.*

The analysis can be summarized in the following diagram:

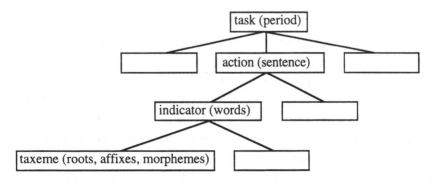

Fig. II.2.6. Hierarchy of composite computer-based signs.

All these definitions have been analytical, since they are based on the relations of the units to other units. But we may also be interested in how the units themselves are built, that is, in their internal structure.

Let us look inside the action "draw freehand". As we recall, the pencil icon follows the movements of the cursor, and when the button is pressed, it leaves a black trace on the "paper". The pencil is signified by an interactive sign, with an icon as its permanent feature and its location as a transient one, whereas the paper is denoted by an object sign with color as one of its transient features that is influenced by the interactive pencil. When the pencil is used to draw on the paper, the joint changes of pencil and paper denote an action that may be paraphrased "I am drawing on the paper with the pencil".

The cohesion between mouse and cursor location, and between mouse press and color change on paper is clearly the decisive factor in the sign formation. It is this cohesion that makes the sign appear. Cohesions of this kind are called *directions*:

- *Direction*: a cohesion between component signs that *establishes* a composite sign

In language we have a clear intuition about some items being more independent than others. For example roots are relatively independent since they can occur alone *(talk)* while inflectional morphemes like the past tense in *(talk-ed)* are parasitic upon the root, since they can never occur alone, the morpheme presupposing a root. By a *characteristic* we mean a unit that consists of these parasitic elements, viz. elements that are the presupposing variable functive in a function:

- *Characteristic*: a unit composed of elements that can enter direction as the variable functive

All other elements are called *themes*:

- *Themes*: units that are not characteristics.

Characteristics thus consist of taxemes that can be evoked by other characteristics or themes and establish a composite unit.

The drawing action can be described as a composite sign in which the transient features of paper color and pencil location are characteristics, and the permanent features of pencil icon and paper window are themes. The action is established by directions between paper color and pencil location, that is: it is the regularity with which the paper is colored in the locations where the pencil moves that makes us see an action and interpret it as drawing.

Color and location changes are characteristics since they cohere, and neither can occur without the pencil icon and paper window, while icon and window can occur without changes of color and location.

Although it may not be possible in general to define two disjunct classes of characteristics and themes, I believe that it can be done in a particular system, and possibly within a particular interaction style. In the Macintosh interface, icons and characters are nearly always themes defining the identity of a sign, whereas all handling features and some transient features like color, location, inversion, and size are changeable characteristics of a sign that may enter directions with similar features in other signs and thereby help establish new composite signs.

Summarizing we can say that

- Composite signs are established by directions between their parts.
- It is often possible to segment a composite sign into two parts, a theme and a subordinate characteristic, of which the latter category can presuppose the former, but not conversely.

The procedure as formulated in glossematics

The previous section introduced the analytical procedure informally applied to computer-based signs. For readers who may want to know how the procedure originally was developed to analyze language, I repeat the same arguments in a form that is closer to glossematic terminology and uses linguistic examples.

The analytical procedure is divided into analysis and synthesis. Analysis first.

Analysis

A glossematic analysis[1] of computer-based signs can be sketched as follows: imagine that you are observing a skilled person using one or more systems for some purposeful work. You want to analyze this process into smaller units according to their functional dependencies, starting with the larger ones, and cutting it into smaller and smaller pieces. At any stage of the analysis, you know the larger units which have already been analyzed and you can investigate the functions between the units of the level you are working at, but you know nothing of the internal structure of the units - you have not got that far yet.

The first thing we are looking for when moving down through the text is whether the parts can have the same functions as their wholes. Chapters,

---

[1] Hjelmslev 1942-43. See also Mortensen 1969.

sections, paragraphs, and periods have this property, but the parts of periods do not:

- *Lexias* are the last elements that alone can function as the wholes of which they are parts without any catalysis.
- *Lexemes* are parts of lexias, viz. they are the first elements that cannot function as the whole of which they are parts without catalysis.[1]

On the content plane, periods are lexias, and sentences are lexemes, since the period *If you want something done right, you have to do it yourself* does not presuppose other elements, whereas one of its parts *if you want something done right* cannot itself function as a period without catalysis.

In Section I.2.2.1 (The Work Process), I transferred the distinction between lexias and lexemes to the work process, defining the *task* as a work process lexia, and the *action* as a lexeme. I use the same terms about the symbolic computer-based work process: computer-based lexias are called tasks, computer-based lexemes actions.

We continue our descent through the text, now looking for units that cannot function as lexias, even if they are catalyzed: we find that

- *Syllabeme*s are the last elements that alone can function as lexias, provided they are catalyzed.
- *Syllabemes* are parts of syllabias, viz. syllabias contain syllabemes as parts[2].

On the content plane, words are syllabemes, whereas parts of words, e.g. morphemes, cannot function as periods at all.

When we have found the syllabemes, we continue segmenting the text, until no cohesions can be found any more and the text cannot be divided further:

- *Taxeme*s are the elements yielded in the last division of the text, based on syntagmatic cohesions[3].

The content plane taxemes are called *plerematemes*, and comprise roots, derivatives, and verbal and nominal morphemes. Expression plane taxemes are called *cenematemes* and include vowels, consonants, tones, and accent.

---

[1] Hjelmslev 1948-49-50: 13.

[2] Hjelmslev 1948-49-50: 15.

[3] Adapted from Hjelmslev 1963a: 137. His definition reads: *virtual element yielded at the stage of analysis where selection* [viz. determination, PBA's note] *is used for the last time as the basis of analysis,* where virtual means: *cannot be taken as the object of a particular analysis,* viz. cannot be cut into smaller pieces in the concrete text, but can possibly undergo a universal, text-independent, decomposition.

The computer-based plerematemes constitute the minimal content invariants of the interface. The Edit-menu described in Section II.1.2.4 gives examples of computer-based plerematemes: the inversion paradigm inverted|non-inverted codes the semantic opposition selected | not selected, while the color paradigm black|grey codes possible | impossible. These plerematemes are similar to morphemes, since they require the presence of a "root", in this case the meanings of *cut, copy* and *paste*[1].

Similarly, the cenematemes are the minimal invariant expression units: black | grey, inverted | non-inverted, etc., and have also already shown their usefulness in systems design as defining a machine-independent level of description, cf. Section II.1.3.1.

Synthesis

When we arrive at the last step of analysis, we are still not finished. Now we begin to move in the opposite direction, describing how the larger units are constructed from smaller units. Hjelmslev uses different terms for analytic and synthetic terms, so to the analytic concept of lexeme corresponds the synthetic concept of *nexus*, and to the syllabeme corresponds the *syntagmateme*.

Since we need some building blocks to construct the syntagmateme and nexus, the taxemes are divided into categories according to their functional properties. I use only a very basic division, namely that of *themes* and *characteristics* introduced in the previous section. These two classes are distinguished according to their ability to enter cohesions, called *directions*, that *establish* a new composite sign.

That a cohesion between component signs *establishes* a composite sign simply means there is a cohesion between the cohesion of the component signs and the complex sign, and the example from Section I.2.1 can be used again[2]: in Danish, the cenematic period is established by two modulations, a rising and a falling tone, the first presupposing the second.

The exact function between the composite sign, the period, and the function that establishes it (the presupposition between the tones) is open to de-

---

[1]The concept of plerematemes is not foreign to traditional computer science. System development methods which see the system as a description or modelling of the real world, such as Jackson 1983, start by setting up units that seem to correspond closely to plerematemes:
"In the entity action step, we begin to define the subject matter by describing the real world for the system in terms of entities and the actions they perform or suffer. The developer considers all the people, things, and organizations which might be taken to be entities, and all the events which might be taken to be actions." *Jackson 1983: 40*
According to Jackson, these elements may not merely be cenematic elements ("must not be merely an action of the system itself", op. cit. p. 40) and they must be atomic, all of which accords well with the plerematic interpretation, so Jackson's entity-action step seems to be akin to plerematic analysis.
[2] Hjelmslev 1948-49-50.

bate. For example, if we find that the presupposition can establish other units than the period (e.g. in ʹ*mmm* or ʹ*mmm*ʹ*mmm* with *mmmm* as its theme), whereas the period always requires the tone function, then the period presupposes the presupposition between the two tones, but if the tone function cannot occur in other contexts, there is interdependence between the period and the tone function.

In a similar way, the plerematic nexus[1] is established by an interdependence between nominative and tense/mood.

Elements that can enter direction as the variable functive are called fundamental characters, and units composed of fundamental characters are called *characteristics*. Units that are not characteristics are called *themes*. Thus, characteristics contain taxemes that can be evoked by other characteristics or themes and establish a composite unit.

In verbal language, roots and derivatives are plerematic themes whereas morphemes are plerematic characteristics. Vowels and consonants are cenematic themes, tones and accent cenematic characteristics.

It follows from the definition that a characteristic can presuppose another characteristic (as when the number of an adjective presupposes the number of a substantive) or a theme (as when a case presupposes a particular preposition), and a theme can be presupposed by another theme (as when derivatives presuppose roots), but *a theme can never presuppose a characteristic.* Thus, a root can never owe its presence to a morpheme.

II.2.1.2. Sequential syntagms

After having established the descriptive framework, I shall look into the structure of sequential syntagms, i.e. patterns of sign tokens that follow each other in time: how are they constructed, how can they be described, and which guidelines can be set up?

The task (periods)

The *task*, corresponding to periods and consisting of actions, is the smallest part of a sequential chain that can function in the same context as the unit of which it is a part. Tasks can be identified in the following way: suppose we have a sequential chain X+Y+Z and we want to know if Y is a task. If Y can be divided into two parts A+B and it turns out that our data contain both X+A+Z and X+B+Z then Y is probably not a task, since it consists of two parts that can occur in the same contexts as Y. If, on the other hand, our data

---

[1] The description is borrowed from Diderichsen 1949.

fail to contain X+A+Y or X+B+Y and we consider this to be no coincidence, then Y may be a task consisting of two actions A and B.

The reason for putting in safe-guards like "probably" and "may" is that we are concerned with the schema behind the usage we investigate. To say that Y is a task and that A and B are actions is to assert that the syntagmatic types they belong to are such that Y's type can occur independently, while the schemas underlying A and B cannot. In the actual chain, we will most often find that a chain A that is part of the larger chain Y cannot replace Y in the concrete instance due to the particulars of the situation. In the following example, there are three periods although the last one presupposes the middle one due to the anaphor *it*.

I looked for the house. I discovered the house. I entered it.

They still form three separate periods since the reason for the presupposition is not in the patterns they follow, but in the topic of the story. However, they can easily be compacted into one period

I looked for the house, which I discovered and entered.

where *which I discovered and entered* presupposes *I looked for the house*. The reason for this presupposition is no longer the topic, but the underlying syntagms, the former being a subordinate clause, the latter a main clause.

In the following I shall give a few examples of tasks, once again using the Macintosh Edit operations.

I am writing a document and want to *delete* a piece of text. First I select the text, and then I select the *cut*-operation, whereupon the text disappears. Is the delete operation a task? Yes, for the following reason: since I can delete anywhere in the writing process, *delete* is not a part of a task. Its own two parts, however, are clearly actions, since choosing the operation presupposes that a piece of text has been selected. Furthermore, *selecting text + selecting cut* follows a very general pattern in graphical interfaces, *select object + select operation*, where the latter part presupposes the first one.

Analysis of tasks is not so easy as in language, since computer systems tend to create much more specific constraints than those inherent in natural semiotic schemas. Consider for example the activity of moving a piece of text to another place. The chain I am producing will then have the form X + *move* + Y, where X and Y are the events taking place before and after moving the text. Now, *move* can itself be divided into two parts, *move = cut + paste*. Is *cut* still a task, or is it an action? The key question is whether both X + *cut* + Y and X + *paste* + Y can occur alone elsewhere in my writing activity. It is clear that the first sequence can and will occur, since I use it in the first example to delete parts of text, but the second sequence, X + *paste* + Y, cannot occur without being preceded by either a *copy* or a *cut*. Therefore *move* contains at least one part that cannot occur in the same surroundings in which it itself occurs, and one could argue that *move* is a task consisting of two actions, *cut* and *paste*. Against this interpretation speaks the fact that the presupposition is not due to any underlying pattern, but simply to the particular functions of the three commands. On the one hand, the presupposition from *paste* to *cut* or *copy* is invariant in all tasks - on the other hand it does not belong to a general underlying pattern.

Here is another example: I want to do a search in the Fourth Dimension data base depicted in Section II.1.1.2, for example *Find all employees called "Smith"*. I express searches like this by three main chains. First I choose the Search command, whereupon the Search Editor appears. Secondly, I specify search criteria, in the present case by the operations Click "Last name" + Click "Is Equal to" + Write "Smith". More criteria can be entered by adding a conjunction, e.g. "and" and repeating the same pattern over again. Thirdly, I click the OK-button, causing the result of the search to be presented. Since the second and third parts presuppose the first part, they are not tasks but actions. Like the first example, this task is an instance of a more general syntagm used to set actor signs in motion: first specify the parameters to the actor, then start it.

The last example is from the game Dark Castle. In the scene called Trouble 1 many events happen simultaneously, some of which contract a simple constellation: bats hunt the hero, rats run on the floor, the guard marches back and forth. These events are independent and therefore tasks according to the definition. Some of them can be broken down into parts that exhibit functional dependencies. For example, when the hero comes within a certain distance, the henchman, who is whipping prisoners, stops whipping, turns in the direction of the hero, and begins whipping in his direction. The changed behavior of the henchman presupposes a certain minimal distance of the hero, and the outcome of the blows they subsequently exchange presupposes the manner in which they are delivered. These elements are therefore parts of a task.

What is the point in this discussion? Does it really matter whether something is a task or an action? Yes it does. The borderline between tasks and actions, periods and sentences, is important since it is a borderline between freedom and restrictions. In language for example, the period structure is outside the clutches of the linguistic schema: it belongs to stylistics and is very much a field for exercising personal skill and taste. Once inside the period, our choices are heavily constrained by the syntax of e.g. English or Danish.

Another aspect of tasks and periods is that they are - or should be - ways of chunking large chains into smaller coherent wholes, and marking actions and sentences as more and less important in relation to each other.

In the following, I shall use the period as a model for presenting normative suggestions of what a good task may look like. I cannot exhaust the possibilities, but shall only give one or two examples, and "leave the rest to the reader".

Cohesion between tasks. In language, periods can be made to cohere in many ways[1]. One important means of cohesion is sharing of nominal elements, expressed by the theme-rheme structure, determiners and anaphors. One period can present a person or object in rheme position, while the next period places it in initial theme position and adds new information about it:

Once upon a time there was *a prince. He* was very handsome...

Another common pattern of cohesion is pairs of indefinite and definite references to the same object, e.g.

Wash and core *six cooking apples.* Put *the apples* into a fireproof dish.

or a full noun followed by pronominal reference:

Wash and core *six cooking apples.* Put *them* into a fireproof dish.

Transferring these means of expression to tasks could lead to the principle that elements from one task, e.g. those denoting objects, must be reusable in subsequent tasks[2]. For example, if a task produces a new file, then this object must be represented in such a way that it can be used to express subsequent tasks like moving, deleting, or filing. In the Macintosh Finder, a file is represented by an icon, moving is expressed by dragging the icon, and deleting by dragging it into a waste basket icon. The icon's location on the screen both expresses the result of a previous task and can be used as a part of the following task. In text-based systems, full file names should be replaced by copying facilities or pronominal shorthands like "it".

There are of course many other methods for creating cohesion between periods that can be transferred to task design: classical rhetorical devices like parallelism, antithesis and ellipsis serve to indicate similarities and dissimilarities between periods, and conjunctions and adverbials to describe particular relations between them.

Internal structure of tasks. Periods should be neither too simple nor too complex. If they are too simple, e.g. only consisting of one sentence, then it is

---

[1] See e.g. Halliday & Hasan 1976.
[2] This principle is akin to the concept of "inter-referential I/O" described in Draper 1986: 339.

difficult to mark the cohesion and unity that the reader expects from the text, but if they are too long and complex, the reader may become lost in the structure, and the writer may be tempted to create dependencies that have no meaning.

The same can be said of tasks. In particular, care should be taken that all dependencies between the actions of a task have a meaning. The clauses constituting a period should be related by definite semantic relations expressed by conjunctions or adverbials, for example conditions, intentions, reservations, effects, reasons, causes, etc., and similar relations should be perceivable in tasks. In games, the component actions come in pairs that are related as cause/effect, attack/counterattack, discovery/reaction, intention/outcome, threat/parrying, means/end. For example, in Dark Castle, the bats attacking and the hero responding by throwing rocks at them can be seen as attack and counterattack, and the pair discovery/reaction is clearly the intended interpretation of the episode where the henchman stops whipping as the hero approaches, turns in his direction and attacks. In graphical interfaces, selecting an object is presented as a means to achieve the goal of manipulating the object[1].

The main clause of periods should present the key meaning of the period, and the subordinate clauses be related to this key meaning. Furthermore, there is a limit to how much subordinate information may precede the key meaning, since the reader is only able to interpret the subordinate information correctly when she knows the key meaning it is to be related to. The same is true of tasks. One of the actions will often be a key action, and the rest are preparations for or modifications of the key action.

Menu searches often involve selecting subordinate actions that belong to a task whose key action is first accomplished when the relevant menu item has been found. If too many preparatory menu selections have to be made before the wanted action can be performed, the task begins to lose its balance and unity in the same way as the following period:

> Provided that it does not rain tomorrow and if my car, which is not in too good shape, works, *I shall come.*

A better balance is achieved, if the key meaning is moved to the middle

> If it does not rain tomorrow, *I shall come,* provided my car, which is not in too good shape, works.

---

[1] The particular relations between the actions of a task are interesting, since they can reveal important properties of the semantic universes of the systems. For example, in many games, Dark Castle included, the death of hero or antagonists is interdependent with physical contact. The precise details may differ: the rat and the bat can only kill the hero by direct contact, whereas the guard can also kill at a distance, namely by firing arrows. But the basic semiotic law remains: contact is lethal!

or right to the beginning

> *I shall come*, if it does not rain tomorrow and my car, which is not in too good
> shape, works.

The balance of a menu-based task can be changed in a similar way by placing some of the subordinate actions after the key action.

Tasks and actions, periods and sentences. The work language of the situation in which the system is used gives its own articulation of the work process, one that need not coincide with the one that can be manifested in the system processes, but since workers need to talk about their work with colleagues, the two articulations ought not to be too different. This means that the tasks should be describable as periods, and actions as sentences in the work language, so if the user describes a piece of work in one simple sentence, the interface should present it as one action or a task consisting of only one action. The sequence *cut + paste* above violates this rule, since it consists of two actions, while I will clearly use one sentence, *I have moved chapter 1 behind chapter 3*, to describe the event. Similar conceptual discrepancies between system and language are not hard to find. An administrative hospital system for example does not allow patients to be moved from one ward to another - they have to be discharged from the first ward, and admitted to the new one.

Interface versus system processes. Since tasks are defined as signs, they describe the interface, viz. the work habits of the user, and not the system processes, viz. the possibilities offered by the designer. However, each chain used to manifest a task must of course be included in the system process. The ideal case is of course that the system processes coincide with the set of chains that manifest tasks, but since this ideal is impossible to achieve, we will always have shortcomings (tasks the user wants to accomplish but which cannot be manifested in any system process), excesses (system processes that do not manifest any task the user wants to do), and mismatches (system processes may have net results that can be interpreted as the result of a desired task but their structure cannot be interpreted as one task).

The action (sentences)

Analytically, actions are defined as parts of tasks that cannot occur in the same contexts as the task without catalysis (cf. the previous section). The action *Cut object* presupposes the action, *Select object*, and therefore it cannot occur in the same context as the task of which it is a part.

In graphical interaction, the internal structure of actions very often consists of two to four signs whose transient and handling features cohere in some way. Thus, the action *I move the paper with the scrollbar box from* Section II.1.2.1 is established by concurrent cohesions between changes of the location of mouse, scrollbar box, and the lines of the text. If the mouse moves up, the scrollbar does too, and the text lines move down. Functions like these are well known in classical linguistics, where they go under the name of rection, and judging from the example, rection seems to be just as important in establishing computer-based syntagms as in verbal ones.

The general concept of rection is defined as follows:

- *Rection* is a dependence between single members of two or more paradigms that takes place whenever the paradigms in question occur in a relation that may be stated in functional terms[1].

The following two main types can be defined:

Concord (most often called *agreement* now) is a type of rection in which a certain member of one item of a given category is always accompanied by the same member of another item of the same category. In language, the number morphemes of subject and verb often agree, and in our case, there is agreement between mouse and scrollbar movement direction. *Government* is a type of rection in which a certain member of a paradigm is always accompanied by a certain, different member of another paradigm.

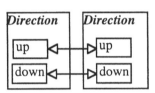

Fig. II.2.7. Agreement between cursor and mouse movements.

The classical example of government is between paradigms of prepositions and case-endings.

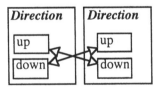

Fig. II.2.8. Government between mouse and text movements.

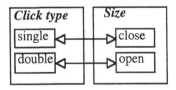

Fig. II.2.9. Government between mouse button and window size.

If two paradigms contracting government belong in the same category, the government is homo-categorial. In the scrolling example above the mouse and text enter homo-categorial government, since the text goes down when the mouse goes up, and vice versa (Fig. II.2.8).

---

[1] Diderichsen 1949: 134-155.

Government between members of different categories is called hetero-categorial. If the action of opening and closing documents is expressed by double or single clicking, respectively, on the document, then the paradigms of clicking and size contract hetero-categorial government (Fig. II.2.9).

The description above is based upon the hypothesis that the abstract principles for establishing actions and sentences are the same. Sentences consist of words that have themes (e.g. roots) and characteristics (inflexion), while the sentence unit is established by agreement and government between the characteristics. Similarly, actions consist of smaller signs whose permanent features (e.g. their icon) are themes and whose transient and handling features (e.g. location and clicking) are characteristics that establish the action by means of agreement and government.

This seems to fit graphical interfaces, but what about textual interaction? Let us look at the PGP-system introduced at the Postal Giro Office in Stockholm (cf. Section I.1.1).

On the face of it, we should expect the framework to fit here too since it was after all originally developed for verbal language, and we do find that verbal computer-based actions can contain grammatical patterns from verbal language. The construction Imperative Verb + Object is for example very common, as in the PGP system's menus where we have items like

Verb	*Object*
Create	Job
[Skapa	Job]
Move	this document
[Flytta	detta dokument]
Fetch	a document
[Hämta	Ett dokument]

However, the fact that we also find constructions that do not occur in the verbal language makes us begin to suspect that verbal interaction may in fact be a quite different thing from verbal language. A good example of such constructions is the pattern Attribute +Value, which is also very common in the PGP-system. The screen image for data entry illustrated in Fig. II.2.10 is mainly constructed upon this pattern.

Film, tr [transaction code], *belopp* [amount], *konto till* [account to], etc. are attributes, and the numbers values. When to these superficial differences we add the fundamental difference that verbal computer-based actions normally involve more screen components than the command items, and that they, like all other computer-based signs, contain handling features and actions, we arrive at the conclusion that verbal interaction, as well, is a unique type of sign whose likeness to verbal language is mostly parasitic, cf Section I.2.4.2.

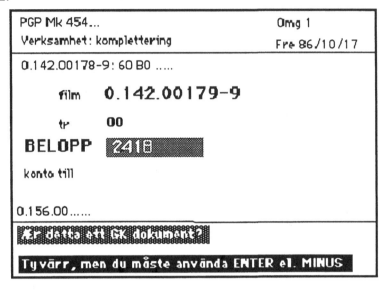

Fig. II.2.10. Screen image for data entry in the PGP system.

The handling features of verbal interaction mainly consist of keystrokes that are echoed on the screen by letters; the typical actions associated with verbal interaction fall in four main types, since a piece of text can

- disappear: for example, the command *delete filename* would erase a filename in a directory, and in line-oriented systems, the command name would disappear when *return* was pressed,
- appear: *create filename* would insert a new filename in a directory,
- substitute another piece of text: *rename filename to filename* replaces a file's name with another name,
- be concatenated with another piece of text: when letters are typed the system will echo by concatenating the letter shapes on the screen.

The PGP-system illustrated above is not a pure textual system since the letters have transient features like size, inversion, and color, but the main processes still consist of pieces of text appearing and disappearing. For example, the warnings and advice in the bottom of the screen are made to disappear by pressing the ESC key, finishing a card causes the next card to replace it, moving into another subview replaces the task name in the upper part of the screen with another, and choosing a command in a menu that appears in the lower part of the screen replaces the current menu with a new one. Finally the status information on top of the screen (machine number, group number, and Section number) is concatenated as the information is entered.

In the following I shall take a closer look at a purely textual system, my example being the small toy operative system described in Section I.2.4.1.

Suppose I have implemented the system in the following way: the commands are typed in at the bottom of the screen, each command disappearing when the next command is entered. On top of the screen is the status information, including a directory of the available files on the disc and a field named *current file* that displays the name of the file being worked upon at the moment. The following table shows the possible combinations of command name, filename in File Directory, and filename in the Current File field. Each command is described by two lines: the first line shows the items on the screen before issuing the command, and the second line the situation after executing the command.

Occurrence of/ *Command:*	*Command*	*<filename>in* *File Directory*	*<filename> in* *Current File*
Take Out A	-	+	-
	+	+	+
Put Aside A	-	+	+
	+	+	-
Create A	-	-	-
	+	+	+
Discard A	-	+	+
	+	-	-
Maintain A	-	+	+
	+	+	+

The diagram says for example that before the command *Take Out "MyFile"* is typed, *MyFile* must occur in the File Directory but not in the Current File field, as illustrated in Fig. II.2.11. After typing, *MyFile* also occurs in the Current File field (Fig. II.2.12).

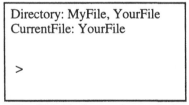

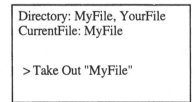

Fig. II.2.11. Screen image before typing the command.   Fig. II.2.12. Screen image after typing the command.

A functional analysis of this system consists of observations like the following: like *Put Aside* and *Maintain*, *Take Out <filename>* presupposes the <filename> in the directory, since the commands cannot be issued if the file is not already on the disc, and together with *Create*, it is presupposed by the <filename> in the Current File field, since the <filename> would not occur there, had one of the commands not been issued.

The actions expressed by the system do not only consist of the command name; they consist of three elements, the command name, the *Directory,* and the *Current File* indication, and are established by the dependencies these elements contract.

We also see that signs in pure textual systems differ from graphical signs in that they have no transient features[1] that can contract rection with each other. The functional dependencies between screen elements that establish actions hold between themes, not between characteristics.

The difference from verbal language is now clear: verbal language is only manifested in a concurrent chain, whereas verbal interaction also involves sequential chains. The definition of a verbal sentence does not contain change as a pertinent feature, but verbal interaction does.

This last difference can be illustrated very nicely if we try to transfer descriptive techniques from language analysis to computer-based signs. Let us take transformational grammar as an example. Below I have used a transformational rule to describe the action of *taking out a file*. The first part of the rule gives a structural description of the "screen-text" that must be satisfied in order for the rule to apply, and the second part describes changes of this structure.

Taking out a file

"Directory" $Filename_1$ + "Current File" $Filename_2$ + "Take Out " $Filename_1$ =>

"Directory" $Filename_1$ +"Current File" $Filename_1$

If the screen is represented by a syntax tree generated by a grammar like the following

Screen	->	StatusPart + CommandPart
CommandPart	->	Verb + Object
Verb	->	"Take Out"|"Create"| "Discard",....
Object	->	Filename
StatusPart	->	DirectoryPart + CurrentFilePart
DirectoryPart	->	"Directory" + {Filename}*
CurrentFilePart	->	"Current File" + Filename

---

[1] Of course it would be possible to consider the visibility property of textual signs a transient feature, but then the distinction between permanent and transient features loses its meaning, and it would be impossible to say that a sign did not occur, since then it always occurs, with only the visibility property changing.

the transformation will replace the *Filename* constituent under *CurrentFilePart* with that under the *CommandPart*, and subsequently remove the *CommandPart*:

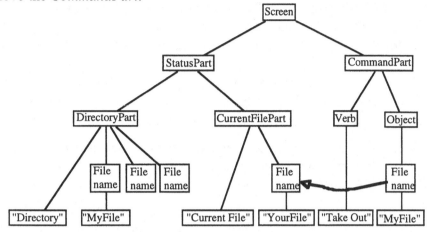

Fig. II.2.13. A transformational description of textual interaction.

There are three points to be made:

- It has been necessary to change our interpretation of transformational grammar. When it is used to describe verbal language, the two parts of the rule relate verbal signs, e.g. sentences, to each other, but the rule itself does not describe a sign. This is so because natural language does not exploit change as a means of expression. Computer-based signs do this, and one way to capture this feature is to let the transformation itself be the action part of a sign.

- In the special case of textual interaction, sign-oriented programming can benefit by borrowing concepts and methods from formal linguistic theories like e.g. transformational grammar or Montague grammar. The states of a computer system are then viewed as a large syntax tree, including both the visible parts of the screen and the invisible data structures, and the transformations of the system are viewed as mappings from one tree to another governed by transformational rules. The permanent features of textual computer-based signs are properties of texts, they will typically not possess transient features, and their actions can be described as transformational rules.

- The formal grammar is used as a programming perspective that views program executions as manipulation of structured texts. The reason for applying this perspective is not that the machine is assumed to possess a faculty of language, but rather that since program executions are interpreted as texts by human users, it is a good idea to use linguistic concepts to construct and understand them.

In the preceding section, I used linguistic analogies to propose guidelines for constructing good tasks, and I shall do the same here with actions. I offer two suggestions that both come from analogies with their linguistic counterparts, sentences:

Rhythm: actions should have characteristics corresponding to tones that delimit the action on the expression plane. For example, it seems to be a good idea to use the tension-relaxation pattern to establish an action:

> One of our main arguments is that we use tension and closure to develop a phrase structure to our human-computer dialogues which reinforces the chunking of the mental model that we are trying to establish.   *Buxton 1986*

Case structure: the action should contain a set of cases also found in sentences (see Section I.2.2.1 for a discussion of the case concept). The argument is similar to that used previously, namely that workers need to talk about their work and this is easier if the content form of the interface is not too different from that of the work language. The argument also works in the opposite direction: it is easier to learn a system if users can rely on their own language when interpreting it.

The obvious question is then: how do we design the action parts so that their roles in the action become analogous with cases in a sentence? The typology of signs in Section II.1.2.1 was partially designed with this purpose in mind. Interactive signs can enter actions as instruments, while actors can play the role of agent or cause. Object signs perform well as objects, while controller and layout signs are good as locatives.

The indicator

The indicator is the smallest unit that can function as a task, provided it is catalyzed. To see the importance of this concept, consider the task of drawing a connector in the Design program. Drawing a connector presupposes drawing at least two objects, which the connector can connect. Often these objects are not drawn immediately before the connector; for example, the user may draw all the boxes of his diagram before drawing any connectors.

Fig. II.2.14. Indicators showing that boxes have been drawn. From Design.

In this case, it is important that the actions of drawing boxes are represented on a screen by indicators that enable the user to infer the previous action and possible subsequent ones. In Design, the drawing of boxes results in the indicators shown in the diagram, signifying that two boxes have been drawn.

Fig. II.2.15.

When this indicator is encatalyzed correctly as an assertion about two previous actions, namely that two boxes have already been drawn, the user can continue his task, connect them, and produce the indicator to the right.

Summarizing, the syllabemes of interactive signs must indicate which actions have been carried out, which types are available and which available ones are possible now.

The first effect, showing which actions have been performed, can be achieved by a tense-like inflection. For example, a Macintosh document can be selected and opened, giving us three different states:

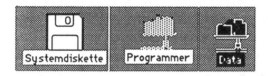

Fig. II.2.16. Indicators showing the status of documents. From the Macintosh Finder.

(1)   The document has neither been selected nor opened (unmarked)
(2)   The document has been selected and opened (expressed by a grey mask)
(3)   The document has been selected but not opened (expressed by inversion)

The second effect, indicating the type of available actions, is often achieved by rhetorical devices such as metaphor, metonym or synecdoche.

Some items of the menu from Fullpaint (Fig. II.2.17) use a combined metonym and metaphor. The tool is substituted for the action, giving us metonymical designations for movements (hand) and painting (pencil, rubber, bucket, brush, etc.), and then these designations are used as a metaphor for what is going on in the program. Other items use only metonymies, denoting

the action by denoting the result, so that a sign creating a rectangle is denoted by a rectangle, and so on.

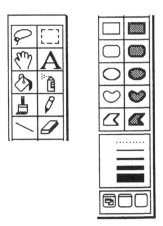

Fig. II.2.17. Metaphors and metonyms in Fullpaint.

Narrative structure: text and story grammars

I have now described computer-based syntagms up to the level of tasks.
Although it may certainly be open to debate whether written or spoken texts
exhibit sufficiently stable structures above this rank, like the argumentative
and narrative structures of text[1] grammar and narrative[2] grammar, such structures definitely exist in some computer systems, particularly in games. Our
Breakout game can again serve as a simple example.

Like any game, it ends with a particular element that we can call the
Ending Event, which either consists in the player missing the ball and losing,
or the point where all the bricks have been smashed, in which case the game
is won. The Ending Event is contrasted to the rest of the game by using verbal code, as illustrated in Section II.1.1. The episodes preceding the Ending
Event consist of one or more rounds. Except for the decreasing number of
bricks, no round has function to another round, and therefore they merely
enter constellation with each other. In other games, the later rounds may presuppose the earlier ones, for example in that the difficulty level is increased,
but this is not the case here, and I shall disregard the concept of round, since
it has no other function than giving you an extra chance, even if you have
lost. The part preceding the Ending Event is then a repetition of turns consisting in two parts: a Beginning Event, consisting in the ball flying towards
the left, and an Attempt on the player's part to move the paddle in such a

[1] Van Dijk 1980.
[2] See e.g. Todorov 1969, Bremond 1966, 1970, 1973, Greimas 1970, Prince 1973, Pavel 1973,
Propp 1975. Meehan 1977, Johnson & Mandler 1980, Bøgh Andersen 1981, Black & Bower 1980.

way as to hit the ball, in order to make it smash a brick. The Outcome Event of this attempt can either be missing or hitting the ball.

Since the turn of *Beginning Event + Attempt* must be classified as a task because its parts cannot occur alone, the game shows functional dependencies above the level of tasks, namely an interdependence between a sequence of turns and the Ending Event. The game must end in a particular way.

Other games exhibit much more complex super-task functions. The success of later tasks in adventure games for example depends upon a correct performance of earlier tasks, like picking the right weapons, talking to the right persons, or going in the right directions. These dependencies belong to the form of the games, since they are invariant for each game.

Such functions are studied by story grammars, of which there are three main types.

Logical grammars (Todorov 1969, Greimas 1970) describe stories as movements in a conceptual landscape, e.g. from a negation (not rich) to an assertion (rich), or between antonyms (danger I security, having fun I boredom).

Syntactic grammars (Bremond 1966, 1970, Propp 1975, Prince 1973, Johnson & Mandler 1980) use grammar as a metaphor for story structures, emphasize part-whole structures, and describe the story by some grammatical formalism. Johnson & Mandler use a transformational grammar, and Propp a slot-and-filler grammar.

Means/end grammars (Meehan 1977, Black & Bower 1980, Bøgh Andersen 1981) describe the conflicts and courses of actions as composed of means, ends, and preconditions (see Section I.2.2.1), and basically view stories as problem solving.

The description of the Breakout game above is in fact based on a simplified version of a syntactic story grammar described by Johnson and Mandler 1980:

STORY	->	Setting And EPISODE
EPISODE	->	{Beginning event Cause DEVELOPMENT}*
		Cause ENDING
DEVELOPMENT	->	COMPLEX REACTION Cause GOAL PATH I
		DEVELOPMENT Cause DEVELOPMENT
COMPLEX REACTION	->	Simple Reaction Cause Goal
GOAL PATH	->	Attempt Cause OUTCOME
OUTCOME	->	Outcome Event I EPISODE
ENDING EVENT	->	Ending Event I EPISODE

A story starts out with a Setting that introduces the protagonist of the first episode, including optional statements about time, locale or props. Then follow one or more episodes, each episode consisting of three parts: the BEGINNING, which is an event that causes the protagonist to react, the DEVELOPMENT, in which the protagonist may react emotionally to the initial event, either by spontaneous acts or by constructing and carrying out a plan which has a certain outcome, and the ENDING, which tells about long-range consequences of the DEVELOPMENT. The concrete parts of the story are defined in the following way:

Setting: introduces protagonist, including optional statements about time locale, or props: the screen layout of Breakout.

Beginning Event: causes protagonist to react: the ball flies to the left.

Simple Reaction: emotional response of protagonist caused by Beginning Event: anxiously following the ball with one's eyes.

Goal: what the protagonist plans to do about the Beginning Event: making the ball hit a brick.

Attempt: planful act protagonist carries out to achieve Goal: moving paddle in order to hit ball.

Outcome Event: represents either success or failure of Attempt: hitting or missing ball.

Ending Event: long range consequences of DEVELOPMENT: game stops and player either wins or loses.

Although super-task structures are mostly found in games, Laurel 1986 suggests the use of drama theory in general design:

> As a student of theater and dramatic criticism, as well as a software designer and researcher, I am impressed again and again by the applicability of dramatic theory to the problems of interface design.   *Laurel 1986: 67-86*

If her idea is realized, for example in the design of a word processor or data base, it would mean that the work process will be staged to a much larger degree than we are used to. To give one example, unlike games, word processors normally have no structure corresponding to the global narrative structure DEVELOPMENT + ENDING , but it is not hard to imagine suitable endings for word processors: it could consist in some kind of summary of your work when you quit your program, telling you what you have accomplished so far and how it might relate to future work. Whether this would be actually useful is difficult to judge, but the idea is fascinating.

II.2.1.3. Concurrent syntagms[1]

In the preceding section, the main emphasis was on sequential syntagms, and concurrent syntagms were only seen as a means for establishing the sequential ones: for example, the action was defined as a sequential unit, but could be established by concurrent agreement and government between its parts. However, there are properties of computer systems that are most easily described with a point of departure in concurrent syntagms. I shall comment on two, the *scene* and the *subview*, and use the Word 3 screen below as an example:

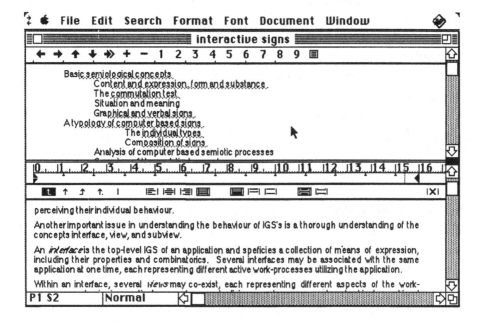

Fig. II.2.18. Subviews in Microsoft Word.

The screen contains two windows that denote the same document but in different ways. The uppermost, the Outline view, gives a bird's view of the text, only showing its rough outline of chapters, while the lower one, the Text view, presents a detailed view of a part of a page, in the size it will have when printed. Different actions are possible in the two views. For example, the Outline but not the Text view contains commands (the arrow buttons in the upper part of the window) that are used for changing the level of chapters and sections. Thus, selecting the chapter heading "The commutation test" and clicking the left-arrow will raise ("promote") the chapter to the

---

[1] This section is based upon Bøgh Andersen & Lindskov Knudsen. Unpublished.

same level as "Basic Semiological concepts", while the right-arrow will lower ("demote") it to the level of "The individual types". There are other actions that are not allowed in the Outline view, e.g. type text and change font style, which are possible in the Text view, where promotion and demotion of chapters can only be done indirectly.

How can we understand and describe this? Let us start by recording what happens when we use the system. If we record the concurrent chains consisting of work object plus task, we will get something like this:

Outline. Promote, Outline.Demote, Text.Type, Text.ChangeFont

Promote and Demote can occur with the Outline view, and Typing and Change Font with the Text view. Thus, the available operations in Word 3 are partitioned into (nearly) disjoint subsets, such that each subset belongs to a particular view of the text.

If our point of departure is the total paradigm of operations comprising every operation of the system, in the example <+Promote +Demote+Type +ChangeFont>, the operations of one view can be described as a paradigm in which the operations of the other views are typically negated:

Outline. <+Promote +Demote -Type -ChangeFont>
Text. <-Promote -Demote +Type +ChangeFont>

If we denote the paradigm allowed in the Outline view by P, we say that the actions of paradigm P can occur whenever the outline view is shown, although of course they need not, but they cannot occur in any other contexts, so P presupposes the Outline view (+Outline.P, +Outline.P̲, -Outline̲.P, +Outline̲.P̲). I shall call the Outline and Text views *scenes*, because functionally they are like a theater scene with props and wings that are a necessary prerequisite for a certain set of actions to be performed; thus, the formal definition of the scene concept runs as follows:

- *Scene*: a concurrent syntagm of object signs and interactive signs presupposed by a paradigm of tasks.

Note that the definition concerns a particular *paradigm* of tasks, not the individual task. It is perfectly possible for a task to be performed in more than one scene.

Beside being a example of scenes, the screen above also can be used as an example of the *subview* concept. The two windows are intended to signify the same document, seen from different perspectives. This effect is achieved by concurrent agreement and government relations between the two windows.

Agreement: The headings in both widows agree since they contain the same characters, so if a heading is changed in one view, the change shows up in the other. The same is true of the first line of paragraphs.

Government: the relation between indentation in the outline view and the style in the text view is a good example of hetero-categorial government. Each part of the text in the text window has a particular style, controlling the layout of the text (font, size, format, spacing, margins, etc.). The name of the style is shown in the bottom line of the window. In the example, the style is "Normal". Some of these styles of the form *Level <number>* are used for headings, and there is government between the degree of indentation in the outline view and the level number of the style in the text view, so if a heading is promoted in the former, the level number is decreased in the latter.

Agreement and government are the essence of the subview concept. We wish to represent the same object in different ways, each presentation being tailored for particular kinds of tasks. The two views must have something in common, since otherwise the user would not be able to identify the common referent of the two views. This makes agreement necessary. On the other hand, since the idea is that the user needs to see the object in different ways, there must be differences in the representations, but some of these differences must be related: change of a property in one representation shows up as changes of other properties in the other representation. Therefore (hetero-categorial) government is also necessary.

It is not necessary that all elements in the two windows be related by agreement and government. On the contrary, many elements occur only in one window, and not in the other one. For example, except for different level numbers, differences of style are not represented in the outline view, and the same is true of the main text of the paragraphs. Thus, most changes of style and corrections of paragraph text in the text view do not show up in the outline view.

The subview concept is defined as follows:

- *Subviews*: two or more signs signifying the same referent by means of agreement between some features, government between others.

In the Word example, the two subviews are also two different scenes. This is quite common, since different task paradigms often require different perspectives on an object. However, we can also have subviews that do not belong to different scenes: databases can for example be displayed in tabular form or in various graphical displays which are not scenes at all because no tasks are associated with them.

The Scene

In the definition of the scene, I have included all tasks that can be done in that scene, but since some tasks can be done in more than one scene, this means that paradigms of different scenes can overlap: for example, the Edit tasks and window and file handling like opening, scrolling, and printing can be done in both scenes. In a system description, I would like to exclude these common tasks and signs from the individual scenes, since they do not characterize them, and assign them to a category of scenes.

The issue may be clearer if we turn to literary texts. Suppose I read a book taking place in northern Sweden. Then the mountains and moors of the Lappish landscape will be part of all scenes of the book and cannot be used to characterize the individual scenes, which must be differentiated otherwise, e.g. by the persons involved or by the time. A good writer will present a general description of the landscape in the introductory chapters, and later only supply specifics of the situation.

The same is probably useful in computer-based scenes, and a description of a program configuration based upon the notion of scenes will then include two levels:

- *A category of scenes* presupposed by the paradigm of tasks possible in all. This may include a description of the window managing system (which is not unique for the individual scenes), of printing facilities (which can be done not only to texts but also to pictures), and disk-operations like opening and closing files.
- *The individual scenes* presupposed by the task paradigms only possible in the particular scene.

It may come as a surprise to many readers that the *program* concept does not enter into my description at all. The reason is that from a semiotic point of view, this concept is irrelevant, since it is defined by the manner in which scenes are manifested, and not by the functions it contracts to other sign elements of the system. In fact, from this point of view, it is a fault if shifts between programs show up too clearly, since they are just "noise", expression features without relevant content.

I think that this line of thought might be extended even further. One should not think of design as designing a program, but as designing a set of scenes that in the use situation will interact with other scenes designed by others and already known to the user. Since the user will try to squeeze all scenes into the same semiotic system, the interpretation of any one scene is partially outside the control of the designer, since it will depend upon the other scenes the user is working with. Designing should be seen as adding a few new scenes to a book that has already been written, marketed and purchased[1].

Scenes are constructed in different ways in different types of applications, and are heavily influenced by the non-computer part of reality that has served as a model for the application. In tool-like programs, the scene denotes scenes of work where tasks are grouped according to the position of the worker in relation to the work object, reminiscent of the example described in Section I.2.2.1, where a mechanic collects all the tasks that must be done in the engine compartment, and performs them together, no matter whether they are logically connected or not. In some games, the scenes correspond to the theatrical notion of scenes, a closed piece of action taking place on a location with props that are significant and motivated with respect to the actions.

The common feature of both notions is a set of tasks that is intimately connected to their surroundings. The mechanic must be in the engine compartment in order to dismount the gas line, and conversely, what he can do in the compartment is to remove or fix the car parts there. Similarly, Hamlet must be in the graveyard in order to discover the skull of Yorrick, and the logic of theater requires that his being in the graveyard eventuates in actions that could only happen there.

Video games not only draw on theatrical effects but also exploit filmic types of scenes based upon difference of perspective:

- An *onlooker* scene presents an overview of the game in a schematic form with a few slow movements, few standardized symbols, no interactive signs, and a "vertical" perspective (seen from above). This is the perspective for detached reflection.
- The *participant* scene presents the game in the form of a situation (i.e. actors and layout) with fast movements, with elaborate icons, interactive signs, and a "horizontal" perspective (seen from the ground), the perspective for hot-headed involvement.

Sometimes one of the perspectives dominates. In Theater Europe all important actions are done in the onlooker perspective, the combats of the participant perspective having no effect on the game, while in GATO, the situation is reversed, since the onlooker perspective is only used for information and no actions can be performed here.

In tool-like systems like Word 3, the unity of the scenes comes from a particular consistent representation of the work object, with the particular task

---

[1] This conception seems to be part of Apple's future policy for integration of programs, as exemplified by the introduction of AppleEvents that enable one program to use facilities in another program.

paradigm being motivated by the representation. However, the unity can also reside in the task paradigm whose members are united by common features. This is the case in the PGP-system of the Swedish Postal Giro, which is designed to be useful in routine work with a certain division of labor. Its scenes are constructed to support different subtasks of the overall routine. The system contains at least three different scenes, associated with three major tasks.

The first scene (shown in Section II.2.1.2) concerns data recording and its work object is a single card. The only task possible is typing in missing information, and when one card is completed, the system automatically presents the next one.

When an error occurs, the subtask of checking off must be performed, and the system changes to the error correction scene below.

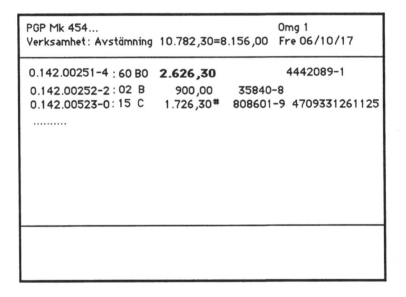

Fig. II.2.19. The error correction scene in the PGP system.

Now the work object is no longer the individual card, but the batch to which it belongs. The reason is that an error is not a property belonging to the individual card, but to a whole batch that must tally. Typing is no longer possible, but instead the worker can send excess cards or batches to a so-called "flier file", where other workers can fetch it, cards can be removed completely, or batches can be "abandoned", viz. marked as faulty and destined for re-examination.

Internal and external reporting is supported by a third scene, where the work object is *lådor*, electronic boxes containing cards that are sent to the data-processing department for electronic book-keeping. The scene is purely informative, only allowing the worker to request information in various layouts:

```
┌─────────────────────────────────────────────────────────────┐
│ PGP Mk 454.29                                                 │
│ Verksamhet: Lådor                              Ons 86/10/22   │
│                                                               │
│                        Alla lådor                             │
│                                                               │
│  Låda  Log.   Fys.   Omgång    Status                         │
│        Dok.   Dok.                                            │
│                                                               │
│  1     8191   4782     77      är fysiskt sänd (band 1)       │
│  2     2482   1430     25      är fysiskt sänd (band 1)       │
│                                                               │
│                                                               │
│                                                               │
│  1=lista job/omg  2=Sortera job/omg. 3=Dok i job/omg.....     │
│                                                               │
└─────────────────────────────────────────────────────────────┘
```

Fig. II.2.20. The reporting scene in the PGP system.

Subview, view and focus

Whereas the scene is defined by functions between signs for objects and signs for tasks, the subview relation is a relation between two or more signs that present the same object in different ways. It is natural to collect all subviews of the same object under the heading of a view. A *view* is then all subviews that refer to the same object. Some systems, including Word 3, can handle more than one view at the same time, each one containing more than one subview.

The Macintosh Finder gives good examples of the view and subview concepts. On the screen in Fig. II.2.21, there are two views called "Del 4" and "Del 2".

They are views since they refer to different sets of documents, but each of these views contains two subviews, because the contents of a folder can be presented either as a set of icons or as lines of text. Each expresses different concepts and/or allows different operations. For example, the icon subview contains two content types, a *kind* type expressed by icons, and a *name* type expressed by characters, while the text subview contains the additional type of *size* and *modification date*. Movement of objects is only possible in the icon view, not in the text view.

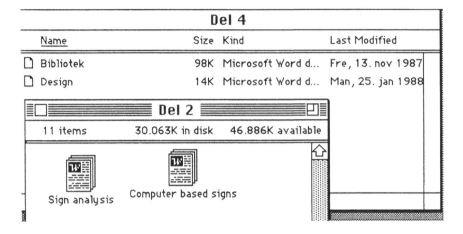

Fig. II.2.21. Views and subviews in the Macintosh Finder.

There is one last possibility that is commonly exploited, namely to simultaneously present different parts of the same object within the same subview. I shall call this sign type a *focus*. The subviews in Word 3 can be split up in two focuses, each showing a different part of the document in the general perspective defined by the subview (Fig. II.2.22).

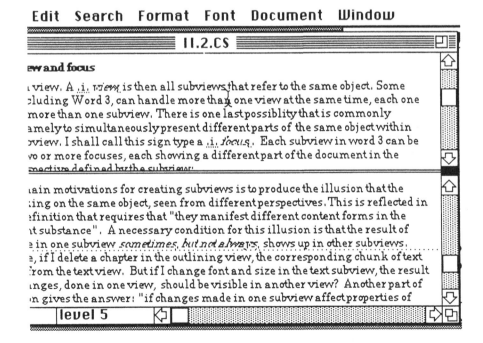

Fig. II.2.22. Focuses in Microsoft Word.

The three sign types, view, subview, and focus, differ with respect to their contents: their reference and their method of presenting their reference. In the framework of this book, the sign types can be differentiated in the following way:

1. Same content substance
    1.1. Same content form: Focus
    1.2. Different form: Subview
2. Different content substance: View

Even if these signs are basically defined semantically, they have counterparts on the expression plane, since conventions for distinguishing them have been established. In the Macintosh world, two expression types are used, namely *windows* and *panes*, of which windows denote a particular view, while the panes of a window denote subviews or focuses within the view.

Windows are often manifested as rectangles signifying the work object. Functionally, windows form constellations, since one window does not presuppose another window, and therefore operations like closing, opening and moving belong to this sign type. In addition windows may be re-sized and scrolled.

Panes[1] are parts of a window: they appear, disappear, and move together, but can be scrolled separately.

The nature of subviews

The subview is the most interesting of the three concurrent sign types, because it creates the illusion that there is something "solid" inside the machine, that the system can view and interpret from different angles. A very simple way of describing views accepts this illusion by defining subviews as signs that manifest different content forms in the same content substance, and requiring that if changes made in one subview affect properties of content substance that are distinctive in another subview, then the expression units of the latter should change according to the commutation test. For example, if I change font and size in the text subview of Word 3, the result should not show up in the outlining view because font and size do not commute here, and if I change the part-whole relation in the outlining view, the effect should not be visible in the text subview because parts and wholes are not systematically expressed in this view.

It is as if the machine uses signs in the same manner as humans do: it looks at something, interprets it according to the content form of its semiotic sys-

---

[1] "Sometimes it's desirable to be able to see disjoint parts of a document simultaneously. Applications that accomodate such a capability allow the window to be split into independently scrollable panes".   *Apple Computer 1984: 31.*

tem, uses the commutation test to find the expressive distinctions that code the content distinctions, and manifests the sign on its screen.

This analysis is contrary to the basic assumptions of the book, that computers can only manipulate the substance of the expression plane of signs and that the sign and its contents exist as a relation between system and user, not inside the machine. From this point of view, there can be no solid objects inside the plastic box, nothing the machine can move to and from, and look at from different distances, and it must all be interpreted as an illusion created by a clever use of agreement and government. But how, then, can such illusions be programmed?

One way of doing it is to write a basic description that either expresses all distinctions of the individual views or contains sufficient data to calculate them, and then define rules that translate the basic description into the views and re-translate operations done in the views back to operations on the basic description[1]. Now, if the basic description is invisible to the user, it can be made to create an illusion of a solid object that can be viewed from different angles, but the basic description itself is just another sign and since the rules of transformation are purely formal, working only on the expression level of the basis, we can safely remove the content plane of the signs from the computer and relocate it in the user interface again.

The particular feature of subviews, namely articulating the same content substance by means of different content forms, is really a semiotic illusion created by functions between the sign expressions that allow one expression to be translated into another.

In order to make this concrete, I shall give a simple illustrative library example. The *basis* is completely traditional, it is simply a collection of periods that describe books:

- A book has a *title*, is written by an *author*, has a *topic*, is placed on a *shelf*, and is in a particular *state*.

The *topic* can be a conventional classification system, for example

Computer science
   Systems Development
   Interface Design
Linguistics
   Semantics

---

[1] Graphical programming uses such techniques: the basic description is called a World Model and consists of a geometrical description of the points in space occupied by the depicted object. If the description is three-dimensional, the translation rules must project it onto a two-dimensional surface, and map this surface onto screen coordinates. See Foley & van Dam 1984.

Syntax
Morphology

In our little toy system, there are three *shelves*, to the left, to the right, and in the front of the room. Systems development books are placed on the left shelf, interface design on the right, and all linguistics books in the front.

A book can be in different *states*: it can be lendable or not lendable (e.g. manuals and dictionaries), borrowed or returned.

In our library, the users and employees perform five different types of tasks:

Searching for books:
    by topic
    by author
    by title
Locating books on shelves
Circulation control: tasks that change the state of a book,
    from lendable to borrowed to returned to lendable.

Our five tasks necessitate seeing the set of books from different perspectives. The topic of the book is irrelevant to circulation control, and the physical location is irrelevant to book searches - it first becomes relevant when the borrower has decided to actually take the book home. Therefore I define five views, one for each task.

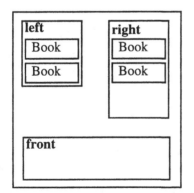

Fig. II.2.23. The physical location view.

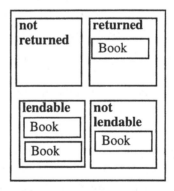

Fig. II.2.24. The circulation control view.

In all views, Author and Title *agree* since they serve to identify a book to the borrower, so if I change the author of a book in one view, it shows up in all other views. In addition, the inversion characteristics of a book *agree*. If I select a book in the topic-view, the book is also selected in the location-view and circulation-control view, enabling me to see the location and status of a book I have found by topic.

The physical location view (Fig. II.2.23) is used by borrowers to locate the book physically. It presents a schematic drawing of the physical shelves, and expresses the content "a book is on a shelf" in a graphical code where a shelf is coded as a large rectangle, a book as a small one containing author and title, and the relation "is on" is coded as "contains".

The circulation control view (Fig. II.2.24) uses the same code, only now "Large rectangle contains small rectangle" means "the book denoted by the small rectangle is in the state denoted by the large one".

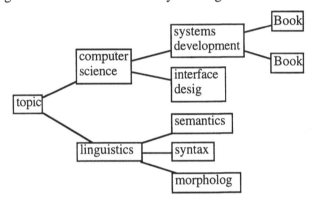

Fig. II.2.25. The topic view.

The topic view (Fig. II.2.25) uses the tree as a means of expression. If a non-terminal node dominates another nonterminal node, it means that the topic denoted by the first is a subtopic of the topic of the second, and if it dominates a terminal it means that the topic of the nonterminal is the topic of the book denoted by the terminal node.

Finally, there should probably be two textual views, one in which the books are ordered by title, and one in which they are ordered by author.

The five views are different ways of viewing the same set of books, and the differences must be defined by *government* relations. There will be one kind of government between the topic and the shelves: if the topic is *systems development*, then the location must be left, and if it is *interface design*, it must be right. These government relations must be maintained, so that if a book is reclassified from *systems development* to *interface design*, the system shifts its location from the left to the right shelf and issues a request to the librarian to move the book. The shelves also enter government with circulation control. If a book is borrowed or returned but not yet put back, it should not show up on the shelves at all, but changing the status of the book from *returned* to *lendable* should make the book appear somewhere on the shelves, depending on its topic.

Besides agreement and government we notice that content distinctions that are invariant in one view can be variants and not expressed in another view. For example, reclassifying a book from semantics to syntax will not show up in the physical location view, since all linguistics books are on the same shelf. Similarly, no changes in the circulation control will show up in the topic view, because the status of a book does not commute in this view.

We can program this by translating changes in one view into changes of the basic description, and then regenerate the other views by translating the basis back to them.

To give an example, the translation T for the circulation control view could be: A *book* is translated as the author designation concatenated with the title. The translation of the *location* of the book, which is one of the rectangles *left, right,* or *front*, must contain the translation of the book:

T(book) = Author(book) + Title(book)
Contain(T(PhysicalLocation(book)), T(book))

T will only express differences of author, title and physical location, whereas all other properties of the book are variants that do not show up.

Each time an operation is done, government must be maintained. If we change the physical location, we must check whether this means a reclassification of the book that should show up in the topic-view, and conversely, reclassification operations should check if the book should have another location. In this example, a simple table like

Physical location	*Topic*
left	systems development
right	interface design
front	semantics
front	syntax
front	morphology

will do the job. The two tables are analogous to paradigms, e.g. paradigms of prepositions and cases, the relation between them is hetero-categorial government, analogous to the government between preposition and case.

II.2.2. Styles

It is common to speak about different interaction styles, e.g. command style versus menu style. In this section, I shall describe three style parameters, and my main point is that *style norms are relative:* they must be discussed in relation to specific kinds of work contexts. For example, although bureaucratic prose can certainly be criticized and made more understandable by learning from journalists, it is not reasonable to transfer the journalistic style wholesale to public administration. The reason is that although both may perform informative functions, there are other functions that are unique to one of the types. For example, journalists must entertain, which is not an obligation of public servants. Conversely, public servants may be entitled to request something of the citizen or to grant permissions to her, which a journalist has no power to do. Since language is used to perform different functions, we cannot expect the same stylistic ideals to apply in both cases.

By the term *style* I understand

- a systematic preference for a subset of a full set of semiotic choices, a preference that can be related to the use context and has consequences for the means of expression.

To a large degree, this covers common usage of the term. For example, bureaucratic style is used by public administration and (in Denmark at least) it is characterized by favoring complex clause structure (where coordinate main sentences is an alternative), by nominalizations (where clauses could have been chosen), by preferring neutral words (contrasting to emotive ones) and by presenting the conclusion after the premises (where journalistic style does the opposite).

These choices are connected to the work context of the public servant: complex clause structure can be necessary to express a complicated decision unambiguously, and nominalizations and neutral words correctly reflect the fact that the public servant is not personally involved in the events, and that he is obliged to take an impartial stand in the matter.

The three dimensions for characterizing style I shall use are:

- *Object vs task style:* Are objects or actions most important?
- *Control vs choice style:* Who controls the work process, the designer or the user?
- *Directness vs indirectness:* Are cast-iron illusions good?

II.2.2.1. Are objects or actions most important?

Semantic description

Descriptions can be organized in different ways. One important distinction is whether I see the world as consisting of objects that can be used for various purposes, or whether I see it as mainly consisting of actions and tasks that may involve objects now and then. The following two descriptions refer to the same objects and actions, but clearly they are organized in very different ways:

- *Object-style.* On my table are a pipe, a computer and a batch of paper. The pipe is used for smoking, the computer for programming, drawing and writing, and the paper is used for reading and making corrections.
- *Task-style.* These days I spend my time writing a book and programming small examples. Writing is nerve-racking, so when I write I am a heavy pipe smoker. I normally write the text on my computer, take a print of a dozen pages, read and correct it, and use the computer to record the changes. Programming is more of a pleasure, I do not smoke so much, and normally make no paper printouts of the system.

In the object-oriented style, the main sections cohere because they refer to the same object, and the actions are only entered if they have function to the object. In the task-oriented style, each section refers to the same task, and objects are entered if they happen to be involved in the task.

This difference of composition can also be observed in interface design.

Most of the applications described so far are in object-style, since the modality of verb-signs (e.g. menu items) depends upon the object selected. Consider again the Edit menu described before. The menu items have a modality inflection (impossible|possible) expressed by color (grey | black) and the objects have a focus inflection (selected|non-selected) expressed by inversion (inverted | non-inverted). The system keeps track of the Focus paradigm of the objects, and adapts the Modality paradigm of the menu items to it, marking some commands as impossible, others as possible. These dependencies do not work the opposite way, so choosing an action will not bring forth a menu of the objects it can be applied to.

Whereas the focus of interest of the object style is on objects, task-style systems are about tasks and actions. A good example of the latter is the PGP-system, which is strongly biased towards *task* style. The main decompositions of the program execution in this style express a decomposition of tasks, and objects are entered as they are relevant to the current task.

Means of expression

Task and object dominance can be expressed in many ways, and one important difference lies in the way actions are expressed.

In the object style, the object is expressed by thematic elements like icons, while the typical action does not have permanent features, but only exists transitorily in functional dependencies between characteristics like location, size, or color. In the Fullpaint example, agreement and government between handling and transient features designate actions like drawing and erasing, while the permanent features code work objects like paper and tools like pencils and eraser.

In the task style, actions are expressed by thematic elements, often verbal command names. Functions between handling and transient features are not used for expressing actions, but code meta-actions like starting, ending, continuing, decomposing and specializing tasks. Work objects and tools may not be coded at all.

Since most of my examples have been object-style, I shall concentrate on task-style in this section, and use the PGP-system to illustrate the ways task-style can be manifested.

Menu structure. The task dominance can be seen in the gapping structures of the system's menus. Most often, the items in a menu share a verb and are differentiated by the objects. The first item of the menu can contain a common verb that is presupposed by the rest of the items:

Flytta Detta dokument, Ett dokument, Flera dokument, En hel bunt
[Move This document, One document, More documents, A whole batch]

or the common verb can be repeated in each item:

överge nuvarende BUNT, *överge* nuvarande JOB
[Abandon current BATCH, abandon current JOB]

Finally, the verb can be presupposed from the previous menu. If the item *visa flygare [show fliers]* is chosen from one menu, the next submenu displays a set of objects that all connect to the previous verb :

Flygare, Borttagna dokument, Gamla flygare, Alla flyttade/borttagna
dokument[1]
[Fliers, Removed documents, Old fliers, All moved/removed documents]

In all cases, the main classification is done by the verb while objects are used for subclassification.

Meta-actions. Since in the ideal case the world of task-style systems consists of actions and tasks, the possible actions in this world consist of changing actions and tasks, not of changing objects. Actions that change other actions are meta-actions, and as mentioned above include *starting, executing, ending, continuing, decomposing,* or *specializing* an action. If we make verbal paraphrases of the computer-based actions, the difference between object and task style shows up in the sentence structure. In object style, the sentences have nouns as parts, whereas in task style the sentences'

---

[1] The design is not consistent, and there are examples where menu items are united by a common object: Flytta *dokument* till flygare, Ta bort *dokument* [Move document to fliers, Remove document].

parts are themselves sentences. Where the object-style paraphrase of an action could be

I fill in a form

the task style will embed this sentences as a (deep structure) subject in another sentence, e.g.:

I continue filling in a form

whose deep structure is often represented as *(I fill in a form) continues* with *I fill in a form* as the subject. Similarly, to

I move a document

may correspond to a classificatory sentence like

Moving documents can be moving one document or moving a whole batch

whose subject and attributes are sentences.

The menu choices of the PGP system are good examples of this. Menu items often denote parts of the work process, and the menu hierarchy expresses a classification and decomposition of the whole work process.

In the following example, the meta-action is specialization. The action class *Moving Documents* is classified into four subclasses, *1=Move this document, 2=One document, 3=More documents* and *4=A whole batch:*

1=Flytta detta dokument 2=Ett dokument 3=Flera dokument 4=En hel bunt

Fig. II.2.26. Menu line before specializing
the action *Move this document.*

of which the last one, *4=A whole batch*, is again specialized into *1=Move to fliers* and *2=Remove Document:*

1=Flytta dokument till flygare 2=Ta bort dokument

Fig. II.2.27. Menu line after specializing the action
Move this document.

The specialization action is composed of two parts, namely *select subclass* (either type its number or use arrow keys to move the selection to its name) followed by *execute* (press Enter). Up till now, the document has not been affected in any way. The user is not handling objects but actions.

Summarizing, one can say that object style codes objects as thematic elements and actions as functional dependencies, whereas task style codes actions as thematic elements and meta-actions as functional dependencies:

	Thematic elements	*Functional dependencies*
Object style	Objects	Actions
Task style	Actions	Meta-actions

In object-style, moving a document can be expressed by an object icon plus agreement between document location and mouse location, whereas in the task-style of the PGP-system, it is expressed by action names plus selection.

Rhythm: Task dominance can not only be observed in menu selection, where specialization and decomposition are used for preparing and ending the work process, but also in the actual execution of work that contains signs for initiation, continuation, and cessation of the work. Consider for example the view supporting the task of data recording called *komplettering*, completing, which occupies the lion's share of employee time.

The largest part of the screen is occupied by the card to be completed. A card is represented by four to five *fields* containing *film number* (a number assigned to card and microfilm by the OCR-reader), *transaction code* (the card type), *amount, account to* (the account to which payment is made), and *account from* (the account from which payment is made).

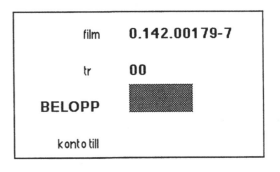

Fig. II.2.28. Screen image for data recording in the PGP system. Prompting for *amount*.

Each field consists of a non-writeable *attribute*, denoting the type of the field, and a writeable numeric *value*. When input to one field is completed, the system shows the next field to be processed, and when a card is finished, the next card is automatically shown. In the example, film number and transaction have been completed, and the worker is about to enter *belopp* [amount]. The amount value is inverted, and furnished with a cursor.

The worker types in the amount in the grey inverted BELOPP-field (Fig. II.2.29), and when the Enter-key is pressed, the system prompts for KONTO TILL [account to], which is the next field (Fig. II.2.30).

The designer has taken great pains to describe the *transition* from one action to another.

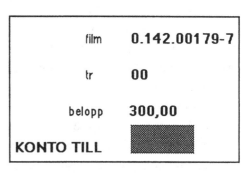

Fig. II.2.29. Screen image for data recording in the PGP system after *amount* has been entered.

Fig. II.2.30. Screen image for data recording in the PGP system. Prompting for *account to*.

The thematic elements, viz. field names and values expressed by alphanumeric characters, are inflected in a combined tense and modality paradigm, consisting of three members: *Past* (fields that are completed), *Present* (the field to be completed now), and *Future* (fields to be completed later). The inflection is denoted by a very skillful exploitation of three transient paradigms, *Size* (Large, Small), *Case* (Upper, Lower) and *Inversion* (Inverted, Non-inverted):

	Attribute	*Value*
Past	small, lower	nonempty, large, non-inverted
Present	large, upper	nonempty, large, inverted
Future	small, lower	empty

There is homo-categorial government between the fields: in the example above, if *amount* is present, *account to* will be future, and if *amount* is past, *account to* will be present.

A very clear symptom of the task dominance is the fact that changes of work objects are not marked. For example, although the individual slip logically belongs to a batch representing the total payments from a single customer, transition from one batch to another is not represented differently than transitions between slips within the same batch. Instead, the main syntagm of work is two filling-in operations bound together by government expressing the concept of *continuation* from one filling operation to the next, and the major breaks in work are caused by errors, a property of tasks.

The structuring principle of the interface is not objects, but rather the structure, rhythm and flow of work. With a musical analogy, one can say that the system sets the beat of work.

Work context

As has already transpired, the difference between object and task-style rests on a basic difference in perspective, in how one looks at the work process, so choice of style is to a large degree a choice of the way the user is invited to see her work.

Not any perspective fits any kind of work. If the focus of a good social adviser is not to be on the administrative procedures but on the client, it would be a complete misunderstanding to give him a task-style system whose main cohesive force stems from administrative rules and which guide him through a case in the most efficient way. The situation is different at the Postal Giro. Although the particular task style did in fact not fit very well with the workers' own interpretation of their work, some kind of task style is not unmotivated: the work involves many thousands of similar cards, none of which can attract the same attention as the unhappy client in the welfare department, it is tempo work, where speed is important and the individual parts are simple and short, and the Postal Giro is a large bureaucracy based on explicit rules for work procedures and divisions of labor. The complexity of the Postal Giro does not so much reside in its work objects, but in its organization.

The answer to the chapter heading, *Are objects or actions most important?* is then: it depends upon the type of work in which the system is used. In some kinds of work, the cohesive force lies in the objects, in other kinds in task structure, and this must be reflected in the interface.

II.2.2.2. Who controls the work process?

The issue of control is important in systems design. At one end of the scale, the system can be designed to offer very limited possibilities for actions, prompting the user for each step she takes, and forcing her to choose one particular way of doing things where several would have been possible. At the other end, the system may offer a large range of actions, and it is the responsibility of the users to select the appropriate ones. In recent literature on man-machine interaction, there has been a clear tendency towards giving control to the user. Rasmussen 1980 criticizes the philosophy of accident prevention in plant control for mostly consisting in

> recommendations for better training together with "stricter administrative control of the adherence to instructions"   *Rasmussen 1980: 98*

and suggests himself that computer systems that provide more relevant information may be a better solution. The tool ideal for computer systems set up in the Scandinavian trade union project UTOPIA also emphasizes that the locus of control should be in the worker: to label some means of production as tools should require that they

- are means to fashion material into a more refined product,
- are under *complete* and *continuous manual* control of the worker,
- are fashioned for the use by a skilled worker to create products of good use quality,
- are extensions of the accumulated knowledge of tools and materials of a given labor process. *Ehn & Kyng 1985 [my italics]*

Laurel 1986 suggests "direct engagement" as a design ideal where the user feels that she is working with the fictitious referent of the system, not with the system itself, and lists three factors that contribute to this goal, one of which is interactive range:

Interactive range describes the range of choices available to users at a given moment in the interaction....First-personness is most completely realized at the extreme end of each of the interactive variables' continuum: Frequency is continuous; range is infinite; significance is maximal. *Laurel 1986: 78-79*

In this section I shall comment on two questions.

The first one is: What does it mean that the system controls the user? My comments will be that control properties are not properties of the system itself, but of the interface, viz. of signs manifested in the system processes. These properties can be described as relations between action paradigms.

The second one is: How should control be distributed between system and user? My comment is the same as in the preceding section: there is no absolute optimal balance of control, rather it depends on the type of work process that the system is intended for. Designing a system is to design preconditions for work, and designing the balance of control is to design the work process itself.

What is control?

As appears from the quotations, control has something to do with the action possibilities available to the user. In general, the more possibilities, the more control.

My first point is that when we count the possibilities we should not count the possible signals the user can enter into the system but rather the contents of these signals, in particular the actions and tasks they signify. To see this, compare a system where the user types in amounts of money, to a system where she can choose between 10 different commands denoted by numbers from 1 to 10. In the first system, the user can input all possible numbers that can be stored in the machine, whereas in the second one, she can only input numbers from 1 to 10. Still, this does not make the first system offer more choices than the second one because in the first example, all typing of digits may signify the same action, namely *entering the amount,* while the 10 different digits in the second example may signify ten different actions in the work process.

Thus, counting possibilities must be preceded by the commutation test in order to determine which signals signify the same or different actions.

As the first quotation above shows, the control issue is closely related to the issue of standardization. Standardization is a social process that is active in many other areas, as well as in systems design[1].

Traffic control is a very good example, and I shall use it to define the notion formally. At one end of the spectrum, consider a person walking across a meadow. His action paradigm includes actions like Stop, go Forward, go Back, turn Left and turn Right. The meadow generates a category of paradigms of the following type, where all paradigms except the full one are negated:

{+<+S+F+B+L+R>
 -<-S+F+B+L+R>

 ...

 -<-S+F-B-L-R>...}

Idealizing a bit, we can say that on the meadow the full paradigm is available all the time, and at no place do we have defective paradigms like <-S+F+B+L+R> where stopping is impossible, or <-S+F-B-L-R>, where only forward motion is possible.

At the other end of the scale we have the highways that are the most standardized means of communication. Of course, the category of paradigms generated by the Danish highways does not contain the full paradigm <+S+F+B+L+R>, but instead has at least three different defective paradigms:

The *rest-areas,* where stopping and driving forward are allowed:
   <+S+F-B-L-R>
The *exits*, where driving forward and turning right are allowed:
   <-S+F-B-L+R>
The *proper roads,* where only forward motion is allowed:
   <-S+F-B-L-R>

Standardization can be described as a relation between two categories of paradigms[2] A and B generated by the same context.

---

[1] The following example is inspired by Jervell and Olsen 1983, ch. 7. I use the term *standardization* instead of their *formalization,* since I wish to reserve the latter for formalization in the mathematical sense.
[2] On categories of paradigms, see "System and Process" in Section I.2.1.

B is a standardization of A if

- A's context is articulated in special *subcontexts* in B. Formally it means that A contains fewer asserted paradigms than B. The meadow contains only one asserted paradigm whereas B contains three, articulating the highway into three subcontexts, the rest-areas, the exits, and the road proper.
- Each paradigm of B is defective since it contains *fewer* action possibilities than the paradigms of A. Formally this means that the paradigms of B contain fewer asserted members than A. The one paradigm of the meadow asserts all five actions, while the three paradigms of the highway only assert one or two actions each.

Fixing one sequence of actions where several are possible is one special way of achieving standardization.

Suppose for example that three main actions are involved when an employee is travelling for her company: Applying for money, Receiving money, and Using money.

The most inflexible rules would be that only one sequence is allowed, Applying + Receiving + Using. In this case the context consisting of these three actions would contain exactly one member: after applying only receiving is possible, and after receiving only using is allowed. The category of paradigms generated by this context would look like this:

{-<+A+R+U>

...

+<-A+R-U>
+<-A-R+U>}

Suppose now that any sequence is possible, so that using can be followed by receiving or applying, or receiving can be followed by using or applying. After each action the full paradigm is possible, generating the following category:

{+<+A+R+U>

...

-<-A+R-U>
-<-A-R+U>}

Clearly, the first category is a standardization of the second one according to the definition.

Work context

The PGP-system is a good example of how important the control issue is in practice: when should control be left to the worker and when should the system control her?

Roughly speaking, the solution in the system is to let the machine have control under normal routine typing (*komplettering* [complete, record data]), but transfer it to the worker under error handling (*avstämning* [balance, check off]). One of the managers is very conscious about this and says:

> When you are completing, the machine as it were tells you which items on the card should be completed, by telling you what is not read.
> But when you have completed and are balancing, then the operator has the ball all the time, so that the operator chooses whether he wants to continue correcting or as it were put aside the batch.

However, generally the coordinator wants the worker to be in control:

> It was quite difficult to explain to the system people that built the system how we as it were wanted to keep this feeling intact, that on the one hand the operator must have control over the machine all the time, and instead demand of the system that it checks if the operator makes errors, and then the system must handle this in a nice way.

The control issue is closely related to the wish to create some kind of job feeling.

> We thought that it is important that you keep the feeling all the time that you finish something. I do not hand it over to somebody else.

These quotations from practice interpret design of the control aspects of the system as design of the work process, and I concur in this interpretation. In the present case, the work process is divided into two different types: the routine part (in which speed is important and where choices should be few) and the problem-solving part (where more choices should be available).

The machine control in the routine part is achieved through sequencing the four main actions: the system moves the text cursor automatically from one field to the next, so that typing film number, transaction code, amount and account numbers always takes place in this sequence. Thus the category of paradigms generated by routine work will contain many defective paradigms, e.g.

{+<+type film, -type transaction, -type amount,...>
+<-type film, +type transaction, -type amount,...>
+<-type film, +type transaction, +type amount,...>...}

The controlling role of the system is underlined in the help messages where the system presents itself as some kind of benevolent supervisor:

Keyboard buffer full.

You are too fast on the keyboard. It should not happen too often.

I'm doing my best

The benefit is increased speed, and the costs seem to be slight. Although the workers' freedom is constrained, this freedom seems superfluous since one sequence can be just as good as the other, and most workers would probably choose a fixed pattern anyway. There is no point in offering system processes that are more flexible than the work schema that actually is manifested in them.

If we record the category of paradigms in error-correction, the difference from routine work immediately appears, since here we will essentially have one paradigm where all members are asserted, while all other defective paradigms are negated:

  {+<+Move document, +Fetch document, +Take away document,
  +Abandon batch, +Search Document...>....}

The features of standardizations are clearly much less pronounced, and there are good reasons why the manager is right in avoiding standardization here. Although it would be possible to articulate the error situation into sub-situations according to probable error type, and only offer the relevant commands for each sub-situation, the grounds for such classification may turn out to be insufficient so that too many false classifications may occur: for example, a deficit may be due both to a missing card, to writing errors on the customer's part or to typing errors by the workers. In addition, such control would run counter to the organizational goals that the system is intended to fulfill, namely to replace the old assembly line organization with a more modern organization where workers are responsible for a coherent set of tasks.

These two considerations are important when considering standardizations: are they possible without hampering the work process or decreasing the quality of the product? Do they agree with the organizational ideas of the work place and do they enhance the desired type of work culture?

II.2.2.3. Cast-iron illusions?

The last stylistic issue concerns the degree of illusion that can and should be achieved. While the object/task distinction pertains to the way actions are coded, and the control/choice distinction to the properties of action paradigms, the realism/non-realism opposition concerns which plane of the sign should be brought to the user's attention, the content or the expression plane.

A common ideal is that computer systems should be designed in such a way that the user can forget the computer, viz. the particular means of expression, and concentrate her attention solely on the contents. The unobtrusiveness of the interface is a main point in Bødker 1987, who advocates *transparency* as a design goal :

"Through the interface" tells us that a computer application, from the user's perspective, is not something that the user operates *on* but something that the user operates *through* on other objects or subjects. ...When I use a text editor to write this chapter, the user interface supports my work on the form and content of the document, and if the user interface is a good one I am capable of forgetting that I actually work with a computer between the document and myself.   *Bødker 1987: 1*

Sign structure

Older systems are often criticized for putting a barrier between the user and her real work because they were difficult to handle and forced her to focus on the means of expression: the spelling of commands, complicated syntax, difficult input units. With the availability of graphical signs, designers saw a new opportunity for hiding the ugly signifiers, coining phrases such as *direct manipulation* and *direct engagement.*

Directness can be achieved by a particular sign structure. According to Hutchins et al 1986, directness has two important aspects:

Semantic directness: Is it possible to say what one wants to say in this language? That is, does the language support the user's conception of the task domain? Does it encode the concepts and distinctions in the domain in the same way that the user thinks about them?   *Hutchins et al 1986: 100*

Articulatory directness: ...articulatory directness has to do with the relationships between the meanings of expressions and their physical form. ...There are ways to design languages such that the relationships between the forms of the vocabulary items and their meanings are not arbitrary. One technique is to make the physical form of the vocabulary item structurally similar to their meanings.
                          Hutchins et al 1986: 109-110

Both types of directness consist of identities.

Semantic directness consists of identity between the content of the interface and that of the work language. The mail example from Section I.2.4.2 violates this ideal, since although I wanted to *read* a document, the interface provided only means of expression for *saving* it, *closing* the mail system, and *opening* the document.

Articulatory directness consists in identity (or similarity) between the content and expression plane of the computer-based sign, that is: motivated signs.

If these conditions are fulfilled, direct engagement, where the user feels as if he manipulated the objects of interest directly himself, and not indirectly through the computer, can occur:

> *Direct engagement* occurs when a user experiences direct interaction with the objects in a domain. Here, there is a feeling of involvement directly with a world of objects rather than of communicating with an intermediary...
> At a minimum, to produce a feeling of direct engagement the system needs:
> /.../
> • The interface to be unobtrusive, not interfering or intruding. If the interface itself is noticed, then it stands in a third-person relationship to the objects of interest, and detracts from the directness of the engagement.   *Hutchins et al 1986: 114-115*

Thus, it seems as if everybody agrees that a good interface is one that lets the user focus his attention on the object and goals of his work, and not on the tool, an ideal that can be summarized in one formula: *A good interface lets the user focus his attention on the content plane of the computer-based signs, and directs his attention away from the expression plane.*

Work context

Although this stylistic ideal sounds natural and sensible, it is not without problems. Some of these have been discussed for at least 50 years in literary theory in relation to the literary schools of naturalism and realism. In relation to systems design, the problems can be divided into two levels, a philosophical/political level and a practical level. I shall start with the first[1].

Literary realism has been criticized for presenting the signified as a natural phenomenon that exists before and outside the signifier, whose role is precisely to express and communicate it. Realism has no concept of meaning production and cannot see that signifier and signified are re-created simultaneously in one and the same semiotic process. In realism, signifier and signified are united, and in this blending, the signifier destroys itself or becomes transparent. It lets the concept represent itself, as it is, without reference to anything other than its own presence. Language is seen as if it replaces or is identical to the real world. This imaginary identity between signifier and signified is a prerequisite for the latter's ability to present itself as *vraisemblable*, as a commonly accepted view of the world that cannot be questioned.

This discussion does not seem to have influenced systems design, since the very effects that are criticized in literary theory are viewed as desirable effects in computer interaction. For example the following quotation recom-

---

[1] The following arguments are based on Coward & Ellis 1977.

mends that the signified should suppress its signifier and present itself as a natural part of the real world:

> The expressions of a Direct Manipulation output language must behave in such a way that the user can assume that they, in some sense, are the things they refer to.
>
> *Hutchins et al 1986: 97*

Although this discussion has mainly taken place in literary circles, the methodology of structuralist linguistics clearly supports such arguments. Its cornerstone is the commutation test, without which we have no tools for isolating and describing linguistic units empirically, and this test will always define expression and content units simultaneously, so, from a scientific point of view, stipulating pre-existing and independent contents is pure metaphysics, as we have no way of observing them. A semiotic approach to systems design therefore must take the literary discussion seriously.

As far as I can see, the critique of realism has two main points:

- Realism presents meaning creation in an erroneous way: it presents the signified as existing prior to the signifier, whereas in reality, signified and signifier are created in the same dialectical process.
- Since realism presents meaning as given and natural, it prevents a critical attitude towards it, and tends to mix up reality and fiction.

Besides being a general problem in a world where television, magazines and film to a still larger degree replace the real referents by signs denoting them, there are special applications where serious damage can be done if fiction and reality are not clearly separated, for example economic models and control room systems.

Economic models are only approximations to the real economy; they rest on particular assumptions, and they can be inhomogeneous in that some calculations rest on relatively firm ground, while others are only educated guesses. If the economist is to assess the validity of the model's predictions, he must know the assumptions of the model, and be aware of the differences in the validity of the individual calculations. A critical attitude towards sign production, and a keen consciousness of the mode of sign production is clearly necessary here.

The same critical attitude is necessary for operators of a control room system whose signs are produced in a complex process: the signals are generated by gauges mounted on the machinery, travel through cables to the system, are aggregated and processed here, and finally presented on the screen. All along this route are sources of errors. In both cases, inattention to the way meanings are produced can have fatal consequences: economic disasters and catastrophes in atomic plants.

A less dramatic but more general argument against a cast-iron realism is that it may invite conservatism in use and design instead of invention and change. Proponents of direct manipulation are in fact quite aware of this danger:

> But if we restrict ourselves to only building interfaces that allow us to do things we can already do and to think in ways we already think, we will miss the most exciting potential of new technology: to provide new ways to think of and to interact with a domain. *Hutchins et al 1986: 118*

The gist of the preceding is that real-life work is not always focused on the work objects, but in certain situations the workers need to step outside the work and focus on its technical and organizational preconditions, and in the particular case of computer-based work it means that they need to concentrate on technical properties of the system itself - they need to disclose the signifier. This is of course true when dramatic errors occur, but our recordings from the Postal Giro project also turned up other daily events: one is *mystery solving,* where the workers try to interpret system behavior they do not immediately understand, another is *forecasting,* where they invent work methods and try to figure out whether the system will allow them. In both types of conversation, the workers have stopped working in the usual sense, since their focus of attention in no longer on the payment slips, but on the system itself and the work procedures it allows.

Thus, work normally contains two types of language usage, talking *in* a situation and talking *about* a situation[1]. In Halliday's words:

> Here the distinction between the language of *playing* a game, such as bridge or football, and the language of *discussing* a game becomes clear. In the former situation, the language is functioning as a part of the game...whereas in the latter, it is part of a very different kind of activity, and may be informative, didactic, argumentative, or any one of a number of rhetorical modes of discourse. *Halliday 78: 223*

As the quotation indicates, the linguistic schemas underlying the two types of situations can be quite different. For example, the soccer game allows short shouts like *Pass!* among the players and disallows arguments with the referee. In the locker room, *Pass!* has no sense, but criticisms like *You should have passed to me, stupid, don't do so much on your own* are relevant, and arguments with the referee are no longer punished.

When we talk *about* a situation, our utterances not only have function to other utterances and actions of the speaking situation, but also to actions and utterances of another situation. Strategy discussions between coach and players in the locker room are of this kind, serving to establish or change the

---

[1] Barthes 1957.

general schema of playing. Their utterances still have function to other *utterances* of the speaking situation (question/answer, proposal/rejection, etc.), but not to its *actions*. In fact, they have no function to particular actions at all, but to the *action schema* of the football match.

The shouts of the football match are language *in* a situation, since they have function to utterances and actions in the same situation, whereas the strategy discussion is language *about* a situation, since it has function to utterances of one situation and actions of another situation.

Most work contains both modes: in the following conversation from the Postal Giro, M stops Y from closing down the OCR-reader, since she may have cards that must be re-read, and both M and Y speak *in* the work situation (these conversations are treated more fully in Section III.2.3):

M: Vänta, jag har ett rött jobb som jag fick nu, man kanske kunde droppa nåt
Y: Ja
M: Jag ska kolla
[M: Wait a minute, I've got an urgent batch here I just got, maybe we could drop something
Y: Yes
M: I'll check]

Whereas these utterances only have function to actions *in* the situation in which they are uttered, here serving to prevent a colleague from doing something, the next (forecasting) conversation has function to another situation than the speaking situation. The topic of the conversation is the appropriate time to change the date of the system, the danger being that data transmission through the local network will close down when the next day's date is entered:

X: Jo vi kan slå in datumet, för måndan, men vi kan ju inte börja köra kort, för då kommer det ju in i sa- i låda två.
Y: Den har jag stängt nu
W: Men går det att göra så
Z: Dom stängs automatiskt, när du sätter på den
X: Datakomben ja
W: Ja men kan den va stängd, den kan vi väl inte stänga, innan vi har sänt iväg våran låda.
Z: Nä men den stängs väl automatiskt, när vi har sänt iväg lådan, så har jag fattat det.
W: (...) den där

Z: Den kan man ju i stort sätt göra dagavslut på, innan man är färdig, gjorde vi
inte så därnere? I och med att man är färdig med sina röda jobb, då kan man ju
ställa om.. dagavslut på den där

[X: Well, we can enter the date, for Monday, but we can't start running cards
through, cause they'll wind up in - in box two

Y: I've closed it now

W: But can you really do that?

Z: They close automatically when you start it up

X: The datacom, right

W: Yes, but can it really be closed, we can't really close it before we've sent off
our box

Z: Nope, but it probably closes automatically when we've sent off the box, that's
how I thought it worked

W: (...) that there

Z: You can on the whole finish off the day's work on it, before you're done, did-
n't we do it that way down there? Once you've finished your red jobs, you can
reset it...finish the day's work on it]

The topic of this conversation is future work situations and the utterances
serve to set up guidelines for these situations. The workers use the opening
and constraining[1] functions of their language to build a work schema, setting
up action paradigms like <enter date, close "datacomben", send box> and
<run cards, send box> and syntagmatic functions between them (*enter date*
prevents *run cards)*.

The two modes of speaking require different types of information and different ways of organizing it. This is already apparent in the two examples of
which only the latter contains complex sentences, and an even clearer contrast appears if we compare the language of the workers in the work situation to managerial language, which is typically about work situations. I shall
do this at length in Part III, but to give an impression of the differences, I here
briefly list some characteristics of the language of a manager at the Postal
Giro which were absent or rare in the language of the workers.

The manager did not describe the tasks of the shop floor with verbs but
used noun phrases containing a nominalized verb:

Så gör man ungefär 500 *kompletteringar* per timme samtidigt som man sköter då
buntavstämning, undersökning och allting som tillhör.

[They do about 500 *completions* per hour at the same time as they take care of *batch
checking, investigating,* and all the other things involved]

---

[1] The concepts are described in Section I.2.2.4, "Functions between Work Context and Language".

The reason is that just as the payment slips are the work object of the shop floor workers, the tasks themselves are the manager's work objects. Since the purpose of his work is to change the tasks, his language contains finite verbs (slå ihop [combine], bryta [break]) describing a change of the tasks denoted by the nominalized verb:

> Vi ska försöka vinna det steget att försöka *slå ihop* datafångsten med kompletteringen och det försöker vi göra genom ett decentralt data system...man *bryter* den där kopplingen då vad det är som en bokföringsavedening egentligen ska göra.
>
> [We'll try to get to the point where we try to *combine* the data intake and completing, and we try to do this with a decentralized computer system...we *break* that link about what an accounting division is really supposed to do]

or transitions from one task to another

> Det här *gick över till* ett genomförandeskede
> [This *turned into* a step of carrying out ...]
>
> och dom *kom* så att säga väldigt tidigt *i kast* med såna här grejer som att *göra* kravsspecifikationen *färdig*
> [And they *came into contact* with this sort of thing very early as it were, this bit of *finishing off* the demand specifications]

which is also his responsibility.

Note in all examples that the association between worker and task is not expressed by subject + finite verb, but is thematized in a subject + abstract verb (göra, sköta) + nominalization construction. The reason is that the association of workers and tasks is in the focus of managerial work, since planning and reorganizing work means to move workers from one task to another.

These observations show that there are clear linguistic differences between speaking in work and speaking about work. Broadly speaking, when you speak *in* a situation, your are submerged in it and use finite verbs and sentence progression to communicate the flow of events you experience, while if you speak *outside* it, your attitude is more detached, the events appear more like objects, and you often use nouns to denote them while verbs and conjunctions describe their interrelations.

Since not only managers but also workers need to speak and reason in these two modes, it follows that the maxim of hiding the signifier in computer systems needs to be modified. Systems should not only support "direct engagement" but also give information appropriate for "detached reflection".

"Direct engagement" interaction supports execution of work, while planning and controlling work functions need a more detached bird's eye view of the working process, so designing these two views is really designing how planning, execution, and control should be organized in the enterprise. Therefore, the basic design goal cannot be just to create as much direct involvement as possible, but must consist in creating a balance of computer support for both direct involvement and detached reflection that corresponds to the desired organization of executive and managerial functions.

Returning to the literary controversy, I believe that designers could learn a good deal from the alienation *(Verfremdungs)* technique of Brecht's theater. In Brecht's view, *Verfremdung* means that although the objects on the stage must be recognizable, they should be presented as strange and foreign phenomena that make the audience wonder and reflect. *Verfremdung* means the opposite of direct engagement, namely to make the known world strange.

I agree with Brecht that the realism controversy is really a political issue and in the case of computer technology concerns the organizational role users should play. Cast-iron realism prevents the user from getting ideas for modifying her tool and changing her working conditions because the technical workings of the system are so to speak sealed up. The Macintosh system I myself use is a good example of this. If a user wants to go beyond its friendly user interface, he enters a completely new world consisting of *files, forks, resources,* and similar strange creatures he has never encountered in the use situation. However, this is clearly not a technical necessity but must be seen as an - in my view misguided and unfounded - assumption about the roles users wish to occupy.

Other systems are constructed more transparently, being built upon one conceptual apparatus at all levels. The ICL Perq is based on Pascal and most of what happens in the system can be understood if you know this language. The same is true of some Xerox machines based on LISP. However, these systems are not ideal either: it takes too much effort before you are able to do anything interesting, because they lack a gradual transition from usage to development. Ironically enough, the system I know that most elegantly guides the user from merely using systems to developing them is designed for Macintosh computers. This is the Hypertalk language described in Section I.2.4.3 (Design as Language Politics), and the method it employs can to a large degree be described as "disclosing the signifier" or "replacing the real meaning with the formal meaning".

The conclusion of this discussion can be summarized thus:

- Work normally consists of both direct engagement and detached analysis and invention.
- These two modes of work require different semiotic focuses. The former focuses on the signified, the latter sometimes also on the signifier.
- The realistic style fails to support analysis and invention and must be modified, possibly based on the dramaturgy of Brecht.

II.2.2.4. Computer stylistics. Conclusion

In the beginning of this section, I deliberately defined style as "a systematic preference for a subset of a full set of semiotic choices, a preference that can be related to the use context and that has consequences for the means of expression". The gist of the three discussions of style is that design ideals are not absolute, but - as the definition indicates - must be related to types of situations. Thus, although the tool style of the UTOPIA project demanding that computer systems be

1. means to fashion material into a more refined product
2. under *complete* and *continuous manual* control of the worker,
3. fashioned for the use by a skilled worker to create products of good use quality
4. extensions of the accumulated knowledge of tools and materials of a given labor
   process   *Ehn & Kyng 1984*

is a good ideal for computer support for skilled handicraft workers, it is difficult or impossible to apply to industrial unskilled work, like that of the Postal Giro.

There is no material that is refined to a product, since the Giro is a service organization, and this alone makes it difficult to apply points 1 and 3. Point 4 can apply but only to a limited extent, since the work is unskilled and can be taught in a couple of weeks, and the same is true of point 2. If your task is to take care of 200 more or less identical cards and type the numbers that have not been optically read, it is just irksome to have to position the cursor yourself at the next place for typing, and if there are fixed rules for solving problems, the system should not indicate a degree of freedom that is not real. It is easier and more truthful if the system tells you where to type next, and which rules are applicable.

This relativistic attitude does not mean that anything goes, but rather that style discussions must be contextualized, and that within a certain context it is meaningful and possible to set up stylistic ideals. It is not sensible to apply the stylistic ideals of journalistic prose to the administrative language of bureaucracies, because the two contexts are different and their language must fulfil different functions. But this does not mean that bureaucratic prose cannot be criticized and better guidelines invented.

In the same way, although the PGP system of the Postal Giro should not be judged on stylistic ideals from handicraft work, it is perfectly sensible to try to set up guidelines for design of systems for routine, rule-based, unskilled work. The characteristic nature of such work is that it is cooperative although cooperation is often disguised in the division of labor, and good systems should support and explicate these features. A set of guidelines similar to the UTOPIA list could demand that the system should support workers in

- coordinating work
- sharing data
- communicating
- getting overviews of task structure and organization
- getting explanations and descriptions of existing work rules.

With these remarks I close Part II of the book. The emphasis in this part has been on computer systems, with the working context serving as a point of reference. In Part III, Language, Work, and Design, the perspective is reversed; the main topic is now a department at the Postal Giro in Stockholm, a concrete work place where computer systems are used, and the purpose is to present techniques for making descriptions of the work environment that can be used as a basis for systems design.

PART III. LANGUAGE, WORK, AND DESIGN

Introduction

In Part I of this book I presented a general framework for understanding language and computers, and in Part II showed how to apply this framework to analysis and design of computer systems. What remains to be done now is to broaden the scope of our analysis, and show how the same framework can be used for describing and designing computer systems in a practical context of work. In order to do that I need a concrete example, and I shall use data from the 1986 project at the Postal Giro Office in Stockholm, "Professional language in change", mentioned in Section I.1.1.

Before I start on this last stage of the journey, I think it would not be out of place to make a short summary of what has been accomplished so far.

Although the theoretical framework of the book is not natural science but a structuralist tradition of semiotics and linguistics, the project of the book is a part of an ongoing paradigm change in computer science itself: from seeing the computer system as a self-sufficient mathematical *object*, the focus is gradually being shifted to the *relations* between system and work context. An important practical motivation for this shift is simply that it hopefully will enable us to construct computer systems that meet the needs of the users in a better way. However, the shift is also theoretically motivated by the structuralist framework, since structuralism is characterized by focusing on relations, not on objects, as the real existing phenomena. For example, in Saussure 1966:117 it is emphasized that the values in a linguistic system are not pre-existing objects, but relations:

> When they [i.e. values] are said to correspond to concepts, it is understood that the concepts are purely differential and defined not by their positive content but negatively by their relations with the other terms of the system.

I have taken this principle to mean that many important properties of computer systems cannot be defined as properties of a physical object but as relations between the system and its use context.

The most important example of conceptual changes of this type is the change in the concept of interface introduced in Section I.2.3.3 and used throughout Part II. From being a piece of software, patched upon the real system to ease access to it, the interface has been redefined to become the most important aspect of the system. The interface is a sign system manifested in computational processes that people consciously or unconsciously create when using and interpreting the computer system. Neither to the users nor to the theory do the system process and structure have any independent

332

existence, but only exist parasitically as a manifestation of a semiotic schema, always interpreted and articulated by means of a semiotic form that determines which physical properties are pertinent and which not. This does not mean that the system considered as an object and product is irrelevant, but, as Floyd 1986 advocates, it means that the product view of the system must be subordinated to the relational view (or process view, as she calls it).

Since the interface, understood in this broader sense, is the ultimate criterion of success or failure of a system, and since the interface cannot be constructed as a physical object can be constructed, but emerges from the complex interactions between the actual physical system and its use context, it follows that system development is only partially controllable. A system developer is in much the same situation as other producers of symbolic material like authors or play writers: they can hope that their intentions will be realized on the opening night, and if they are talented their hope may often come true - but in principle they can never be sure.

In this view, the role of the computer system is basically that of a *medium* - a physical substance in which signs can be manifested, one that can be - and is - used for communication. On this level of generality, it is not different from other media like the book, the telephone, the radio, the theater, the television, or the movie. However, the media perspective invites us to focus on those properties that are special to the computer and consequently should be the basis of a computer aesthetics. Like the other media, the computer has physical properties that make some means of expression central, others marginal but available, and others unavailable. The unique feature of theater is the actual presence of the actors and the events. It's all happening now! This feature is absent in films, but on the other hand they can achieve a realism of setting with which theater never can compete. In a similar way, the characteristic feature of computer systems is the availability of handling features. The active hand movements of the "reader" are an essential ingredient of computer-based signs, and therefore were incorporated in the sign typology set up in Section II.1. Because of the handling features, the computer medium differs from the older ones in having properties also known from tools. This shows up in the interpretation of the signs. In many systems, some signs are interpreted as work objects and tools, while others signify actions done to the objects. But the fact remains: what we see are not objects, tools, and actions - we see and use signs signifying these phenomena.

The media perspective described in this book shares some assumptions with other current perspectives on computers, but differs from them in other respects. From object-oriented programming and its associated perspective, the physical model metaphor, it has borrowed the notion of objects - which are reinterpreted as signs - consisting of properties and actions. However, from a media perspective, saying that the system models or is similar to the part of the world it refers to is too imprecise and borders on metaphysics since it is difficult or impossible to specify what this similarity relation would consist of. When the model idea is abandoned, we have also to abandon the idea that system structure can be built from a system analysis of the topic of the system. Instead, the system is seen as a sign system, and programming and design as activities that aim at creating signs. To denote this I coined the term *sign-oriented programming*, suggesting a similarity to object-oriented programming. System processes are seen in analogy to performances of a play, and it is suggested that analysis of the work context, in which this performance is to take place, can be used as a basis for building the system structure. Like a playwriter who must always have the theatrical situation, its effects and its audience in mind when writing the plot, the designer must also all the time have *his* theater in the back of his mind: the available hardware, the tasks to be accomplished, and the meaning system inherent in the work register.

This does not, however, mean that analysis of the topic of the system is irrelevant, but in line with the general argument it must be subordinated to and guided by work analysis. There will be no "natural" representation of the topic; rather, the selection of information and the manner in which it should be structured depend upon the tasks and culture of the users.

The media perspective is clearly incompatible with the AI-paradigm that endows the computer with some kind of language faculty, and either hopes to learn something about humans by building systems, or, conversely, to invent new techniques[1] by studying human cognitive behavior. Still, some of the techniques of AI are also interesting from the media perspective, not as scientific hypotheses about human cognitive processes, but as technical support for them. For example, if we look at text-based systems from a media perspective, we may want to interpret the system states as a huge text with a certain syntactical structure, and system processes as syntactic transformations of it (cf. Section II.1.2.1).

So far the exposition has been rather theoretical, and therefore the purpose of the sections that follow is to show what the theory can be used for in practice. I try

- to argue for the theory's general relevance by showing that what is important in the theoretical framework presented so far can also be important in a practical system development project.

---

[1] E.g.Winston 1977: 1.

- to give concrete examples of how to analyze the existing work organization in which the system is to be used and how to use this analysis
  when constructing the system structure. This part is essential: if the
  change of focus from the system to the relations between system and
  context is to gain any momentum, feasible techniques for basing systems design on analysis of work and language must be developed. I
  illustrate the constructive use of the analysis by re-designing a small
  part of the actual PGP-system based upon the linguistic data collected.
- to show how to describe the actual changes that have taken place.
  This activity is often classified as technology assessment, but must be
  regarded as an essential part of system development if we accept the
  assumption that the constructive activities are only partially controllable and predictable. We then need some techniques to see if what we
  intended to happen, in fact did happen.

Since I cannot hope to cover all these theoretical topics in the last 100 pages,
I have selected the following for further elaboration:

Language as interpretation. Semantic fields in the Postal Giro.
The first topic concerns Halliday's ideational functions. In large organizations with an elaborated division of labor different groups will interpret the
organization and work in different ways. Each group will select one part of
the organization as the topic for their conversations and ignore others, and
they will introduce distinctions into it that are interpretable from their educational and organizational background and relevant for their particular tasks.
For example, in the accounting department, raw materials are classified according to the budget plan, while in the production department, people may
distinguish between the items according to where they are stored and what
products they are used for.

The data from the Postal Giro showed clear differences in the way different
groups interpret the "same" work process, and since this must be expected
to be the normal case, it is important that systems designers be conscious of
whose language they base their design upon, and how their design relates to
the work language of the actual users. In addition, large integrated systems
like the PGP-system must serve different groups of users, each employing its
own conceptual structure.

Apart from the ways particular work processes are interpreted, more general differences of interpretation can be important in systems development.
The issue may even be the basic interpretation of the organization itself, and
this was in fact the case in the development of the PGP-system. The basic
mode of operation of the Postal Giro is not very complicated: customers pay

their bills by sending in brown envelopes (*bruna kuvert*) containing payment orders (*betalningsorder*), or handing in the forms at a post office,
which then sends them (now called *missiv*, dispatches) on to the Giro. The
paying out is done by depositing the money in electronic accounts and
mailing the receipts and statements of account to the payee.

Traditionally, these work processes were seen as *production*:

> Since 1948 a part of the administrative work at the Postal Giro has been called pro-
> duction. However, this so-called production or work does not imply any manipulation
> of material. The Postal Giro does not have any real product.[1]

and this has set its stamp on the way many working processes are organized
inside the Giro. There was a strong division of labor, work was rule-governed, and problem-solving consisted mainly in discovering which rules to
apply and when to send the problem on to special sections - not in creating
new methods. A project coordinator we interviewed describes the old work
organization as an assembly line where "speed had the highest priority, and
if problems occurred, then put it aside, the next link in the chain can take
care of it. The operator did not need to know what she did".

Tasks were normally designed so that one person could do them, and the
medium of communication was mainly oral, either face-to-face or via loudspeaker. In the accounting department, mechanical tools such as coding machines and adding machines were employed, but the product of the department was sent to a computer department where the actual accounting was
done.

Seen from the inside of an accounting department, the work does not appear as service but as manipulation and transport of paper[2], and this is also
the view reflected in the old work language described in Section I.1.1.

However, as appears from the quotation, seen from the customer's point of
view, the Postal Giro does not produce any goods, but provides *services* by
helping customers to pay money to other people. The new computer system
was designed to support organizational changes that - to some limited degree - meant a change from pure production to a more service-oriented way
of seeing work, and the data showed that certain semantic changes in fact
did take place when the system was introduced: organizational and technological changes can change meaning systems, although not always in the
way intended.

The content form of language[3], in particular its paradigmatic aspect, is a
good framework for describing such elusive notions as "interpretations",

---

[1] Grip & Sundström 1984: 169.

[2] Holmqvist & Källgren 86: 7.

[3] See Hjelmslev 1954.

"perspectives", and "conceptual structure" - always assuming that we do not need to know what goes on inside the mind, but are satisfied with describing what people say. I shall introduce a particular variant of the content paradigm, the *semantic field*, and show how it can be used to describe differences between the interpretations of different groups, differences between work language and computer systems, and changes in work language.

I shall also by examples show how knowledge of the structure of semantic fields, often called *distinctive features* and in glossematics termed *glossemes*, can be used in systems design.

Language as action. Language games in the Postal Giro.

The next section deals with another of Halliday's main functions, the interpersonal functions, the action aspect of language. Language is not only used for discriminating and articulating reality, it is also used for acting in this reality. As was already illustrated in Section I.1.1, speech is organized in shorter or longer exchanges that are united to a whole by having a particular function to the real world: in the work place, exchanges are used to coordinate work, to solve problems, to teach, or to order people to do something. Exchanges that have this property were called *language games* in Section I.2.2.4, and I do approximately the same thing here as in the section on semantic fields: describe language games before the introduction of computers, after their introduction, and the changes that could be observed in the data.

Whereas knowledge of semantic fields is useful for understanding the basic concepts that should be expressed by the system, and the way they should be structured, study of language games tells us which kind of information is needed when. For example, problem-solving requires information, both about the work objects and about the rules to apply, while information about the progress of work is necessary to perform work coordination. To get ideas for redesign, I look at three games, *mystery solving, forecasting,* and *problem solving*, and ask whether insufficient or wrongly structured information causes the game to be played badly or to terminate prematurely at a point where continuation is desirable.

Task analysis. Controlling control

In this section I discuss the issue of control described in Section II.2.2.2. Although the general idea is to analyze work practice, set up the schemas behind it, and design the system so that it supports them, making signs and sign parts available when they are needed in work, the exact nature of this support is by no means clear.

For example, how much of the work schema should be built into the system? The workers sit with a job of cards, and each job is segmented into

batches that contain all payments from a particular customer. We may observe that processing the last card from one batch is always followed by processing the next card from the next batch, except when the job is finished.
The two actions thus form a presupposition, processing next batch presupposing processing the last card in current batch. If we were to build this
function into the system, it would mean that it automatically provided the
next batch when the previous was finished. This would give control to the
system, a general system feature of systems built in this way for routine jobs.
But if we build large parts of the current work schema into the system, we
may make it difficult to change work organization and methods of work,
since we would have to re-program the system each time an organizational
change takes place.

My suggestion is to use the distinction between invariant and variant task
structure, so that the former is incorporated into the system and cannot be
changed by the users, while the latter can be specified and changed in a
user-oriented programming language. Thus, work schemas should be implemented in levels, some of which are open to user tailorability, and some of
which are not.

Division of labor and cooperation.

Most work involves division of labor and cooperation, and these issues
also bear on design of computer systems. Again the Postal Giro gives a good
example since it is a large organization with more than 5000 employees and
a full-blown bureaucratic structure. The accounting section that is described
in the following pages is only a part of a *bokföringsavdelning* [accounting
department, "Girobokföring"] that contains:

- Six accounting sections [*bokföringssektioner*]: handle receipt, coding,
  and mailing of payment orders.

and a number of special offices that take care of problems and errors:

- Offices [*expeditioner*]: handle non-routine tasks:
  Avdelningsexpedition: handles all customer errors.
  Granskningsexpedition: relays unusual messages, handles cash pay-
  ments, and checks security of cheques.
  Ändringscentralen: checks punched material.
  Underskottsexpedition: handles accounts with deficit.

Outside our accounting department, we find:

- Revision (*girorevisionen*, GR): controls in- and outgoing payments for
  the Postal Giro.

- Registration (*Giroregistrering*, GG): updates information about accounts, addresses, etc.
- Investigation (*Giroundersökning*, GU): takes care of complaints and errors.

and probably still more than we learned about during the project.

Divisions of labor and bureaucracy often disguise actual cooperative processes. To some degree, the two concepts are different ways of looking at the same thing. Consider for example the division of labor between the accounting department and the computer department. The former enters data that cannot be optically read, and the computer department handles the actual book-keeping. This is a clear-cut instance of a division of labor: one group is assigned one set of tasks, and another group another set of tasks. However, if we focus on the work object and not on the tasks, it could also be described as a form for cooperation: two groups handle the same work object. My main point is that it would be a good idea in systems design to focus on the cooperative aspects, and play down the division of labor. This would enhance the employees' opportunities for understanding the larger organization of which they are a part, and for actually helping each other when it is needed.

On feasibility

Are the methods presented feasible? The amount of intelligence gathering and analysis required may seem daunting, and even in vain since the language investigated will change, precisely as a result of the new computer system.

It is no secret that empirical work is time-consuming, but it is not so bad as to be unrealistic. In my experience, much can be gained by applying different techniques to different quantities of data. One can for example learn much by close-reading and analyzing small transcribed portions of the tapes, and hypotheses, based on little data, can be corroborated by quick and fast analyses of larger portions of tape, which may even not need to be transcribed.

However, there is a need for computer-based tools for speeding up the process, and if we want to get a good impression of the silent parts of the work, we will need video recordings and tools for analyzing them too.

There is also a need for research in families of work languages (e.g. the work language of nursing, journalism, shipping, travel agencies, theaters, and hospital kitchens, just to mention a few that our students have investigated), so that a designer may gather much of the required knowledge from literature studies, and only needs to concentrate on the specific properties of his costumer. In fact, there is already a considerable bulk of research on terminology of languages for special purposes. The problem in this research is that the terminology recorded is the "official" terminology and real life recordings may show quite a different picture.

The benefit of the methodology presented in the following is a much better empirical anchorage of design since our point of departure is what people actually say and do, not what they or others believe they are saying or doing. In addition, the necessary changes of work concepts can be made much more explicit and conscious.

The general idea is to use the analysis of the data

- as a basis for making the users aware of their own language and concepts,
- as an aid to the designer for better understanding the work he is designing for, and
- as a basis for consciously changing some of the concepts as they are transferred to the system.

I do not treat user cooperation, although this is an important topic in itself, but only give methods for doing the analysis, and suggestions as to how it may relate to design.

III.1

Language as Interpretation. Semantic Fields in the Postal Giro

III.1.1. Perspective differences at the Postal Giro

When we enter a large organization like the Postal Giro, we will be exposed to a large inhomogeneous mass of written and spoken language: we listen to the speech of workers engaged in work, interview them and talk to them, read manuals and look at the screen images they work with, and talk to management in offices removed from the shop floor. Although many of these verbal exchanges clearly refer to the same physical phenomena, the linguistic forms can be quite different. It soon appears that each linguistic form is adapted to the particular function the speaker fulfills in the total structure of work processes and power relations in the organization. Each sub-language expresses a particular *perspective* (on perspective, see Section I.2.2.2) and reveals a partial truth about the organization.

In the development of the PGP system there was one major issue that in a nut-shell illustrates the intricate interplay between language, perspectives and position in the division of labor. In semiotic terms, the issue was simply the relation between signifier and signified, in this specific case taking the form of a disagreement between union and management about electronic scanning of paper forms.

Management wanted to get rid of all paper by optical scanning of the paying-in-forms and wanted all subsequent work involving the cards to be done by means of electronic card images on a video screen. The union demanded that the basis of data recording should still be the paper forms, so that a direct feeling of the amount of work remained intact. The union succeeded in preventing electronic scanning of paper forms.

The reason why the union wanted to keep the reference of the electronic signs, declining to work only on a symbolic representation, was that to the workers, the distinction between sign and referent is ontological, between reality and non-reality:

We don't like to work *only* with the screen and not feel something *tangible*

To the project manager, however, the difference is not philosophical, but more a practical question of choice of medium, and he seems to view paper as some kind of a burden:

The other alternative was originally to work with an image technique, *get rid of* our dependence on the documents and work with electronic images instead.

The dispute, as well as the differences of wording, reflects a difference of perspective that again is caused by the division of labor. To the *workers*, the paper form is not a sign in the daily work, but a physical object that is manipulated and transported. What they see is an electronic sign and its reference, the paper forms. Therefore, a loss of the paper is a loss of reality. The *manager*, however, also works with the economic services of the Postal Giro, and he sees money and money transactions as the reality. To him, the paying-in forms are just signs signifying economic transactions. In his view, computer-based signs are just as good as paper-based ones, both are just signs for something outside the Postal Giro, and computer-based signs may have certain advantages.

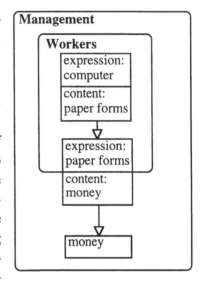

Fig. III.1.1. Division of labor and semiotic structure.

The following example from our recordings shows that the disagreement is not only theoretical: introduction of the PGP system did in fact change the balance between reality and unreality on the shop floor.

There is at least one exception to the decision to have both sign and referent present in the work situation: some cards, *C-kort*, are complete in the sense that all data are machine-readable. These cards are extracted by the optical reader and are not intended to go on to the work place, nor is the electronic representation of the C-cards shown during normal *komplettering* [completing]; they act as *ghost signs* in the sense that they only indirectly reveal their existence by contributing to the sum of the batch.

In the following example, the worker has a batch with only a payment-order, but no cards. She wonders if the batch originally contained a C-card that was picked out by the the OCR. She looks at the screen showing the complete batch, but sees no representation of a C-card:

> Nu letar jag efter den här, det här kortet är borta, och om de *skulle* ha blitt läst på rätt sätt här, bakom på de här C-kortet, *skulle* det ha kommit fram.

[Now I'm looking for this one, this card is missing, and if it *had* been read right here, back here in the C-slips, it *would* have been shown]

The important feature is the modality: *skulle ha* [had] signifies an unreal, past, and conditional meaning: if they had been read, then they should have appeared. But they have not appeared, so they have not been read. Compared with the coding machines, the computer has made reality problematic, similar past conditionals never being used about the coding machines. They occur now because computer systems, qua signs, can hide parts of their processes, only certain symptoms being accessible.

I like the paper/screen example because it shows that basic theoretical concepts of semiotics can contribute to explaining major disagreements in practical systems development. Although the paper/screen issue was also an economic issue, it seemed genuinely difficult for management to understand why the workers wanted to keep the paper, because the two parties saw the work process from different perspectives.

An overview of the difference between the interpretations of the organization is helpful for understanding controversial issues, and a good method for achieving this is to compare a series of utterances with similar topics but produced by speakers with different organizational roles. In the following, I shall present some examples of this technique.

III.1.1.1. C-slips[1]

The topic of the three utterances below is the *C-kort* [C-cards, C-slips] mentioned above. C-slips are cards on which every piece of information is preprinted and machine-readable, and in principle, these cards should stay at the optical reader, and never reach the work stations.

Text (a) has been taken from a recorded interview with the coordinator, (b) from a recorded interview with an instructor who teaches the use of the system at the office level, and (c) from a recording of the authentic work language on the "office floor". In (a), the interview takes place in the office of the interviewee, in (b) at a table in the accounting department, and in (c) at a work station.

(a) The coordinator :

> One of the purposes of the Optical Character Recognition is of course that one can read everything optically - directly, that is - for example our paying-in C-

---

[1] The first three pages of this section are an extract from Holmqvist 1988b. With permission from the author.

slips; because they have complete rows of optic codes, and so they never have
to be passed on to B 25.

(b) The instructor:

They code a lot of C-slips that have this optic area - the machines are able to
read it, and so they read the slip and we don't have to touch it - when we put it
into the frame, the machine reads it and then we lift the blue box, and then they
are ready.

(c) The work situation:

E: Well, I think you should do like this: you take a small piece of paper, and then
you attach it to the C-slip to show that it is a C-slip. Later, when you have got
it back, then you put everything in this box.

X: Well, I'll have to leave this till tomorrow morning, then I'll give it to her, because I had one today that I left for her - a slip that was missing, something that
she had cut out - we'll take that too, and then I'll put back this C-slip when she
... well

E: Because she is bound to see that one too if you leave it for her, she wants to
see the C-slip too.

In the first two examples, the interviews take place outside the work situation and they deal with the same part of the working process. In the third
example, the speakers work while they talk, and use language to intervene in
and comment on the process in which they both take part. The difference between (a) and (b) is that the person in (a) does not normally take part in the
working process in question, whereas the person in (b) does.

The different organizational roles of the three speakers are reflected in
their language. The coordinator in (a) rejects people as well as activities. He
sees the work processes as atomic "things"and therefore uses nominalizations

the optical recognition,

whereas the instructor in (b) uses tensed verbs to describe the same process
as consisting of events that follow each other in time:

we put it into the frame,
the machine reads it,
we lift the blue box

The coordinator goes on to talk about the work station through which the
"flow" of work objects does not pass:

so they never have to pass the B 25.

Contrary to this, the instructor does not talk about the "flow" and the work stations; she talks about the people who work at the work stations and the things they have or do not have to do:

> we never have to touch them.

The main difference between the two can be summarized by saying that the coordinator focuses on the work object and describes the paradigm of machines it visits (<OCR-reader, B25>) whereas the instructor focuses on the worker and her machines and sets up a paradigm of actions done and work objects processed (<code, read, touch, put, lift>).

Although they describe the same part of the working process, the coordinator presents it as an abstract procedure, whereas the instructor describes it as a concrete one. To her, the paper documents they are talking about (the "C-slips") are concrete objects that can be observed:

> a *lot of* C-slips

and which can be physically manipulated:

> *put* it into the frame

whereas to the coordinator, they are categories:

> *for example* our paying-in C-slips

in a data flow where the machines represent spaces for the material to pass through

> they never have to *pass* the B 25.

If we compare the last sentence to a nearly synonymous one of the instructor

> we never have to touch them

we note that the in the coordinator's sentence, the subject is the pronoun *they* denoting the work objects, whereas the coordinator has the pronoun *we* denoting the workers as subject. If we accept the interpretation of cases given in Section I.2.2.1, namely that they are used to arranging the items of the sentence by rank of saliency, we can say that to the coordinator, the work objects are the salient features of the scene of production, and the machines are circumstantial, while to the instructor the workers are the main actors, and the work objects and actions the setting.

(a) and (b) are similar in that the attitudes to the working process are of a general nature. Both persons are able to describe the general premises of the process without including definite time and space descriptions. This is demonstrated by their choice of indefinite pronouns, for instance:

one can read [Sw:*man* kan läsa]
everything one can read [Sw:*allt man* kan läsa]
a lot of C-slips [Sw:*en* massa C-kort]

and temporal/causal relations combined with timeless present tense:

because they have ... *and so* they [på dom finns *ju*... *alltså så*]
when we put ...*then* [*när* vi lägger... *så*]

(c) is different in that its description of the working process is not of a general nature; instead, language is used to intervene in and comment on the tasks. This means that the statements are bound to time and space, and there are no general explanations of the working process - only specific comments. When they talk about the work objects, they use the definite article, as when they talk about a specific C-slip, which can be pointed out in the room:

then I'll put back *this* C-slip [sen lägger jag tillbaka *det här* C-kortet]

There are also definite personal pronouns:

then *you* attach [så sätter *du* på]
then *I'll* put back [sen lägger *jag* tillbaka]

The actions they talk about take place within a certain period of time:

leave this *till tomorrow morning* [får ligga *till i morgon bitti]*

and in a certain sequence of time:

take a small piece of paper, *and then* ... [ta en liten lapp *och så* ...]

with time-specific perfect tense:

later when you have gotten it back, *then*... [*sen* när ni har fått tillbaks det *då*...]

These three small examples have revealed very different ways of looking at work, differences that reveal themselves in a preference for particular grammatical choices: persons or work objects as subject, finite verbs or nominalizations, indefinite or definite pronouns and nouns, and timeless or time-specific present tense. It is important that a system developer know that such differences in perspective exist in organizations, because the description techniques of computer science are closer to some perspectives than to others. The coordinator's perspective is for example very close to that inherent in data-flow descriptions. Like the coordinator's sentences, data-flow diagrams focus on data, not on the data-processors:

The inversion of viewpoints occasioned by Structured Analysis is that we now present the workings of a system as seen by the data, not as seen by the data processors. The advantage of this approach is that the data sees the big picture, while the various people and machines and organizations that work on the data see only a portion of what happens. As you go about doing a Structured Analysis, you will find yourself more and more frequently attaching yourself to the data and following it through the operation. I think of this as "interviewing the data".   *DeMarco 1978: 49*

The example shows that - like all other professional languages - the professional language of computer scientists is not a general, but a very specific way of looking at things, closely connected to their work responsibilities in the project. The perspective can be shared by some user groups, which may have no difficulty in reading the specifications and finding relevant information here. However, other groups in the project may find it difficult to extract relevant information from the specifications, for example information about the impact of a proposed system on their working conditions, because the descriptions express a perspective on their work that is foreign to their professional language. Therefore flow-oriented specifications should be supplemented with other kinds of descriptions, for example scenarios that indicate how a typical work day will look when the new system is put to use.

A similar result is reported from the Florence project where a group of nurses were asked to write flow-descriptions of their work:

Wall-graphs do not fulfil the demand of containing what the nurses consider important in their work...wall-graphing was [not] about nursing as the nurses experience their profession...Deciding which descriptive techniques (and description languages) should be employed is an important power factor in getting one's view of what is important in work and organization recognized.   *Bjerknes et al 1985: 104 ff*

The solution to the problem is to recognize computer science language as a rather specific language, well suited for some tasks, but unusable for others, and to see to it that the project provides additional information written in other stakeholders' languages.

III.1.1.2. Perspectives on change and time

In order to show that the difference between these three small examples was no coincidence, I shall give one additional example of differences of interpretation and perspective. This time the topic is not work objects, but different conceptions of time and change.

The next two quotations are from the same speakers, and their joint topic is the organizational change they had just experienced. Previously, *kodning* [coding] and *rättning* [correction] were performed by different persons, whereas under the new system, the corresponding tasks of *komplettering* [completing] and *avstämning* [checking off] is the responsibility of the same worker.

Coordinator:

> We are going to gain a step by trying to merge the data input with completion, and we try to do that by a decentralized computer system where we work with a network consisting of twelve smaller data input systems.
>
> [Vi ska försöka vinna det steget att försöka slå ihop datafångsten med kompletteringen och det försöker vi göra genom ett decentralt datasystem där vi då jobbar med ett nätverk bestående utav tolv mindre data(fångst)system.]

Instructor:

> Which was the greatest difference, well, it was just what I said that in the old system others had to take over the work after we got through. But in the new system no one has to do that, but if he's checked and it balances, then it's ok, it only goes up to the computer room and there they run a "match and spray" and then a sorting run and then we get the material back.

The coordinator describes the change in one sentence *merge the data input with completion* [slå ihop datafångsten med kompletteringen], because in his language, the change itself is a concept, explicitly expressed in a word *merge* [slå ihop]. In the language of the instructor, however, the change is distributed over several sentences. It is not explicitly expressed in a word, but implicitly through the narrative: in the old system others had to take over the job after us, but in the new one nobody has to do that. In the language of the coordinator, the change is a property of tasks, whereas the instructor sees it as a property of persons.

The next examples illustrate a similar difference. Their common topic is the way the development process was organized. Whereas the coordinator sees the process as a process of changing the relations between types of agents and tasks:

The coordinator:

> Then there were a few people who worked with manual routines. And there our, well what we call our instructor group, functions as it were both with working with manual routines, but also as it were working with training, so that we actually put together into one and the same group both manual routines and training

giving us two paradigms, one of persons <people, instructor group, group> [Sw: personer, handledargruppen, grupp] and one of tasks <manual routines, training> [Sw: manuella rutiner, utbildning], the instructor in the next quotation keeps her own person constant and generates a paradigm of the different episodes she experienced and the relations she had to other persons: <went on courses, made study visits, was at the exhibition, went and

looked> [Sw: gick på kurser, gick på studiebesök, var på mässan, gick och titta]:

> *The instructor:*
> We went on different courses here at the Giro office and out at the Burroughs plant in Kista and then we made a few study visits...We were at the exhibition, technical exhibition, and visited various units here at the Giro office and suchlike. For example we went, all the terminals in the Giro office...we went and looked at their texts, what they looked like, and measured the screen and the text, how big it was, right, of course we were involved in helping to decide that we got this setup.

The coordinator seldom codes the agent-task relationship as subject and finite verb, but prefers a dummy verb (göra [do], sköta [take care of]) combined with a nominalization:

> So they *do* about 500 completing per hour and at the same time *take care* of the batch checks, investigating and all suchlike.
> [Så *gör* man ungefär 500 kompletteringar per timme samtidigt som man *sköter* då buntavstämning, undersökning och allting som tillhör.]

> Then it was also self-evident that the requirement specification should as it were be *made* by the personnel as close to the office "floor" as possible.
> [Sen var det också självklart att kravspecifikationen skulle då så att säga *göras* utav personal som va så nära golvet som möjligt]

Just as the agent can be described apart from the task, the task is seen as a composition of individual subtasks. Part/whole relationships and decomposition are important concepts in the coordinator's language:

> Every system *consists of* decentralized optical readers called S49 zero zero, and terminals for completing and checking, correcting work. [...] *divide* it up into the number of sub-jobs which are the batches, the number here, and if, for example, if I have, this is just how you do it when you go to this flier file, where you have for example 300 cards and it actually *consists* of 20 batches.

The time paradigm of the coordinator is different from that of the instructor. He lives in a historical time consisting of different epoches, and when he says

> If we had stuck to the coding machines [Sw: blivit kvar vid kodningsmaskinerna], for example, it wouldn't have been possible to finish the entire batch in the same way and then go on to the next batch,...

the phrase *stick to the coding machines* [bliva kvar vid kodningsmaskinerna] does not mean that one day he stayed with a coding machine instead of walking somewhere else. His time unit is not the working day, but the year or the decade. He never describes a work task from the inside, but focuses on the external relations between a set of tasks using a paradigm of aspectual verbs like <start, turn into, engage in, finish> [börja, gå över till, komma i kast, göra färdig], as in the the next quotation:

> If one *starts* from the moment when we decided we would, that this *turned into* a stage of carrying it out.
>
> [Om man *börjar* från det ögonblick när vi bestämde oss för att vi skulle att det här *gick över till* ett genomförandeskede]
>
> And they *got involved* very early in things like *finishing* the requirement specification.
>
> [Och dom kom så att säga väldigt tidigt *i kast* med såna här grejer som att *göra* kravspecifikationen *färdig]*

These observations can be summarized in the following way. The universe of the coordinator is biased towards the paradigmatic dimension of language. It consists of paradigms of tasks and workers, and the semantic operations he performs upon them consist in changing the paradigms themselves (e.g. *merge the data input with completion* [slå ihop datafångsten med kompletteringen]) and the relations between them (e.g. *we actually put together into one and the same group both manual routines and training*).

The universe of the instructor is more focused on the syntagmatic dimension of language: it consists of a sequence of events where particular persons do different actions and experience different events.

These characteristics are very clearly related to the work responsibilities of the coordinator. The coordinator is responsible for the long-term changes, not for the individual work process, and he has a right to regroup tasks and change the relation between worker and task.

III.1.2. Definition of semantic fields

Since - as we have just seen - differences of interpretation exist in large organizations and since the system, qua semiotic system, cannot help expressing its own interpretation, a tool for comparing conceptual structures would be of good help in systems development. In the following I shall present one such concept, namely the *semantic field*. Traditionally, semantic fields have been used for comparing the lexical structure of different languages and different states of the same language. Semantic fields are

> closely-knit sectors of vocabulary, in which a particular sphere is divided up, classified and organized in such a way that each element helps to delimit its neighbors and is delimited by them.   *Ullman 1962: 245*

As mentioned in Lyons 1979:258, one of the problems in semantic field theory is: how is a semantic field defined (which signs belong to it and which do not), and according to what criteria can two sets of signs be said to cover the same semantic field?

A field is often defined by a set of common semantic components that all members must share[1] and a small set of components that distinguish them. However, I want to avoid the notion of "components" since it suggests that meaning consists of a set of things that somehow "glue" to the sign-vehicle, an idea that fits badly with the view that meaning is differential and can only be understood from the situation in which the differences are used. To be compatible with the contextual point of view, componential analysis must be reformulated as contrasts like

boy | girl = man | woman ≠ boy | man = girl | woman

asserting that there are situations where the difference between boy and girl is the same as that between man and woman and that this difference is different from that between boy and man, which again is the same as that between girl and woman. Instead of phrasing the results in terms of such relations, it is of course possible to phrase it in terms of the endpoints of the relations and say that boy and man contain a component that is not found in girl and woman, although it is somewhat misleading from a structuralist conception of language.

I shall use the common term *distinctive feature* to denote the meaning distinctions that structure a semantic field. The corresponding term in glossematics is the *glosseme* concept defined in Section I.2.1, "Parts and Wholes". In Hjelmslev's formulation, glossemes are simply the smallest elements the theory leads us to establish, the irreducible invariants[2].

Component, distinctive features, and *glosseme* denote by and large the same phenomena, but the perspectives are different. Whereas the term *component* suggests that the units in question are parts of words and therefore adhere to them and move when they move, the term *glosseme* is a part of a framework that focuses on relations and differences and neither invites nor warrants this objectified view. *Glossemes* are differential, they are established by contrasting signs, *and in situations where the contrast does not occur, it*

---

[1] Saussure 1959: 126 himself mentioned this type of paradigmatic relation (the example is *enseignement| instruction| apprentissage | education*), and many empirical descriptions are based on this idea, e.g. Bendix 1966: 32.

[2] Glossemes are different from taxemes, since taxemes are the smallest pieces into which a text can be segmented, while glossemes are units that are constructed by making a universal, text-independent classification of the taxemes. Thus, glossemes can be viewed as properties of the taxemes. I shall use the same idea, but since my corpus of analysis is always the situational language, my glossemes will be much more concrete than the ones Hjelmslev envisioned.

cannot be recorded and therefore does not exist. The following quotation
of Umberto Eco stresses this transitory nature of the sign relation:

> A sign is not a fixed semiotic entity but rather the meeting ground for independent
> elements (coming from two different systems of two different planes and meeting on
> the basis of a coding correlation)...
>
> Thus signs are the provisional result of coding rules which establish *transitory* cor-
> relations of elements, each of these elements being entitled to enter - under given
> coded circumstances - in another correlation and thus form a new sign.   *Eco 1976: 49*

I concur in these formulations, and when I use the concept of semantic field
it is under the assumption that distinctive features used to set them up are
not components inherent in the words but differences generated by situational contrasts. As discussed at length in Section I.2.1, this again implies that
the meanings generated by comparing signs that do not contrast in any real
situation are non-existent from a scientific point of view. For example, the internal contrasts between *man, woman, girl, boy* are surely operative in many
situations, because we treat children and grown-ups differently, both in
words and actions, but since there are probably no registers that need to distinguish between e.g. petrol and scissors the "components" that set them
apart simply do not exist.

In Section I.2.1, I concluded that, even if the same words occur in two situations, one is not allowed to transfer contrasts from one situation to the
other without investigating the new situation properly. To illustrate what
this principle means in a real situation, let us look at words for work objects
at the old Postal Giro organization, namely *blue, yellow* and *brown envelopes*[1]. According to our principles, we have to find a situation in which
they actually contrast. The task called *öppning* [opening] is a good candidate. It occurred in the morning when work material arrived at the accounting department. Some material is enclosed in brown envelopes: those marked
with a cross contain cheques and are called *checkar*, while the remaining
ones are just called *bruna-kuvert* [brown envelopes] with a single-word
stress and tone, indicating a lexicalized construction. From our knowledge of
general vocabulary, we may be tempted to assign a semantic feature of color
to *bruna-kuvert*, but since it does not contrast to envelopes with other colors
but to *checkar* and *missiv*, whatever distinctive features are relevant to the
bruna-kuvert, color cannot be among them.

However, there are other tasks in the Postal Giro where color is relevant. It
turns out that the non-lexicalized form is used in another department called
Ljusgården, where the incoming mail is first sorted and the workers have to
separate brown from blue and yellow envelopes. Here *bruna kuvert* [brown

---

[1] Holmqvist 1986: 48, Bøgh Andersen & Holmqvist 1986.

envelopes] are in practice contrasted to other phrases by means of the color adjectives and color can therefore safely be said to be part of its content, but this feature cannot be transferred to the accounting department, where the phrase enters a different paradigm altogether.

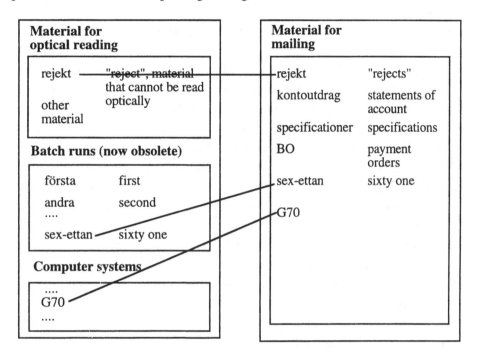

Fig. III.1.2. Semantic fields and the meaning of terms depend upon the division of labor.

The example is not unique, but typical, and I shall add another one which illustrates the point even more clearly (see Fig. III.1.2[1]). We move from the morning work to the early afternoon and look at the language used during the task called *inläggning* [putting in] where the material opened in the morning is put into envelopes and mailed back to the customers. We find a well-defined semantic field of materials for mailing, articulated according to its time of arrival and the working process applied to it: *BO* [payment orders], *kontoutdrag* [statements of account], *rejekt* [rejects], *sex-ettan* [sixty-one], and *G70*.

Rejekt (reject) means "material arriving at the reception desk in small batches that must be fetched and sorted by hand into the large batch of automatically sorted material from the data processing department". The latter

---

[1] A more detailed exposition is found in Holmqvist 1986 and in Bøgh Andersen & Holmqvist 1986.

is called *G70*. Finally, *Sex-ettan* (sixty-one) means "the last material for mailing".

If we leave the accounting section and take a look inside the data processing department, we find the same three words, but here they enter into different semantic fields.

Here *rejekt* means "material rejected by the optical reader", and contrasts with material that is correctly processed. *G70* is the name of an accounting system that was introduced in 1970, and is also used to denote a special department. Thus *G70* contrasts with other computer systems and departments. *Sex-ettan* has only a historical meaning in the data processing department. Previously, it meant "the first part of the sixth batch run", but at the time of the investigation, the number of batch runs had decreased.

These are examples of the kinds of semantic fields that are clearly useful to a systems designer: if we are constructing computer support for work in the section, it is useful to know that the workers need to distinguish between *bruna-kuvert, checkar,* and *missiv* in the *öppning* task, and between *BO*, *kontoutdrag, rejekt, sex-ettan,* and *G70*, in the *inläggning*. At the same time, these fields exemplify a more limited concept than the traditional notion of semantic fields, so the question is now how to characterize the concept theoretically.

In general, semantic fields are paradigms of content units like words or stems, and we will normally only be interested in comparing two such paradigms if they articulate the same substance. There are cases where we can immediately establish the identity of the substance: a particular object and its parts, a process and its parts, collections of objects or processes. Contrastive linguistics and dialectology offer many studies of this kind.

However, since we want to be able to relate language to work, we are not interested in any old collections of objects or actions: the substance must be a set of actions that the worker has to distinguish in order to perform the work process, or a set of tools or objects of work that he should choose between at some point of the work process. In addition to contrasting in the verbal chain, the paradigm we are interested in must also contrast in the task chain.

Thus the issue at stake here is simply: which kind of context do we use when we collect the paradigm? We can distinguish between language- and task-motivated paradigms in terms of the context in which their members are collected:

- A *language-motivated paradigm* consists of a set of mutually exclusive signs that can occur in similar environments in a verbal context.

- A *task-motivated paradigm* consists of a set of signs articulating mutually exclusive actions that can occur in similar environments in a task context.

Both paradigms are linguistic paradigms, but the members of the first one are collected in the same linguistic context, and may e.g. consist of a set of transitive verbs that all can occur with an object, while those of the second one are collected in the same work context and could consist of all the terms for work objects that one needs to distinguish at a given point in the work process.

Given these definitions, we can define semantic fields as follows:

- A *semantic field* is a language-motivated paradigm that is also task-motivated.

Language- and task-motivated paradigms need not coincide.

For example, a task-motivated paradigm can contain members that do not form a language-motivated one. When an error occurs in data entry in the accounting section in the new Postal Giro organization, there are mainly five different things that can be done to the offending batch

(1)   Move a card: skicka, flytta den *till flygare*
(2)   Fetch a card: *hämta* den
(3)   Hand in the batch: *lämna in* den *i buren*
(4)   Destroy the batch: *macka* den, *ta bort* den
(5)   Abandon the job: göra ett *rött job*, *överge* den

These actions are different, and the tape recordings show that they are marked as different in the language of the workers.

One distinction is for example between faulty batches that should be taken care of now (3) or later (4):

Instructor:
Det där får du macka bort eller lämna in i buren
[As for that one, either destroy it or hand it in]

Macka bort [destroy] means that the batch is removed from the day's work, and to be taken care of later by some special unit, who decide what to do, whereas *Lämna in i buren* [hand in] means that the batch is immediately given to the special unit.

Another important distinction is between batches with too many cards and batches with too few cards. In the first case, the rule to follow is to send it to the flier file (1), whereas in the latter case, the appropriate action is to search for the missing card in the flier file (2).

Finally, (1) and (4) are different in that (1) *Flytta* [move] is used when an excess card is removed from the batch, while (4) *macka* [destroy] is used when a faulty batch cannot be processed but must be taken care of by a specialist. In the following quotation, *macka bort* and *flytta dokument till flygare* are presented as mutually exclusive options:

> Ska jag *macka bort* den, det är tretusen, ...den där har jag tagit, *"flytta detta dokument till flygare"*?
> Men det ska du inte göra, du ska ju macka.
> Får jag göra om den nu?
>
> [Should I *destroy* it, it's for 3000...I chose this one, *"Move this document to flier"*.
> But you should not do that, you were supposed to destroy it.
> Can I redo it now?]

However, although tasks denoted by the five expressions alternate in the work practice and therefore are an action-motivated paradigm, there is no single language paradigm in which the distinctions can be made. The primary candidate for such a paradigm would be the verbs:

> Skicka [send], flytta [move], lämna in [hand in], hämta [fetch], macka [destroy], ta bort [take away], göra [do], överge [abandon]

but here only *ta bort, lämna in, macka,* and *överge* [take away, hand in, destroy, adandon] are able to effect the discrimination, while *göra, flytta* and *skicka* [make, move, send] are so empty that other paradigms like adverbials (*till flygare, [to the fliers]*) and noun phrases(*rött job, [red job]*) are necessary too. Although a verb + object construction is sufficient in *ta bort kort [take away card]* a similar construction with the verb *flytta, flytta kort (move card),* is too imprecise and needs to be expanded to *flytta kort till flygare [move card to fliers].* The two groups do not form a language-motivated paradigm, since the first group can be described as verbs plus optional particle, while the latter group are complete verb phrases.

Although task- and language-motivated paradigms can differ, I believe that language in general will tend to make them merge into one paradigm, because in this way the structure of language would support the structure of tasks. One method for achieving this is the process of lexicalization, where complex phrases are treated as single words. I believe that the *brown envelope* example above is typical of the way semantic processes operate: a particular situation requires the language to articulate a limited set of distinctions, and the language user simply constructs a new field by "stealing" appropriate linguistic material from older fields. Unfortunately the stolen goods come from an adjectival field but have to fit into a field dominated by nouns. Lexicalizing *bruna kuvert* to *bruna-kuvert* neatly solves the problem.

Since the concept of semantic fields given here requires the paradigm members to be language- as well as task-motivated, it is a measure of how well language fits work. Large and well-structured semantic fields with few glossemes mean that language is able to distinguish between work-relevant concepts in an economical and systematic way.

III.1.3. Using semantic fields for analysis

Semantic fields can be used to depict differences in the way two or more languages articulate the same substance.

III.1.3.1. Systems specification, interface and work language

The first example shows how the structure of semantic fields depends heavily on the tasks and responsibilities of the language users, and in addition demonstrates how difficult it is to predict whether the semantic structure suggested by the system is relevant and will in fact be adopted by the users.

I first contrast the requirement specification of the PGP system and the work language of the accounting section that uses the system; the relevant semantic field is defined by the substance "transport of data and paper from the section to the computer department".

As will be remembered, when a job is completed and corrected its electronic version is locally put into data-structures called boxes. When a box is full, it is sent to the computer department via the local network, and its physical counterpart (the grey plastic boxes) is carried off to the mailing department.

The first diagram describes the situation as seen from the system designers' point of view:

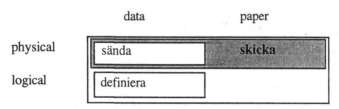

Fig. III.1.3. The designers' semantic field
of data transport.

They use *skicka* about physical transport, regardless of whether it is data or paper and reserve *sända* for physical transport of data. Logical transport of data has its own verb, *definiera*.

I have used two sets of distinctive features to structure the field. The first one, the data versus paper opposition, is easy enough: it uses the substance of the work objects to distinguish between the processes. The second set, physical versus logical transmission, is more technical, since it distinguishes between the physical process of transmitting objects through some channel, and the logical process of verifying and identifying the transmitted objects at the receiver end of the channel.

The next diagram presents the situation as seen from the accounting department's perspective:

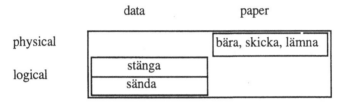

Fig. III.1.4. The workers' semantic field
of data transport.

The workers articulate the field into two main parts: transport of paper and transport of data, and they use different verbs for the two parts: *bära, skicka, lämna* are used for paper, whereas *sända* means to transmit data, and *stänga* to stop transmission of data.

This pattern is no coincidence, but is repeated in the verbs for manipulating work objects that are also divided into two different categories, one consisting of verbs that are used about paper (*skriva på, skriva dit, skriva under, måla, måla över, [write, sign, paint]*) and another containing verbs for manipulating the electronic card (*slå, slå in, trycka, trycka på, trycka ner, slå fel [hit, press, enter]*). "Du behöver inte *skriva* det dit"[You don't need to write it there] is an example of the former, while "För att jag *slog* in den här" [Because I entered this one] exemplifies the latter.

The diagrams show that the distinction between physical and logical transport is not operative in the users' language and the reason is that they do not see the physical transport on their terminals. It happens behind their backs and is not relevant to their work tasks. What is important to them is the difference between data and paper, because sending paper by means of plastic boxes is a quite different task from sending data, which is done at the work stations. However, to the designers, this distinction is important. To ensure physical transmission of data through a cable is one task, and to define the transmission logically for the receiving machine is quite another thing. In fact, it seems as if their main articulation is between physical and logical.

Let us now look at the structure presented by the system itself. The system uses the term *dokument* to denote electronic cards, and when necessary distinguishes between electronic cards and paper cards by means of the adjectives *logisk [logical]* and *fysisk [physical]*. However, these adjectives were not adopted by the workers, since, as indicated above, they used verbs to distinguish between transport of electronic and paper cards.

I never heard the workers use adjectives or nouns to make the distinction, as in expressions like *logical document;* in fact, it seems as if their nominal system treats the data and paper objects as the same:

If I ...send *it* to the flier, then we must send *it* - register it today, but it might be that they send *it* back to this [guy], Karlsson.

In *send it to the flier, it* must refer to the electronic document, since *the flier* is a file, but in *they send it back* the pronoun must refer to the paper cards, since it is the paper that is sent back to the customer. Thus, pronouns in the same anaphorical chain can refer to the electronic document and the paper card and the same verb *send [skicka]* is used[1].

The next example shows the same lack of distinction between data and paper in the lexical choices:

But you understand, you have to put the *card* [Sw:*kort,* paper card] in the flier box, if you have put a *card* [*kort,* electronic card] in the flier, and then I'll have to look in this flier box.

The first occurrence of the word *card* refers to the paper card, the second to the electronic card, since *flier box* denotes a physical plastic tray, and only paper cards can be placed there, while *flier* denotes a file, where only electronic cards can be placed.

Thus, the workers tend not to use the data versus paper distinction in their nouns. Even if the system consistently uses the term *dokument* for the electronic sign, and the manual tries to distinguish between *dokument* and *kort,* the work-language uses the same word *kort* for both data and paper.

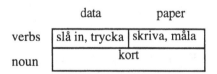

	data	paper
verbs	slå in, trycka	skriva, måla
noun	kort	

Fig. III.1.5. The data-paper distinction in the work language.

---

1 Note that although *skicka* can be used for both data and paper inside the department, it cannot denote data transmission from the accounting department to the computer department.

Summarizing, the workers interpret the distinction between paper and its electronic representation, not in terms of the "objects" themselves, but in terms of the actions applied to them.

Whatever the reason may be for this phenomenon, it reveals a basic difference of semantic organization between workers on the one hand and system and designers on the other hand. The examples show that it is very difficult, maybe impossible, for designers to abstract away from the relevance criteria of one's own work, and imagine what may be relevant to the users. Who could have guessed that the users want to distinguish between data and paper in their verbs but not in their nouns?

The difference between interface and work language is illustrated in an even more conspicuous way in the next example. It was already mentioned in Section I.2.4.2 as an illustration of discrepancy between the semantic fields of interface and work language.

The substance of the fields consists of the main work tasks done by means of the system. As mentioned before, the system articulates this substance into at least three segments, *komplettering* (recording data), *avstämning* (correcting data) and *annan behörighet* (including e.g. inspection of fliers, entering new date, etc.). The articulation is partly based upon functional, partly upon organizational criteria, but the staff use a different criterion, namely physical location. They lump *komplettering, avstämning* and *annan behörighet* together under the term *registrering*, and add a new member to the paradigm: *köra* or *stå* [run, stand]. These latter terms cover work at the OCR-reader, while *registrering* means "work at the work stations"[1].

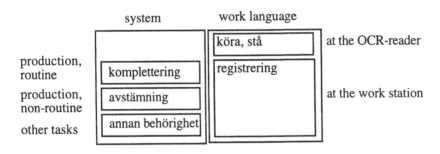

Fig. III.1.6. Task designations. Differences between system and work language.

---

[1] There is a possible historical explanation for the meaning of the word *registrering*. It existed at the department before the introduction of the PGP-system, where it was used to denote cheque-processing, which was already computerized. At that time *registrering* meant "work at the terminals" and contrasted to *kodning,* which was done by physical coding machines, so when new "terminal work" was introduced, it too was called *registrering,* no matter if its contents were quite different from cheque processing.

The absence of an analogy to *köra, stå* in the system is simply due to the fact that work at the OCR-reader and work at the work stations involve two different programs that do not "know" anything about each other.

The fact that a program knows about a smaller part of reality than the workers is also the explanation of the next difference. In principle, the PGP-system only distinguishes between two states: either a batch tallies or it does not. The first state is unmarked, whereas the second one is expressed by the warning *VARNING: Denna bunt balancerar inte* [this batch does not tally] accompanied by a beep-signal. The manual and the work language, however, have a much finer articulation of the same situation: the payment orders may lack a signature, the customer may have added it up incorrectly, the amounts of money on the order may differ from the amounts on the individual cards, etc., etc. If we compare the two fields, we get the following picture:

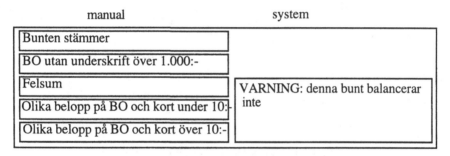

Fig. III.1.7. Error designations. Differences between system and work language.

Note that the boundary between correct and incorrect cards is different: payment orders without a signature are classified as incorrect in the manual, but the system does not issue warnings, since it has no access to the physical card where the signature is.

The final example shows that although semantic fields of the computer system and the work language may contain the same members, they may have a different structure. To the paradigm of five error-correcting actions described above there correspond four system commands:

(1) Flytta Dokument till Flygare ($\approx$1) [Move document to fliers]
(2) Hämta Dok ($\approx$2) [Fetch document]
(4) Ta bort Dokument ($\approx$4) [Take away document]
(5) Överge nuvarande BUNT ($\approx$5) [Abandon batch]

but they are not expressed as one paradigm by the system. As the following fraction of the menu hierarchy shows (Fig. III.1.8), 1 and 4 are described as a unit in opposition to 2^1, a classification that can be found elsewhere in the hierarchy.

One plausible explanation is that *Flygare* [fliers] and *Borttagna Dokument* [removed documents] are implemented in the same way. If this is true, it is a very clear example of designers transmitting a semantic structure that is probably relevant in their own work situation to a use situation where it is ir-relevant.

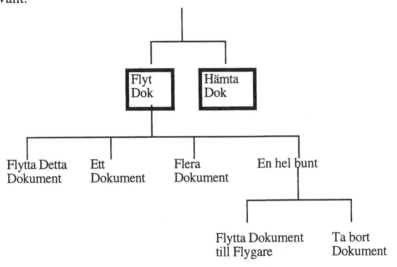

Fig. III.1.8. Task classification in the system.

Summarizing, one can say that even if care was taken to base the system upon "old Giro Words", its basic semantic structure in several ways differs from that found in the work language. The next question is naturally: what would the system look like if its basic semantic organization had been taken from the work language? Before I answer the question, I shall briefly show how to use semantic fields to describe the conceptual changes that occurred as a consequence of the new system.

III.1.3.2. Changes of semantic fields

Semantic fields can also be used for describing technology-motivated lan-guage changes. Again the technique is to define similar areas of substance and to plot the sign variants of two language periods on them.

---

1 The fat boxes mean that the command is entered via a function key. The other commands are acti-vated by choosing menus on the screen. We see that *Flytta Dokument till Flygare* and *Ta bort Dokument* are classified as specializations of the general command *Flytta Dokument* entered by a function key.

In the first example, the substance is the work material for the old task of *kodning* [coding] and the new task of *komplettering* [completing]. The figure compares the nomenclature from the old paper-based work process with the new nomenclature of the computer-based version.

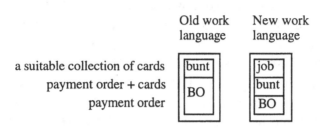

Fig. III.1.9. Change of work object designations.

A *bunt* in the old language was all the material that was processed in one coding task. It consisted of parts called *BO's* that in turn consisted of a payment order from a particular customer plus paying-in forms.

In the new language, the word *job* (probably borrowed from the language of informatics) has been introduced in the space previously occupied by *bunt*, pushing *bunt* into the space below, which is now partitioned into two parts: the payment order is now called a *BO*, and the order plus paying-in forms (previously called BO) are renamed *bunt*. The change is caused by the nomenclature of the PGP system.

A possible motivation for this change can be organizational. *Bunt's* meaning in both fields is *work object*, but whereas the work object previously was defined physically as a paper batch of a certain size, the new work object is defined economically as documents that belong to the same economic transaction. If this interpretation is correct, the system is used to communicate the new conception of work, saying: *you are no longer only responsible for performing a certain number of mechanical tasks on a paper batch - you are responsible for completing an economic transaction.*

III.1.4. Using semantic fields for design

In the previous sections I have given many examples of divergence between system and work language, and a natural question to ask is: how can we use knowledge about the work language in design, and what might the system have looked like, had the work language been used as a basis for design?

The first thing to note is that there can be no question of copying or translating work language into computer-based signs. There are two reasons for this: firstly the computer is another medium than the verbal language, and this alone prohibits direct copying. The other reason is that systems development normally also means organizational change, as the Postal Giro case nicely illustrates: changes of task structure, of division of labor, of responsibilities and rights, and of values and norms.

The key concept is to use work language as the point of departure for inventing new computer-based signs. It is more like making a film version of a novel than translating a book from one language to another.

In this section, I shall show how to use semantic fields to get ideas for design. My point of departure will be the observation that the semantic fields of the system are different from those of the work language, not only on a superficial level, but in the very glossemes that are used to structure them. Many signs in the actual PGP-system are related by part-whole relations (the referent of a sign is a part of the referent of another sign) and hyponomy (the referent of a sign is a subclass of the referent of another sign), but these glossemes are not operative in the work language. The following piece of conversation illustrates this very well. Hilkka, one of the workers, has just noticed that a classification of the work process appears on top of the screen, and asks the instructor:

> Here it says "completion", up here, but later, when I'm done with the batch, it's "production", how come?

and receives the answer that

> It says precisely all the time what you do.

However, Hilkka does not sound convinced, and in any case has not noted it before we asked. Inspection of the data shows that Hilkka is perfectly right in being skeptical about whether the system really "says what she does". It turns out that her basic distinctive features are not part-whole and hyponomy but rather *here* versus *there* and *having* versus *missing* versus *wanting*.

Like the librarians in Section I.2.4.1, she frequently uses paradigms of transport and location, describing movements and locations in relation to herself. Work objects can *gå där, komma, komma fram* [go there, come, come forth].

> Det här *kommer* inte *fram.*
>
> XE5, jag vet inte om det är den eller den där stora, ..., du vet allting *går ju där* sen.
>
> Den här e inte så lämplig för att då *kommer* alla kortena.
>
> Och om de skulle ha blitt läst på rätt sätt här, bakom på de här C-kortet, skulle det ha *kommit fram.*

[This doesn't appear clear (lit: *come forth*).

XE5, I don't know if it's this one or the big one there...you know, everything
winds up (lit: *go*) *there* later on.
This isn't really so appropriate, because then all the cards *come* up.
And if they had been read in the right way here, behind these C cards, it would
have appeared (lit: *come forth*).]

and she presents her own actions as a journey in a landscape of cards and
tasks, describing the surroundings from her present location: *komma till, gå
till, gå tilbaks till, vara, sitta* [come to, go to, go back to, be, sit], for example:

Eva Britt! när den frågar om tretti öre måste jag *gå till* C-korten och titta att det
är rätt?
Ja för att när jag väljer - jag kan ju *gå tillbaks till* menyn, och då väljer jag vilket
jag gör.
Nu är det produktion och när jag *sitter* i komp då är det komplettering.

[Eva Britt! When it asks about 30 öre (cents), do I have to *go back* to the C
card and check that it's right?
Well, since when I choose, I can *go back* to the menu and then choose what
I'm going to do.
Now it's production, and when I'm *sitting in* "comp", then it's completion].

Her own actions on the work objects either remove them from her: *lägga åt
sidan, skicka, lägga där, ta ut, ta bort* [put aside, send back, place there,
take out, take away], for example:

Så *lägger* jag det *åt sidan.*
Då *lägger* jag den *där.*
Då måste jag *ta bort* den här varningssignalen.

[Then I *put it to one side.*
Then I *put it there.*
Then I have to *take away* this warning signal.]

or bring it nearer to her: *hämta* [fetch]

Jag kunde ha *hämtat* också.
Och nu måste jag gå och *hämta* C-korten innan jag kan fortsätta.

[I could have *fetched* also (about data).
And now I have to go and *fetch* the C card before I can continue (about paper).]

Although the distinction between *here* and *not here* is closely related to the
distinction between *having* and *not having*, presence often implying pos-

session, as in the phrasing *nu har jag C-korten framme* [now I have the C cards in front of me] cards can be absent but still in possession as in *men jag har ju de - korten har jag i flygaren* [I have the cards in the flier].

She can have or get work objects: *ha, ha framme, ha uppe, få, få fram, ta* [have, get, take]

> Och så *får* jag namnet på jobbet för varje får sin egen.
> Så sexton, från 14 till 16 då är det C-kort, då har den id- fält här, det är kundi-den, men här hade den inte summan {piip} jag *får* alltid- så, här *har* jag, det är typ noll, då är det ingen information alls härnere------ här *har* vi C-kort, nu ser jag att där måste jag *ha* och där måste jag *ha*.
> Så *tar* jag den här nya arbetskonto.

> [And then I *get* the name of the job because each one has its own.
> And sixteen, from 14 to 16 it's the C card, then it has this id field here, it's the customer id, but here it didn't have the sum [beep], I always *get*, so here I *have*, this is type zero, then there is no information at all down here...here we *have* the C cards, now I see that I have to *have* (something) here and there.
> Then I *take* this new work account.]

but she can also lack or lose them: *sakna, överge, inte ha, inte få* [miss, abandon, not have, not get]

> Men nu står det att jag *har ingenting,*
> För det är inget kort, det *saknas.*
> Men jag *har inte* det kortet på 447.

> [But now it says that I haven't *got* anything.
> Because there's no card, it's *missing.*
> But I *don't have* the card for 447.]

Verbs of possession are not only used about her relation to the work objects, but also about the work objects themselves that *have, want to have, or should have* something:

> C-korten *har* hela informationen här.
> Är det A-kort *vill det ha* både kontonummer och summa.
> Nu har jag lärt mig 87501 *ska alltid ha* summan, så man kan lära sig om man bara vill.

> [The C card *has* the entire information here.
> If it's an A card, it needs (lit: *wants to have*) both account number and sum.
> Now I've learned 87501 *should* always *have* the sum, so you can learn it if you really want to.]

These verbs can be arranged in a semantic field structured by three sets of features:

location versus *possession*
positive versus *negative* versus *modal*
(result of) *process* versus *state*

	location		possession		
	positive	**negative**	**positive**	**negative**	**modal**
(result of) process	COME, FETCH komma, komma till, komma fram, hämta	PLACE, SEND lägga åt sidan, skicka, gå där, lägga där, ta bort	GET, TAKE få, få fram, ta	ABANDON överge, inte få	WANT, MUST vill ha, ska ha
state	BE, SIT: vara, sitta	NOT EXIST finns inte	HAVE ha, ha framme	LACK inte ha, sakna	

Fig. III.1.10. Semantic field of task designations in work language.

where positive location = here, negative location = there, not here. Komma = come, lägga (åt sidan, där) = put (to one side, there), ta bort = take away, hämta = fetch, skicka = send, få = get, ta = take, överge = abandon (vill, ska), ha = (want to, must) have, vara = be, sitta = sit, sakna = miss.

The worker does not look at the data from a detached bird's eye perspective, but views it from her own position, using *mine* and *here* as her points of reference. In addition, her conception of these landmarks seems to be positively charged, whereas *there* or *theirs* are negatively charged, since she uses the phrasings *finns inte, har inte, sakna* [is not found, does not have, is missing] about items that are located in other places or possessed by others.

I find this way of organizing the world quite sensible. In design it can be supported by declaring attributes of *possession* and *location* in all system objects that designate work objects. The precise value of these attributes represents the status of the work object. To give a few examples:

The card I am working on at the moment will be owned by me and be located in a batch that is located in a job that in turn is located on my desk. When I send a superfluous card to the flier file its properties change: it is no longer owned by me but by the whole department, and any worker is entitled to take it if needed. Also it no longer is located in the current batch but in the flier file.

A job can also be located in different places and owned by different people. The current job is of course located at my desk and owned by me, which means that no other worker can see it nor manipulate its items. If I cannot solve an error in the job, I can abandon it, making it a so-called *red job*. Red jobs can still be possessed by me because I may want to give them another try later and therefore wish to prevent others from taking them. On the other hand, I may also want to give them up completely and transfer their possession to my colleagues in my section. When a job is finished it becomes a so-called *green job*, I lose possession of it, and its location is changed from my desk to the area of the section. Later, after the job has been checked against the paper jobs, it is put into a box, and sent to the computer department, which then owns it. It means the section has neither access to it nor can see it anymore.

These examples show that the two attributes can be used to represent important aspects of the system objects denoting work objects. In addition the attributes have the advantage that they are easy to give a visual expression to.

Ownership can be expressed by a closed contour: persons within the smallest enclosure in which the work objects are placed are co-owners of the objects. To a certain degree, this symbolization is copied from the plan-layout which expresses the same symbolic content.

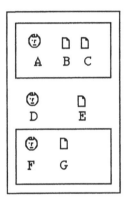

Fig. III.1.11. Graphical representation of ownership.

My objects are placed at my desk, which again is placed within mobile walls that set each section apart from the others in the large office landscape of the department, which itself is confined by solid walls. In Fig. III.1.11, A owns B and C, F owns G, and A, F and D together own E.

The location of the worker is implicitly assumed to be at the bottom of the screen, and the location of the work objects can be symbolized by their distance from the bottom and the color of the surrounding area: the higher up and the darker the background, the greater the distance (Fig. III.1.12).

The work objects near me are placed in the white rectangle at the bottom of the screen. Here we find the current job, batch, and card together with the red jobs I want to keep for myself. Those farther away, e.g. the work objects of the section, are in the light grey area, and include the jobs my colleagues are working at, the finished "green" jobs and the boxes into which the jobs are "packed". Outside the section, in the dark grey representing the whole department, we find the flier file that the whole department can use, and possibly the "destroyed (mackade)" batches that cannot be processed but must be sent back to the customers.

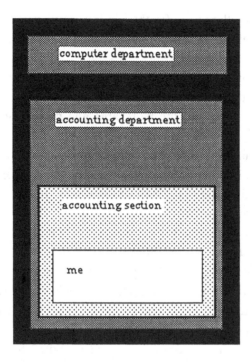

Fig. III.1.12. Graphical representation of location.

Finally, if we cross the black area and enter the computer department, we meet the boxes we have sent there and which are now irretrievably outside our jurisdiction.

I have now described some properties of the system objects, but analysis of the actions they are to perform or that can be done to them still remains. To get ideas for actions, I take a new look at the data, this time not from the paradigmatical point of view, but from the syntagmatical.

The sentences of the workers are built according to a limited set of syntagms, and in my design I shall at least use three types, two of which are exemplified in the material above:

- *Transport:*
  Work Objects or Worker move[s] Somewhere
  Work Objects or Worker is/are placed Somewhere
  Worker moves Work Object Somewhere
- *Possession*
  Machine or Work Object possesses, wants to posses, or does not possess an Object

> Worker possesses, wants to possess, does not possess, comes to pos-
> sess, or loses possession of an Object

These syntagms can all be used for the administrative part of the work: locating, moving, and taking or losing possession of data. Here are a few examples:

Work Objects moving by themselves can be used if the system is to supply
the next card or batch after the previous one has been finished. The card or
batch will "itself" move into the work area and make itself ready for data
entry.

Worker moving is useful if the screen is not large enough to hold the total
amount of information above. The cursor can be used to denote the worker,
and if it moves against the upper part of the screen, it will scroll and display
the part of the layout that "lies outside the screen". Thus, the screen is presented as a pane through which a certain part of the plan layout can be seen
and which can be "tilted" to make other parts visible.

Worker moves Work Object will typically be used in problem-solving situations, where the worker and not the system should decide whether to move
a superfluous card to the fliers or fetch a missing card from them.

In the routine part of the work another frequent schema expressing affecting (e.g. *för att jag slog in den här* [because I typed in this one]) can be
used:

- *Affecting:*
  Worker affects Work Object or Machine

Obvious examples are: entering amount, account number, film number, etc.

Note that at the moment I have only fixed the contents of the computer-
based signs. I have still not decided how to express them, since this is a
choice of style that I wish to postpone until Section III.2.4.2, where more
data has been considered.

III.2

Language as Action. Language Games in the Postal Giro

III.2.1. A psychological definition of language games

In the preceding section, I showed how to use semantic fields of lexical material for various purposes: when the system developer enters the organization she can use them to get an impression of conceptual differences of the organization, when she starts doing particular applications she can use them to design the general data structure, and when she has made a prototype, semantic fields are useful for evaluating its reception and for redesigning it. Finally, researchers studying the general effects of computerization on organizations can use semantic fields to record language changes in the organization, and use these data as a basis for setting up hypotheses about changes of culture and cognition.

However, language is more than a vehicle for interpretation and description. Besides the ideational functions, language also has an action aspect that is subsumed under Halliday's interpersonal functions.

Although it is not a bad idea to start with the ideational aspect, since professional languages are registers and tend to differ in vocabulary, the action aspect is equally important in systems development. Language in work situations is not only used to interpret and *describe*, but also to *act* verbally, and in a similar way, computer systems are used as media for distributing work, giving orders, and reporting. Designers not only need to know which kind of information is needed and how it should be structured semantically, they also need to know when it is needed and for which purposes.

Since we are now focusing on the action aspect of language, an important requirement of the descriptive concepts we need is that they must be able to relate the internal linguistic structure of the utterances to their external functions relative to other linguistic and non-linguistic events. How will the actions evoked in the addressee differ when we remind, request, or order him to do something?

Pragmatic theory has addressed this issue, in particular the speech act theory expounded in J. R. Searle's book "Speech acts"[1], and several computer

---

[1] Searle 1977.

scientists have tried to use his ideas in analysis of information systems[1]. He was one of the first to treat the action aspects of language systematically, but his approach has two problematic features in this context. Firstly he treats only the action aspect of single utterances, but - as mentioned in Section I.2.2.4 - in authentic speech it is often a whole *sequence* of utterances that has function to work. Secondly, his description is basically psychological, since his classifications are based upon what speakers intend or believe. To my mind, this is a serious problem, because there are no linguistic methods for determining what goes on in people's heads. Therefore the analysis will ultimately rest upon commonsense criteria, and will be difficult to combine with the normal stock-in-trade of linguistic methodology. The problem may not be so serious when you work with your own utterances, because then you know what you intended by saying them, but it becomes a real obstacle when the data is authentic speech produced by speakers from a country and a culture you do not know yourself. How can I ever classify an utterance in my tapes as a *request* if I first have to ascertain

- that the hearer is able to do the action,
- that the speaker believes that the hearer is able to do the action,
- that it is not obvious to both speaker and hearer that the hearer will do the action in the normal course of events of his own accord, and
- that the speaker wants the hearer to do the action[2].

My objection is not that Searle's analysis is wrong or uninteresting. The problem is rather that linguistics, as I understand it, *is not a psychological, but a social and behavioral science.* Searle's concepts have to be translated into these terms, and I shall modify his ideas in two ways. First I shall change the relevant units of analysis from a single utterance to a group of utterances which I call a *language game*, and next I shall change the psychological definition to a linguistic one, trying to get rid of the notions of purposes and beliefs.

Holmqvist 1986 offers the following psychologically oriented definition of language games in her book on the Postal Giro language:

- *Preliminary psychological definition:*
  A language game can only be identified by the results the actions have in a given situation.
  A language game is a closed unit of interaction in the sense that when the last word has been said, nobody is required to continue the line of argument, since the goal has been reached or abandoned.

---

[1] E.g. Goldkuhl 1984a and b, Winograd & Flores 1986.
[2] Searle 1977: 66.

A language game consists of sequences of verbal acts that mutually presuppose each other, and form a well-defined unit in relation to other acts, since they can be subsumed under the same purpose[1].

Although the actual result of the game (corresponding to Searle's perlocutionary effects) has been entered into the definition, the purpose is retained, and it gives no clues as to which linguistic observations could be used as a basis for identifying types of games.

The concept of language games exemplified above can be characterized in the following way: it focuses on the *syntagmatic* aspect of language in opposition to semantic fields, which essentially present a *paradigmatic* analysis. It views language as *action*, i.e. as a way to influence the environment, as opposed to viewing language in its capacity of description and discrimination, and it places the emphasis on purposes and *results*, as opposed to focusing on the *process*.

From the flow of observed verbal acts, we select those that *depend* meaningfully upon each other, discarding those that belong to other games. This is important, since several games can be played simultaneously, and some games can extend over days or months. The opposite course of action would be to select everything that is said during a certain period of time, i.e to use *temporal contiguity* as a criterion.

Finally, the language game concept stresses the *rule-governed* aspect of language in opposition to *creative* or artistic use of language.

The game metaphor implies that the acts can be classified into *moves*, that the sequence of moves is partially governed by rules that are known to the participants, and that the moves have a function in relation to the purpose of the game.

In some cases, the game metaphor can be extended further. We can define a *stake*, composed of items that can only be possessed by one of the players. The purpose of the game is to gain possession of the largest amount of items. This makes it possible to define concepts of *winning* and *losing*, the individual speech acts being classified as moves, counter-moves and evaluations. The strategic view of language we express in this way is interesting because it can be combined with organization theories that analyze organizational behavior in terms of strategy, tactics, and opportunism[2].

The following example, a small game from the old Postal Giro organization, shows how to use the strategic view on language games at the micro level[3]:

---

[1] Holmqvist 1986: 22. See also Severinson Eklundh 1976.
[2] See Ciborra 1985, who adapts the American school of institutional economics to analysis of information systems.
[3] Bøgh Andersen & Holmqvist 1986b: 11.

A: Rosa, will you punch for two seconds?

B: Just two seconds? I'm going up in a moment.

A: When?

B: Well, when she is finished with that list.

[A: Rosa stansar du två sekunder?

B: Två sekunder bara? Jag ska gå upp sen!

A: När då sen?

B: Ja när hon blir klar med den där listan.]

The item at stake is *free time*. A wants to go on an errand, and asks B to take over her job. B, on the other hand, is about to go to lunch.

In her first move, A requests B to take over her job for two seconds. At the Postal Giro, an official system of work distribution exists according to which colleagues can help each other for a short period of time. Thus, B's first move is a request for help.

In the second line, B makes a counter-move: she makes an ironic comment on the "two seconds", since she knows that it makes no sense to punch for a couple of minutes, and she adds an argument supported by the official work distribution scheme: she is scheduled for lunch. One of the implications is that A is not playing according to the rules of the game: she is cheating. The game is really about work distribution, not help. In this case, the pre-conditions for making a request are not fulfilled, since A has no right to tell B to punch. This has to be done by the supervisor.

However, A has not given up yet, and her next move is a question about when B is going to lunch. After all, B may have time for punching. No, B's countermove is to deny this implication, she is just about to go.

The game is not concluded by verbal means. A recognizes her defeat by resuming her punching. The free time at stake was won by B, not by A.

Besides being useful for micro-strategic analyses of this kind, the purpose-oriented definition can be used to set up a typology of language games[1], as the following list shows. I have appended the examples from Section I.1.1 as illustrations:

Work organization

(1)   *Ordering* aims at allocating tasks to the employees and is typically done in the morning (example 6).

(2)   *Work distribution* aims at dividing a task or set of tasks among several people, either because some of the employees are idle, or because the amount of work is too large to be finished within the deadline (example 7).

---

[1] Holmqvist & Bøgh Andersen 1987.

(3)   *Work coordination* aims at coordinating workers working with the same task (example 1).

(4)   *Work priority ordering* aims at changing the priority of tasks so that one task is moved in front of another.

(5)   *Help* denotes utterances produced when one worker calls in a colleague to take over that part of the job for which the latter for some reason is better qualified.

(6)   *Control check* aims at verifying that the task is carried out correctly or in the manner ordered (example 10).

(7)   *Supervision* aims at controlling the manner and speed of the work.

(8)   *Reporting* aims at informing the person in charge about the current state of the work.

Task

(9)   *Problem-solving* denotes utterances that are used to solve an unexpected problem: these may be a monologue or dialogue (examples 2, 3, 8).

Reproduction of social relations and knowledge

(10)   *Instruction* aims at giving an employee knowledge about tasks or work organization (examples 5, 9).

(11)   *Talk-in-the-work (shop talk)* does not refer to the actual work in which it is embedded; however, its topic is still events in the place of work, and it serves to reproduce common knowledge and social relations.

(12)   *Greetings* aim at reproducing social relationships and keeping the channels of communication open.

(13)   *Comments* on a specific problem may serve to establish a common understanding of what the problem or its solution is (example 4)

(14)   *Exclamations* are used as outlets for emotions and at the same time as signals to co-workers about work progress.

Machinery and tools

(15)   *Requesting tools* serves to give information about the availability and location of tools.

(16)   *Warnings* serve to protect tools, raw materials, or humans from damage or accidents.

I have used this classification in Section I.1.1, and shall continue to use it in the following pages as a basis for developing a more purely linguistic taxonomy.

III.2.2. A linguistic definition of language games

The next step is to translate the psychological definition into a linguistic one that retains most of the valuable insights of the former definition.

One of the demands of a linguistic definition is that it should not abstract the actual linguistic coding away, but be close to actual language and sensitive to the actual formulations of the speakers, and, as mentioned previously, another requirement is that it must be able to relate the internal linguistic structure of the game to its external functions to other linguistic and non-linguistic events.

To illustrate the requirements, let us look at the difference between *work distribution* and *help*. In the typology, there are four games aiming at allocating tasks to workers:

- ordering
- work distribution
- work coordination
- help.

If we abstract the linguistic coding and the communication situations away, the same thing happens in the four cases: workers are assigned to tasks. On this level of abstraction, there will only be one function, but this does not describe the social reality at this place of work, where there exist different codings and use situations that set the functions apart. In the Postal Giro, *ordering* is different from *work distribution*, since orders are given in the morning in the form of written schedules, whereas *redistribution of work* (called *jämning* [levelling]) takes place during the day. Both *work distribution* and *work coordination* are used when two or more workers are involved in the same task, but in the repair shop data from Section I.1.1, they are coded differently: work distribution takes the shape of agreements, *if I rivet the rear linings...then you can take these off,* whereas work coordination can consist of short phrases uttered during actual work, *higher up towards you - straight up - there, right there...it has to be there...there, right there.* At the Postal Giro, work coordination in this sense hardly exists.

What we need is a definition that explicitly relates the working context function of the language games to their internal linguistic structure. Let us start with this internal structure.

III.2.2.1. Internal structure of language games

The Rosa example above shows that it is necessary to know a lot about the situational context in order to make a correct interpretation of the way the rules are actually put to use in language games. In this example we need information about

- the work organization (who distributes work?)
- the specific task (why does it not make any sense to punch for a couple of minutes?)
- the means of production, tools and raw materials (what do the punching machines look like?)
- the informal social relations (may colleagues help each other outside the written schedule?)
- demands of efficiency and profitability (why may the punching machines not be idle?)
- the roles (employee vs supervisor).

The language games we will be working with are of this situation-specific type, and therefore the syntactic description of their constituent utterances will be different from those found in grammar textbooks that cover a whole national language. The utterances of a particular type of situation will exhibit fewer syntagmatic patterns and the possibilities for filling the individual slot of the syntagm will be limited.

The syntagmatic concept we need in this case is similar to the frame notion in Minsky 1975, and to indicate this similarity, I shall coin the term *sentence frame*.

A good illustration of the concept can be found in the analysis of flight control work in Falzon 1983. To give an example of his analysis, consider the following sentence, uttered by a flight controller:

climb level 230

Its frame, called the *change level* frame[1], contains the following slots:

Slots	Action	Nature	Relation	From	To	Time
Fillers	vertical	level	above or below present level	present level (default)		now (default) or at pilot's discretion

Fig. III.2.1. Sentence frame for change of level.

---

[1] Falzon uses the term *schema*, but since this terms already has a technical glossematic meaning in the present book, I shall replace it by *frame*. The example is found in Falzon 1983: 26.

The description says that the action must be *vertical*, and its nature has to do with *levels*. The relation between the present and future position of the airplane must be *above* or *below*. Some of the fillers of the *from* and *to* category are default fillers. If nothing else is said, the origin of the action is the *present level*, and the time is *now*.

After the frame has been evoked, the words of the utterance are used to fill the categories of the frame, or to reject the frame as a wrong choice. In the present example, a default rule is used to fill *time* with *now* since the sentence does not explicitly mention the time.

The flight controller example exhibits all the characteristics of frames:

- Each situation type generates a special collection of frames. Not all work tasks consist in moving an object up and down, but some, like data entry at the Postal Giro, may consist in manipulating an object and therefore replace the cases *source* and *destination* with *instrument* and *object*, while others, like nursing, are concerned with human feelings and needs, and therefore may employ cases like *experiencer* and *beneficiary*.
- Default filling of slots. If nothing else is said, the *from* case is filled with *present level*.
- Limited set of fillers available for each slot. Time can only be filled with *now* or *at pilot's discretion*, not with e.g. *at dinner time* or *yesterday* or *next year*.

Falzon implemented the frames in a program, and ran it on the transcript of the tape recordings. Most sentences were analyzed correctly, but in unusual situations the air traffic controllers switched codes, and the programs were unsuccessful:

> The language of the controllers is not homogeneous. Most of the time, the language they use is a technical dialect, in which vocabulary and syntax is highly restricted. However, they may use other expressions and a different vocabulary in less usual situations.   *Falzon 1983: 31*

This observation delimits the validity of the frame concept: it can describe the controller's knowledge of standard situations, and give an account of how this routine knowledge is used in interpreting utterances, but it seems unable to account for the shift of code caused by "break-downs".

One possible way of defining types of language games is to use the sentence frames that dominate their internal structure. This is the method employed by Andersson 1983: 64 ff, who uses two main parameters to classify communicative functions:

- *Paraphrase:* the individual functions are defined by an abstract paraphrase indicating some change or state in work organization, e.g. *Reporting:* of products: *X has been produced,* and of persons: *A has produced.*
- *Roles:* hierarchical/non-hierarchical relations are used to distinguish variants of the functions, e.g. *Work distribution:* hierarchical: *You do X and you do Y,* and non-hierarchical: *You do X and I do Y.*

In spite of their different terminology, Falzon's and Andersson's concepts are similar in that both work with partially filled sentence forms. The similarity becomes clearer when we reformulate Falzon's *change level frame* as one of Andersson's paraphrases: *Airplane moves up or down (from present level now).*

If Andersson's method of defining the games in terms of a question frame that has to be answered, or a statement frame that has to be instantiated, is feasible, we would have come closer to a purely linguistic definition, which immediately makes it easier to set up hypotheses about the detailed verbal characteristics of the individual games: if a particular game for example is defined by a certain combination of question-slots, we will expect the semantic fields corresponding to these slots to have a fine-grained articulation while others need only a few distinctions or are already default-filled with one item.

Let us use these notions to redefine some of the games in the preliminary psychological typology in a work context where workers act on some object. A preliminary glance at the Postal Giro data indicates that a general sentence frame for work processes of this type could look like this:

someone	do	acting on	something	in some way	sometime

and the individual game types can be defined by different distributions of the question-slots (italicized below):

Work distribution: who should begin doing it when?

Someone	should begin	acting on	something	in some way	sometime

Supervision: is she doing it?

Someone	*is*	acting on	something	in some way	now

Reporting: has she done it?

Someone	has	acted on	something	in some way	now

Reporting:has it been done to it?

Someone	*has*	acted on	*something*	in some way	now

Work coordination: what should I do now?

I,you	should	*act on*	*something*	in some way	now

Instruction: how should she do it?

Someone	should	act on	something	*in some way*	sometime

In work distribution, the question concerns the actor and the time, while the action and the object are given (who should begin doing it when?). The problem is the *who*, not the *manner* and not the *what*. Therefore the actor and time slots should be finely articulated, while the manner case is irrelevant. Conversely, in instruction the implied question concerns the *manner* (how should she do it?), and the actor and time slots are irrelevant.

The question analysis seems to work well, but should only be taken as a heuristic that is a symptom of more abstract concepts. There is no particular reason why we should postulate a question-formed "deep-structure" of the games. The real insight hidden behind the question-analysis is that the games can be distinguished by particular combinations of the two kinds of paradigms introduced in Section I.2.2.4, namely the open and closed paradigms. In order to emphasize their different communicative roles, I shall rename them *focus* and *background* paradigms.

Focus paradigms are open in the sense that at the beginning of the game, each member of the paradigm can be chosen. The game is concluded when a member has been agreed upon or the game abandoned. Thus, the worker paradigm is a focus paradigm in work distribution. *Background* paradigms are closed paradigms in the sense that at the beginning of the game, the member(s) have been chosen. Verbally, this means that either they are not expressed at all or they are verbally backgrounded and do not change during the game. Furthermore, since a game has to have background paradigms but may possibly not have focus paradigms, it is likely that the category of focus paradigms presupposes the category of background paradigms.

The particular configuration of focus and background paradigms provides a definition of a particular language game. Work distributions, for example, could be defined by the focus paradigm of worker and time and the background paradigms of task and manner. Conversely, instruction is defined by having worker in the background and manner in the focus.

Summarizing, we can say that the utterances of language games can be described by sentence frames consisting of focus and background paradigms, and the particular combination of focused and backgrounded paradigms characterizes a specific game type.

But utterance syntagms are not the only syntagms to be discovered in language games. Utterances contract cohesions with other utterances and build *move*-structures that are also characteristic of a game type.

Move-structures can be described at more than one level of abstraction. The most abstract level describes functions that recur in any language game. *Moves, counter-moves, evaluations* is one set, *request, accept, negotiation, renegotiation, withdrawal, declaration* is another one[1]. On this level of abstraction we could say that the four utterances in the Rosa example fall into two pairs (also called *adjacency pairs*) consisting of a request and a response to the request. One analysis could be that the response presupposes the request, since *Rosa, will you punch for two seconds?* can occur without an answer and still count as a request, whereas *Just two seconds? I'm going up in a moment* cannot count as an answer without a request.

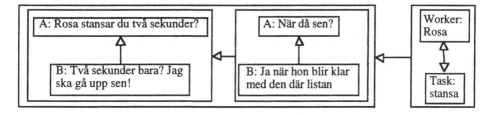

Fig. III.2.2. Functional analysis of move structures.

Also, the second pair *A: When?* + *B: Well, when she is finished with that list* presupposes the first one, since the conversation could have ended after B's second turn, while A's third turn does not make sense without the two first turns.

However, the structures yielded by such analyses are rather general, and if the data are to be useful for design, we must also try to capture the specifics of the task and the organization. One method to accomplish this is to contrast the individual moves, and record their mutual meaning differences. As an example, let us look again at the first two moves in the example:

---

[1] Winograd & Flores 1986: 65.

A: Rosa, will you punch for two seconds?
[A: Rosa stansar du två sekunder?]

B: Just two seconds? I'm going up in a moment.
[B: Två sekunder bara? Jag ska gå upp sen!]

A is *requesting* B to punch, and B is referring to her scheduled lunch break. The relation between the moves consists in B referring to a part of her future schedule that will make her unable to do what A requests. She is not referring to personal wishes or desires, as might have occurred in other contexts, but to her place in the fixed work schedule. This specific relationship between the two moves can be called a *disenablement*. It is not because she is personally against it, she is just not able to do it! By classifying the second move as a disenablement, I have inscribed the analysis in a bureaucracy where detailed rules exist that enable or disenable the employees independently of their personal wishes.

Now, let us compare

B: I'm going up in a moment!
[B: Jag ska gå upp sen!]

B: Well, when she is finished with that list.
[B: Ja när hon blir klar med den där listan.]

The relation between these two moves is the opposite: the second move refers to a part of the schedule (a colleague finishing a piece of work) that will enable the part referred to in the first move to happen (the speaker having her break). The second one enables the first one, and the relationship could be called an *enablement*.

We shall later see that move-structures of this level of concreteness can be used to further characterize the game types and their organizational context. At present, the following two points are important:

- like all other concepts in this book, the move-concepts is relational. The property of being a disenablement is not a property of the utterance *I'm going up in a moment* but is a value it acquires by contracting a function to a preceding request *will you punch for two seconds?* Therefore statements about move-structures are basically relational: their form is: "the relation between move A and B is the same as/is different from the relation between move C and B".

- the context in which these judgments are made is the situation type, and therefore the move-types will not be the general ones mentioned above, but situation-specific ones.

Let us now turn to the external functions, corresponding to Hjelmslev's analytical definitions.

III.2.2.2. External function of language games

In the psychological definition, the function of the utterance was described by its purpose, and we need to translate this concept into linguistic terms.

The concept of purpose captures an important property of language games, namely that they have function to non-verbal phenomena that the speakers wish to to change. Consider the following game of work distribution (S = supervisor):

S: They are short of people at check control. Can anyone go over there?
A: I was there last week.
B: I have to be at the dentist at eleven o'clock.
S: But in the afternoon they have a part-timer coming.
B: Well, I'll go then.

[S: Dom har ont om folk på Checkringningen. Kan någon gå över dit?
A: Jag satt där i förra veckan.
B: Ja ska va hos tandläkaren klockan elva.
S: Men på eftermiddagen har dom en deltidare som kommer.
B: Då går jag väl då.]

Holmqvist 1987: 80. Holmqvist & Bøgh Andersen 1987:339

Obviously, the utterances have function to a task performed at Check Control. In particular, this task *presupposes* the utterances, since it would not have been performed, had the utterances not been uttered.

As clearly appears from the example, the utterances do not necessarily bring about the task, since objections and disobedience are possible.

However, if the task is not performed, its absence will be marked as something special that may entail reproaches, and perhaps even dismissal.

This pattern can be used as a characteristic of the class of games called *directives*[1].

Directive

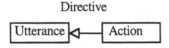

Directives are utterances that contract presupposition with a task.

In this typology, directives include games like *ordering, work distribution, work priority ordering, help,* and *warnings.*

---

[1] Clark & Clark 1977: 88.

The opposite function, the utterance presupposing the action, defines a class we may call *representatives*, including *control, supervision,* and *reporting*. In all these cases, the utterances would not have been uttered if the action had not occurred, although the action will often occur without the utterance.

A class of *coordinative* games can be defined by interdependent actions and utterances: the utterance occurs only in the presence of the action, and vice versa. The work coordination example from Section I.1.1 is a good example of this.

Finally, we can define a *commentative* type, including talk-in-the work, in which action and utterance contract constellation. Neither is necessary for the other.

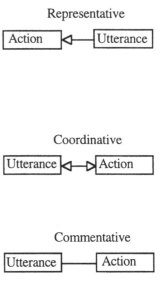

The preceding games all had function to specific tasks, bound to time and place. However, there is also a group of *regulative* games that are presupposed by the *schema* that manifests the tasks and actions. Another way of putting it is that regulative games has function to a set of tasks, not an individual one.

These games are normally played by management, but in the 1986 Postal Giro data, at least one game of this type is played on the shop floor, namely *instruction* and *forecasting*. The function of instruction is to reproduce an existing work schema, not to create it.

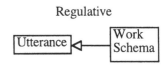

The external functions of the individual game type can be further specified. What characterizes work distribution within the directive group is that it reassigns a worker to a task, and the established function between worker and task is probably in many cases an interdependence, since work distribution has failed if the task is performed by another worker, or the worker performs another task. In addition, this interdependence between worker and task presupposes a particular situation, e.g. a particular place and time, since the worker is not just requested to do the task in the above example, she is requested to do it at a certain place (Check Control) and at a certain time (now).

The functional description of the purpose of these games is easy to relate to their internal structure. For example, since work distribution establishes a function between a person and a task, the interpersonal function of modality is expected to occur (our example contains two modals : *kan, skall* [can, must]) and to contain the "personal", deontic variants, as opposed to the "impersonal", epistemic ones in problem-solving games. Whereas the worker paradigm in work distribution is expected to contain many members (the example: *någon, jag, deltidare* [someone, I, a part-timer]) the place and task slots are not at issue and are expected to be filled with one fixed member or by none (the example has one fixed member of the place slot, *Check control*, and the task paradigm is even more backgrounded, since it is not explicitly filled, the supervisor assuming that the workers know what the task is).

The result of the preceding is the following linguistic definition of language games:

- *Analytic definition:* a language game is the smallest verbal unit that contracts cohesions with non-verbal actions. Games can be classified in types according to the functions they contract.
- *Synthetic definition:* A language game consists of a presupposition from a set of focus paradigms to a set of background ones. Games can be classified according to which paradigm types are focus and background, respectively.

I shall use this definition in the following sections to describe language games at the Postal Giro before computerization and the way they changed, and I shall subsequently show how this concept can be used in design of computer systems.

However, before I proceed I want to elaborate on a point that was hinted at in Section I.2.5. Using the concept of language games as a basis for design means that we assign the same roles to computer-based signs as we have just done to verbal utterances. Thus, the system will be decomposed into sign types according to the function they perform in relation to work.

As illustrated below, we will have signs that are presupposed by actions, and therefore are used in directive language games.

Other signs will occur only if certain actions have been done or a certain state of affairs obtains. The latter, which include many data bases and logs, are representatives, since they presuppose actions or states of affairs, and are interpreted as assertions about these actions and states.

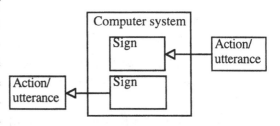

Fig. III.2.3. Language game perspective on computer systems.

This way of decomposing a computer system is different from the standard input-process-output model.

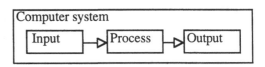

Fig. III.2.4. Data processing perspective on computer systems.

The former decomposes the system into components according to their function to the work environment, whereas the latter uses internal technical criteria for decomposition (collecting data from peripheral units versus storing it on disc or presenting it on printer or screen). In the perspective of the present book, the former decomposition should be the primary one, while the latter may be useful later when the modules are actually constructed, for example because data entry modules may share many routines for handling disc, readers, or keyboard although they are parts of completely different language games.

III.2.3. Using language games for analysis

This section serves two purposes: to illustrate how the concepts can be applied to empirical material, and to give an impression of language games at the Postal Giro before computerization.

III.2.3.1. Language games at the Postal Giro

The language game of work distribution
I start by analyzing the language game of *work distribution*.

(1) Holmqvist 1987: 38

A: Rosa stansar du två sekunder?

B: Två sekunder bara? Jag ska gå upp sen!

A: När då sen?

B: Ja när hon blir klar med den där listan.

[A: Rosa, will you punch for two seconds?

B: Just two seconds? I'm going up in a moment.

A: When?

B: Well, when she is finished with that list.]

(2) Holmqvist & Källgren 1987: 59

A: Birgit, ska du in på ändringscentralen?

B: Ja.

A: Tar du med det hära? (Turns to C) Har du någon rosa lapp? (Which B can take along. C gives a slip to A. who gives both to B. B looks at them)

B: Nä, det här är fel. Det måste va en typ på en tjugi...en makulering
   (C writes something on the slip)

C: Så här?

B: Mm

[A: Birgit, are you going to the change center?

B: Yes.

A: Could you take these along? (Turns to C) Have you got any red slips?
   (Which B can take along. C gives a slip to A. who gives both to B. B looks at them.)

B: Wait, this one is wrong. It must be one of those twenty...a cancel. (C writes something on the slip.)

C: Like this?

B: Uh-huh]

(3) Holmqvist 1987: 80

A: Ja nu är jag klar med kuverten.

Chef: Ja då kan du hjälpa Lena med checkarna.

[A: OK, now I'm finished with my envelopes.

Supervisor: OK, then you can help Lena with the checks.]

(4 = 7 in Section I.1.1) Holmqvist 1987: 80

Bass: Dom har ont om folk på checkringningen . Kan någon gå över dit?

A: Jag satt där i förra veckan.

B: Ja ska va hos tandläkaren klockan elva.

Bass: Men på eftermiddagen har dom en deltidare som kommer.

B: Då går jag väl då.

[Supervisor: They are short of people at check control. Can anyone go over there?

A: I was there last week.

B: I have to be at the dentist at eleven o'clock.

S: But in the afternoon they have a part-timer coming.

B: Well, I'll go then.]

This game aims at dividing a task or set of tasks among several persons, either because some of the employees are idle (3), because it is easier (2), or because the amount of work is too large to be finished within the allotted time (4).

The focus paradigms clearly include workers and time:

Workers:

jag /du /hon /Lena /Dom på checkringningen/ någon/ deltidare/ Rosa /Birgit

[I/ you/ she/ Lena /people at check control/ anyone/ part-timer/ Rosa/ Birgit]

Time:

nu/ då/ sen/ När då/ förra veckan/ klockan elva/ på eftermiddagen/ två sekunder/ när hon blir klar med den där listan

[now/ then/ in a moment/ at eleven o'clock/ in the afternoon/ two seconds/ when she is finished with that list]

and there is a rather large paradigm of verbs denoting transitions between tasks:

Task transitions:

är klar / blir klar med /hjälpa /gå över / ska gå upp/ ska in/ ska va /tar med/

[is finished/ help/ go over/ is going up/ go to/ have to be/ take along]

whereas the task paradigm itself is a rather small background paradigm:

Tasks:

stansar/ satt där [punch/ was there]

This is as expected and the only surprise is that objects of work is rather well articulated:

Object of work:

kuverten/ checkarna/ listan/ det hära/ rosa lapp

[envelope/ checks/ list/ these/ red slip]

As mentioned in the previous section, the move structures consist in pairs of utterances, the first of which is a request and the second enables or disenables the first by referring to rights and obligations in a rule-governed context of work. The *disenablement* relation covers relations like *Rosa, will you punch for two seconds?* ≈ *I'm going up in a moment,* and *Can anyone go over there?* ≈ *I was there last week,* while the *enablement* relation is exemplified by *OK, then you can help Lena with the checks* ≈ *OK, now I'm finished with my envelopes* and *Can anyone go over there?* ≈ *But in the afternoon they have a part-timer coming.*

Comparing to instruction

Let us now see if the method can differentiate between different games by comparing work distribution to *instruction*, a game aiming at giving an employee knowledge about tasks and work organization. Instruction is often performed as a part of work, and the verbal explanations are mingled with nonverbal acts:

(5) Holmqvist 1987: 93

Chef: Vill du visa Åsa hur man öppnar?

A: Du har aldrig gjort det här förut? Först tar du ut checken, så kollar du att numret stämmer...att den är underskriven. (B takes out check and card.)

A: Nej, ta bara ur checken och håll kvar kuvertet.

B: Är det bara det här jag ska kolla?

A: Jag kollar det här och sen lägger jag checken här och sen stämplar jag.

B: Den här har inte skrivit kontonummer.

(A rises and looks at B's check.)

A: Nä då får du skriva det. (Stays and looks). Och sedan ska du sortera upp, om det är över 25.000 ska du lägga checken för sig och kuvertet för sig.

[Supervisor: Can you show Åsa how to open?

A: You've never done it before? First you take out the check, then you see if the number matches... that it has been signed. (B takes out check and card.)

A: No, just take out the check, but keep the envelope.

B: Is this the only thing I'm supposed to check?

A: I check this and then I put the check here and then I stamp it.

B: This one hasn't written the account number.

A: Well, then you'll have to write it. (Stays and looks.) And then you should sort them, if it's more than 25,000 crowns, put the check and the envelope in separate places.]

The most striking difference from work distribution is in the worker paradigm. In work distribution, the articulation of the workers is important since the question is: *who is going to do it?* Thus /you/ and /I/ commute, so *I'm going up in a moment* has a different meaning than *You're going up in a moment*. But as mentioned in Section I.1.3, in some of the moves in instruction, the paradigm of worker designations does not commute at all, so that *I* and *you* are mere variants. Thus *First you take out the check* means the same as *First I take out the check* and *I put the check here* the same as *You put the check here*.

The reason is that the work process that is taught is single-person work and the focus is on how to perform the task, not on the worker doing it.

The time paradigms also show differences related to the different games. Acts are part of the instruction game, because the instructor is teaching by doing. Therefore, time indications in instruction are relative and imprecise *(förut/ först/ så/ sen/ då)* [before/ first/ then], acts being placed chronologically, relative to previous acts in the game. Work distribution does not contain any non-verbal acts, since the purpose of the game is precisely to determine who is going to do it. Since the time relations concern acts that are outside the game, they have to be more precise and absolute (*på eftermiddagen, klockan elva*) [in the afternoon, at eleven o'clock].

Finally, there is an interesting difference in the articulation of the tasks. The terms of instruction articulate a task with a conventional name (*öppna*, [open]) into a sequence of concrete acts (*tar ut/ kollar/ håll kvar/ lägger/ stämplar/ skriva/ sortera upp*) [take out/ keep/ put/ stamp/ write], whereas work distribution articulates *transitions* between tasks (*är klar/blir klar med*) [is finished] or mixing of tasks (*hjälpa/tar med*) [help, take along], not the tasks themselves.

Major differences are also found in the move contrasts. We do not find relations of enablement-disenablement. The relation between *First you take out the check* and *No, just take out the check, but keep the envelope* is clearly different from that between *Rosa, will you punch for two seconds?* and *I'm going up in a moment*. The former relation could be termed *correction*: the first move contains an instruction from the teacher which the learner tries to carry out, and the second move corrects the action by giving more details.

Comparing to problem-solving

The third game I will compare is *problem-solving*. As the name indicates, the aim of problem-solving games is to solve an unexpected problem. Typical problem-solving differs from instruction in that the solutions are not general, and the knowledge cannot be repeated directly in new situations, but rather serves as a analogy or comparison.

(7) Holmqvist 1987: 96 (=8 in Section I.1.1)

A: Are you going to keep that one later?

B: Well, I don't know, there was a number I changed that I had to go and look up in the book, do I have to change it in the list, do you think?

A: The hell with it.

(8) Holmqvist 1987: 97

A: Lena, this one is 143 crowns out.

B: It shouldn't be out, should it?

A: Nope.

B: Well, then you/ well, then you/ You aren't out by that amount anywhere else, are you?

A: Not in the batch I've been working with.

B: Well, then we'll have to take it out and then we write a slip saying "under wrong cover" and then we send it on down.

(doubtful silence from A)

B: Just write "under wrong cover" or "put under wrong cover" or something like that, they'll understand.

(A goes away, but comes back after a while.)

A: Hey, now I've found another cover.

B: You did, huh, well, and it fits in there?

(9) Holmqvist 1987: 99

(A is sitting checking, B comes over with a card she doesn't know what to do with.)

A: Well, I wouldn't worry about it, there should be a register card for that one.

B: Did you say that I should take the register card for this one?

A: Yeah, this one, yeah/nope, there's no giro there.

B: The hell with it then.

(B goes away and comes back after a minute or two.)

B: Eva, when all this is sent on, should it be put in some special place?

A: That gets sent in the tube.

The external function of the problem-solving games is similar to work distribution in creating a cohesion between worker and action or task, but with respect to focus and background, they are opposites, since in problem-solving, the worker is the given background while the task is the problematic issue, whereas work distribution takes the task for granted and focuses on the worker.

Therefore the commutation between *I* and *you* is suspended in several cases, so that *Well, I wouldn't worry about it* is synonymous with *Well, you shouldn't worry about it,* and the task is articulated into concrete subtasks, as in instruction: *change a number, look up in the book, change it in the list, write a slip, take register card for [ta registerkort på], send in the tube [skickas i röret].*

Since the work is rule governed, the solution to problematic situations is not to invent some suitable course of action, but to identify the rule that should apply in this case. One could say that the network of rules is fixed and determined from above. However, in some situations it is not clear which rules to apply, and the task of the workers is to fit these situations into the existing rule network. In the following series, the first move describes a *problem definition*, and the second move identifies the corresponding *rule to be followed.* This pair can be called *rule seeking*

Problem:

> Lena, this one is 143 crowns out.

Rule:

> then we'll have to take it out and then we write a slip saying "under wrong cover" and then we send it on down.

Problem:

> there was a number I changed that I had to go and look up in the book, do I have to change it in the list, do you think?

Rule:

> The hell with it.

Besides rule-seeking, problem-solving often contains a relation that could be called *error determination*: the first part refers to a possible error, and the second part confirms or disconfirms the possibility. For example, *You aren't out by that amount anywhere else, are you?* suggest a particular error type, and the following *Not in the batch I've been working with* disconfirms it. The properties of a particular language game depend both upon its external function and its work context: work distribution and problem-solving are good examples of this. The articulation of the worker and task transitions of work distribution is due to the external function of the game, whereas the relation of rule seeking is motivated by the fact that the work context is rule governed. If the context had not been rule governed, the move articulations would probably contain different dyads, e.g. *rule-invention*. In the same way, the fact that tasks have only one participant is responsible for cancelling the commutation between *you*, *I* and *we* in instruction that otherwise is operative in other tasks involving several persons.

With these few examples I have tried to show that the language concept can be used to differentiate different types of games, that the analysis can be done mainly by traditional linguistic methods, like collecting paradigms, and that the result of the analysis can be related to the function of the game relative to the work context.

III.2.3.2. Language game changes

After having given an impression of the games played before introduction of the PGP-system, I shall now describe changes in three of these games, namely problem-solving, instruction and internal reporting, and describe two new games, forecasting and mystery solving.

Problem-solving and instruction

In the new situation, work is still rule governed, specific courses of actions being governed by specific conditions, so we still have rule seeking. However, the paradigm of errors and rules has grown since the individual worker is responsible for a larger part of the working process. This causes the problem-solving situations to become longer, since there are more conditions to investigate and more actions to choose between, but the general structure is much the same as before.

A typical problem-solving game in the new organization can start in this way with error-determinations:

E: That is an adding mistake.

Y: Yes.

E: Yes, it is.

...

E: Card missing?

X: Well, I didn't have the card then, you know, then I put it to one side, for the time being, though we'll sit on it, now we *fetch job, enter job number 1*, it was the first job, you see.

and end with a rule-seeking of considerable length:

E: You'll have to destroy it or hand it in the box.

X: Right, that's it.

E: He's, he's...

X: Well, let's see now, then I should, then I'll destroy the whole batch.

E: Let's see, hmm, it's sure to be scan, this one's going to be a real mess.

X: Wait a minute, let's see, my mind's a blank.

E: What are you going to do?

X: No, I'll destroy it.

E: Are you going to destroy the whole batch?

X: Sure, why not?

E: Well, you can if you want to, or else you can just turn in this one, and then they'll take care of it now.

X: Yeah, I could do that, too, right.

E: But then you'll have to do it like this...

X: Like this?

E: Do it like this, I think: take a little slip, and then put it on the C card, and tell them that it's a C card, then when you get it back, then you put it all in this box here.

[E: Det där får du macka bort eller lämna in i buren.

X: Ja just det.

E: Han har ju, han har ju..

X: Ja, vänta nu får vi se, då får jag ta, då mackar jag bort hela bunten.

E: Nu ska vi se mrmrmr, det är säkert scan, det ska bli korv av det här.

X: Vänta nu, få se, å nu står det still.

E: Vad ska du göra?

X: Nej jag ska ju macka det...

E: Ska du macka bort hela bunten där?

X: Ja skulle jag inte det?

E: Jo det kan du göra om du vill, eller också kan du lämna in det här, då så får dom fixa det här nu.

X: Ja det kan jag också göra ja, ja.

E: Mmen då får det vara så här alltså.

X: Så...?

E: Gör då så här tycker jag, ta en liten lapp, å så sätter du på C-kortet och talar om, att det är ett C-kort, sen när ni får tillbaks det, då lägger ni alltihopa i lådan här [1].]

Another difference is that discussions of the consequences of a solution are often appended to the conversation. The reason for this is partly that the work organization is new, but also that the workers have got more responsibility.

Analysis of tape recordings like these can provide many good ideas for design and redesign of the system. We will learn which errors typically cause trouble (*sum error* versus *missing card*), the words they use to describe the errors (*felsummering* [sum error] versus *kort saknas* [card missing]), and which kinds of questions they would like to answer. In the problem-solving data, we found questions like

- Which account type (*bank account* versus *personal account*) corresponds to a given account number type?
- Where can a missing card be located?
- What does a plus on the screen mean?

The system can be made to support such conversations by providing relevant information at the right time.

When the problem has been defined, the workers must choose the right rule to apply and this decision also generates questions: in the example, the choice is between destroying the batch, *macka bort,* or handing it in, *lämna in i buren.* The system could support this part of the problem-solving game by presenting the possible rules to the workers and the conditions under

---

[1] The box for uncompleted jobs.

which they apply. I shall later give an example of a re-design based on analysis of problem-solving conversations.

The next game I shall comment on is *instruction*.

The data contain many examples of where a worker teaches a colleague how to perform various tasks. When the system was introduced, some workers were appointed instructors and given formal training. Afterwards they helped and taught their colleagues on the shop floor. The teaching is informal and integrated into normal work.

If we compare to the instruction games before computerization, we note an important difference in the situational context. In instruction in a non-computerized context, the teacher issues a direction, the learner executes it, and the teacher interprets the learner's action and possibly corrects it, cf. example 5 above. The same pattern was found in the garage, cf. example 5 in Section I.1.1. Both directions and corrections are interpretations produced in the situation. For example, the determiners and pronouns are bound to objects that either both persons can see or to nouns previously introduced in the conversation.

In the computerized work context, the actions of the learner are symbolic and therefore already interpreted by the designer. Therefore, the teacher's situation-specific interpretation of the actions gives way to *quotations* of the canned, situation-independent interpretation.This is clearly illustrated in the following example, where the instructor E helps X to obtain a job which has previously been processed by a colleague. The underlined phrases are quotations from screen or keyboard.

E: Vi tar det här igen, <u>hämta.</u>

X: <u>Slå in jobnummer</u>, ja men det missar det blir samma igen då.

E: Nä då.

X: Jasså <u>inge.</u>

E: <u>Det finns inge mer arbete i detta job</u>, då är det bara för att hon hade inte gjort klar bunten därborta.

X: Nä nähä.

/.../

E: Där <u>eskar</u> du då, så att du får fram den.

X: <u>Nästa bunt.</u>

[E: We do this again, <u>fetch</u>.

X: <u>Enter job number</u>, well if it is wrong, then it'll be the same one again.

E: Well then.

X: Well, it says <u>nothing</u>.

E: <u>There is no further work in this job</u>, that's only because she hadn't finished the batch over there.

X: Oh, uh-huh.

/.../

E: Then you <u>esc</u> so that you get it.

X: <u>Next batch.</u>]

Consider how the first two remarks cohere. In her first remark, the instructor tells X what function key to use by quoting the keyboard labels *(we do this again, <u>fetch</u>)*, in the next X quotes the screen for the next command she uses *(<u>Enter job number</u>)*, and remarks on the resulting feedback *(Well, it says <u>nothing</u>)*. The cohesion is not effected by means of linguistic textual functions like anaphoric chains or theme/rheme structures, but by the sequence of signs presented on the screen. The global dialogue structure is to a large degree structured by the system, not by the speakers.

The frequent use of quotations in instruction games is interesting for several reasons. The first reason is that it emphasizes the educational functions of the system interface. The concepts of the interface must be designed in such a way that they can be used for teaching purposes, because they will by necessity be part of instruction games. The other reason is that instruction is one of the most clear and tangible loci for language change. In instruction, the interface and the work language meet for the first time and gradually form a computer-based register. The users are trying out new terms for the first time; some of them may never be used again outside this particular use situation, whereas others will enter the language of the department and become a part of the meaning potential always at their disposal.

After having discussed changes in existing language games, I shall now describe three new kinds of games.

Internal reporting

In an organization based on a division of labor, coordination between tasks is important, and computers can be used to give better information to workers about work progress by their colleagues.

Before the PGP-system was introduced, work progress was reported every half hour to the reception desk. Each section reported how many boxes they had coded, and the information was routed to the head of department, who calculated when work could be finished, contacted the computer department, and redistributed work *(jämning)*.

Now, however, the module for *external reporting* of the PGP-system also enables decentralized *internal reporting*. It is possible to see how much work the individual sections (which at the time of recording only included two) have completed, and our data include several conversations where this information is discussed and used. In the following conversation, the workers are doing another job, entering a new date, and information about work progress accidentally attracts their attention:

X: Today's date.
E: The next day.
X: It's tomorrow, whoops, right, we have three jobs left
E: They have one each.
X: And they have six on (seventeen).

[X: Dagens dato.
E: Nästa dag.
X: Det ör morgondagen, oj oj oj, jaha, vi har tre job kvar.
E: Dom har varsitt.
X: Och dom har sex på sjutt(on) ja.]

What is going on in these conversations where the workers interpret information on the screen describing the work progress of their colleagues? Let us take a closer look at it. The screen shows information like

Section	Total Jobs	Completed Jobs
17	66	62
18	91	88

signifying that the total number of jobs of section 17 is 66, and that 62 are completed. Is it reasonable to say that the workers of section 17 communicate this information to those of section 18?

According to the definition of communication given in Section I.2.2.4, it *is* communication, since communication was (carefully) defined as a presupposition from an act to a symbolic act or object, and the information in the reporting view above is clearly a symbolic object which is presupposed by the conversations.

However, from a psychological point of view, the signal transmission cannot unreservedly be classified as communication, since it is not intended. When a worker defines or completes a job and thereby changes the numbers under *Total Jobs* and *Completed Jobs*, she is not intending her keystrokes to form a message to be interpreted by a receiver but is just working. Without her will or intention, the system intercepts her signals, processes them, and composes a sign describing what she is doing.

This phenomenon is quite common: for example, when a person enters data into a data base, she is not in control of the way the data appears in the output, since this depends upon the query and the rest of the data in the base. Compared to other media, the computer is unique in being able to manipulate the ingoing signal and combine it with other signals, so that the outgoing signal is an aggregation of many data coming from different sources and forms a message that none of the "senders" may intend or know of.

This new feature is often considered a liability and potential danger, because the "sender" has lost control over his message. This concern is real enough, and is based upon the fact that computer-based signs can hide some of the language games users take part in. Workers may believe that they are partaking in a language game of ordering and internal reporting, whose participants are employees on the same department, whereas in reality they also partake in external reporting, since the data is tapped, aggregated and sent to a third terminal or printer, where an external report of the work load is produced for management[1] .

However, since the ability of computers to manipulate and "distort" messages is one of their main characteristics, a purely defensive strategy is of no use, since it will only result in limitations and restrictions, not in invention and creativity. The above examples show that data tapping and unintended communication can in fact have useful purposes for the providers of information, as well. It can make the work place more public, making the work organization and work progress transparent to the workers, thereby supporting them in coordinating their work, and enhancing decentralization and self-management.

What should be required of systems like the PGP system is that the hidden communication be made explicit and presented as real communication, partly because senders have a right to know which kind of communication they are participating in, partly because the information can then better be used for coordinative purposes by the users themselves.

Forecasting. Building the new work schema

The external function of *forecasting* is to build up an understanding of the constraints between actions and consequences of actions, including both worker and computer system. Forecasting was very infrequent and short before computerization, but occupies a fair portion of our tapes. The focus paradigm of forecasting is dependencies between actions, expressed by modality *(can, must)*, mode (conditionals), and temporal conjunctions *(when, then, before)*, the thematic question being: *is it possible to do task A before task B?* Forecasting differs from instruction, the other regulative, in that in the former two or more persons together *create* a schema, whereas in the latter one person is *reproducing* a schema.

---

[1] Bøgh Andersen & Mathiassen 1984.

In the next example, a group of workers discuss the correct sequence of the subtasks *sända iväg låda, slå in datum, stänga datakomb, köra kort* [send box, enter date, close "Datakomb"]. They know it is possible to change the date to tomorrow's date, but have been told that this causes the system to close the transmission line from the accounting department to the computer department, so that no more material can be sent.

(10)

A: Well, we can enter the date, Monday's, but we can't begin to run the cards, because it'll wind up in ...box two.

B: I've closed it now.

C: But can you really do that?

D: They close automatically, when you start this one.

C: Yeah, but can it be closed, I mean, we can't close it until we've sent off our box.

D: No, but it probably closes automatically when we've sent off our box, that's how I understood it.

D: On the whole, you can balance the day's books on that one before you're done, didn't we do like that down there? Once you're finished with your red job, then you can reset...the day's books on that one.

C: On that one, right, and then she said that you could reset that one, but if you reset it, then it says that the *datakom* is closed. Yup, and if it closes, then we can't send off our box.

D: Well, there must be some block on it, I think that the only way that was on the course that was important about this, it was, because we had excercise material, otherwise that's all supposed to be automatic, you're not supposed to think of all that, 'cause my God what errors you might get otherwise, you just can't allow such errors, there have to be blocks put in.

Although task designations occur frequently, they do not form a focus paradigm since they do not substitute in similar contexts as they would have done in problem-solving. Instead, the focus paradigm is the *relation* between tasks like enablement, presuppositions, entailment and prevention.

To see this, consider the beginning of the game. Here we have a modal contrast between *can* and *can't:*

> We *can* enter the date
> We *can't* begin to run the cards

a temporal/modal contrast between the perfect *have closed* [har stängt] and the modal *can do* [gå att göra]:

> I've closed it now.

But can you really do that?

and a temporal contrast between *when* [när] and *before, until* [innan]:

They close automatically, *when* you start this one.
[Dom stängs automatiskt, *när* du sätter på den.]

We can't close it *until* we've sent off our box.
[Den kan vi väl inte stänga *innan* vi har sänt iväg våran låda.]

It probably closes automatically *when* we've sent off our box.
[Den stängs väl automatiskt *när* vi har sänt iväg lådan.]

If the game had been conventional problem-solving with function to a particular action, the contrast would not have been between modality and temporal sequence, but between tasks (Are we going to *enter the date* or *run cards?*), but since the game has function to an emerging work schema, it is the relations between actions that are focused upon. Forecasting produces an interpretation of the system in terms of a fragment of a work schema, and it is no coincidence that the systematization efforts results in a work schema, not in a technical description of the computer system. We find the same tendency to view the system in close connection to the work schema in the worker-written manuals that consistently interpret the keys and commands in terms of actions, opportunities for or purposes of actions, or properties of work objects.

Solving mysteries: maintaining the computer-based register

Computer-based work is always subject to two kinds of interpretations coming from the two components of the computer-based register: the designer's conception as it appears via screen responses and the workers' as it can be heard from their oral conversations.

Sometimes these twin interpretations do not concord, the computer-based register threatens to fall apart, and the function of the mystery-solving game is to reconcile and connect the two interpretations.

Mystery-solving differs from forecasting in that it has no direct function relative to tasks, but merely results in an interpretation. It is similar to problem-solving in that it is motivated by errors or events that look like errors, but whereas the workers in problem-solving are obliged to find and correct the error, the participants in mystery-solving have no such obligations.

Mysteries are caused by a mismatch between the interpretation intended by the designers, and the interpretations generated by the workers in terms of the tasks they are doing. The workers believe they are doing one thing but are informed that they are doing another. This clash of interpretations can cause users "not to know what they are doing". Our data contains small as well as large mysteries, but all follow the same pattern. First we have a *mystery description* that consists of two parts: a description of the task I believe I am doing and a quotation of an incomprehensible system response that gives the system designer's interpretation of what I did. In one small conversation, a worker has entered data into a card before the computer has finished processing the previous one, and the system issues a response that makes no sense for the current card, only for the previous one. The worker describes the task she believes she was doing *(I entered the transaction code on this card)* followed by the inappropriate interpretation by the designer *(later it came up that it did not tally on the previous one)*. After a mystery description follows often an *explanation invention* given in everyday terms. In the present case, the workers explain the mystery by saying that the computer has to think a bit *(den måste tänka ett tag)* before it is ready for the next card.

The following episode presents a major mystery that challenges the workers' basic understanding of what they are doing and involves four to five people, including an instructor. The workers discover that fliers remain in the flier file, although they know that all fliers from today have been removed[1]. The conversation starts with a mystery description

L: Hey Anki, what's this?

L: Two, why, what's this, these are fliers, I see that it was a flier.

A: But it was empty yesterday, but this has to be a check flier, right?

L: Well, this is strange, I don't understand this, look here when I sit here, look, "Number of fliers 8".

A: But, 8...what day was it, the 8th, right?

L: But the number of fliers here.

A: ...370, well I didn't think it looked...

L: Well, we had that before, but they disappeared, after all, you know, the ones we had.

A: Here's the payment order too.

that thematizes the inconsistency between the system's interpretation of the events *(these are fliers,"Number of fliers 8")* and the worker's own interpretation of her action *(they disappeared, after all)*.

---

[1] I do not know the precise course of events leading up the mystery, but it could have been something like the following. During the completion task cards are moved into the flier file, and other workers who are missing the cards fetch them. At the end of the day, inspection of the flier file results in the message *Number of records = 0*, since all fliers have been fetched. The next day, however, one of the workers by coincidence takes a look at the fliers, and reads the message *Number of records – 8*, which she interprets as *a lot of fliers stay on.*

How can fliers remain in the file when we have removed them? She begins inventing explanations: maybe they are *removed cards*, which she remembers can legally stay on in the system from one day to another because one of the instructors made sure of that? This explanation is not accepted and the mystery is redescribed in more detail. An instructor is summoned, and she suggests that their interpretation of the events is wrong and the system's right by suggesting that they have done a different task than they believe they did, looking at old fliers instead of new fliers: *Maybe you are in "old fliers"?* They immediately try to verify the explanation, and in the meantime go on inventing new explanations like *Maybe you can go back and see them a certain number of days* and recounting the previous mystery which turned out not to be dangerous. Verification proceeds, and the conversation continues along the same pattern with invention of possible explanations and verifications. The final hypothesis is that the fliers stay on in the system for three days, and then disappear and they generate a prediction that will verify the hypothesis

> Y: They'll probably disappear later.
> L: Yes, I think so, with the others that disappeared.
> X: We'll find out when the new ones come in.
> Y: They'll be gone for sure on Monday.

The conversation can be viewed as a combat between two interpretations: the system's and their own. The battle rages back and forth, sometimes they insist upon their own interpretation, sometimes the system's gets the upper hand, as when the instructor suggests that they had not been doing what they believed they did. The tapes show that they are beginning to tackle these situations of conflicting interpretations by developing a collective language game which has a striking similarity to the normal scientific ways of arguing. First a mystery description consisting of a conflict of interpretations: *these are fliers* versus *they disappeared.* Then invention of three explanations, (1) they are not looking at the fliers but at removed cards, (2) they are looking at "old fliers", or (3) the fliers stay on for three days, of which the last is chosen as the most probable. Finally they suggest a method for verifying the selected hypothesis.

The lessons to be learned from these examples are the following:

- The users are not only using the system as a tool, they also want to understand it, and when understanding fails, they make it an object of "scientific" investigation.
- The users' only access to important parts of their work objects and tools goes via computer-based signs.

It is instructive to compare this situation to situations where the old coding machines malfunction:

A: Kerstin, where's that envelope you use to clean the machines?

B: Here.

A: If you put me on this machine tomorrow, I'll cut your head off, it just keeps giving me grief.

Holmqvist 1986: 73

The workers can themselves clean the physical machines by physical means, and malfunction does not initiate research projects but grumbling. While dirt can be seen and removed manually, mysteries and bugs in a computer system are properties of computer-based signs calling for analysis and explanation, not for a piece of cleaning paper.

- The conversation is not very well supported by the system and contains more repetitions and unverified guesses than necessary. The designers who provide the computer-based signs must keep in mind that they should not only inform the users of the daily routine work, but that *it is also their responsibility to provide signs that enable users to understand the system in breakdown situations,* because breakdowns are certain to occur and signs are the users' only access to the system.

III.2.4. Using language games in design

After having looked at the language games played in the new work organization and suggesting that analysis of the conversations could be a good help to design, the time has come to substantiate these claims. The language games I shall be interested in are games in which some moves presuppose that certain information is available on the screen. The problem-solving games are of this kind, since the system must present information about the faulty batch in order for the workers to discuss which course of action to take.

In situations like these, two types of symbols will occur: the worker's utterances and the computer-based signs on the screen, of which the former will often contain quotations of the latter. The utterances will typically presuppose the computer-based signs, since the former cannot occur without the latter, whereas the screen can display information that does not generate conversations.

The quotations can be more or less loosely integrated into the verbal language. At one end of the scale, the screen quotations can occur as an independent isolated unit of discourse, as when an utterance consists of one complete screen quotation: *Det finns inge mer arbete i detta job.* [There is no more work in this job.]. In other cases, the screen fragment is a part of an utterance, but the internal structure of the expression does not correspond to its external syntactic function in the utterance. It is for example not uncommon to use command names as objects, without regard to their syntactic structure. In *nu kan jag... ta "sök efter frånkonto"* [Now I can take "search from-account"], the phrase sök efter frånkonto is object, but its structure is an imperative sentence, which normally cannot occur as an object. In some cases, screen elements are completely integrated in the work language. For example, key designations like ESC (the escape key) and the verifiera [verify] command can be turned into verbs with full inflection *där eskar du* [There you ESC] and *När du ska verifiera då...* [when you verify then...].

Analysis of the move structure of these games can teach us which information must be available at which time, and one possible guideline is simply that *the syntactical dependencies between the computer-based signs should be the same as those that hold between the verbal moves they support.* As a simple example, consider the relations between the query and answer part of a data base system. If the conversations in which the data base is used consist of a part in which the query is discussed followed by a part in which reference is made to both the answer and the query, then the system should contain a two member syntagm, query entry + answer list, of which the latter should presuppose the former. The query can occur alone, but the answer list is always accompanied by the query. The rationale behind the conversation structure could be that output cannot be evaluated and discussed without reference to the input, and therefore it would be bad design if the output simply replaced the input on the screen, thereby building a paradigm and not a syntagm.

The same rule can be applied at a lower level of detail where we can compare the period and sentence structure of the games to the structure of the computer-based signs. A university administration may be interested in getting statistics of how students move from one major to another, and in conversations and reports want to make statements like *Many students stop studying linguistics and start on computer science* that contain subordinate (deep structure) clauses like *(study linguistics)* embedded in main clauses with aspectual verbs like *stop* and *start.* Conversations like these will not be properly supported by data bases only expressing simple statements like *Smith studied linguistics in 1987. Smith studied computer science in 1988.* Another simple example is the topic-comment structure of the sentences. If conversations normally use the name as topic and have the student's registration number as comment *(Smith has registration number 1234),* then the system should not do the opposite, presenting information like *(Number*

1234. Name = Smith). At a more abstract level we can describe the topic of the conversations and use that as a basis for deciding which information types should be provided by the system.

III.2.4.1. Support for problem-solving

I shall start by demonstrating how the structure of moves in a language game can be used as a basis for design, and my data is the problem-solving conversations of the tapes. As will be remembered, problem-solving games consist of *rule-seeking,* that again consists of a *problem definition* and an indication of the *rule to be followed.* The latter can optionally be followed by a detailed *method discussion,* for example concerning the exact sequence of keystrokes to use. *Error determination* is an optional subgame serving to define the problematic situation. It consists of a *possible error* followed by an indication of whether the conditions for the error are *satisfied* or not.

There is government between the error types of the *problem definition* and the actions of *the rule to be followed.* For example, *card missing* governs the action *search for it in the flier file,* while *sum error under ten crowns* is corrected by *changing the sum,* and *missing signature* requires the worker to *destroy the batch.*

The structure of the game is approximately as follows:

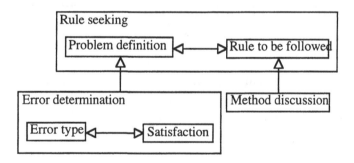

Fig. III.2.5. Functional analysis of problem-solving conversations.

At present the rules sought in problem-solving conversations are listed in written manuals together with the conditions under which to apply them, and one idea for improving the system would simply consist in having them on-line. It might make them easier to change when the work organization changes, and users would not have to shift their attention from screen to table to consult them. In addition, presentation of general rules could be combined with system-generated suggestions about which one to choose. In the sketch below, problematic situations are shown to the left, and the rules to be followed to the right. The system puts a check-mark next to the most probable error and also next to the rule (or rules) to be followed. Clicking a check-marked error type brings more detailed information to be used in error determination and clicking the rule to the right presents information about how to apply it .

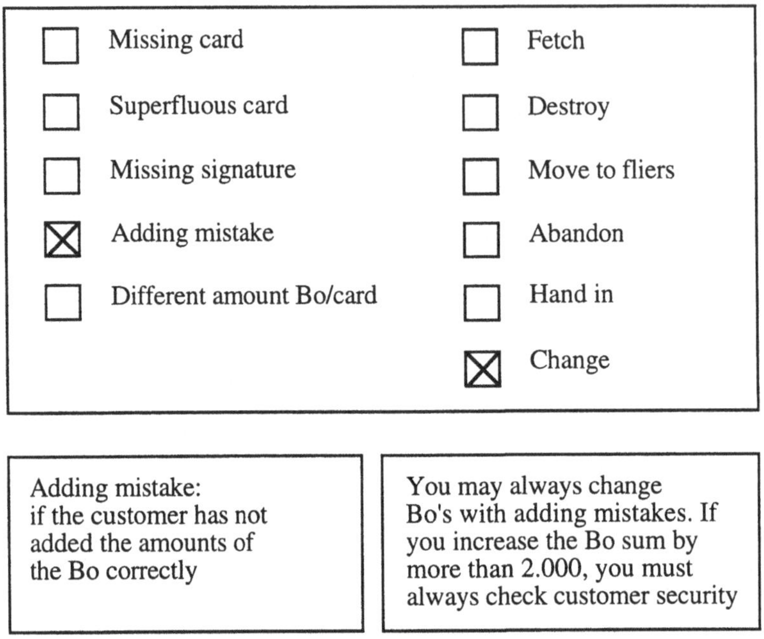

☐	Missing card	☐	Fetch
☐	Superfluous card	☐	Destroy
☐	Missing signature	☐	Move to fliers
☒	Adding mistake	☐	Abandon
☐	Different amount Bo/card	☐	Hand in
		☒	Change

Adding mistake: if the customer has not added the amounts of the Bo correctly

You may always change Bo's with adding mistakes. If you increase the Bo sum by more than 2.000, you must always check customer security

Fig. III.2.6. Support for problem-solving conversations.

Note how the interface mirrors the syntactic dependencies between the moves of the problem-solving game. The error+ rule signs always appear together, because error definition and discussion of the rule to be followed are interdependent, one presupposing the other, whereas the other two signs below are optional since the conversation parts they support are optional. In addition, the government between error type and rule are signified by check-marks.

III.2.4.2. Presence is not enough

After having considered the move-structure, I shall now comment on the sentence structure, and its relation to the structure and style of computer-based signs.

In Section II.2.2.1, I defined object style as a particular way of coding objects and actions: actions are coded as directions between transient and handling features, while objects are coded as permanent icons. This coding achieves a certain kind of similarity between expression and content since it codes user actions by graphical processes, and user objects as stable graphical objects, and the hypothesis is that similarities of this kind enhance a feeling of direct engagement.

Section III.1.1 showed that at least a part of the work language is suited for coding with direct manipulation techniques, since it is used for acting *in* the work situation, not for describing it from an outside vantage point.

But the new analytical language games of forecasting and mystery solving described in Section III.2.3.2 reminded us that there are language games where the workers want to stand back from their involvement, making classes of tasks and their interrelations the theme of discourse.

Thus, the workers need to look at the work from two different perspectives and these perspectives should be supported by two different styles of interaction.

This idea, that different types of tasks require different kinds of symbolic support, is not new. Rasmussen 1983, discussing systems design for process plants, argues that there are three main types of actions: skill-based behavior (which covers automated, only partially conscious actions), rule-based behavior (which consists in following stored rules), and knowledge-based behavior (in which goals are explicitly formulated and methods for achieving the goal constructed). Three types of behavior exploit different types of signs: signals (which have no symbolic meaning but only function as stimuli), signs (which refer to specific stored patterns of behavior) and symbols (which are associated with concepts that can be used in analysis and problem solving). Rasmussen & Lind 1981 suggest that process plant operators need display information on different levels of abstraction: one kind of information to answer questions of the "why" type, another for "what" questions, and still another for "how" questions.

In the following, I shall discuss which consequences can be drawn with respect to screen design in the PGP system if we want to support the two perspectives found in the tapes.

The involved perspective

In the *involved perspective* where the speaker talks *in* a situation, cf. Section II.2.2.3, the focus of speaker attention is on the current goal and the relevant objects, the tense of the utterances is present, their agents are the speakers, pronouns are used instead of nouns, deixis (here, there) instead of prepositional phrases (on the table), the context of the utterances is known by the speakers and therefore not verbalized, the utterances often consist of simple sentences or parts of sentences, and cohere with the work process, not with preceding or following utterances.

The typical sentence in these conversations is a simple sentence with a verb denoting a task, and noun phrases designating worker, work objects, and tools, for example: *jag ska macka bort den* [I am going to take it away].

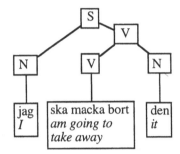

Fig. III.2.7. The involved perspective. Typical sentence structure.

This kind of perspective can be facilitated with an object-style interaction intended to make workers experience the work process as a presence.

The objects denoted by noun phrases are coded as permanent icons, and the processes expressed by the verb are coded by directions between transient and handling features of the icons.

Process ~ verb ~ directions between transient and handling features
Objects ~ noun phrases ~ permanent features

An additional argument for having some kind of similarity between expression and content is that the computer system itself is built as a mirror image of the paper system (cf. the introduction to Part III), and the users need to check if the states of the two systems correspond. For example, if the system asserts that a certain job is unfinished (a red job), then the corresponding paper cards should be placed in a certain tray with a red header, and if a data box is sent to the computer department, then the corresponding plastic box should also be on its way. Since the system is built as a mirror image, it is important that users can easily check if the image is true; thus I believe that it will be helpful to them to design the screen as a stylized picture of the physical work place and its objects.

The detached perspective

But besides involved perspective, we also find examples of detached perspective where the speakers talk *about* a situation. The clearest examples are found in mystery-solving and forecasting. The focus of speaker attention is no longer on the current goals of the work but on actions and relations between actions, either past events as in mystery-solving:

But isn't it something we cancel*led*, cancel*led* out, we had them from *the 6th*, before, that *stayed there for two days*.

or possible future events in forecasting:

and then she said that you could reset that one, but *if* you reset it, *then* it says that the datakom is closed. Yup, and *if* it closes, *then* we can't send off our box.

The tense of the utterances is *past* (mystery solving) or *future/conditional* (forecasting), their agents may be other persons than the speakers or may be indefinite, *descriptive phrases* are used instead of pronouns and deixis, the context of the utterances is presented and partially described by the speakers, the utterances can consist of *complex sentences* with subordinate clauses, and they *cohere internally*, not with the work process that is suspended.

The typical sentence could be represented by *men ställer man om den, så säger den att datakom stängs* [but if you reset it, then it says that the datakom is closed]. It consists of three sentences, of which the first one is a subordinate adverbial to the second one.

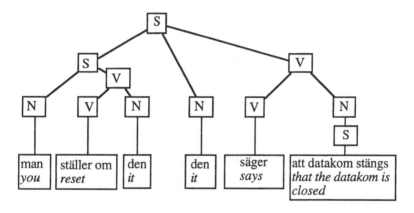

Fig. III.2.8. The detached perspective.
Typical sentence structure.

An even clearer example of detached perspective is found in the coordinator's speech from Section III.1.1. He uses complex sentences in which the noun phrases contain nominalizations with a verb kernel. Example: *slå ihop datafångsten med kompletteringen* [merge the data input with completion] (see Fig. III.2.9).

These sentences are very difficult or impossible to paraphrase in object style. In this latter example, it would mean that the verb of the main sentence *(slå ihop)* should be coded by transient features of its noun phrases, but they are themselves verbs and should also be coded by transient features. So the verb *slå ihop* [merge] would have to be coded by changes of changes! To me, this concept is difficult or impossible to envisage - direct manipulation seems to be like first order predicate calculus in that although it allows one to describe properties and relations between objects it does not allow properties of properties, and relations between relations.

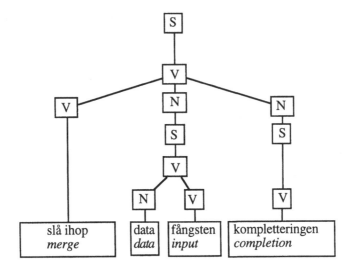

Fig. III.2.9. The detached perspective.
Typical sentence structure.

To support detached conversation I believe that some kind of textual task style interaction is the most appropriate: tasks are then represented by permanent features, e.g. verbs, and not by cohesions between handling and transient features, and there is no difficulty in representing verbs whose cases contain sentences or nominalizations.

On the basis of this data and reflections, I wish to make two major modifications in the redesign.

III.2.4.3. Support for mystery-solving: logging the past

Firstly, I propose that the topic of the system should not only include the present state of thousands of cards as it does now, but also past and future actions. The former could be achieved by letting the system record a selection of the actions performed, and providing facilities for playing this log. Such a log would be helpful in the *mystery-solving* situation previously described, where the workers cannot understand why fliers that have been removed from the flier file continue to stay in it. By playing the log backwards and forwards, the workers would have had opportunities for discovering patterns in the fliers' behavior. At present, mystery-solving conversations consist mostly of guesswork, and much time is spent on them because the workers want to understand the rules, not only comply with them. Given a log, a future conversation about fliers like that in Section III.2.3.2 could run as follows:

L: Hey Anki, what's this?

L: Two, why, what's this, these are fliers, I see that it was a flier.

A: But it was empty yesterday, but this has to be a check flier, right?

L: Well, this is strange, I don't understand this, look here when I sit here, look, "Number of fliers 8".

A: But, 8...what day was it, the 8th, right?

L: But the number of fliers here.

A: ...370, well I didn't think it looked...

L: Well, we had that before, but they disappeared, after all, you know, the ones we had.

/.../

X: We checked yesterday, but we didn't have any flier left then.

L: I don't understand why they pop up.

At this point, the workers can play the log in order to verify a hypothesis about what happened since yesterday:

L: Let's play the log from yesterday morning.

X: OK. Look there, now the fliers start to come.

L: And now they start to disappear - look, this was mine I remember.

X: Four o'clock - all fliers are fetched as we thought.

L: Now the date shifts - hey, look, all the old fliers pop up again!

Replaying the log has now told them that they have not made any mistakes, for example by looking into the file of old fliers as the instructor in the real conversation suggested. The next step would be to set up hypotheses about the rules governing the behavior of the fliers:

X: Maybe you can only go back a certain number of days to see them.

Y: Yes, I believe that too - maybe they just stay on for two or three days.

X: Let's go back three days and see what happens.

And playing the log may in fact verify that the fliers pop up and stay on for three days:

X: It is them, all right.

L: They're the ones we removed.

X: They seem to stay on for approximately three days.

Y: And then they disappear.

L: The ones from today should have disappeared on Monday.

In what follows, I shall continue to use the method of rewriting conversations. It simply consists in looking at existing conversations, discovering lines of arguments that could be improved, or ideas that were not explored further because the necessary information is lacking, and then sketching facilities that might enable the required pieces of conversation. There are two advantages in this technique:

- It is based upon real events, which curbs tendencies to design facilities that have no connection with real needs.
- It concretely shows the future uses of the facility.

The actual PGP-system does contain logs. However, one log is only about technical events in the machine, such as *Checking pool readability, pool-size = 20505600* and is clearly addressed to the technicians. Other logs are used for reporting, but although the wording to some degree is taken from the work language, it also contains technical passages, passages which the tapes showed to be difficult for the users to understand and use.

It is important that the facility describes the events in terms of the work process, not in terms of system features, since the tapes show that workers always interpret the system's behavior in terms of work.

Building the system upon two perspectives amounts to creating two main subviews, both denoting the same topic, but using different concepts and means of expression.

Object style

The object style will be used in routine work like data entry and some problem-solving situations. It shows a world of work objects in which the worker can act according to the sentential schemas listed in Section III.1.4, two of which concern transport of work object and worker:

(1)   Worker moves Work Object Somewhere
(2)   Work Objects or Worker move[s] Somewhere

Fig. III.2.10 that shows *my desk* elaborates the first proposal a bit more.

It shows two collections of work objects, the current batch and the fliers. They are denoted by scrollable windows that can be opened and closed. Each line of the window denotes a work object and the user can move a work object from one collection to another by selecting it and dragging it from one window to the other.

Let us first look at action type (1), where workers move work objects. Although the workers use synthetic expressions like *macka* [destroy, cancel] and *hämta* [fetch], I want to make interaction uniform and express all actions in the same analytical way, namely as dragging an item from one list to another, thereby also making the contents of the actions conform to the schema (1): *Worker moves Work Object from Source to Destination.*

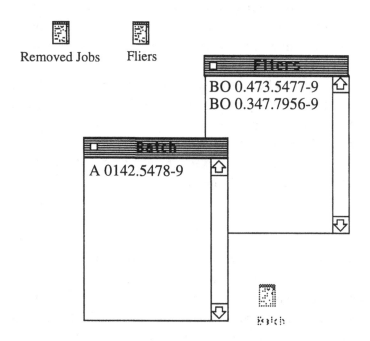

Fig. III.2.10. Interaction based on analysis of work language.

Thus, instead of saying *Remove Document* I shall use the more circumstantial *Move Document from Current Batch to Removed Documents.*

The expression form of the interaction will consist of three invariants:

(1) *Selection in list* (manifested by the handling feature of pressing the mouse when the cursor is located on a list item followed by the transient feature of highlighting the items selected).

(2) *Dragging* (manifested by agreement between the location of mouse, cursor, and the selected item).

(3) *Deselecting in list* (manifested by the handling feature of releasing the mouse button when the cursor is within a new list, followed by insertion of the item in the list).

All parts are invariants, since they pass the commutation test. Consider for example *Selection in Fliers, Dragging, Deselecting in Current Batch,* which means *Fetch Document.* If we exchange the two lists in the first (selection) part and the third (deselection) part, we get *Selection in Current*

Batch, Dragging, Deselecting in Fliers, which has a different meaning, namely *Move Documents*.

As mentioned in Section III.1.4, schema 2 can be used for two different purposes. *Worker moves Somewhere* is useful for handling the fact that the screen cannot hold all the necessary information. One method for displaying hidden information while still staying within the basic spatial metaphor of the design is to make the screen scroll and display the invisible area above or below the visible part, when the cursor hits the upper or lower border of the screen. If the cursor denotes the worker, this event is naturally interpreted as *Worker moves forward or backwards*.

The other one, *Work Objects move Somewhere,* can be used for automatizing parts of the work process. For example, the first card from the next batch can itself pop up on the screen when the last card from the current batch is finished.

Verbal task-like style

In addition to object style, I want the system to be able to paraphrase these actions in a verbal task style. In mystery-solving, a window can present descriptions of the actions done, e.g. "Film number xxxx has been sent to the flier file" or "The job has been abandoned" or "Batch xxx has been taken away", and in non-trivial problem-solving games, it suggests the type of error and possible courses of action ("Missing card. You might find it in the flier file" or "Card xxx may be superfluous. If you remove it the batch will tally").

An important argument for adding such verbal paraphrases to the graphical one is that although we may easily log the graphical interaction and make it available for replay during mystery-solving games, the concepts it expresses are poorly suited for this kind of discussion, since it will only contain a huge amount of simple analytical statements like

(1)   Worker moves Document from Batch to Fliers.
(2)   Worker moves Document from Fliers to Batch.
(3)   Worker moves Document from Batch to Removed Documents.

In discussions, these phrasings are long and circumstantial and lack synthetic concepts that are good for discussing and thinking. To remedy this, we may introduce the concept *take away = move from batch to Removed Documents,* giving (3) the synthetic paraphrase

(4)   Worker took away Document.

In a similar way, introduction of *fetch = move batch from Fliers to Batch,* will reformulate (2) as

(5)   Worker fetched a document.

The following list shows a sample log generated by my prototype.

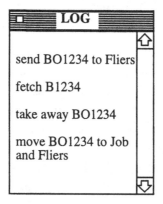

LOG

send BO1234 to Fliers

fetch B1234

take away BO1234

move BO1234 to Job
and Fliers

Fig. III.2.11. Sample log from prototype.

However, still more synthetic concepts are needed. Consider for example the sentence

(6)   Men dom försvann ju [but they disappeared].

from the "mystery of the fliers". It describes the behavior of *all* fliers in the example, condensing many statements of the form *Worker moves Document from Fliers to Batch* to one, so what is needed is not merely another expression form, but also another content form articulating the same content substance as the graphical interaction. This is an exciting challenge to linguistics, which here can use its sophisticated analytical tools for purposes that may turn out to be more useful than those defined by AI. Here all the horsepower of the linguistic engine will be used for making people, and not the system, more knowledgeable.

The basic linguistic problem involved is one of translating from one language to another, but since we want it done automatically and the system can only handle expression units, we must write rules relating the graphical expression form to one or more verbal expression forms in such a way that the contents substance of the two are interpreted as identical but their forms as different.

The *case* concept (which was described in Section I.2.2.1 and later suggested as a tool for structuring computer-based actions in Section II.2.1.2) turns out to be useful again. It can serve as a common point of reference for both codes since both verbal and graphical signs can be analyzed by means of cases. Here is a simple example of a possible translation rule:

- the name of the list component of the selection is put into the source case,
- the name of the deselection part is put into the destination case,
- if the middle part is *dragging*, the verb "flytta"[move] is put into the verb slot.

This rule will translate graphical actions into sentences like *flytta BO1234 från bunt till flygare* [move BO1234 from batch to fliers].

However, as mentioned previously the workers often use shorter and more synthetic phrasings. For example, *source = Bunt* is the unmarked case that is never verbalized, and the system should mirror this by deleting the source case in this situation. In addition, if the destination is "Removed cards", the work language has special words "ta bort, macka" [remove, destroy] that allows the destination case to be deleted also. Thus, *flytta BO1234 från bunt till borttagna kort* [move BO1234 from batch to Removed Cards] can be shortened to *Macka BO1234* [Destroy BO1234]. If the destination is "Flygare" [Fliers], the verb "flytta"[move] must be replaced by "skicka" [send], giving *skicka BO1234 till flygare* [send BO1234 to fliers].

The above examples show that direct manipulation style often involves a semantic analysis of the action: thus, *Destroy card* is analyzed and expressed as *Moving card from Current Batch to Removed Cards*. Are there any guidelines for doing this kind of analysis?

One place to look for ideas is the linguistic concept of *aktionsart*[1]. The concept denotes semantic schemata for articulating actions, schemata that are found in many languages. Such schemata are set up, both to represent meaning differences between the verbs, and to account for their distribution with respect to time adverbials, tense, and aspect. Vendler 1957 for example classifies verbs in four main categories:

A. Process verbs
  1. Activity terms *(push a cart)*
  2. Accomplishment terms *(draw a circle)*
B. Non-process verbs
  1. Achievement terms *(win a race)*
  2. State terms *(love somebody)*

---

[1] See e.g. Noreen 1904, Ryle 1962, Vendler 1957, 1967, Lindroth 1906, Pollak 1920, 1934, Meyer 1927/28.

The difference between A and B is that A-verbs can take the progressive ing-tense, which the B-verbs cannot. Within the process verbs activity terms are differentiated from accomplishment terms by the fact that they can occur in questions like:

For how long + Verb

but not in sentences like

How long did it take to +Verb

Thus *push* is an activity verb since we have

For how long did he push the cart?
*How long did it take him to push the cart?

while *draw a circle* is an accomplishment since we have

*For how long did he draw the circle?
How long did it take him to draw the circle?

Vendler explains this difference by the content form of the two classes of verbs. Both A-verbs view the action as an activity having temporal extension, but whereas accomplishment verbs add a result or climax that must be reached if the action is what the verb claims it to be, the activity verbs have no such requirements:

Thus we see that while running or pushing a cart has no set terminal point, running a mile and drawing a circle do have a "climax", which has to be reached if the action is to be what it is claimed to be. *Vendler 1957: 145*

The verbs of the problem-solving work are all accomplishment terms: the middle part, *dragging*, corresponds to the activity with a temporal extension, and the third part, the destination of the cards, corresponds to Vendler's climax or result.

If it is true that these time schemata have a general validity for human language, they could be used as a basis for designing direct manipulation actions.

III.2.4.4. Support for forecasting: simulating the future

Adding an unreal future to the system would be useful in the language game of *forecasting* described in Section III.2.3. Here the workers try to set up functions between actions, and their focus is upon modality (possible/not possible), mode (conditional/non-conditional), and conjunctions (temporal, causal, etc.). One obvious possibility for supporting this kind of conversation would be to add an "irrealis" to the system, e.g. as a small toy data base, where errors or stupid actions would not have fatal consequences. With such a tool, the workers could use the system in an exploratory mode: settle the correct functions between sending a box, entering new date, closing the transmission line, and processing cards by experimenting, and not by guessing, as they do in the example. It may sound like this, given the new facility:

C: Can we close the data valve before we send our box?

D: I think it closes automatically when we have sent the box, but let's try. No - we can't send the box when we have closed the valve.

D: But can we enter a new date before we are finished? Let's see. No, if I enter the new date, it says that the data valve closes. And when it has closed, we cannot send the last box.

The system should enable the workers to shift between object- and task-style interaction. Although some kinds of situation favor one style (e.g. data entry and object style but mystery-solving and task style) other situations exhibit a shift from engaged to detached perspective.

If an error is not too difficult to locate, the problem-solving conversation can be carried out in an engaged perspective, whereas other problems make the workers step back from work and reflect upon the consequences of the solution. Most of the previous examples are of the latter kind, but there are also problem-solving situations that do not exhibit any of the characteristics of the perspective of detached reflection, as the following example demonstrates:

Z: Hey, look, this card is missing.

Y: But here, look, it should be between these ones, it should be between these ones.

Z: Right, it got in the wrong place, I thought. I haven't abandoned anything this time.

The conversation is short and contains none of the characteristics of problem-solving games since there is neither definition of the problem nor discussion of which rules to be followed. The conversation itself is simply a work comment, and the problem-solving is a routine case for the worker.

III.2.4.5. Support for internal reporting: cooperation and division of labor

When computers replace mechanical tools, the functions between the parts of the working process change. The typical situation before computerization is that tasks and tools are interdependent: a task can only be done by means of specific tools which in turn can only be used for one (or a few) tasks. In addition, this interdependence presupposes a specific location: although other tasks can normally be done in a particular room or building, the task must be done there since the tools are there. This was the case at the Postal Giro before computerization. For example, coding requires the availability of a coding machine, which could only be used for coding. The machines were placed at certain tables, so the coding also requires the worker to be at a specific place.

After computerization, these functions change. The computer can run more than one program, and therefore can be used for many tasks, so the *interdependence* is replaced by a *presupposition* from task to tool. In addition, terminals and workstations can be placed anywhere where current and data transmission are available, so the task no longer *presupposes* a particular location - the location-task function is reduced to a mere *constellation*.

These changes remove some of the necessity to perform work in the Giro building in Stockholm. Employees in the local postal offices could probably do some parts of it from remote terminals or workstations, and whatever the benefits of this could be, a designer certainly ought to have it in mind when providing facilities for cooperation. Although at present the cooperating workers can see and hear each other, there is no guarantee that this assumption will continue to hold, and then the needs for cooperative tools may increase by an order of magnitude.

The system could be prepared for this kind of situation in two ways:

- By adding concepts that are directly concerned with cooperative processes, and expressing existing disguised cooperation in terms of these concepts.
- By adding new facilities for cooperative processes within the building.

Although the work is cooperative in the sense that there exist dependencies between the tasks of the workers, it is not presented as such. One example is the action of fetching a flier from the flier file after a colleague has placed it there. The task is not presented by the system as a cooperative activity, but had it been understood as such, more cooperative facilities might have come to mind, e.g. a facility that would enable people not only to wait for the missing flier, but to broadcast an inquiry over the local network, as was done orally before computerization.

Once introduced, the notion of people cooperating might be used for building tools for work distribution. As mentioned above, the present system supports reporting since it keeps a record of the progress of work, and the facility is used in the new language game of internal reporting, described previously. The conversations often are initiated when the workers are using the reporting screens for other purposes, as in the following example where they incidentally notice how work is progressing in the twin section:

A: (checking their own work) Yes it looks nice at least, but we ought to see if we have anything more now.

B: Have you looked?

A: No, I didn't look at the one I looked at.

A: (looking at the reports from the twin section) Look here, they have two jobs left on the 142, do you remember, it is the one we had to take away yesterday.

We did not observe that the workers used the information for other purposes than pure information, but it is not hard to imagine how a present-day conversation like the following

A: Have you run that much?

B: Yes, this is what we've done, they've probably done approximately the same.

C: (checking the data records and the paper cards against each other) Shall I choose "all boxes" then?

D: No, but we can do all the boxes then.

B: Then we'll see.

D: Yes here it comes, "box one, box two, box three".

B: This one is "current", it must be the one that "eighty" are working on.

in the future could be continued in the following fashion where the information is actually used for work distribution:

A: This one is "current", it must be the one that "eighty" are working at.

B: They haven't finished yet, you see. Look at all the material they have, they won't be finished by four. Maybe we should lend them a hand.

A: Ok, I'll suggest to them that we take two hundred cards. (Mails the proposal through the system. The overworked section accepts gladly, and releases the material, so that X can move it into the electronic desk of her own section.)

Another symptom of a hidden cooperative process, this time between the accounting and computer departments, is the *data valve* metaphor mentioned in Section I.2.4.2. The relation between the accounting section and the computer department is cooperative, since work in the former department (sending data) is presupposed by other work processes (finishing work on the received material) in the latter. Therefore, instead of explaining a failure to send data as "you cannot send because the valve is closed", I would prefer "You cannot send because the computer department people are busy with other things" or "You cannot send because the computer department people are using the space you need to store your data". The first explanation is a fiction without any connection to the real nature of the Postal Giro, while the latter interpretation refers to an important characteristic of the organization, namely that 5,000 people work there and that the work of the individual is closely knit together with the work of others. Again: from a semiotic point of view, the computer system is not merely a tool, but also a medium that should communicate relevant information to its users.

If I add representations of workers and organizational units to the basic concepts of the redesign, I can represent requesting and giving help in problem-solving, distributing work within the department, and coordinating work between the accounting and computer departments in the same way, namely as cooperative processes. If I stay within the basic conceptual structure already set up, the addition can be made in the following way:

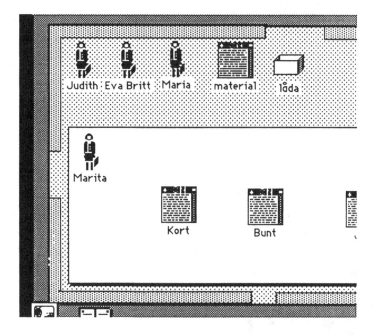

Fig. III.2.12. Prototype with representations of people.

Representations of the owners of work objects are inserted in the confines that define their "properties". The picture below shows Marita's work station. She is placed within the boundaries of her desk, while her colleagues in the section are placed within the boundaries circumscribing the section's objects.

The worker icons can be clicked, launching an instant mail ("talk") connection[1] between the workers. Thus instead of conversations like these

---

[1] Xerox offers this facility on some of their workstations.

W: No, now I have to go and fetch someone, now I've got a bank giro.

Z: What, bank giro?

W: Yes.

W: We are beginners you know, somebody has to teach us, but they are never around [she gets help].

W: No, this is just going on the work account.

something like the following happens: she clicks on Maria's icon, uses the instant mail to request help, and sends the screen image with the problem to her colleague.

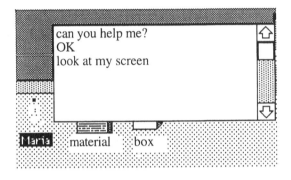

Fig. III.2.13. Support for help.

This facility may not be very necessary within the section now, since people can see and hear each other, but may turn out to be useful to support decentralized work distribution within a large department. In the redesign, a section does not have access to the material owned by other sections, but can see a graphical representation of the progress of work.

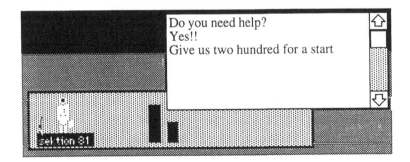

Fig. III.2.14. Support for work distribution.

In the example in Fig. III.2.14 the black columns show that section 81 is clearly falling behind, another section that has just finished its work discovers it, clicks the section icon which again opens the instant mail connection. After having confirmed that help is sorely needed [Do you need help? Yes!!], section 81 removes 200 cards from its own pile of material and puts it into that of the finished section [Give us two hundred for a start].

III.3

Task Analysis. Controlling Control

In the preceding section, I showed how to use work and conversation patterns as a basis for design. In this last section I discuss principles for building these patterns into the system. What does it mean to "put work patterns into the system"? To what degree should it be done? How should it be done?

As my example I shall use the data entry parts of the data entry *(registrering)* process classified as control style in Section II.2.2.2. Here I noted that the PGP-system is in control in this part of the work process and guides the worker through a fixed standardized sequence of operations:

film number, transaction code, amount, account to, and account from

In addition, it automatically provides the next card of the same batch, and the first card of the next batch when the last of the previous batch is finished and the batch tallies. If it does not tally, it enters the *completing* subview. The system *supervises* [1] the user's work, and directs the worker's attention to and from the screen by means of error messages like

Tyvärr, men det är fel kontrollsiffra för denna film.
[Sorry, but the control digit of this film is wrong]

VARNING: Denna bunt balanserar inte.
[Warning: this batch does not tally]

a type of control which was consciously introduced by the developers: they wanted to "stop a phase where you work with the card, and initiate a phase where you work with the screen".

I have already classified this standardization of work as a "frozen" variant structure. Before the batches are put into the OCR-reader, the workers can shuffle them around without any consequences, but once inside the machine, the system freezes a random order and makes it invariant as long as the task takes.

---

[1] The system's role as supervisor is very clearly expressed in some of the system's help messages where the system speaks in the first person:
Keyboard buffer full. You are too quick on the keyboard. It should not happen too often. I do my best.
Two keys pressed simultaneously. You have pressed two keys simultaneously. ...When this happens I cannot be sure which one you meant. Then I have to stop you and ask you not to press two keys simultaneously.

There are probably good reasons for this: for example that it makes it easier to keep a good rhythm and to keep track of how much data has been processed correctly and how much remains. Still I think that one should be cautious when using the system to promote a particular variant of a task to an invariant, because it may make organizational changes and development more difficult than necessary.

In Section I.2.3 I described the development of human behavior as a dialectical interplay between schema and usage. On the one hand, usage is always usage within some schema: if we do not comply with the linguistic schemata of our country or our work place, our fellow beings cannot understand what we say, and our speech does not count as communication but as gibberish. On the other hand, the schema changes through fluctuations of usage: small deviations or innovations spread, become systematized and at some point enter the schema as invariant features. As emphasized by Eco 76:131, normal language usage does not merely consist in applying rules to expression units to get at their meaning - it just as often consists in inventing rules for interpreting virtual signs that we do not yet know and that are not covered by the existing rules of the codes we know. Eco quotes Peirce for a good example of this process: Peirce visited a Turkish province and met a man upon horseback, surrounded by four men holding a canopy above his head. The canopy was clearly a sign for something, but Peirce did not know the correct rule to apply, so he invented one by saying that the expression element *canopy* means *honor*, and furthermore inferred that its specific meaning in this context was *governor*: *having a canopy* means *I am the governor*. Confronted with a virtual sign, Peirce in one step invented a rule of interpretation (canopy-> honor), and applied it in the context (honor - governor).

Eco's point is that this kind of abduction must be considered a customary social reflex, because "otherwise the principle of the flexibility and creativity of language would not hold"(Eco 76:133).

Now, if a computer system does not allow such deviation and innovations at the level of usage, it prevents the process of abduction doing its work, it deprives the user of experimenting, of inventing new ways of doing things that at first glance may seem as incomprehensible as the Turkish canopy, but in the next moment may give rise to a rule that gives it meaning and later may enter into the established work schema of the organization.

I think the data entry part of the PGP-system has these unfortunate properties, because it promotes one variant to an invariant, and does not allow other variants to develop. However, the method to overcome this problem is not to remove the standardization from the system, but rather to make part of the system structure more similar to a semiotic schema.

As mentioned in Section I.2.3.3, a system structure and a semiotic schema function in different ways. Whereas the system processes must stay within the system structure and normally cannot modify it, schema and usage are interdependent and mutually influence each other.

Although it may be neither possible nor desirable to transfer the dialectics between language usage and language schema fully to computer systems, the gap between using and changing a system must be bridged to some degree, if the system structure, as in the present case, is used to denote a work schema. The reason is that work practice and sign usage change over time and give rise to changes of their underlying schemas, and if the corresponding parts of the system structure remain unchangeable, the system will be experienced as an obstacle and hindrance to doing what one wants to. Therefore some degree of interaction between system process and system structure is needed.

I addressed this question in Section I.2.4.3, where I suggested different ways of easing the transition from just using a system to modifying it, but I did not discuss the borderline between tailorable and non-tailorable system features.

In the following I take up this question. The first thing to note is that the exact degree of flexibility is by no means obvious. The maximum degree would be obtained by selling a programming environment to the Postal Giro, leaving all structuring to the employees. Since this is clearly absurd, the problem is to delimit the properties of a system that should be modifiable by users. I think that the following guideline would be useful, even if it is not particularly radical, since it essentially allows users to create "paraphrases" of the system:

- *Guideline for tailorability:* The properties of the system structure that denote variant properties of the task should be modifiable by the users.

In the present case it would mean that a tailorable part should be added to the system, enabling the workers to change the cohesions between most of the actions in the data entry part. Now, according to which principles could such a facility be constructed?

Let us first see which kind of standardization we have in the data entry module. It turns out that the standardization can be described as a government from work objects to actions. For example, if the last digit in a field has been entered, the system provides the first digit of the next field of the card by moving the cursor down to it. If the field is the last one, it gets the next card in the batch, and positions the cursor in the first digit in the first empty field.

The government is defined on a parts/whole structure of work objects that is depicted in the following tree:

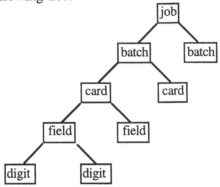

Fig. III.3.1. Part/whole hierarchy of work objects.

If we use Halliday's nets to describe the government from this tree to the worker's actions, we will need four paradigms, corresponding to each work object, *digit, field, card,* and *batch.* Each paradigm discriminates only between two kinds of items, *last* and *non-last,* and the value *last* of a component is the entry condition for entering the larger object it is a part of and retrieving the next component. For example, if there are no more digits in a field, the field paradigm is entered to display the next field and its first digit.

These facts are represented in the diagram below, which explicitly views the properties of the work objects as a system (in Halliday's sense) that imposes structure on the task in the same way as linguistic systems impose structure on sentences in systemic grammar.

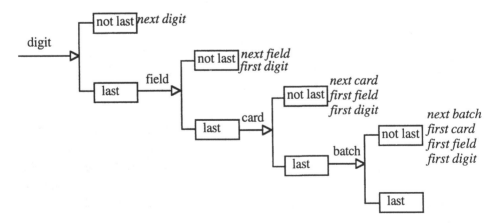

Fig. III.3.2. Systemic net description
of work object government of tasks.

The description above is neutral as to whether the computer system or the worker inspects the work object and performs the actions. Thus, the field subsystem could be manifested in two ways:

(1) The worker inspects and manipulates the work object: the situation *not last field* can be displayed as in the actual PGP-system, where the layout

AMOUNT 241 ▮

means that the amount field has not been completed, whereas the term *last field* can be represented by a screen that only contains fields with the layout

amount **241 8**

If the current field is not the last one, the worker must herself move the cursor down to the first digit of the next field. If it is the last one, she must move the next card of the current batch into the work area.

(2) The system inspects and manipulates the work object. In this case, the system will contain a component that advances the cursor to the next field or displays the next card of the batch.

The gist of the preceding discussion is that the user should be able to choose whether she wants (1) or (2), that is: whether a variant of the work schema should be part of the system structure or whether she wants to maintain it herself.

How do we conceptualize these notions in a program? One possibility is to set up a system component, *a user model,* that can receive the same messages from the work object as the worker (e.g. last field) and perform the same actions on it as her (e.g. take next card). In the present case, the model can receive the message *Last* from the work object and send *Next* and *First* to it:

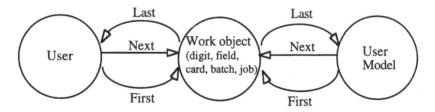

Fig. III.3.3. Object-oriented description of user, work object, and user model.

A user model is sometimes thought of as a hidden representation of the user, through which the programmer tries to infer the intentions of the user and make the system respond according to these intentions. In the present case, however, the user model is not hidden, rather it is the user's own description of those parts of her work practice she wants the system to do. It is not a psychological model made by others, but a self-portrait painted by herself.

The purpose of the user model is to represent all control concerning variant structures. Thus, it may contain rules like

Object User model:

Message	Action
Last digit	send "Next" to Field send "First" to Digit
Last Field	send "Next" to Card send "First" to Field

The work objects must contain handlers that respond to the messages First and Next:

Object Digit:

Message	Action
Next digit	*if* there is another digit in the current field *then* display it *otherwise* send "Last digit"
First digit	*if* there is a first digit in the current card *then* display it *otherwise* send "Last digit"

I have not specified the receiver of "Last digit"; the idea is that the message is first sent to the user model, and if the model has no handler for it, it is routed to the user. By inserting and deleting message handlers, the user can then determine which messages are handled by her model and which by her.

Here is an example of how it could work: if the worker has processed the last digit in the last field of the current card, the digit will send "Last digit" to the User Model. The model will send "Next" to the field object, but since there are no more fields on the card, the field will respond with "Last Field". This makes the model send "Next" to the card. After having got the next card, the model sends "First" to the field (the Last Field handler) and the digit (the Last digit handler).

Suppose now that the worker wants to take her cards herself, but still wants the system to handle the fields on the same card. Then she removes the message handler for "Last field" from the user model and now the procedure is as follows: the digit still sends "Last digit" to the model that responds by sending "Next" to the field, which sends "Last field" to the model. But now the model has no handler for this message, and relays it to the user by displaying the situation: all fields are processed. Then the user takes the next card, and selects the first field. Finally, the Last digit handler ends its work by displaying the first digit of the field.

The model must be programmable by the user. The actual design of the programming interface should probably be done in levels. At one level, there could be buttons labelled with action names taken from the work language, e.g. *take card* and *take batch*. Pressing these buttons would cause the system to perform the actions automatically, so for example if *choose field* and *take card* but not *take batch* are pressed, the system will itself move the cursor from field to field, and provide a new card within the same batch, but will not get another batch when the current one is finished.

However, designing this facility is also an opportunity for teaching the workers something about the actual workings of the system[1], so in addition to having buttons, windows could display the actual change of code that takes place when a button is pushed. The code itself should be designed as a profession-oriented programming language as envisioned by Nygaard 1984, cf. Section I.2.4.3.

Thus, when the worker is in control of the cards, the system would display

Message	*Action*
Last Field	none

When the *take card* button is pushed, it changes to

Message	*Action*
Last Field	send "Next" to Card
	send "First" to Field

showing that this is how the system will respond to the message. With experience the worker learns what the changes of code mean in her work, and if the code uses concepts related to her work, she may gradually come to bypass the buttons and enter code directly into the window.

I believe that user tailorability is useful at least in situations where introduction of computer technology is coupled with a gradual change of the division of labor, as at the Postal Giro, because it would make it easier to experiment and to adapt the system to the desired work organization. However, much thought must be given to the facilities provided. For one thing, users may not change their private system in such a manner as to become incompatible with the rest of the organization; moreover, the tools

---

[1] Cf. the principle proposed in Section I.2.4.3: "Experiences gained from using the system should be applicable for modifying and changing it".

provided should fit the actual needs and concepts as they show up in daily work.

A system built along these lines can be envisioned as follows: its stable kernel is a tool box providing a collection of signs denoting tools and work objects. These signs can immediately be combined into actions by the users themselves. In the present case the kernel might offer the following signs:

Work objects: job, batch, card, and field
Tools: cursor
Actions: taking job, batch, card, field, and digit. Entering digits

These tools can be used immediately, but no cohesions between the actions are supported at delivery. As the workers use the system, task patterns begin to emerge, possibly one resembling the actual pattern supported by the PGP system. As they stabilize, the users want the system to provide them and therefore enter them into the user model.

REFERENCES

ANDERSEN, N.E. et al. 1986. Professionel Systemudvikling [Professional Systems Development]. Copenhagen: Teknisk Forlag.

ANDERSEN, P. BØGH & HALSKOV MADSEN, K. 1987. Design and professional languages. Presentation at the symposium"Computers, cognition & epistemology", Institute of Psychology, University of Aarhus, 24-26/4, 1987.

ANDERSEN, P. BØGH & HOLMQVIST, B. 1986a. Fagsprog og fagorienteret systemutvikling [Professional languages and profession-oriented systems development]. Utvalgte SYDPOL-aktiviteter. Oslo: SYDPOL-sekretariatet.

ANDERSEN, P. BØGH & HOLMQVIST, B. 1986b. A toolbox for analyzing work language. In: J. D. Johansen et al (eds.): Pragmatics and Linguistics. Odense: Odense Univsity Press.

ANDERSEN, P. BØGH & KJÆR, A. 1982. Artificial intelligence and self-management. Journal of Pragmatics 6: 321-355.

ANDERSEN, P. BØGH & L. MATHIASSEN. 1984. Semiotics and informatics: The impact of EDP-based systems upon the professional language of nurses. In: Readings on Cognitive Ergonomics - Mind and Computers(226-247), ed. Van der Meer et al, Springer Verlag. Also in Journal of Pragmatics 10: 433-458. 1986.

ANDERSEN, P. BØGH & L. MATHIASSEN. 1987. Systems development and use. A Science of the truth or a theory of lies. In: G. Bjerknes, P. Ehn & M. Kyng (eds.): Computers and Democracy. A Scandinavian Challenge. 395-419. Avebury, Aldershot.

ANDERSEN, P. BØGH & LINDSKOV KNUDSEN, J. 1989. Semantics for interactive graphical systems. Unpublished.

ANDERSEN, P. BØGH & NIELSBY, O. 1981. PROTEUS - en programmeringsfilosofi baseret på selvforvaltning [a programming philosophy based on self-management]. SAML 8: 53-100. Institute for Applied and Mathematical Linguistics, University of Copenhagen.

ANDERSEN, P. BØGH et al. 1987. Research Programme on Computer Support in Cooperative Design and Communication. IR 70. Computer Science Department, University of Aarhus.

ANDERSEN, P. BØGH. 1973. Handlinger og symboler. Elementer af handlingens syntaks [Actions and Symbols. Elements of the Syntax of Actions]. Copenhagen: Akademisk Forlag.

ANDERSEN, P. BØGH. 1974. Om brugen af generativ grammatik til sprogbrugsbeskrivelse [On the use of generative grammar for description of language usage]. In: NyS 6:37-63. Copenhagen: Akademisk Forlag.

ANDERSEN, P. BØGH. 1977a. Sproget på arbejde [Language at Work]. GMT.

ANDERSEN, P. BØGH. 1977b. Simulering af sprogbrug på datamaskine med særligt henblik på en vurdering af programmeringssproget SIMULA. [Simulation of language usage on computers]. In: SAML 3: 45-78. Institute for Applied and Mathematical Linguistics, University of Copenhagen.

ANDERSEN, P. BØGH. 1979. The syntax of texts and the syntax of actions. In: J. L. Mey (ed.): Pragmalinguistics: Theory and Practice (283-330). The Hague: Mouton.

ANDERSEN, P. BØGH. 1981. FANGORN: a special-purpose language for the humanities. Computers and the Humanities 15: 227-242.

ANDERSEN, P. BØGH. 1986. Semiotics and informatics: computers as media. In: P. Ingwersen, L. Kajberg & A. Mark Peitersen: Information Technology and Information Use. Towards a Unified View of Information and Information Technology (64-97). London: Taylor Graham.

ANDERSSON, J. & M. FURBERG. 1974. Språk och Påverkan. Stockholm: Aldus/Bonniers.

ANDERSSON, L.G. 1981. Språk och arbetsliv - tankar och termer (Language and work - thoughts and terms). Department of Linguistics, University of Stockholm.

ANDERSSON, L.G. 1983. Arbete och kommunikation på Volvo (Work and communication at Volvo). Department of Linguistics, University of Stockholm.

APPLE COMPUTER. 1985. The Macintosh user interface guidelines. In: Inside Macintosh. I.27 - I.70. Reading, Mass: Addison Wesley Publ. Comp.

BANNON, L. 1989. From Cognitive Science to Cooperative Design. In: N. O. Finnemann (ed.): Theories and Technologies of the Knowledge Society. 33-59. Center for Cultural Research, University of Aarhus.

BARLEY, S. R. 1983. Semiotics and the study of occupational and organizational Cultures. Administrative Science Quarterley. 28: 393-413.

BARLEY, S. R. 1986. Technology as an occasion for structuring: Evidence from observations of CT scanners and the social order of radiology departments. Administrative Science Quarterley. 31: 78-108.

BARTHES, R. 1957. Mythologies. Quoted from the 1970 edition. Paris: Éditions du Seuil.

BAZELL, C.E. 1949. On the neutralisation of syntactic oppositions. In L. Hjelmslev (ed.): Recherches structurales 77-86. Nordisk Sprog- og Kulturforlag, Copenhagen.

BEDRIFTSKLUBBEN VED A/S HYDRAULIK. 1974. Bedriftspolitisk handlingsprogram. [A program for shop political action]. Oslo: Tiden Norsk Forlag.

BENDIX, E.H. 1966. Componential analysis of general vocabulary. International Journal of American Linguistics.Vol 32, part 2, no. 2.

BERRY, M.1986. Is teaching an unanalyzed concept? In Halliday & Fawsett 1987: 41-93.

BIRTHWISTLE, G.M. et al. 1973. SIMULA BEGIN. Stockholm/Philadelphia: Studentlitteratur/Auerbach publ.

BJERKNES, G. & T. BRATTETEIG. 1985. "The application perspective is a frame of reference for understanding development of computer based systems for nurses". 8th Scandinavian Research Seminar on Systemeering, Århus.

BJERKNES, G. et al. 1985. Gjensidig læring [Mutual learning]. Florence report no. 1. Department of Informatics, University of Oslo.

BJERKNES, G. et al. (eds.). 1987. Computers and Democracy. Aldershot: Avebury.

BLACK, J.B. & G. H. BOWER. 1980. Story understanding as problem solving. Poetics 9: 223-250.

BODEN, M.A. 1977. Artificial Intelligence and Natural Man. Hassocks: The Harvester Press.

BOLTER, J. D. & M. JOYCE. 1987. Hypertext and creative writing. Hypertext '87 Proceedings. 41-51. The ACM: New York.

BRATTETEIG, T. 1983. Kommunikasjon i systemutvikling [Communication in systems development]. Diss. Institute of Informatics, University of Oslo.

BREMOND, C. 1966. La logique des possibles narratifs. Communications 8: 60-76.

BREMOND, C. 1970. Morphology of the French Folktale. Semiotica 2: 247-276.

BREMOND, C. 1973. Logique du récit. Paris: Éditions du Seuil.

BURKS, A.W. 1970. Essays on Cellular Automata. Urbana: University of Illinois Press.

BUXTON, W. 1986. Chunking and phrasing and the design of human-computer dialogues. Proc. of the IFIP World Comp. Congress. 59-64. Dublin, Ireland, Sept 1-5, 1986.

BØDKER, S. & P. EHN. No year. CSCW - an ideal for the few or a process for the many. Unpublished.

BØDKER, S. 1987. Through the Interface - a Human Activity Approach to User Interface Design. Ph. Diss. Computer science department, University of Aarhus. DAIMI PB-224.

BØDKER, S., P. EHN, J. LINDSKOV KNUDSEN, M. KYNG & K. HALSKOV MADSEN. 1988. Computer Support for Cooperative Design. Computer science department, University of Aarhus. DAIMI PB-262.

CARD, S.K & A. HENDERSON. 1987. A multiple, virtual-workspace interface to support user task switching. In: J. M. Carroll & P. P. Tanner (eds.): Human factors in computing systems and graphics interface. 53-59. Conference Proceedings. Toronto.

CHOMSKY, N. 1957. Syntactic Structures. The Hague: Mouton.

CHOMSKY, N. 1965. Aspects of the Theory of Syntax. Cambridge, Mass: MIT Press.

CHOMSKY, N. 1968. Language and Mind. New York: Harcourt, Brace & World.

CHOMSKY, N. 1976. Reflections on Language. Fontana/Collins.

CHOMSKY, N. 1980. On Binding. Linguistic Inquiry 11: 1 -46.

CIBORRA, C.U. 1981. Information systems and transaction artchitecture. International Journal of Policy Analysis and Information Systems. Vol. 5, no. 4: 305-324.

CIBORRA, C.U. 1985. Reframing the role of computers in organizations: the transaction cost approach. In: Proceedings of the sixth International Conference on Information Systems. Indianapolis, Indiana. 57-69.

CLARK, H.C. & E. V. CLARK. 1977. Psychology and Language. New York: Harcourt, Brace & World.

COMRIE, B. 1977. In defense of spontaneous demotion: the impersonal passive. In: P. Cole and G. M. Sadock (eds.): Syntax and Semantics: 8. Grammatical Relations. 47-58. New York: Academic Press.

COWARD, R. & J. ELLIS. 1977. Language and Materialism. Developments in Semiology and the Theory of the Subject. London: Routledge & Kegan Paul.

DEMARCO, T. 1978. Structured Analysis and System Specification. New York: Yourdon Inc.

DIDERICHSEN, P. 1949. Morpheme categories in modern Danish. In: L. Hjelmslev (ed.): Recherches Structurales.134-155. Copenhagen.

DIDERICHSEN, P. 1962. Elementær Dansk Grammatik [Basic Danish Grammar]. Copenhagen, Denmark: Gyldendal.

DIJK, T.A. VAN. 1980. Macrostructures: an Interdisciplinary Study of Global Structures in Discourse, Interaction, and Cognition. Hillsdale, N.Y: Lawrence Erlbaum.

DRAPER, S.W. 1986. Display managers as the basis for user-machine communication. In: Norman & Draper 1986: 339-351.

DREYFUS, H. & DREYFUS, S. 1986. Mind over Machine. Glasgow: Basil Blackwell.

ECO, U. 1977. A Theory of Semiotics. London: The Macmillan Press.

EHN, P. & M. KYNG. 1985. A tool perspective on design of interactive computer support for skilled workers. In: M. Sääksjärvi (ed.): Proceedings from the Seventh Scandinavian Research Seminar on Systemeering, Helsinki 1884. Also in DAIMI PB-190, Aarhus University, Denmark.

EHN, P. 1988. Work-Oriented Design of Computer Artifacts. Arbetslivscentrum.

EHN, P. & M. KYNG. 1987. The collective resource approach to systems design. In: G. Bjerknes, P. Ehn & M. Kyng (eds.): Computers and Democracy. A Scandinavian Challenge. Aldershot: Avebury.

FALZON, P. 1984. The analysis and understanding of an operative language. In: B. Shackel (ed.): INTERACT' 84: 437-441. Amsterdam: North-Holland.

FALZON, P. 1983. Understanding a technical language. Rapport de recherche 237. Rocquencourt: Institut National de Recherche en Informatique et en Automatique.

FILLMORE, CH. J. 1968. The case for case. In: E. Bach & R.T. Harms (eds.), Universals in Linguistic Theory. 1-90. London, New York, Sydney, Toronto: Holt, Rinehart and Winston.

FILLMORE, CH. J. 1977. The case for case reopened. In P. Cole and G. M. Sadock (eds.): Syntax and Semantics: 8. Grammatical Relations. 59-81. New York: Academic Press.

FISCHER-JØRGENSEN, E. 1966. Form and substance in glossematics. Acta Linguistica Hafniensia 10:1. 1-34.

FLOYD, C. 1987. Outline of a paradigm change in software engineering. In: Bjerknes, G. et al. (eds.) 191-212.

FOLEY, J.D. & A. VAN DAM. 1984. Fundamentals of Interactive Computer Graphics. Reading, Mass.: Addison-Wesley Publ. Comp.

GAINES, B.R. & M. L. G. SHAW. 1984. The Art of Computer Conversation. Prentice Hall International.

GAMBERG, H. 1986. Symbols and Values of Strategic Managers. A semiotic approach. Helsinki: The Helsinki School of Economics.

GOLDKUHL, G. & K. LYYTINEN. 1982. A language action view of information systems. SYSLAB report no. 14. Göteborg, Sweden: Department of Computer Sciences, Chalmers University of Technology and the University of Göteborg.

GOLDKUHL, G. 1984a. Modeling communicative acts in information systems. HUMOR 1984-04-18. Göteborg, Sweden: Human-Infological Research Group, Department of Information Processing, Chalmers University of Technology.

GOLDKUHL, G. 1984b. Understanding computer-based information systems through communicative action analysis. HUMOR 1984-12-06. Göteborg, Sweden: Human-Infological Research Group, Department of Information Processing, Chalmers University of Technology.

GREIMAS, A.J. 1966. Sémantique Structurale. Paris: Larousse.

GREIMAS, A.J. 1970. Du Sens. Essais Sémiotique. Paris: Éditions du Seuil.

GREIMAS, A.J. & J. COURTÉS. 1979. Semiotique. Dictionnaire raisonné de la théorie du language. Paris: Hachette. Danish translation by P.Aa. Brandt & O. Davidsen 1987.

GRIP, A. & L. SUNDSTRÖM. 1984. Postgirot i Stockholm [The Postal Giro in Stockholm]. Stockholm: Arbetslivscentrum.

HAIMAN, J. 1974. Targets and Syntactic Change. The Hague: Mouton.

HALLIDAY, M.A.K. & J.R. MARTIN. 1981. Readings in Systemic Linguistics. London: Batsford Academic and Educational Ltd.

HALLIDAY, M.A.K. & R. HASAN. 1976. Cohesion in English. London: Longman.

HALLIDAY, M.A.K. & R. P. FAWSETT (eds.). 1987. New Developments in Systemic Linguistics. Vol. 1. London: Frances Pinter.

HALLIDAY, M.A.K. 1975. Learning How to Mean. Explorations in the Development of Language. London: Edward Arnold.

HALLIDAY, M.A.K. 1976. System and Function in Language. Oxford, U.K.: Oxford University Press.

HALLIDAY, M.A.K. 1978. Language as Social Semiotic. The Social Interpretation of Language and Meaning. London: Edward Arnold.

HALLIDAY, M.A.K. 1985. Systemic background. In: J.D. Benson & W.S. Greaves (eds.): Systemic Perspectives on Discourse, vol.1. 1-15. Norwood, New Jersey: Ablex publ. Comp.

HANSSON, H. et al. 1974. Bild och Form [Picture and form]. Skolförlaget Gävle.

HJELMSLEV, L. 1938. Essais d'une théorie des morphémes. Actes de IV Congres international de linguistes. 140-151. Also in Hjelmslev 1971: 152-164.

HJELMSLEV, L. 1939. La notion du rection. Acta Linguistica 1: 10-23. Also in Hjelmslev 1971: 139-151.

HJELMSLEV, L. 1942-43. Sprogteori. Unpublished lecture notes. University of Copenhagen.

HJELMSLEV, L. 1943. Language et parole. Cahiers F. de Saurre 2: 29-44. Also in Hjelmslev 1971: 69-81.

HJELMSLEV, L. 1948-49-50. Grundtræk af det danske udtrykssystem med særligt henblik på stødet [Elements of the Danish expressive system with special regard to the "stød"]. Copenhagen: Selskab for Nordisk Filologi, Årsberetning. 1948-49-50.

HJELMSLEV, L. 1948. Le verbe et la phrase nominale. In: Mélanges de philologie, de littérature et d'historie anciennes offerts a J. Marouzeau. Paris. 253-281. Also in Hjelmslev 1971: 165-191.

HJELMSLEV, L. 1954. La stratification du language. Word 10: 163-188. Also in Hjelmslev 1971: 44-77.

HJELMSLEV, L. 1954. Sprogets indholdsform som samfundsfaktor. Det Danske Magasin 2: 1-7. In French "La forme du contenu du language comme facteur social" in Hjelmslev 1971: 89-95.

HJELMSLEV, L. 1963a. Prolegomena to a Theory of Language. Menasha, Winsconsin: The University of Wisconsin Press. First edition 1961. Translated from "Omkring Sprogteoriens Grundlæggelse". University of Copenhagen 1943, reprinted and published by Akademisk Forlag, Copenhagen 1966.

HJELMSLEV, L. 1963b. Sproget. Copenhagen: Berlingske Forlag.

HJELMSLEV, L. 1971. Essais Linguistique. Paris: Les Éditions de Minuit.

HOLBÆK-HANSSEN, E, et al. 1977. System description and the DELTA language. Oslo: Norwegian Computing Center.

HOLMQVIST, B. & ANDERSEN, P. BØGH. 1987. Work language and information technology. Journal of Pragmatics 11: 327-357.

HOLMQVIST, B. & G. KÄLLGREN. 1986. Postgirot som Språkmiljö I (The Postal Giro as language environment). MINS 18. Department of Scandinavian Languages, University of Stockholm.

HOLMQVIST, B. 1986. Postgirot som Språkmiljö II (The Postal Giro as language environment). MINS 19. Department of Scandinavian Languages, University of Stockholm.

HOLMQVIST, B. 1988a. Datorisering av språk och arbete [Computerization of language and work]. Department of Information and Media Science, University of Aarhus.

HOLMQVIST, B. 1988b. Work and perspective. Report of The 11th IRIS. The 11th Information systems Research seminar in Scandinavia. 276-296. Department of Informatics, University of Oslo.

HOLT, A. 1986. Primitive man in the electronic work environment. Presented at the conference on electronic work, Milan, March 1986.

HOPCROFT, J. E. & J. D. ULLMAN, 1969. Formal languages and their relation to automata. Reading, Mass.: Addison-Wesley Publ. Comp.

HUTCHINS, E. L., J. D. HOLLAND & D.A. NORMAN. 1986. Direct Manipulation Interfaces. In: Norman, D.A. & S.W. Draper (1986) 87-125.

HÅNDLYKKEN, P. 1977. Rapport fra et systemutviklingsprosjekt der resultater fra Delta-prosjektet er brukt i praksis. Oslo: Norwegian Computing Center.

HÅNDLYKKEN, P. 1983. A critical view on the use of modelling methods in system development. In: M.I. Nurminen & H.T. Gaupholm (eds.): Report on the sixth Scandinavian Research Seminar on Systemeering. 48-77. Bergen: Institute for Information Science, University of Bergen.

JACKSON, M.A. 1983. System Development. Englewood Cliffs, New Jersey: Prentice-Hall.

JERVELL, H.R. & K.A. OLSEN. 1983. Hvad Datamaskiner Ikke Kan [What Computers Can't Do]. Copenhagen: Rosenkilde og Bagger.

JOHNSON, D.E. 1977. On relational constraints on grammars. In: P. Cole and G. M. Sadock (eds.): Syntax and Semantics: 8. Grammatical Relations. 151-178. New York: Academic Press.

JOHNSON, N.S. & J.M. MANDLER. 1980. A tale of two stories: underlying and surface forms in stories. Poetics 9. 51-86.

JOSEFSON, I. (ed.). 1985. Språk och Erfarenhet. [Language and Experience]. Stockholm: Carlsson.

JØRGENSEN, C. 1979. Ska vi danse [Shall we Dance]. Copenhagen: Wilhelm Hansen.

KAASBØLL. J. 1986. Intentional development of professional language through computerization. A case study and some theoretical considerations. Paper for the conference on System Design for Human Development and Productivity: Participation and Beyond. Humboldt-Universität zu Berlin: Berlin, German Democratic Republic.

KAMMERSGÅRD, J. 1985. On models and their role in the use of computers. In: Preceedings of the Working Conference on Development and Use of Computer-Based System and Tools. The Computer Science Department, University of Aarhus. 241 - 261.

KATZ, J.J. & J.A. FODOR. 1963. The structure of a semantic theory. Language 39: 140-210.

KATZ, J.J. 1972. Semantic Theory. New York: Harper and Row.

KNUDEMANN, J.O. 1980. Registre og Kontrol [Registers and Control]. Copenhagen: Informations Forlag.

KRUEGER, M.W. 1983. Artificial Reality. Reading, Mass: Addison-Wesley Publ. Comp.

LABOV, W. & D. FANSHEL. 1977. Therapeutic Discourse. New York/ London: Academic Press.

LAKOFF, G. & M. JOHNSON. 1980. Metaphors We Live By. Chicago: The University of Chicago Press.

LANZARA, G. F. 1983. The design process: frames, metaphors, and games. In: Briefs et al. (eds.): Systems Design For, With, and By the Users. 29-41. Amsterdam: North-Holland.

LARSEN, S. FOLKE. 1980. Egocentrisk tale, begrebsstruktur og semantisk udvikling. Nordisk Psykologi. 32: 55-73.

LARSEN, S. FOLKE. 1981a. Knowledge updating. Psychological Report 6:4. University of Aarhus: Institute of Psychology.

LARSEN, S. FOLKE. 1981b. Specific background knowledge and knowledge updating. Psychological Report 6:4. University of Aarhus: Institute of Psychology.

LARSEN, S. FOLKE. 1984. Kognitionens logikker. Handling, sprog og datamater. [Logics of cognition. Action, language and computers]. Psyke & Logos. 5: 221-242.

LAUREL, B.K. 1986. Interface as mimesis. In Norman, D.A. & S.W. Draper (1986) 67-86.

LEECH, G.H. 1969. Towards a Semantic Description of English. London: Longman.

LEHMAN, W.P. 1974. Proto-Indo-European Syntax. Austin & London: Univ. of Texas Press.

LÉVI-STRAUSS, C. 1964. Le Cru et le Cuit. Paris: Librairie Plon.

LIGHTFOOT, D.W. 1979. Principles of Diachronic Syntax. Cambridge: Cambridge University Press.

LINDENMAYER, A. 1968. Mathematical models for cellular interactions in development I-II. Journal of theoretical biology 18. 280-299, 300-315.

LINDROTH, H. 1906. Zur Lehre von den Actionsarten. Beiträge zur Geschichte der deutschen Sprache and Literatur. 239-260.

LUND, L. et al. 1972. Motivation - til fordel for hvem? [Motivation - who benefits?]. Copenhagen: Røde Hane.

LYONS, J. 1979. Semantics 1. Cambridge: Cambridge University Press.

LÖFGREN, L. 1968. An axiomatic explanation of complete self-reproduction. Bulletin of Mathematical Biophysics 30: 415-425.

MADSEN, K. HALSKOV. 1988. Breakthrough by breakdown. Metaphors and structured domains. IFIP WG 8:2: Information Systems Development for Human Progress in Organizations. Amsterdam: North-Holland Publ. Comp.

MADSEN, O. LEHRMAN & B. MØLLER-PEDERSEN. 1988. What object-oriented programming may be - and what it does not have to be. In: ECOOP '88 European Conference on Object-Oriented Programming. Lecture notes in Computer Science 322. Berlin: Springer Verlag.

MALMBERG, B. 1973. Teckenlära [A Reader in Signs]. Stockholm: Aldus/Bonniers.

MARTIN, J.R. 1987. The meaning of features in systemic linguistics. In Halliday and Fawsett (1987). 14-40.

MASUCH, M. 1973. Politische Ökonomie der Ausbildung. Hamburg: Rowohlt Taschenbuch Verlag

MATHIASSEN, L. & P. BØGH ANDERSEN. l984. "Semiotics and informatics: the impact of edp-based systems upon the professional language of nurses". In: van der Veer (ed): Readings on Cognitive Ergonomics - Mind and Computers. 226-247. Berlin: Springer-Verlag. Also in Journal of Pragmatics 10(1986): 1-26.

MATHIASSEN, L. 1981. Systemudvikling og systemudviklingsmetode [System Development and System Development Method]. PB 136, Computer Science Department, University of Aarhus.

MEEHAN, J.R. 1977. TALE-SPIN, an interactive program that writes stories. In: 5th International Joint Conference on Artificial Intelligence. 91-98. Cambridge, Mass.: MIT.

MEYER, E.A. 1927/28. Ruhe und Richtung, Actionsart und Satzton im Neuhochdeutschen. Moderna Språk. 1927: 159-220, 1928: 1-75.

MINSKY, M. 1975. A framework for representing knowledge. In: P.H. Winston (ed.): The Psychology of Computer Vision. 211-280. New York: McGraw-Hill.

MONTAGUE, R. 1976. Formal Philosophy. Selected papers of Richard Montague. Yale University Press: New Haven and London.

MORTENSEN, F. 1969. Sætningsemnet og dets anvendelse i yngre nudansk i en eller flere genrer [The nominal phrase and its usage in modern Danish in one or more genres], Ch.1-2. Ph.D. Unpublished. Institute for Scandinavian Languages and Literature. University of Aarhus.

MOULTHROP, S. 1989. Hypertext and "the Hyperreal". Hypertext '89 Proceedings. 259-367. The ACM: New York.

NEWMAN, W. 1980. Office models and office systems design. In: N. Naffah (ed.): Integrated Office systems - Burotics. 3-10. Amsterdam: North-Holland Publishing Company.

NEWMAN, W. M. & R.F. SPROULL. 1973. Principles of Interactive Computer Graphics. New York: McGraw-Hill.

NISSEN, H-E. l985. A theor-etical(sic!) basis for studies of information systems use and development. 8th Scandinavian Research Seminar on Systemeering, Århus.

NOBLE, D. F. 1978. Social choice in machine design: The case of automatically controlled machine tools, and a challenge for labor. Politics and Society 8. 313-47.

NOREEN, A. 1904. Vårt Språk [Our Language]. Vol. 5. Lund: C.W.K. Glerup.

NORMAN, D.A. & S.W. DRAPER (eds.). 1986. User Centered System Design. Hillsdale, New Jersey: Lawrence Earlbaum.

NORMAN, D.A. 1986. Cognitive engineering. In D.A. Norman & S.W. Draper (1986) 31-65.

NURMINEN, M. I. 1988. People or Computers: Three Ways of Looking at Information Systems. Lund: Studentlitteratur.

NYGAARD, K. 1984. Profession oriented languages. Presented as keynote speech at Medical Informatics Congress Europe, Brussels, September, 1984.

NYGAARD, K. & P. SØRGÅRD. 1987. The persepctive concept in informatics. In: Bjerknes, G. et al. (1987) 357-379.

OWEN, D. 1986. Naive theories of computation. In Norman & Draper 1986: 187-201.

PAVEL, T.G. 1973. Some remarks on narrative grammars. Poetics(8): 5-30.

PETERSON, J.L. 1981. Petri Net Theory and the Modeling of Systems. Englewood Cliffs, NJ: Prentice-Hall.

POLLAK, H. 1920. Studien zum germanischen Verbum, I, über Actionsarten. Beiträge zur Geschichte der Deutschen Sprache and Literatur. 353-425.

POLLAK, H. 1934. Über Aktionsarten und Modi bei 'fast' und 'beinahe'. Moderna Språk(28). 65-74.

PREBENSEN, H. 1967. La glossématique est-elle une théorie? Languages. Vol 6, June. 12-25.

PRECEEDINGS. 1985. Working Conference on Development and Use of Computer Based Systems and Tools - in the context of democratization of work. Computer Science Department, University of Århus.

PRINCE, G. 1973. A Grammar of Stories. An Introduction. The Hague: Mouton.

PROPP, V. 1975. Morphology of the Folktale. Austin and London: Univ. of Texas Press. English translation 1958. Quoted from the paperback edition.

RASMUSSEN, J. & M. LIND. 1981. Coping with complexity. Risø-M-2293. Roskilde: Risø National Laboratory.

RASMUSSEN, J. 1979. On the structure of knowledge —a morphology of mental models in a Man-Machine System Context. Risø-M-2192. Roskilde: Risø National Laboratory.

RASMUSSEN, J. 1980. What can be learned from human error reports. In: K.D. Duncan et al. (eds.): Changes in Working Life. 97-113. John Wiley & Sons.

RASMUSSEN, J. 1983. Skills, rules, and knowledge; signals, signs, and symbols and other distinctions in human performance models. IEEE Transactions on Systems, Man and Cybernetics, vol. SMC-13 no. 3.

RASMUSSEN, J. 1986. Information processing and human-machine interaction. New York: North-Holland.

REICHENBACH, H. 1947. Elements of symbolic logic. New York.

RUUS, H. 1979. Sproglig betydningsanalyse [Linguistic content analysis]. Nydanske Studier(10) 161-198.

RYLE, G. 1962. The Concept of Mind. Published 1949. Quoted from the paperback edition. Middlesex: Penguin

SACERDOTI, E.D. 1977. A Structure for Plans and Behavior. New York: Elsevier.

SANDSTRÖM, G. 1985. Towards Transparent Data Bases. Lund: Studentlitteratur.

SAUSSURE, F. DE. 1966. Course in General Linguistics. New York: McGraw-Hill.

SCHANK, R. & R. ABELSON. 1977. Scripts, Plans, Goals and Understanding. Hillsdale, New Jersey: Erlbaum.

SEARLE, J.R. 1977. Speech Acts. Cambridge: Cambridge University Press.

SEVERINSON, K. EKHLUND. 1986. Dialogue Processes in Computer-Mediated Communication. Malmö: Liber Forlag.

SHNEIDERMAN, B. 1986. Designing the User Interface: Strategies for Effective Human-Computer Interaction. Reading, Mass.: Addison-Wesley.

SMITH, D. C. et al. 1983. Designing the Star user interface. In: P. Degano & E. Sandewall (eds.): Integrated Interactive Computing Systems. 297-313. Amsterdam: North-Holland Publ. Comp. Also in BYTE 7:4. 242-282.

SPANG-HANSSEN, H. 1961. Glossematics. In: C. Mohrmann et al. (eds.): Trends in European and American Linguistics. 128-165. Antwerp: Spectrum.

SVENDSEN, G. 1986. Kartlegging og Analyse av kontorarbeid [Investigation and analysis of office work]. DIAS/11/86. Norwegian Computing Center, Olso.

SVENDSEN, G. et al. 1987a. Beskrivelse av analysemetoden WAND [Description of the analysis method WAND]. Norwegian Computing Center, Oslo.

SVENDSEN, G. et al. 1987b. WAND editor - User's guide. Norwegian Computing Center, Olso.

TODOROV, T. 1969. Grammaire du Décaméron. The Hague: Mouton.

TWAY, P. 1976. Verbal and nonverbal communication of factory workers. Semiotica 16:1. 29-44.

ULDALL, H.J. 1967. Outline of Glossematics. Copenhagen: Nordisk Sprog- og Kulturforlag.

ULLMAN, S. 1962. Semantics. An Introduction to The Science of Meaning. Oxford, U.K.: Basil Blackwell.

VENDLER, Z. 1957. Verbs and times. The Philosophical Review . 143-160.

VENDLER, Z. 1967. Linguistics in Philosophy. Ithaca, N.Y: Cornell University Press.

WHORF, B. L. 1970. Language, Thought, and Reality. Cambridge, Mass.: The MIT Press.

WINOGRAD, T. & F. FLORES. 1986. Understanding Computers and Cognition. Norwood, New Jersey: Ablex.

WINOGRAD, T. 1983. Language as a Cognitive Process. Vol. I: Syntax. Reading, Mass.: Addison-Wesley Publ. Comp.

WINSTON, P.A. 1977. Artificial Intelligence. Reading, Mass.: Addison-Wesley.

WIRTH, N. 1971. The programming language Pascal. Acta Informatica 1. 35-63.

WOODS, D.D. 1984. The cognitive coupling of man and machine. In: Operatør-kommunikationsproblemer [Operator Communication Problems]. 1 - 10. Copenhagen: Dansk Automationsselskab.

WYNN, E.H. 1979. Office Conversation as an Information Medium. Ph.D. dissertation. Department of Anthropology, University of California, Berkeley.

YOURDON, E. 1982. Managing the System Life Cycle. New York: Yourdon Press.

INDEX

Printed in the United States
By Bookmasters